A question of MURDER DOWN UNDER

COLIN O'NEILL

Cover by Melinda Childs @studioorchard

Internal design by Alana Lambert

First printing: April 2026

Paperback ISBN 978-1-7638691-4-1

eBook ISBN 978-1-7638691-5-8

NATIONAL LIBRARY OF AUSTRALIA

A catalogue record for this work is available from the National Library of Australia

Distributed by Lightning Source Global

ALSO BY COLIN O'NEILL

From Vietnam Nasho to Catching School Crooks

A Question of Arson

The April Fool's Day Lawyer

CONTENTS

PROLOGUE

Murder is generally regarded as the most reviled crime within society. Unfortunately, Australia, often referred to as "the lucky country", has certainly not been lucky when one looks at its history of murders. It begs the question of what actually is murder? Some scholars describe it in the way Sir Edward Cloke[1] defined murder. His classic and common law definition determines such an act as:

When a person of sound mind and discretion, unlawfully killeth any reasonable creature in being and, under the king's peace, with malice aforethought either express or implied.

Another word to aptly define murder is also the noun "homicide". The first known use was around the Middle English period in 1350 and in the simplest term, a homicide is defined as 'the killing of one person by another'. It can also be defined

1 Sir Edward Cloke was Chief Justice of the King's Bench1613-1616 and is often viewed as the greatest jurist of the Elizabethan and Jacobean eras. Also see Encyclopedia.com.

as 'unlawfully killing, attempting to kill, or conspiracy to kill another person'.[2] In other words, with 'malice aforethought'.

What we have witnessed, time and time again, is that it's not just confined to the murder of one person but also the act carried out by serial killers. As you will read, murder/homicide can take many forms. In its simplest term, the guilty act[3] of murder must be accompanied by and proven, that the offender killed the person with the necessary intent or, in its Latin term, the mens rea.[4]

In the event the necessary elements cannot be proven to charge a person with murder, a charge of manslaughter5 may follow. However, thanks to the Lord Justice of England, the century old legal maxim, "*Justice must not only be done but must also be seen to be done*"[6] has in many instances, fallen over as a well-established legal principle. Thanks to a favourable consideration by well-meaning public prosecutors, time and time again, defence lawyers are able to negotiate a deal. This has resulted in a charge of murder being withdrawn, following the acceptance by the defendant of a guilty plea to manslaughter,

---

2 See the Australian and New Zealand Standard Offence Classification (ANZSOC).

3 Guilty act is derived from and known as 'Actus reus' being the Latin term.

4 In criminal law mens rea means guilty mind being the mental state of the person who is accused of committing a crime. The Latin phrase in full is defined as actus reas non facit reum nisi mens sit rea.

5 The Cambridge Dictionary definition of manslaughter is the crime of killing a person unintentionally or without planning to do it.

6 This well-known aphorism was laid down by Lord Hewart in the case of *Rex v Sussex Justices* [1924]1 KB 256.AII ER Rep 233.

caused by either an unlawful and dangerous act or negligence, also known as involuntary manslaughter.

Other murder-related offences to take into consideration include: workplace manslaughter, single punch manslaughter, known as the coward's punch, infanticide and culpable or dangerous driving causing death. Even a suicide pact, with one person surviving, may see a charge of murder reduced to manslaughter.

But I am getting ahead of myself. Firstly, we need to look at earlier cases of murder.

Murders down under have been recorded as far back as the early to mid-1820s and include the cannibalistic efforts of Alexander Pearce, who was serving time in the penal colony of Van Diemen's Land, now Tasmania. He escaped with six other convicts but, due to food being scarce, Pearce killed, then ate, one of his fellow inmates. When police caught up with him, they even found some human remains in his pocket. Pearce's other claim to fame was in 1824, when he became the first convicted felon to be executed under the now established Supreme Court framework.

Van Diemen's Land also witnessed the despicable actions of convict bushranger, Thomas Jefferey. It was a pity that the minor crimes he committed in Bristol, England, saw him transported here for life. He continued with his criminal exploits but now they were accompanied with extreme violence. This all ceased only when he was executed by hanging in Hobart in May 1826, after he and three other convicts committed five murders, one being a five-month-old baby.

Another convict transported to Australia to continue with a life of violence and murder was John Lynch. He would have to be one of the most prolific serial killers in Australian history, being responsible for the deaths of 10 innocent people in 1841 in the Berrima district of New South Wales. Prior to carrying out a number of killings, he had already escaped justice when he was acquitted of killing a fellow convict in 1836. Obviously, encouraged by his luck, he then escaped from a convict gang and murdered unsuspecting carriers along the back roads of Berrima, before killing a farmer and his family.

To show how devious he was, Lynch then possessed their farm using the alias of John Dunleavy, but it all ended in early 1842. Lynch maintained his innocence throughout a subsequent trial for one of his earlier murders but was found guilty in March 1842. He did, eventually, confess his guilt the day before he was hanged and even took local police to the farm, showing them where he had buried the family of four. His other victims included a father and son, whose bodies were later found, as were his other four victims. In total, Lynch murdered 10 innocent victims. A plaque has been placed in the graveyard of the All-Saints Anglican church at Sutton Forest, Berrima, in memory of the family of four.

Ben Hall was a bushranger born and bred in the "lucky country".[7] His murderous gang was named after him and a feature film titled, *The Legend of Ben Hall*,[8] was made in 2016. His gang would remain supreme for some time carrying out many armed robberies across NSW in the early 1860s, including the shooting deaths of two police officers.

In 1865, the NSW government passed the *Felons*

---

7 The title 'The Lucky Country' was a nickname thanks to a 1964 book written by Donald Horne, awarded to Australia recognising its natural resources, weather and history of its reliance on Britain.

8 Gang members also included John O'Meally, Frank Christie, Johnny Gilbert and others.

Apprehensions Act which provided for any named bushranger to be shot on sight by anyone, and without warning. On 5 May 1865, Hall was ambushed by armed police and, as he tried to flee, 30 bullets ended his life of crime.

Another bushranger, Edward 'Ned' Kelly, would also suffer a similar fate but this time it was because of a noose. Kelly was known for wearing a suit of armour designed from plough mouldboards, which probably saved him in the final shootout with police in Glenrowan in rural Victoria in 1880. Kelly was the only outlaw to survive that confrontation but he was captured after being wounded. On 11 November 1880, this 25-year-old convicted bushranger and murderer was hanged at Old Melbourne Gaol.[9]

Domestic violence murder reared its ugly head[10] when 37-year-old Kenneth Brown, killed his younger wife at the Geraldton colonial family farm in January 1876. Brown was a wealthy pastoralist and had only been married to Mary Ann Tinsdale for less than eight years after his first wife, also named

9 This now former jail was built in 1839 located in Russell Street, Melbourne. During its operation between 1845 and 1924, a total of133 prisoners, including Ned Kelly, were executed within its walls by hanging. One of those hanged was also Frederick Deeming, who was convicted and executed for the murder of his family in England and his second wife in Melbourne. Old Melbourne goal is now a museum with some of its area also a part of RMIT University.

10 Current Australian statistics reveal that one woman every nine days and one male every month is now murdered by a current or former partner. A report from the Australian Institute of Criminology also revealed that women murdered by their partners increased by 28% from 2021-22 to 2022-23. Sadly, intimate partner homicides were higher for First Nations women (63%) compared to non-Indigenous women (52%).

Mary, died in 1868, leaving behind their four children. After a minor argument in front of witnesses, Brown put a gun to her head and pulled the trigger.

In those days, a jury of your peers was chosen from only men of European origin. They had to be aged between 21 and 60 and also hold a certain amount of wealth and property. In other words, to be selected on a jury you had to be of the same class and standing as Brown. Given that the jury pool was somewhat reduced, as Perth in Western Australian only had a population of around 25,000, and Brown was considered by all and sundry as a 'bloody good bloke', it would take three jury trials before he was convicted.

The prevailing argument submitted, on behalf of Brown, was a defence of provocation, with Mary being too boisterous and not bowing to his commands. It was also suggested Brown was insane, so how could he possibly be held responsible for her death. Also, one of his leading defence witnesses was his brother, a local court magistrate. After the second trial also failed to reach a unanimous verdict, a third one was held but the court's chief justice was struggling to find sufficient jurors. Eventually, the chief justice did find enough for the jury pool but they were of a lesser social standing than Brown. However, it would only take them a short deliberation to find him guilty and Brown was executed a few days later on 10 June 1876.

Another Brown, this time Irish born Robert Francis Brown, perhaps holds the mantra for being Australia's first mass murderer. As he walked up the steps at Ararat Goal, in September 1883, to be hanged for a murder in Western Victoria, he allegedly confessed to his soon-to-be executioner that he was responsible for another seven murders.

In his own words, 'I have cooked eight, five in Victoria and three in Sydney, and now you're going to cook me.'

The question remains though, was he in fact our first serial killer?[11]

The murderous escapade list is endless. Another chilling example was NSW couple, John and Sarah Makin, known in the late 1880s as "baby farmers". The Makins responded to unmarried mothers seeking adoption of their newly born babies and, after receiving a gratuitous payment, they would then take on the care of the child. Sadly, it was only about making money. Police found the remains of 15 badly decomposed bodies of infants buried in different backyards, where the Makins had lived. It was difficult to determine exactly how they died but given that the majority of these poor young innocents had bloodstains on their clothing, it was considered they had all been stabbed to death.

The Makins were both charged with having on or about 29 June 1892, at Redfern, "feloniously and maliciously murdered…", and also on the same day and place, murdered "a certain male infant whose name is unknown". They pleaded not guilty but a jury of their peers in March 1893 thought otherwise, finding them both guilty but they recommended mercy for Sarah Makin.

Following an unsuccessful appeal to the Full Bench of the Supreme Court, Justice Stephen sentenced them both to hanging and compared their conduct and the burial of each child in their yard, 'as you would the carcass of a dog.'

The learned judge would then go on to say they:

---

11 To this day many still consider that accolade, for want of a better word, belongs to the mutilator, William MacDonald- see chapter 7.

Engaged in baby farming in its worst phase and its most hideous and revolting aspect...ghastly evidence from the years in which you lived testified... that you were carrying on this nefarious and hellish trade, destroying the lives of those infants for the sake of gain.

Sarah Makin was given some mercy, with her sentence commuted to life imprisonment. After serving just over 18 years and, thanks to a petition by her two daughters, who were lucky they didn't suffer the same fate, she was released in April 1911. After a failed petition for mercy, her unlucky husband was executed by hanging in the gallows of the Darlinghurst Gaol.

The conduct of the Makins demonstrated that the legislation enacted by the NSW government in 1892, in order to prevent baby farming activities, was largely useless.[12] This legislation was supposed to be a broad ranging act to regulate the care of infants and children under the age of three years. In order to take a child into care, a Justice of the Peace would sign off a written order which stipulated the registration and payment requirements which were not to exceed the princely sum of 20 shillings. The act also banned baby farmers but obviously was of little use in preventing the escapades of the Makins.

What became known as the Gatton murders of December 1898 still remains unsolved to this day.[13] The lovely rural town of Gatton is situated in what was then known as colonial southern Queensland. It is 90 kilometres from Brisbane, with its name believed to have been adopted from a village in Surrey,

12 *Children's Protection Act 1892* (NSW).

13 Also see chapters 12 and 13 for other cold case unsolved murders.

England. It would also have an unfortunate homicide title, thanks to the triple murder of the Murphy children. They never returned home from a Boxing Day dance festival, which had been postponed without their knowledge.

On travelling back from the local hall in their horse drawn cart, tragedy struck. Michael Murphy was found on 27 December 1898 in a secluded paddock, having been bludgeoned and then shot dead. His two younger sisters, Norah, 27, and Ellen, 18, had been raped and also beaten to death. Their horse had suffered a fatal shot to the head and ants were crawling over the three victims' bodies when found.

It would be fair to say that in those early days, crime scenes were not treated as they are now, which didn't help after police made a number of serious blunders. Not only was the crime scene left contaminated but the rushed autopsy ruled that each had died from a fractured skull. After police were told of shots being heard that fateful night, a fresh autopsy found, in Michael's case, he had been shot dead with a .380 calibre bullet lodged in his skull.

Given Gatton's small population of only a few hundred people, its locals believed it would only be a matter of time before the killer was taken into police custody. It wasn't to be and, in early January 1899, another murder, only 80 kilometres away in Oxley, had interesting similarities to the Gatton murders. A 15-year-old boy was found shot dead, as was his pony, and a postmortem revealed it was by the same type of gun, namely a .380 calibre. What made it even more convincing that a serial killer was now on the loose, were his feet were found pointing west, as were the three Gatton victims.

The Queensland government offered a £1,000 reward but, despite police interviewing a number of suspects, no one was ever charged. A Royal Commission into the Gatton murders took place in late 1899. It was of no surprise that its findings determined that Queensland police were tardy and acted without cohesion, falling well short of expectations by the colony community. The commission also recommended that a particular senior police detective be transferred away from criminal investigations, nonetheless, he went on to be appointed as Chief Commissioner of Queensland Police in 1917.

Jimmy Governor arrived in this world in 1875 but he didn't last long after he went on a murderous rampage. He was the eldest of eight children and his Aboriginal father was known as a hardworking and intelligent man. Sadly, two of his sons, Jimmy and his brother Joe, together with accomplice Jacky Underwood, were responsible for a total of nine murders in NSW during July 1900. Joe was lawfully shot dead by a local farmer as he was a declared outlaw, meaning he could be shot on sight with no questions asked. After Jimmy was captured, he was executed at Darlinghurst Gaol, Sydney on 18 January 1901.[14]

Martha Rendell wasn't in the same league as the Makins but she received some notoriety being the third and last woman to hang in Western Australia in 1909, following a conviction for the wilful murder of her de-facto's three children. Her method was by swabbing their throats with hydrochloric acid and saying they were just taking medicine. This enabled her to witness their pitiful deaths and listen to their cries of sheer agony.

Sadly, these children would then die in what can only be

14 The life and crimes of Jimmy Governor was the basis for the novel 'The Chant of Jimmy Blacksmith' written by Thomas Keneally and a 1978 film of the same title.

described as agonising and slow deaths over a period of months. Rendell went to the gallows on 6 October 1909 and is buried at Fremantle Cemetery. I doubt she would have many visiting her grave but we must wonder about her motive.

It is well established, however, that there are many motives behind the act of murder. The case of the 'message left in a bottle', however, leaves you to ponder why he did it. For all intents and purposes, Andrew Thomas Edgar Archer, known as 'Tom', was a much-liked man and local cricketer, without, at first glance, having any suggestion of lingering mental problems. It was considered he had a loving relationship with his wife and he adored his five children, the youngest being only 10 months old.

On the night of 26 February 1929, their weatherboard home in the small village of Dom, about three miles to the west of Devonport, Tasmania, went up in flames. Little did fire responders know, they were about to find the badly burnt bodies of, not only his wife and five children, but also Archer in the charred remains. His wife, the baby and he were found lying on the floor in the family bedroom. His body lay next to a shotgun. The two sons, aged five and six, were also lying on a bed in the same room, with his eight- and 11-year-old daughters in another room. Other than the remains of Archer, the bodies of his family gave the impression they had died in their sleep, which couldn't be further from the truth.

A coronial inquest followed which determined that, in all likelihood, his family had died prior to the extensive fire. Pellets from the shotgun owned by Archer, were located nearby. Although the bodies were badly charred, it was ruled his family had most likely died by either a blow to their heads, with evidence of fractured skulls, or by being shot. This was supported by various items, including blood-stained clothing. The remains of the shotgun were located, with a cartridge still in its breach. What investigators also found was a message left in a bottle which read, 'This bag and contents are from Tom. Goodbye.'

The question that now left some debate was the motive that resulted in what appeared to be a murder-suicide.[15] It was revealed at the coronial inquest some years prior, that Archer was having mental issues with depression and his doctor recommended he take time off and go away on a holiday. Local neighbours also suggested he was quick-tempered but apart from that, he and his family were held in high regard.

There was a suggestion the family were in financial difficulties but a medical practitioner who saw him just prior to the fatal night, stated he seemed to be in good spirits. There was also evidence tendered from his relatives that it was inconceivable Archer would have murdered his family before killing himself.

The coroner held a different view, despite there being no obvious motive for the murder-suicide and, on that basis, determined that Archer did:

Feloniously, wilfully and with a malice aforethought, kill and murder Mrs Archer and the children…and…Archer, not being of sound mind, died by his own hand by gunshot wounds…

There are many cases that continue to remain unsolved in Australia and notably during the period of the 1920s and 1930s. One was that of 19-year-old sex worker, Jean Morris, who was found dead from over 30 stab wounds in a rooming house in

15 This is now commonly referred to as 'familicide' when a person kills family members, usually their spouse and children, or simply the children as a form of revenge following a separation, before committing suicide.

the rural town of Ayr, Queensland in 1932. She was also known as 'Stiletto Jean' because of the small knife she always carried.

Queensland, at the time, was inundated with migrant Italian canecutters and the notorious gang known as the 'Black Hand'[16] was prevalent, demanding payment of money, or suffer the consequences. Not only was Jean thought to be one of their victims, given that she was known to several of their brethren, but there were others who had been shot to death. One well-known victim was Vincenzo D'Agostino, a Calabrian man and Black Hand leader, who, in a payback killing, was blown up in 1938 in a bakery explosion in Ingham, Queensland.

The abduction and murder of four schoolgirls in separate incidences in Victoria, from late November 1930 to December 1935, also looked likely to be a question of "whodunnit". However, after 36-year-old Arnold Karl Sodeman was teased by a work mate that his car had been seen near the murder crime scene of a six-year-old girl, who had been suffocated after being bound and gagged, Sodeman angrily reacted, leading to him being reported to police.

On the questioning of his whereabouts at the time of this latest murder, he quickly confessed to all four murders. Sodeman became known as the "School-Girl Strangler" and, after a two-day jury trial rejecting evidence of insanity, he went to the gallows at Bluestone College (Pentridge) in June 1936. As to a possible motive, an autopsy revealed he had a degenerative brain damage disease caused by alcohol.

Motive in a murder can be somewhat perplexing at times and indeed raises the question "why?". In essence, I could probably write a whole book on why people kill, with many

16 The Black Hand, or the Olive Peril, was a secret society that had its origins in 18th century Naples.

cases to this day still left unanswered regarding motive, but one I have included resulted in a posthumous pardon nearly 90 years later.[17]

There are also a number of well written books on murder motives ranging from mental disorders to the usual greed-inspired reason. For example, where the perpetrator goes to any length to line their pockets from a prosperous victim or the usual bank holdup, leaving victims in their wake. Revenge also comes to the fore, by way of retaliation for some ill perceived wrong, including gangland warfare payback.

Power raises its ugly head from time to time, even bordering on obsession, hate or even frustration. The latter can stem from a disagreement or conflicting opinion, leading to a violent argument resulting in death. Crimes of passion also take place, whether they be from sexual attraction or a spurned jealous lover, following a domestic argument and taking the path of:

If I can't have you then no one else can.

We also have murder to hide a secret the victim may reveal and murder solely due to the victim's political, religious or sexual orientation. We also see persons charged with murder due to substance abuse, whether it be drugs or alcohol. A recent study of 205 Australians, aged between 15 and 65, when convicted of murder, determined that nearly half had been drinking and most likely under the influence of alcohol at the time of offending.[18]

The fact is, on average, eight out of 10 homicides are likely to take place between people who are known to each other. This

---

17 See chapter 1.

18 The study released in early July 2025 was carried out by senior academics from Griffiths University.

is why detectives, when investigating a murder, unless the crime scene suggests otherwise, initially look closely at the victim's "nearest and dearest". In further examining a number of our cases of murder, the majority have occurred between 6pm and 6am, apart from some during broad daylight. They were most likely to occur in public places, such as parks or in desolate areas, with the victim's remains often moved away from the crime scene and left at a separate location.

Data released by the Australian Institute of Criminology in November 2024, suggested homicide rates for both males and females in Australia have been slowly decreasing since 1990. Regardless, in that period a staggering 9,646 were victims of murder with 65 per cent being males. The worrying trend is the prevalence of family and domestic violence murders, which shows that one woman on average was killed in Australia every 11 days during 2022-23, with one male every 91 days. Other statistics for the year ending 2023 determined that law enforcement in Australia investigated the deaths of 409 victims of homicide and related offences which, in fact, meant there had been an increase of 20 victims when compared to 2022.

What is then left for law enforcement is to determine, not only who did the crime but the motive. While motive is not in any way a required element to prove guilt, if it can indeed be established, it will further strengthen the Crown's case of the burden of proof. If no motive can be determined, strong circumstantial evidence can still lead to a guilty verdict of beyond reasonable doubt that the accused was criminally responsible.[19]

---

19 The burden of proof also referred as the onus of proof, rests with the prosecution to prove the accused's guilt in order to reach such verdict. There is no onus on the defence to prove the defendant's innocence.

Self-defence also from time to time rears its ugly head when a person is left with no choice but to protect themselves or a loved one from harm. Again, this raises a difficult task for investigators to determine whether any such defence at law can be relied on, based on reasonable doubt.[20] Other defences, which may come into play include: mental impairment, duress and even a sudden or extraordinary type of emergency.

There is also a defence of provocation in some Australian states and territories but it is quite restricted in its application and, if accepted by a jury, the offender will be found guilty and sentenced to the lesser charge of manslaughter. Such a defence is centred around significant provocation from the victim, with the person acting violently in response, arguing they were not responsible for their actions causing death.[21]

I don't intend to go into great detail about the applicable legislation that applies in Australian jurisdictions but the usual penalty, if convicted of murder, is imprisonment for life, or such other term as the court should determine.[22] In order to prove murder beyond reasonable doubt, it is useful to set out the core

---

20 See, for example, section 418 of the *Crimes Act 1900*(NSW) and also the case of *R v Katarzynski* (2002) NSWSC 613, which sets out the two main tests to be met in order to make out self-defence. Also see the concept known as defensive homicide which was introduced into legislation in Victoria by the *Crimes (Homicide) Act 2005* (Vic) when self-defence could not be made out but was repealed on 1 November 2014. It now only provides a defence to homicide offences committed on or after 23 November 2005 and before1 November 2014.

21 Provocation as a partial defence to a charge of murder is no longer available in South Australia, Victoria and Tasmania.

22 Any minimum non-parole period that may be applicable varies between each jurisdiction.

elements. However, it should be noted, in some Australian jurisdictions, such elements that apply are left to the definition at common law, however, in other jurisdictions the elements for the offence of murder are detailed or varied by applicable legislation.[23]

Also, depending on the jurisdiction, both voluntary and involuntary manslaughter convictions can carry a penalty ranging from life imprisonment to a maximum penalty of 25 years.[24] To be convicted of manslaughter, such an unlawful killing of another person must lack the essential element of "intent to kill". In other words, the person charged with such an offence did not plan or have any desire to carry out the taking of a life. It can also include situations such as negligence, where the person charged has failed to exercise reasonable care and, as such, it has led to a death.

It should be noted though, concept of negligence is somewhat complex, as the prosecution must prove the accused owed such a legal duty of care and such breach resulted in death. In other words, this form of manslaughter does not require that there was an unlawful act. In Victoria, child homicide is a criminal offence when it is committed by a person whose

23 The legislation that applies is as follows: *Crimes Act 1958*(Vic)-section 3:*Crimes Act 1900*(NSW) section 18:*Criminal Code 1899*(Qld)-sections 302 & 305: *Crimes Act 1900*(ACT)-section 12;*Criminal Code Act 1924* (Tas)-section 157:*Criminal Code Act 1983*(NT)-sections 156-157:*Criminal Law Consolidation Act 1935* (SA)-section 11 and *Criminal Code Compilation Act 1913*(WA)-section 279(4).

24 Sentencing Advisory Council statistics released in June 2023 deemed the most common range of total effective sentences for manslaughter was nine to 10 years imprisonment. Also see for example as to penalty- *Crimes Act 1958*(Vic)–section 5.

conduct resulted in a child under the age of six years being killed in circumstances that constituted manslaughter.[25]

Regarding murder, such core elements are where the accused committed an act or acts resulting in the death of the victim. They were carried out voluntarily and with the deemed "malice aforethought". Simply put, there was the intention to kill or, at the very least, cause serious injury. This then leads to different degrees of murder which can be intentional, reckless or constructive, which means the act of murder is carried out in connection with a crime of violence.

A question of the criminal standard of beyond reasonable doubt with conviction, is then normally the sole responsibility of a jury consisting of 12 people, in cases where a plea of not guilty has been entered.[26] Using Victorian legislation as an example,[27] every enrolled person over the age of 18 years is eligible for jury service, providing they are not disqualified for various reasons. Names are selected at random from an electoral district jury roll and if selected as one of a number of potential jurors, a person will be notified by the Juries Commissioner where they will need to complete a questionnaire on eligibility or provide reasons to be excused.

A panel is then chosen from those liable for jury service,

---

25 *Crimes Act 1958*(Vic) -section 5A- Also carries a maximum penalty of 25 years imprisonment.

26 There is an exception for a judge alone trial if the accused and prosecutor agree. In the event the prosecutor does not agree to a judge alone trial, the court can still make such an order if it considers it to be in the interests of justice to do so. In the event the accused does not agree, the court cannot make such an order. For example, see section 131 of the *Criminal Procedure Act 1986*(NSW).

27 Jury service in Victoria is courtesy of the *Juries Act 2000*(Vic).

followed by a summons and, when required, placed into what is known as a jury pool. Such jurors for the trial then attend court for final selection by way of jury empanelment. They can be subject to any challenge by the defence or asked to be stood aside by the prosecution.[28] Once that process is completed, a jury of one's peers is then finalised. If it is considered a criminal trial will be of some duration, 15 jurors are selected and, prior to the jury retiring to consider its verdict, the jury is reduced by way of ballot to 12. Payment for jury service is at a prescribed rate and varies depending on the trial duration.[29]

Each state and territory has applicable sentencing legislation, which sets out the strict purposes for which sentences can be imposed. These governing principles can be summarised as: just punishment; specific and general deterrence; rehabilitation and denunciation and protection of the community.[30]

Every convicted person then has the right to appeal against any subsequent conviction and sentence. An application for leave to appeal is then determined in accordance with the criteria set out in each state or territory's legislation.[31] If a Court of Criminal Appeal is then to determine that such a conviction should be set aside, depending on the veracity of the appeal

---

28 A potential juror can also ask to be excused, for example, based on knowing a witness who will be giving trial evidence, having particular knowledge of the trial matter, travel, medical or family related reasons.

29 Employers are required under the *Juries Act* to reimburse the difference between the amount paid by the court and what they would normally earn as an employee.

30 See by way of example *Sentencing Act 1991*(Vic)–section 5.

31 For example, see the *Crimes (Appeal and Review) Act 2001*(NSW).

grounds, a new trial may be ordered but only if it is considered in the interests of justice to do so.

An application for leave to appeal against the severity of sentence will only be successful if the court concludes, due to some error in the exercise of sentencing discretion,[32] a more or less severe penalty is warranted by law. In that respect, the court will usually quash the sentence and hand down such other sentence as it deems fit or, in other cases, dismiss the appeal. The High Court of Australia is the final court of appeal for conviction and sentence and questions of law. Any application in a decision by a lower court first requires granting of leave to appeal by the higher court.

Using Victoria Police as an example, since their homicide squad was formed in 1943, initially with a strength of only six detectives,[33] they now have investigated in excess of 4,500 homicides. Given the prevalence of gangland shootings, serial killers, domestic homicides, rampage and spree murders, no doubt they, like all police throughout Australia, will continue to be kept very busy.

I might add that what follows is not a complete and exhaustive analysis of murder down under. To do that, I would need to put together many more books. However, please be warned, some of the selected cases I write about are quite confronting and beyond any sort of human comprehension. But before we proceed any further into murders down under, let's have a closer look at some earlier "mysteries".

---

32 Established in *House v The King* [1936] HCA 40; (1936) 55 CLR 499.

33 The Victoria Police Homicide Squad now has around 80 detectives, analysts and support staff responsible for the investigation of all suspicious deaths, including deaths in police custody.

1
THE GUN ALLEY POSTHUMOUS PARDON

Following Colin Campbell Ross' birth in October 1892, his early upbringing in Fitzroy North, Victoria was not without its challenges. Ross was one of five children whose father passed away in 1900. Surviving on a daily basis would have been difficult for his mother, who was left to fend on her own and take care of her young children. At the age of 11, Ross was not being well educated so he left school early, as did his brothers. He initially worked at a local quarry, followed by employment as a labourer and then graduated to working at an army hospital in Broadmeadows.

The family finances improved to a degree when he was 28 years old, with one of his brothers as licensee of the Donnybrook Hotel, in partnership with Ross and their mother as manager. However, the comfortable life, as he now knew it, was about to radically change due to being sentenced to a term of imprisonment for making threats and in possession of an unlicensed firearm. He was not happy with his then girlfriend and, on her refusing his marriage proposal, he produced a revolver and made threats of 'Marry me or else.'

His prison sentence, however, was suspended, on the proviso he entered into a bond of good behaviour for 12 months and paid a fine for the illegal firearm.

Around April 1921, he and his brothers owned a wine saloon in the Melbourne Arcade near the Eastern Market off Bourke Street, extending from Little Collins Street. His next criminal adventure was an armed robbery in October of the same year. On this occasion, Ross was believed to be involved when one of their drunk customers was shot and it was alleged Ross and a cohort teamed up to share the proceeds from the robbery. Ross was acquitted but his partner in crime was sentenced to six months in prison with hard labour.

One of the problems the Ross brothers had was serving liquor to all and sundry and this once respected "Australian Wine Saloon", as it was then known, started to attract criminals and drunks. The local neighbourhood was not happy because when these miscreants left the wine bar in a drunken state, they would leave behind vomit and urine and also make lewd suggestions to any passing, unsuspecting women.

Ross' life was about to alter dramatically when, on 31 December 1921, the body of a 12-year-old girl with auburn hair was found in Gun Alley, a laneway emanating off Little Collins Street.[34] This poor, defenceless child had been sent on a short errand by her grandmother to a butcher shop in Swanston

34 Gun Alley is now Nauru House in 80 Collins Street which is a 52-storey landmark building being built and completed in 1977.

street and, on picking up the meat, she was to take it to her aunt who lived close by. The delivery of meat never took place.

Sadly, the girl's body was found with her clothes removed and the police concluded she had firstly been raped then strangled, during the afternoon or night of 30 December 1921. It was also apparent she had been washed and then dried to ensure there was no incriminating evidence. Police suspected the murder had occurred most likely around 6pm the day before her body was found.

This chilling murder quickly gained intense media attention with police in the firing line if they didn't quicky solve it. A reward was offered by the Herald newspaper, which was then increased by the state government to one thousand pounds, which in today's terms is around $100,000. Police determined that this young lass was last seen near Little Collins Street around 2.30pm to 3pm, somewhere around the corner of Alfred Place and Little Collins Street. On interviewing several witnesses, including resident arcade shopkeepers, they spoke with Ross and other witnesses[35] and this is where it became very intriguing.

Ross, who was known to police, thanks to his previous endeavours, told them he had seen a young girl, matching the victim's description, near their wine saloon. Other witnesses also confirmed seeing the young girl around this time as well as Ross in the same area that evening. But the story they then

35 Contemporary witness accounts of the February 1922 Supreme Court trial of Ross are from the Argus newspaper, a record of the trial by junior counsel acting for Ross and excerpts of the coronial inquest held in late January 1922. These records would also be relied on by the Supreme Court of Victoria in the subsequent quashing of the conviction of Ross in December 2007.

obtained from a local prostitute would place Ross firmly in their sights. This lady of the night was a frequent visitor to the Ross wine saloon and she told investigators she saw the young lass in a small room off the premises, with two strange men on the afternoon of 30 December 1921.

The girl appeared to be drinking what the witness thought could have been wine, so she commented to Ross that she was certainly very young to be having a drink. Ross allegedly made some gratuitous comment of, 'That is her choice.'

On returning to the saloon 40 minutes later, she then told police the girl and Ross were no longer to be seen. This soon-to-be Crown witness then stated she spoke with Ross on 5 January 1922 and he made a number of incriminating comments, including the young girl was a 'cheeky little devil'. This was despite the newspaper headlines stating she was a good little child. He then made the comment, according to this witness, 'She was just at the age she would feel like as if she wanted a man.'

Corroboration of the murder victim being seen in the wine saloon that fateful afternoon was also obtained from an ex-employee, who had been dismissed by the Ross brothers not long after the October 1921 shooting incident. She provided a description of the girl as being about 13, with auburn-coloured hair and the clothes she was wearing at the time. On reading in the Truth newspaper about a young girl's body being found, she then went back to the wine saloon and asked Ross why he murdered the young girl she had seen him with.

Ross first denied he had done anything wrong but, according to the ex-employee, he then went on to say both he and his brother had sexually interfered with the young girl that evening. According to her version of what Ross had admitted to, he would detail strangling the young lass in a moment of sexual passion. Afterwards, he travelled to Footscray on a train that evening before returning to the premises to place her body in the street.

It came as no surprise that police arrested Ross. On 12 January 1922, he was charged with murder and remanded in custody in the Melbourne Goal. Another witness would further bolster the Crown case against Ross when a prisoner on remand told police of a supposed conversation he'd had with the accused on 23 January 1922, while walking up and down in the prison yard. According to his version of the conversation, it was similar to what police had previously been told.

Ross supposedly confirmed, according to the prisoner, after she drank three glasses of wine, he had sex and, when she yelled out, he choked her. On returning to the saloon by train later that evening, he cleaned blood from the cubicle, took off her clothes and placed the body in some sort of overcoat or blanket and left it in a nearby laneway. As to her clothes, he said he tore them up and disposed of them somewhere along Footscray Road. This prisoner, however, had 27 previous convictions, including making false verbal statements which would become a point of contention due to repeatedly perjuring himself during Ross' trial.

On 20 February 1922, the case against Ross went to trial. The Crown not only relied on the crucial witness testimony and alleged admissions made by Ross but, on "expert evidence" regarding strands of hair on two brown-grey coloured blankets found at Ross' home. The suspect claimed they were from the wine saloon for customers to sit on but the dismissed employee would later say she had never seen such type of blankets at the saloon. These hair strands were examined by a government analyst, a trained chemist, but with very little expertise in examining hair samples. He gave what could only be described as tenuous and contradictory circumstantial evidence.

The analyst initially told the jury that under microscopic examination, the hairs found on the blankets were not a match to sample hairs taken from the deceased, being of a different colour and diameter. However, when recalled by the judge, he then said it was similar to that of the murdered young girl. In their summing up to the jury, the Crown even stated if this witness wanted to 'put the boots into the accused', he would have said it was indeed the hair of the deceased victim but he chose to say, 'it was similar.'

The defence counsel for Ross had a difficult task trying to convince the jury Ross was not involved in any way in the murder. Ross gave evidence denying the conversations and confessions he had supposedly made to the three main witnesses and, further to that, the young girl was never in the wine saloon. At times, Ross would display varying degrees of hostility which, in all likelihood, didn't help his defence. His testimony of events and movements on the fateful day were largely collaborated by family members and other witnesses who supported his denial.

Apart from requesting a more qualified and independent examination of the hair samples, which was refused by the judge, the motivation and perjuring of the three witnesses was also brought into question, with emphasis on the discrepancies in their evidence. Counsel, in his final submission to the jury, said the two women were motivated by a reward offered by the state government, while the prisoner on remand would not only have also profited, but would have expected some leniency in the housebreaking charges he had been facing. Indeed, the trial judge in his charge to the jury, referred to the arguments put forward by defence counsel that the witnesses had not only perjured themselves but were less than credible. Even the Crown agreed they were of bad character.

Needless to say, after a five-day trial, Ross was found guilty by the jury who believed the evidence of the three main Crown witnesses, and of the victim's connection to Ross via the hair sample testimony. He was then sentenced to death by hanging but the jury of his peers would also not escape some punishment, thanks to the Herald newspaper. For unknown reasons, the Keith Murdoch-owned tabloid first prejudiced Ross' trial by publishing his photograph and then also printed the names and addresses of the jury, which ultimately resulted in anonymity for all future serving jurors.

Ross would take his conviction and sentence all the way to the High Court of Australia, stating, in particular, that the trial judge had failed to identify and saliently point out the conflicting weakness with the hair from the deceased child found on the blankets, allegedly from the saloon. In the judge's charge, he stated that one of the classes of evidence was for it to be identical with or resemble that of the victim.

The majority response from the appeal judges was that the trial judge left it to the jury to attach such weight as they would see fit, therefore, there was no error of law. It was interesting that one dissenting judge determined, apart from the confession statements, the case was practically unsustainable.[36]

After being denied a right of appeal to the Privy Council of the United Kingdom[37] and prior to being executed on 24

36 *Ross v The King* [1922] HCA 4; 1922 30 CLR 246.

37 Prior to the enacting of the *Australia Act 1986*(Cth), appeals could be made to the Privy Council including from the High Court and State Supreme Courts.

April 1922,[38] Ross forwarded a letter to his family which, in part, started, 'The day is coming when my innocence will be proved.' Little did he know how long it would take to prove there had been a miscarriage of justice.

The first attempt to clear his name, not only started by his family and supporters forming the Colin Ross Vindication Committee, but his guilt-ridden defence barrister, believing he had failed Ross, penned a rebuttal book.[39] He set out a number of factors which, in his opinion, led to his client being executed for a crime he did not commit. This fight for justice would remain dormant until around 1993, when a former schoolteacher, Kevin Morgan, uncovered a number of interesting facts concerning the Gun Alley Tragedy. He found a number of witness statements which effectively gave Ross an alibi. There was one statement not tendered to the court, of a witness who heard screams of panic coming from another building in Collins Street. It confirmed Ross was nowhere in the vicinity as he was at the wine saloon.

Now, making some progress, it would take a few more years before the hair evidence would come into play, with Morgan finding the original hair samples exhibit which, up until now, had believed to have been lost. This exhibit, which had played an extremely powerful and prominent role in the conviction of Ross, was sent for DNA testing in 1998.[40] The

---

38 The State of Victoria abolished the death penalty in 1975. Ronald Ryan was the last person to go to the gallows and was hanged in February 1967 for the shooting death of a Pentridge Prison warder. (see chapter 6).

39 The Gun Alley Tragedy: Record of the trial of Colin Campbell Ross by T.C Brennan Barrister at Law. Melb 1923.

40 See further Gun Alley: Murder, Lies and Failure of Justice, Kevin Morgan, Hardie Grant Books (Australia) Melbourne Second Edition 2012.

microscopic determination by both the Victorian Institute of Forensic Medicine and Forensic Services of the Australian Federal Police, came to the opinion that the Crown's crucial hair evidence was flawed.

Thanks to the families of both Ross and the victim, the Attorney-General for the State of Victoria sought an opinion of the Supreme Court in a 31-page petition on a point arising from the case of Ross.[41] The petition set out what it claimed to be fresh evidence, which was not available at the time of the trial. If taken into account, it would have affected the outcome in which the jury deemed him guilty of murder. This new and fresh evidence was in respect of the forensic analysis of the hair sample and the flawed character of one witness, namely the remand prisoner.

On 20 December 2007, three judges of the Supreme Court of Victoria handed down their conclusion that there had been a miscarriage of justice.[42] Whilst finding that the testimony was indeed questionable, due to the credibility of the three main witnesses, it was not sufficient to demonstrate alone that Ross was not guilty beyond reasonable doubt.

The hair evidence was another matter though, given that it had played a very prominent role in the trial of Ross. The state and federal forensic analysts were damning in their view. If it had been properly examined in the first instance and then put to the jury, combined with the questionable evidence of the witnesses, such jury acting reasonably would have acquitted Ross.

The hair evidence was critical in the learned judge's

41 The opinion sought was pursuant to section 584(b) of the *Crimes Act 1958* (Vic).

42 *Re Colin Campbell Ross* [2007] VSC 572.

conclusion as both analysts, one recognised as an expert of some world standing, stated that the two hair exhibits were not from the same source. In particular, the hairs recovered from the blankets were not that of the deceased young girl as there was a clear difference in colour, pigmentation and other features.

In reaching their opinion, the justices said in a 19-page determination that:

> *We are not considering this matter as an appellate court. Nonetheless, given the importance of the hair evidence, not only to the confessional evidence, which was vital to the Crown case, but also to the rejection of what otherwise may have been the exculpatory evidence of key defence witnesses, we are driven to the conclusion that there has been a miscarriage of justice as that concept is applied by the appellate courts.*[43]

In reaching such a conclusion the judges also said:

> *It needs to be understood, however, that a finding that there has been a miscarriage of justice does not automatically result in an acquittal. Rather, in a case such as the present one, it would, in our opinion, result in the quashing of the conviction and the ordering of a new trial…in this case no new trial is possible… but that would not prevent a Court of Appeal…from quashing the conviction of Colin Ross*[44]*…The Attorney–General also has the option of granting a pardon independently of this statutory regime…*[45]

43 Ibid-para 87.

44 Ibid-para 89.

45 Ibid-para 90.

On the recommendation of the State's Attorney-General, based on the now credible forensic examination which discredited the evidence used to gain the conviction, the Victorian Governor gave a posthumous pardon to Colin Campbell Ross on 27 May 2008.

While the families of Ross and the victim were pleased with the pardon, which was the only one in the legal history of Victoria at the time, this does not mean it was a declaration that Ross was innocent. As a retrial was not possible, it simply meant that such pardon would be recorded against the conviction of Ross, recognising his culpability could not be conclusively determined.

The final say on the matter, which some notable crime writers might well disagree with, was aptly put by the aunt of the young girl when she stated, in recognition of the pardon:

It is a tragedy for everybody that the actual perpetrator was not caught and an innocent man lost his life.

2
THE 'UNWRITTEN LAW' ACQUITTAL

Audrey Jacob, at 18 years of age, was a tall and attractive young lady who, along with her seven siblings, lived a happy and enjoyable life in Fremantle, Western Australia. In the early 1920s, they lived in a worker's style cottage and, although Audrey's father had been the clerk of courts at the Fremantle Court from around 1906, with his modest income, supporting such a large family was not easy.

Audrey had now met the man who she initially thought she would eventually marry. His name was Claude Arundel. He was a naval officer and after he proposed, they became engaged when she was 20 years old and studying as an art student. However, it wasn't to be as, in early 1924, Audrey became infatuated with 25-year-old ship engineer, Cyril Gidley, introduced to her by her soon-to-be ex-fiancé. He had recently migrated to Australia from the United Kingdom and, according to his few friends, he was nothing but an arrogant and, at times, controlling person.

What would later be revealed in court proceedings, Cyril had somehow managed to seduce Audrey and they quickly became engaged, with Audrey now thinking they would soon have a new life together as husband and wife. In early August 1925, Gidley's controlling and abusive behaviour got the better of him, particularly when he found out Audrey had just received a letter from Claude. Gidley grabbed Audrey and carried her to his room and when she tried to escape from his clutches, he thought it was funny as he pulled her back inside.

He not only had his way with Audrey but left her shattered with bruises on her neck and also broke off their engagement. Her mother, on finding Audrey back at her apartment now crying over what had happened, tried to console her distraught daughter but, understandably, Audrey thought her life as she knew it was all but over.

One of her girlfriends, trying to help the heartbroken Audrey, convinced her to attend the St John's Ball being held at Government House on the night of 26 August 1925. Audrey, although somewhat reluctant, agreed to join her and they both went along dressed as pantomime characters, Pierrot and Pierrette.

Audrey appeared to be enjoying herself, along with the other revellers, dancing the night away in the hall ballroom but that was about to change when she saw Gidley. He was also dancing happily with an attractive girl but Audrey couldn't help herself. She approached Gidley and not only asked what he was doing, but if he would reconsider their relationship. Gidley, in his usual arrogant fashion, told her to go away and stop annoying him.

Audrey, now in a very distressed state, immediately left the building and went home. On undressing and still crying, she noticed a revolver in her bedroom drawer which she had obtained after being robbed by burglars. As far as she was now concerned, her life would be better if she ended it. On dressing in her favourite blue evening gown, she took the gun down to a nearby foreshore but then, on having second thoughts, went to a local catholic church. It appears that she found forgiveness after reciting the Rosary and, as she walked past the local ballroom around 1.30am, the dancing was still underway. Perhaps, if she went inside and had a further chat to Gidley, he would forgive her and they would get back together.

Audrey, now with the pistol covered up with a handkerchief and just as the band were finishing playing "Follow Yvette", approached Gidley and touched him on the shoulder to get his attention. Gidley then abruptly turned to her and said, 'Excuse me, I am dancing with my fiancée.'

Evidence would be later given on behalf of the Crown that Audrey, who was within an arm's length of Gidley, shot him in the head. He staggered a few paces, blood trickling from his mouth and nose, then fell dead on the floor.

According to numerous witnesses, with the orchestra no longer playing their music after hearing a loud bang, she then placed the pistol on the floor and stated, 'I did it,' as she stared at his body. Police, who were on duty at the ball, then took a very calm but dazed Audrey into custody. On being questioned by police, all Audrey said was, 'I would prefer to say nothing.'

Believing her motive was clearly jealousy, she was charged with one count of wilful murder and remanded in custody at the Perth Police Court on 27 August 1925.

On appearing before the local coroner in early September

1925 and now being represented by the affable and brilliant A.G. Haynes of counsel, Audrey pleaded not guilty to the one count of murder. Her parents gave evidence which was refuted by the prosecution, that it was all Gidley's fault. In that regard, they said he was the cause of their separation and that Gidley was nothing but a callous seducer of their daughter. Audrey, sitting alongside her counsel, was observed to have her eyes shut most of the time, including when her parents were giving evidence. The coroner, after stating he didn't need to hear any more testimony, then committed Audrey for trial on one count of wilful murder. She remained in custody at Fremantle Prison.

Although this prison was renowned for being rather hard and regulated with its prisoners,[46] a media report suggested Audrey was allowed a number of privileges while awaiting trial on remand. She was afforded meals that were not the usual prison fare, spending the majority of her time reading, particularly the Bible.

The jury trial commenced on 8 October 1925 before Supreme Court Justice John Northmore,[47] with Audrey vehemently pleading she was not guilty as charged. The jury would hear from several witnesses, including Audrey and her parents, who again painted Gidley as a cruel and controlling

46 Royal Commissions were held in 1898 and 1911 in an effort to reform its operations. It was well known for using its prisoners as labourers for public works, in addition to the usual floggings and time in irons along with numerous hangings. One of its infamous prisoners was bushranger Joseph Bolitho Jones known as 'Moondyne Joe', who had the ability to escape from prison on a number of occasions.

47 His Honour would be appointed Chief Justice of the Supreme Court of Western Australia in 1931 and also served as Administrator (Acting Governor) of the state for two years.

man. Audrey gave evidence that, although heartbroken, she had then determined not to commit suicide. She agreed she still had the gun with her but was walking to her home only a short distance away and it was only by chance that she stopped at the ballroom.

Audrey then, in a grief-stricken voice, said she did not fire the gun on purpose. According to her version of events, she had a bad headache at the time and even had forgotten she was carrying the gun in the white handkerchief. Audrey then stated it must have gone off accidentally when she put her hand up to her head after approaching Gidley.

This accidental version was particularly interesting to the Crown prosecutor who, on cross-examination in front of the jury, asked Audrey to wrap the handkerchief around the gun. She struggled to cover the gun with a standard size handkerchief, with the prosecutor pointing out that no such item was found at the scene of the shooting. In addition, it was most likely suggested to the jury that it would be rather difficult to pull the trigger if it was, in fact, wrapped in a handkerchief.

Her barrister, Arthur Haynes, renowned for his sheer cross-examination skills, was unperturbed. On the face of it, it was an open and shut case of murder. It was expected her defence would be based on one of temporary insanity or perhaps a plea of jealousy and Gidley was shot dead in the heat of the moment. However, the defence had other ideas with a complete denial of murder. Not only did Haynes first rely on it being an accidental shooting but the gun was only in Audrey's possession because she wanted to end her own life. Such planned suicide was all the fault of Gidley, who had left his client in a heartbroken state, after ending their engagement.

His relentless cross-examination of Crown witnesses would be something that law students would look at in years to come, because it was not only vigorous but quite brilliant. As to what witnesses supposedly heard Audrey say following the fatal gunshot, Haynes would put to them it was nothing but a figment of their imagination.

Haynes would then attack the character of Gidley, saying he would abuse and control Audrey, who was just an innocent young woman and didn't deserve such compelling behaviour. What the jury didn't know though, was Haynes had a number of contacts with the local press who were fascinated with what they originally deemed to be "murder in the ballroom". However, thanks to Hayne's influence, the daily press then repeatedly painted Audrey in a glowing light, while carrying out a character assassination of Gidley.

Her deemed counsel would argue that his client had been wrongly accused and in taking evidence in chief from Audrey, Haynes said:

'And did you, Audrey, have any reason at all to kill or hurt Gidley?'

She then replied in a soft voice:

'No, I loved him still, for all his faults. If I could, I'd undo the harm that's been done.'

At this point, scholars would think Haynes would simply rest with nothing more to say, other than rely on as a defence that it was an accident. But no. He had one final ace to play in his pack of cards and left his last argument or, some would say, his final tactic, introducing to the jury a concept known as the "unwritten law". Such a concept had never been used in criminal trials in Australia before and, most likely, hasn't been relied on since. In the early 1900s, it came into prominence particularly in the United States of America and even in France, being relied on in a number of murder trials.

In effect, what it does is present the now-deceased, not as the victim but as the guilty party. Such a picture painted here was of Audrey as nothing but a respectable young woman, who was wronged by Gidley. In other words, it was all his fault. What happens then, it reverses any sympathy for the dead victim to the accused, leaving a jury to approve an acquittal.

Well, that's what happened, even after Judge Northmore reminded the jury of 12 men in his final charge that it was not a written law, only a concept. On the evening of 16 October 1925, Audrey was acquitted after the jury reached such a verdict, deliberating for just over two hours.[48] She left the dock a free woman with rapturous cheers and applause from the public gallery, who stood up in elation, clapping their hands, which was gleefully reported in the press the following day.

Audrey Jacob was now a free woman but decided that living in Western Australia was no longer an option. She eventually married a wealthy American businessman she met in Melbourne, then Audrey would disappear into anonymity but for her acquittal perhaps based on unwritten law.

48 *R v Audrey Campbell Jacob* [1925] Unreported, WASC. Justice Northmore, 17 October 1925 -Transcript of proceedings.

3
PYJAMA GIRL MURDER MYSTERY

At the young age of 24 years, Antonio "Tony" Agostini migrated to Australia around 1927 and quickly became a popular waiter at Romano's restaurant in Sydney, NSW. He soon met a tiny, attractive and well-liked theatre usherette named Linda. Love quickly followed and in April 1930, when Linda was 25 years old, they married at the Sydney Registry Office.

Sadly, Linda also had an attraction to alcohol and when they moved in 1930 to Melbourne, Victoria, their relationship deteriorated. This was to the extent where Tony was very embarrassed about the drinking exploits of Linda and, as a result, there were periods of separation. He was now working for a Carlton Italian newspaper known as *Giornale Italiano*, while Linda was employed as a hairdresser. Their married life continued but with on-going arguments. Around August 1934,

Linda was nowhere to be seen and friends most likely put it down to another one of their separations.

On 1 September 1934, a young woman's remains were found by a local farmer in Albury, NSW, and it was readily apparent she had been murdered. Clothed in yellow silk pyjamas, she had been placed in a sack and pushed down a road pipe. The body had a neck bullet wound and the forehead, in a very battered state and wrapped in a towel, had also suffered extensive wounds.

The lower half, from the abdomen down, had been set on fire, later determined by the use of petrol, leaving what one newspaper headlined as a "black mess". A coronial inquest in 1938, would also determine the injuries had been caused from blows by a heavy blunt instrument. Thanks to the exotic yellow silk pyjamas, the deceased female was dubbed by the media as the "Pyjama Girl".

Police were now left with the unenviable task of trying to identify the remains and track down whoever was responsible. Thanks to prevention techniques, one being the use of a bath of ice, followed by a bath of formaldehyde, the remains remained well preserved. Police were reasonably confident the woman would be quickly identified but, despite many civilians looking at the body, kept at the Sydney University, and much to the frustration of the investigators, she remained unidentified. This was despite NSW police, after using infrared technology, coming to the conclusion they had a Victorian connection from Dalmore in Gippsland, Victoria. This was through identifying the markings DALM and ORE from the towel and sack.

Police tried every other investigative tool they could think of, including examining electoral records after the body had first been located, to find any under 40-year-old women who had not voted in the recent federal election. What appeared to be a breakthrough occurred in 1935, when a person advised police the body was Linda Agostini. However, a number of other witnesses who also knew Linda, on perusing the remains, were of the view it was not her. One middle-aged woman told police it was her daughter, which was even confirmed by a local doctor who also knew the young missing lady. Police disagreed as they were of the view this particular woman had been murdered in Queensland in 1932.

When brought in for questioning and shown the preserved body, Agostini was adamant it was not his estranged wife. He stated she had left him and he didn't know where she was. He even gave the name of Linda's dentist to police so her dental records could be checked. It wasn't Linda as the dental records compared to the teeth in the body didn't match.

Around 1936, Agostini relocated to Perth. Due to World War Two, he was deemed an "alien" in 1940, interned and, after being released in 1944, he went back to working at Romano's restaurant in Sydney. During this period, police were no closer to identifying the Pyjama Girl and it wasn't until March 1944, they had a breakthrough, which was largely due to the efforts of their Commissioner of Police, William McKay.[49]

McKay liked to dine out at his favourite restaurant, unbelievably Romano's. He had known Agostini since he first started working at the dinery in the 1930s. McKay noticed that his waiter mate was not himself. Concerned, the chief asked him

49 William John Mackay was a Scottish born police officer who played a major part in bringing Sydney's underworld to account during the 1920s. He was known as 'Big Bill' and not just due to his size as he was not afraid to mix it with the local crooks. He was appointed Commissioner of Police in 1935.

to come down to the police station for a chat, where Agostini confessed to McKay that Linda had been shot accidentally. In his police statement, he referred to her heavy drinking and how he'd had enough after finding her favourite whisky bottles all over the place. He stated he did not kill her.

Her behaviour, described by him as "unladylike", then progressed to many threatening arguments, especially emanating from a drunken Linda. It all came to an end when, on being woken by her pointing a gun at his head, it went off in the struggle, resulting in Linda being shot. Agostini then stated that in a panic and not wanting to be blamed for her death, he drove the body from Carlton to the NSW border where he tried to hide it, including setting it on fire. Agostini also said he was glad he had confessed as the past 10 years since her death had left him devastated. He was glad the truth had finally come out.

Agostini was charged by Victorian Police with her murder and in April 1944 was committed to stand trial in the Supreme Court of Victoria. As well as the confession, the evidence to be presented at trial also included that the body was indeed Linda, as the initial dental records had been incorrect and they now had a perfect match. In addition, other witnesses made statements that the remains were those of Linda, further identified by freckles on one of her arms, which was matched with a photo taken of her when she was still alive.

The question for the jury now was whether to believe the story put forward by Agostini of Linda being shot accidentally. In view of that, he should be acquitted of murder. In June 1944, despite not believing his story of what had occurred, the all-male jury found him not guilty of murder but guilty of the lesser charge of manslaughter. His Honour Justice Lowe did perhaps have some sympathy for Agostini saying:

My view of the jury's finding is that they thought that you had been for so long sorely tried by your wife's conduct and had been, at the time you attacked her, provoked to the limits of your endurance.

Then again, maybe the learned judge didn't sympathise with him, as he sentenced Agostini to six years jail with hard labour.[50] Agostini would only serve just over three years before being deported back to Italy in 1948 and passing away in 1969.

The mystery of the Pyjama Girl doesn't end there though, with questions still being raised whether, in fact, the body was Linda Agostini.

In a book published in 2004,[51] leading criminologist and academic, Dr Richard Evans, suggested the confession obtained by police from Agostini may have been obtained under duress, as they wanted to get the cold case solved and off their books. In his view, the police statement contained a number of inconsistencies, including the type of head injuries inflicted on Linda, which Agostini said occurred when he dropped her body. However, the autopsy and visual identification revealed her head had been badly beaten. According to Evans, the forced confession also included the weapon that shot her was a revolver when it was a pistol.

What I find interesting though is Agostini told police who her dentist was, so they could check the dental records against her teeth, which then initially suggested the body was not Linda. If Agostini had any concerns by revealing the name

50 *The Penalties and Sentences Act 1981*(Vic) was amended in 1983 to remove hard and light labour imposed as part of a prison sentence.

51 The Pyjama Girl Mystery: A True Story Of Murder, Obsession and Lies, Dr Richard Evans, Scribe Publications 2004.

of her dentist and that he may then be implicated in her death, why did he assist police in trying to identify the remains by nominating the name of her dentist?

The fact the dental records would later determine the body was Linda, reinforces the view Agostini had nothing to hide and it was death by misadventure. Apart from the freckles on the arm that again confirmed it was Linda, Evans also raises an interesting argument that to the body had blue eyes, whereas Linda had brown eyes and a different shaped nose. Linda also had large breasts but the Pyjama Girl was small-breasted.

I will allow you to be the judge and jury in deciding whether the Pyjama Girl remains an unsolved mystery.

4
'AUNT THALLY' THE COMFORT TOXIC TEA KILLER

Caroline Grills came into this world around the late 1880s and would lead a comfortable existence and marry the love of her life, a local labourer, in 1908. They resided in Balmain, NSW, with their five sons and one daughter. Sadly, two of Aunty Carrie's sons, as she was then known with some affection, died during the typhoid pandemic. The family then moved into different houses, mainly situated in Randwick where her husband was working in real estate.

Following the death of her father in 1948, the lovable Aunty Carrie relocated to his home in Gladesville and this now short, dumpy woman seemed to have it all, including grandchildren, followed by great grandchildren. One of her favourite pastimes was baking biscuits and cakes for her extended family, washed down with cups of tea which she would gladly make for them. So famous were her goodies that she would often visit relatives and other friends making sure they ate what was on offer. She would even extend her help in their kitchens, which didn't go unnoticed and was highly appreciated.

Earlier, in the face of a housing crisis in Sydney around 1947, comfortable accommodation became difficult with many families crammed together in small houses and rooms, leading to an infestation of mice and rats. There were tales of sleeping children being bitten on their faces by these large unwelcome rodents. The only way to overcome the problem was to obtain copious quantities of the highly toxic thallium rat poison, which had been in use since 1920 and could be purchased from the local chemist.

When her stepmother became ill, the lovable and kind Auntie Carrie, now wearing thick-rimmed glasses, was the first person to offer to care for her until she passed away at the age of 87. The family were still grieving this loss, which was quickly followed by her husband's aunt dying at the age of 84 years. More grief was to follow, when a brother-in-law of the husband of Grills suddenly became ill and died.

Our short, dumpy great-grandmother obviously felt the family's pain and visited the grieving widow, plying her with the usual biscuits and cakes and making her cups of tea. While this was happening, another sister-in-law passed away but at a much younger age of 60. This meant a total of four family members had now died, the first in 1947.

The other issue was the poor grieving widow of her husband's brother-in-law also fell ill. Her hair was falling out and she was slowly losing her sight. Other symptoms became evident, including nervous disorders and loss of speech. It seemed, no matter how many cups of tea Aunty Carrie gave her, the worse she would become.

There was obviously an unknown illness spreading through her family as the widow's daughter and son-in-law, John, who resided with her, were both suffering the same effects, losing their hair and their sight. However, what was becoming rather strange was when the much-loved aunty didn't visit and supposedly care for them, their health improved.

In March 1952, the local media were reporting a number of rat poison issues, including deaths and repeated incidents of children being bitten while they slept. The article also highlighted the dangers faced with the use of the thallium rat poison, which could be mistaken for a simple household ingredient due to being colourless, no taste and no odour. Upon reading the article, John became very interested and suspicious when it described the medical symptoms if thallium salts were ingested. These symptoms were exactly what he and his wife had experienced.

John decided to have a much closer look at his perhaps not-so-lovable Auntie Carrie, watching her intently when she next visited. What he observed raised warning bells, when he saw her remove an item from the pocket of her favourite dress and then place it into a cup of tea. Without her noticing, he immediately switched the cup of tea with another and then took the contents to local police to voice his concerns.

Police arranged for the sample to be forensically examined and when the tests revealed traces of thallium, they became very interested in Auntie Carrie. Two of the deceased family member's bodies, which had not been cremated, were then exhumed, again finding similar traces of the rat poison. Investigators placed great reliance on the basic principle of 'every contact leaves a trace'[52] and after taking Grills into custody, they also found similar traces in a dress she would often wear when visiting her victims.

She denied any knowledge of her involvement in the deaths. Notwithstanding incriminating testimony at a coronial inquest, with the coroner agreeing Grills was responsible, charges of murder of the four victims and two of attempted murder were eventually withdrawn. This was despite clear unequivocal but largely circumstantial evidence that she was nothing but a killer.

A remaining charge of attempted murder was, however, proceeded with in the Sydney Central Court in October 1953. Supported by her husband, Aunty Carrie still professed her innocence and insisted that police had arranged with her relatives to set her up. She maintained she was only there to look after the eventual victims but each time when disparaging evidence was given against her, she would smile or roll around in fits of laughter.

One of these giggling outbursts was in response to the statement by the Crown Prosecutor, who submitted to the jury that she was:

A killer who poisoned for sport, for fun, for the kicks she got out of it, for the hell of it, for the thrill that she and she alone in the world knew the cause of the victims suffering…

The jury obviously didn't think it was funny as, after only deliberating for 12 minutes, Grills was found guilty of attempted murder. The judge was also not impressed and handed down a death sentence saying:

52 This principle can be attributed to Dr Edmond Locard who also became known as the 'Sherlock Holmes of France' and he set up in 1909 their first police forensic laboratory.

Under the guise of friendship and loving kindness, but with apparent motiveless malignity, you administered poison... condemning her to at least a life of blindness and possibly death...

As Grills was led from the dock, all she could say was, 'I helped to live, not to kill.' She was now facing her own ugly death by way of hanging.[53]

Luck was on her side, not that she allowed her victims the same courtesy, as following an appeal to the Criminal Court of Appeal in April 1954 and, despite the court rejecting the appeal grounds, her sentence was commuted to life imprisonment. Grills would only serve six and half years at Long Bay Prison in the State Reformatory for Women. She had become well known with some affection as Aunty Thally, obviously in recognition of her exploits with the thallium rat poison.

She passed away in 1960 of a bacterial infection and, no doubt, took many secrets to her grave, especially regarding the serving of tea and cakes to her supposed loved ones.

53 New South Wales abolished the death penalty in October 1954, except for treason, piracy and arson in naval dockyards until 1985. Prior to 1954, judges were bound to impose a death sentence for all persons convicted of murder and other serious crimes such as attempted murder. Under section 19A of the *Crimes Act 1900*(NSW) it can now carry a penalty of life imprisonment.

5

LAST MURDERER TO BE FLOGGED

On 1 February 1952, in the early hours of the morning at the Alfred Hospital in Melbourne, Victoria, Constable George Howell died. This was as a consequence of a bullet wound which had entered his stomach and, after travelling upward, lodged in a back muscle. He had been stationed at the Malvern East Police Station and it was not uncommon in those days for police to not only carry out patrols unarmed but also use a bicycle or patrol on foot.

On the night of 30 January 1952, due to a number of thefts of motor vehicles, Constable Howell, who had only been in the force since May 1948, was quietly riding his police issued bike along Dandenong Road, near the Crystal Palace Theatre in Caulfield. Seeing a male loitering near some parked cars, he quietly approached to see what he was up to. A scuffle then took place between the constable and the loiterer, with the suspect dropping a satchel.

After running off with Constable Howell in hot pursuit, the crook turned and shot him once at point blank range. The 25-year-old police officer, although badly wounded, didn't give up and continued to chase after him but then staggered and finally collapsed in an adjacent street, with the offender escaping into the darkness of the night.

Despite now in shock and falling in and out of consciousness, Constable Howell was able to provide a detailed description of who had shot him, to both people who came to his aid and to local police. The homicide squad would take over the investigation, ably assisted by their consorting squad[54] and were able to speak with Howell before he passed away.

The description provided by Constable Howell was that his 5ft 8in attacker was about 25-26 years old, with a solid build and ruddy complexion. He then said he was wearing a rather large pork pie hat with a tweed overcoat, covering what appeared to be brown sports clothes.

His statement, which would later be used in court as a dying declaration,[55] detailed how he observed this male person attempting to force entry into parked cars. After being approached by Constable Howell, he threw a leather satchel at him and, in the pursuit that followed, dropped the satchel

54 The Squad was established in 1931 with the main aim to interrupt criminal gangs by regularly attending racetracks, nightclubs and sly grog shops, the latter which came in existence thanks to the early closing of hotels. In 1980, the squad was amalgamated with the then Major Crime Squad.

55 In 1881, UK Justice Lush stated 'A dying declaration is admitted in evidence because it is presumed that no person, who is inevitably going into the presence of his maker will do so with a lie on his lips'. In 1909, Victorian Supreme Court Chief Justice Maddern stated it should be accepted as if the deceased was in the witness box as 'such a person has no motive to tell a lie'.

which contained a screwdriver, tin snips and a damaged silver brandy flask. After Constable Howell died, medical staff were able to extract a .22 calibre bullet from his back.

At his funeral on 4 February 1952, attended by many mourners which included over 500 uniformed and plain clothes police members, the oration would bring many to tears. Reverend Goy, who also knew Constable Howell personally, said:

> *...We are apt to take our police for granted until something like this happens. Without that police force, there would be chaos and lawlessness leading to anarchy. The police are the guardians of our civil society. In their duty they take grave risks, even make the supreme sacrifice. We honour the name of this young man who made the supreme sacrifice in the pursuit of his duty. He has set a splendid example to others...*[56]

The search for the man who killed Constable Howell, would see police leave no stone unturned trying to identify the culprit. This included taking fingerprints from a number of motor vehicles parked outside the Crystal Palace Theatre. They also brought in for questioning a few known car thieves, all to no avail. After receiving several tip offs from members of the public and given they had an accurate description of who they were looking for, their focus narrowed to a small number of criminal identities. One promising lead was the pork pie hat, which would soon be identified by a victim who had such a hat recently stolen from his Toorak house in an overnight burglary.

56 On the way to the Cheltenham Cemetery to lay Constable Howell to rest, the funeral procession was over a mile long. In September 1952, he was posthumously awarded the Queen's Police medal for bravery.

One particular person of interest, who kept standing out in police enquiries, was the well-built, broad-faced, bull-necked, 31-year-old, William John O'Meally. He had a rather interesting background, born in 1920 as Joseph Thompson in the country town of Young in NSW.

Around the age of 11, after his parents separated, he became a ward of the state for the next three years. He then changed his name in the belief that he was a grandson of bushranger, Johnnie O'Meally, an infamous member of the bushranger Ben Hall's gang. Now out of the control of the state, he began his life of crime, first being sentenced to five days of hard labour, for all things, riding on a train without a ticket.

By June 1936, after assaulting a policeman, he was subsequently incarcerated at the Gosford Farm Home for Boys[57] after being declared an uncontrollable child. But, as it would transpire many years later, he had a penchant for escaping in the dark of night. He didn't stay long at Gosford after breaking out, even being lost for a week somewhere along the Hawkesbury River. By 1952, O'Meally had a total of 42 convictions for assault, five involving police officers. He was released from prison after serving six months for one of the assaults, also riotous behaviour and interesting to police, a number for house break-ins. He would often use aliases when before the courts, such as Gene Thompson or Jospeh Cerzia.

Around 6am on the morning of Tuesday, 5 February 1952, detectives from the homicide squad knocked on the door of his bayside home in Bonbeach, where O'Meally, who worked as a labourer, lived with his wife and young baby. They certainly

57 This home was a reformatory built by its first inmates in 1911 on a 700-acre site on Penang Mountain near Kariong and was officially opened by the NSW Department of Public Instruction in 1913.

had found their suspect when the owner of the pork pie hat, dropped by the Howell assailant, accompanied police and also pointed out a number of other items in the O'Meally house that had, in fact, been stolen from his home in Toorak.

O'Meally was quickly taken into custody and placed in a line up at Russell Street Police Headquarters, which was viewed by a number of witnesses who had been near the Howell murder scene. During a lengthy 16-hour interview, O'Meally told homicide detectives he was not involved in the shooting death of Constable Howell. He said a young man by the name of Ray Campbell was responsible, as he didn't want to be placed under arrest by police again, so he shot Howell. O'Meally did admit to the Toorak house burglary but said he was in company with Campbell at the time but certainly not involved in anything else.

Campbell, when spoken to by police, admitted he had known O'Meally for a number of years but denied any involvement in either the house burglary and the shooting murder. When asked when he last saw O'Meally, Campbell stated it was at least two and half months ago seeing him waiting for a train at the Chelsea station. Campbell also had a good alibi though, as he had spent many months working at a hotel in Queensland and then returned to Melbourne.

As to the pork pie hat, the record of interview went along the following lines, with emphasis added:

> Detective De Vere: Some of your wife's relatives say that a black hat, similar to the one found at the scene of the shooting, was worn by you on January 30, the day of the shooting. What do you say to that?
> O'Meally: (no response).
> Detective Hill: We will ask you again. Some of your wife's

> relatives say that a black hat, similar to the one found at the scene of the shooting, was worn by you on January 30, the day of the shooting. What do you say to that?
> O'Meally: I'm not saying anything about the hat. That hat has got nothing to do with me.

O'Meally appeared in the Russell Street City Court on the afternoon of 13 February 1952 and was remanded in custody, as he vehemently maintained his innocence for the murder of Constable George Howell. Following a three-day inquest in March 1952, Coroner Stipendiary Magistrate Burke was satisfied there was enough circumstantial and witness evidence to commit O'Meally to stand trial in the Supreme Court of Victoria.

His jury trial took place in May 1952 before Justice Coppell and after 10 days of evidence with the Crown calling 41 witnesses, the jury would take just under four hours to find O'Meally guilty. This was despite his continual plea of innocence and stating he was being framed by police. His wife said they were both at home on the night of the shooting. However, the dying declaration by Constable Howell, in which he gave a detailed description of his assailant, was a point of contention raised by his defence counsel.[58] Regardless, it would certainly bear sufficient weight to convince the jury beyond reasonable doubt, O'Meally was responsible for the murder.

Nonetheless, it was submitted that O'Meally knew Constable Howell as they just happened to live in the same bayside suburb of Bonbeach in Melbourne, so he would have named him when he gave the description before he died. That

---

58 See *R v O'Meally* [1952] VLR 499, Supreme Court of Victoria, Coppel A-J 12 May 1952-admissibility of evidence-declarations by deceased persons-whether made in course of duty.

spurious claim was rejected by the jury, as was his contention that Campbell was the murderer. In his final summing up charge to the jury, Justice Copple said:

As far as humanly possible, put out of your mind any sympathy in favour of the accused from the great deal of talk about the young wife, that she had a child, or that he doesn't feel well.

On 23 May 1952, His Honour, on handing down a death sentence that O'Meally was to be hanged for the callous murder, turned to the jury and said:

> *You have, in this case, had a very difficult and arduous task and I think it is only proper I should tell you that in my opinion you have returned the proper verdict. The community will be grateful to you for the service you have rendered in the last fortnight.*[59]

As for O'Meally, on the verge of collapsing, he was led from the dock calling out to his wife, 'Cookie, Cookie,' with her sobbing as he also said, 'I could not do it, I could not do it.' His wife would later be interviewed by waiting media and she told them she was convinced of his innocence and would take any appeal all the way to the Privy Council,[60] if necessary.

She was only right in some respects as O'Meally did appeal his conviction and sentence. He had insufficient funds and with the State Government refusing to fund any higher appeal to the Privy Court. It only got him first to the Full Court of the

59 Ibid- 23 May 1952.

60 Up until 1975, the British Privy Council could overturn decisions of the High Court of Australia on appeal. The Australian Parliament then passed the *Privy Council (Appeals from the High Court) Act 1974*(Cth) to enable the High Court to be the final appeal court.

Supreme Court in Melbourne and then a further appeal to the High Court of Australia. Both were dismissed.

In his first appeal, his lawyers based their submissions on the grounds that Justice Coppel had misdirected the jury in his statement, 'that there was not a shred of evidence...' to support what was being submitted in his defence. Other grounds of appeal included a misdirection by His Honour, again to the jury, to take into account what they saw during a visit to the murder scene. As to the articles found near the scene of the murder and in the home of O'Meally, it was submitted that the trial judge again erred. In that respect, it was that such articles obtained from robberies should not in any way show the accused to be of bad character and, in any event, likely to commit the crime of murder.

On 23 July 1952, the Full Court had no hesitation in dismissing the appeal and said the trial judge had not in any way misdirected the jury, emphasising there was ample evidence for the jury to reach a guilty verdict. O'Meally, of course, couldn't help himself and from the dock, again in a highly agitated state, said:

> *Your Honours, I'm innocent. I still maintain that a miscarriage of justice has been performed. My wife and my child know it as well as the Lord above. I'm sure the public at large realise there has been a miscarriage of justice. The matter will be taken further.*[61]

It was taken further following the Victorian State Government then agreeing to provide additional financial aid to O'Meally, so he could file an appeal to the High Court

61 *R v O'Meally*, [1953] VLR 30 -Full Court-Supreme Court of Victoria, 15-22 July 1952.

of Australia. In August 1952, his lawyers prepared 12 appeal binders totalling 863 pages of evidence in his application for special leave for a retrial. Despite legal argument over many days in early October 1952, with O'Meally still under a sentence of death, it only took its justices 20 minutes to determine that his case was not one that justified the granting of an appeal.

In some way, while O'Meally may have felt wronged at such refusal, luck was still on his side. On 28 January 1953, the Executive Council, in keeping with the Labor Government's opposition to the death penalty, commuted his death sentence to life imprisonment but without remissions. This meant he would remain imprisoned for the term of his natural life, unless a further appeal was made to the Privy Council. However, it was now all over for him as he did not have sufficient funds to lodge such an appeal and the State Cabinet had already announced they would not provide any further funding.

You would like to think that would be the last we would hear about O'Meally as he spent the rest of his days behind bars at Pentridge Prison. Well, think again.

O'Meally had three choices of how he would use his time in prison. He could simply obey the rules and do what he was told by the prison guards. Alternatively, do it the hard way, be a pain in the arse to all and sundry and be nothing but a troublesome prisoner. Escape or, at least, try to escape, was the third option.

O'Meally chose the latter. After playing a football match on the afternoon of 27 August 1955, five hardened prisoners saw their chance and broke out of Pentridge by climbing a rope attached to a prison wall.[62] O'Meally didn't last long, as he was

62 Pentridge Prison in Coburg was established in 1851 and the first to escape from its walls was Scottish bushranger, Frank Gardiner. Bluestone College, as it was also known, would see many a prisoner escape by 1955.

recaptured three hours later with two of his cell mates. The remaining two would enjoy freedom for a few days, committing an armed robbery, before being taken into custody. For this misguided botched attempt, O'Meally would be convicted and sentenced to four years imprisonment, not that it mattered as it was to be served concurrently with his life sentence,

In company with shop burglar, John Henry Taylor, O'Meally would try a second time in late March 1957. Again, he didn't taste freedom for very long, being recaptured 13 minutes later. In their failed attempt, Taylor somehow had a .38 handgun in his possession and would shoot a prison officer, which fortunately only wounded him in the leg. O'Meally, who was armed with a pair of scissors, then grabbed the weapon and engaged in a fierce gun battle with other prison officers, before stealing a motor vehicle from a petrol station in Sydney Road and taking off. Their exploits soon came to an abrupt end when the bonnet of the car flew open and, thanks to a broken windscreen, they crashed into a fire hydrant and were quickly recaptured.

Following charges of escape and wounding with intent to do grievous bodily harm, on 31 October 1957 Taylor would have his existing prison increased by only one year, while O'Meally's sentence of four years and six months again meant nothing as it was also ordered to be served concurrently with his existing life sentence. However, what they both didn't anticipate was an additional order of a flogging of 12 strokes with the cat o' nine tails.[63]

His Honour, Justice Hudson, in delivering this additional curial punishment told them that:

63 Often referred to as 'the cat' and was made up of nine thongs of cotton cord. It was also used as a form of punishment in the early days of the British armed forces.

You are both clearly beyond hope of reform. Simply to sentence you to a further term of imprisonment would be to impose a totally inadequate form of punishment and would provide no real deterrent against further attacks of a like character.[64]

That obviously didn't sit well with O'Meally, now facing the reality of being one of the first prisoners to be flogged since 1943, so he took his appeal all the way to the High Court of Australia.[65] This was on the basis of whether the criminal acts should be punished by whipping[66]. Regardless, five justices on 14 March 1958 refused such application for special leave to appeal, saying in respect of the flogging:

... A study of the reasons which his Honour has, seems to show that he based the sentences on the violence which the shooting involved, but that at the same time his Honour would not have used the power of ordering a whipping as part of the sentence for that crime, had it not been for all the surrounding circumstances, including the fact that the men were prisoners, that they already had broken gaol, that the grievous bodily harm had been inflicted on a prison official and in order to effect an escape and that the men respectively had before them the terms of imprisonment...[67]

Pentridge Prison officials didn't waste any time and on

64 *R v Taylor & O'Meally* [1957] Unreported, Supreme Court of Victoria, Hudson J, 31 October 1957.

65 On 19 December 1957, the Victorian Court of Criminal Appeal ruled that the application seeking leave to appeal be dismissed.

66 *Crimes Act 1928*(Vic)(No 3664)-section 510(2).

67 *O'Meally v R* [1958] HCA 7; (1958) 98 CLR.

April Fool's Day 1958, they delivered the flogging to both men. As was his usual form, O'Meally continuously complained about the wounds he received to his rib cage, which he said were left opened, as were the cuts to his chest and back. Not surprisingly, he was placed back in his cell without any medical attention. His luck by this stage had certainly run out, with his wife divorcing him in June 1965. In February 1966, he spent a number of years breaking rocks and also being placed in solitary confinement, apparently as result of him bashing a warder.

O'Meally though, would be remembered as the last murderer to be flogged in Victoria, with this form of punishment abolished in the early 1970s. He would also achieve the mantle of then being Victoria's longest serving prisoner. After serving 27 years he was released in July 1979. His release on parole was most likely thanks to the "Free O'Meally Committee", who were often seen wearing badges with the same line tag. He could also thank the Victorian Adult Parole Board who recommended his release, which was then ratified by the State Governor, Sir Henry Winneke.

Interestingly, Sir Henry happened to be the lead crown prosecutor in the 1952 murder trial of O'Meally, and now he had the "privilege" of signing the release papers. From all reports, O'Meally lived until the ripe old age of 92, something he didn't allow Constable George Howell.[68]

68 In recognition of his service and sacrifice, the Wimmera Base Hospital Accident and Emergency Ward has one of its areas named the 'Constable George Howell Memorial Resuscitation Unit'.

6
LAST ONE TO BE HANGED

The death penalty, also referred to as capital punishment, is derived from the Latin word *caput*, meaning "head". The usual form of capital punishment includes electrocution, lethal injection, firing squad and hanging. Decapitation is still carried out in a number of Middle Eastern countries but only for certain offences. During the 19th century in Australia, following the arrival of the First Fleet, apart from murder and manslaughter, if you committed an offence, such as burglary, sexual assault, forgery and even stealing sheep, you could be sent to the gallows. By 1901, up to 1900 so called offenders had been executed for their crimes, with the first being convict, Thomas Barrett, who was executed on 27 February 1788 for stealing food.

In 1973, the Commonwealth Parliament of Australia extinguished the death penalty for any federal offence[69] and

69 *Death Penalty Abolition Act 1973*(Cth).

such a sentence has been abolished in all jurisdictions since 1985. In March 2010, the Commonwealth enacted legislation prohibiting any state or territory from reintroducing the death sentence.[70]

Since Federation in 1901 and prior to such abolition, a total of 114 legal executions has taken place, with the last death sentence imposed on Brenda Hodge, who was sentenced to death in Western Australia in August 1984 but such penalty was later commuted to life imprisonment.[71] Ronald Joseph Ryan wasn't so lucky, as he would be 'hanged by the neck until he was dead'.[72]

On 21 February 1925, Ronald Edmond Thompson was born at the Melbourne Royal Women's Hospital. His mother,

---

70 *Crimes Legislation Amendment (Torture Prohibition and Death Penalty Abolition) Act 2010* (Cth).

71 Hodge was convicted of the murder of her de facto partner and after her sentence was commuted to life imprisonment, she would be paroled in 1995. Serial killer, Eric Edgar Cooke, was the last person to be executed in Western Australia when he was hanged at Fremantle Prison on 26 October 1964. Cooke was responsible for at least eight murders and 14 attempted murders during the period September 1958 to August 1963. Western Australia would be the last state to abolish the death penalty for murder with the passing of the *Acts Amendment (Abolition of Capital Punishment) Act 1984*(WA). It remained in place in NSW for all other crimes such as treason until 1985 when it was abolished.

72 Following the execution of Robert Clayton, Norman Andrews and Jean Lee in February 1951 for the torture and murder of well-known bookmaker, William 'Pop' Kent, the Victorian Government would thereafter commute every death sentence, except for Ryan. In 1975, the Victoria Government abolished the death penalty courtesy of the *Crimes (Capital Offences) Act 1975* (Vic).

Cecilia Thompson, was in a relationship with John Ryan, who she later married in 1929. The young Ronald adopted his father's surname and was raised as a Roman Catholic in the leafy Melbourne suburb of Carlton. He then changed his full name to Ronald Joseph Ryan because he also didn't like Edmond as his middle name.

His first "claim to fame" was when he stole a watch from a neighbour and, as his three sisters had been made wards of the state, Ryan finished up in Rupertswood in Sunbury. It was a well-known "school" for those not only seen as wayward but also considered to be neglected.[73] In 1939, at the young age of 14, he left for the NSW country town of Balranald, where he commenced working. At this point in time, he stayed clear of the law and when he turned 25 years old in February 1950, he married the woman of his dreams. With Ryan in full time employment, either as a wood cutter or painter with the State Electricity Commission, they were able to rent a house in Noojee, Victoria, later also being blessed with three daughters.

By 1953, his next brush with the law had occurred, albeit thereafter too frequently. Ryan was acquitted of a charge of arson, purportedly over his rented house burning to the ground and his attempts to allegedly claim an insurance payment. Three years later in 1956, he was placed on a bond over forged cheques, then sent to prison in 1960 over burglary offences, including where he and his cohorts escaped from police while in custody.

Perhaps this was a sign of what lay ahead, apparently not helped by his acquired gambling addiction. After being released

---

73 Rupertswood also known as Salesian College would be named in the 2013 Royal Commission into Institutional Responses to Child Sexual Abuse.

on parole, he was back inside behind bars in November 1964. His sentence, this time for robbery, was eight years jail in 'B' division at Pentridge Prison in Coburg. One of his cell mates was Peter John Walker, who had been sentenced in November 1965 to a minimum term of eight years imprisonment for armed robbery.

In some ways, Walker's early life, having originally grown up in London, would mirror his soon-to-be prison escapee mate. He was shunted to various foster homes after his mother committed suicide by placing her head in an oven when he was aged seven. After relocating to Australia, he would first steal cars and then in his early 20s, he carried out the botched armed robbery.

Prison is a cold and dark place, made even worse for Ryan when he learned his wife had filed for divorce, with his daughters now refusing to visit him. On a warm and balmy day just before Christmas in December 1965 and, after hatching an escape plan with Walker, the two men obtained a rifle from an unsuspecting prison warder, scaled the B division wall and exited through a gate into the prison car park.

By this stage, other warders had been made aware of the fleeing escapees, so they gave chase before Ryan and Walker could drive off in a stolen car. One penal officer was George Hodson. In the ensuing mayhem with Hodson gaining ground, he was shot by a single bullet which entered through his chest and went out his back. He was left to die in the middle of Sydney Road, with four eyewitnesses later making statements that the gunshot was fired by Ryan.

Media outlets warned the public that they were armed and dangerous and urged any witnesses to come forward. You would think the pair would go into hiding but no. They continued on their merry way to commit further crime. On Christmas Eve

1965, Ryan, armed with the same prison rifle and in company with Walker, robbed the Ormond ANZ bank. After driving away in a 1952 Holden sedan, with around 4,500 pounds from the bank safe, two witnesses informed police that one of the armed robbers had told her, 'This gun shot a man a few days ago.' The male who made that remark was later identified by the witness as Ryan.

Both Ryan and Walker then found a safe house, first in Kensington before relocating to a flat in Elwood. Despite the flat owners knowing who they were, they were able to hold a party where copious amounts of alcohol were consumed. When the beer ran out, Walker accompanied the flat owner's boyfriend, tow truck driver, Arthur Henderson, to a sly-grog shop but only Walker returned. Henderson's body was later found in a Middle Park toilet block on Christmas Day 1965, shot through the back of the head. The now distraught flat owner went to police and told them what had happened. She was charged with harbouring criminals but such charge was later withdrawn.

By this stage, the two escapees had taken off to Sydney to another safe house but police were tipped off where they were hiding. A number of armed police, led by the infamous Detective Inspector Ray "Gunner" Kelly and joined by Detective Sergeant Fred Krahe,[74] didn't take long to capture them and place both

74 Gunner was head of the investigation into the 1960 kidnapping and murder of Sydney schoolboy, Graeme Thorne, resulting in the arrest and subsequent imprisonment of Stephen Bradley. Kelly died in 1977 but by this stage his reputation had been somewhat tarnished over corruption allegations. Krahe also had similar allegations, even with suggestions he was involved in the 1972 murder of police informant, Shirley Briffman, the disappearance of Juanita Neilson in 1975 and anti-drugs campaigner, Donald Mackay, in 1977.

men in custody. After being on the loose for 19 days, on 6 January 1966 Ryan and Walker were then extradited to Melbourne.

On the way back from Sydney, Ryan made several incriminating verbal statements to police regarding the shooting of warder, George Hodson. There was also a witness statement from one of the party goers at the Elwood flat, who told Acting City Coroner J.M. Duggan that Ryan said he shot one of the warders. On 4 February 1966, Mr Duggan committed both Ryan and Walker to stand trial on a charge of murder.

On 15 March 1966, in the Supreme Court of Victoria before Justice Starke, Ryan and Walker both pleaded not guilty to the murder of prison officer George Hodson. It was the Crown's contention, without any forensic evidence to support their case, that Ryan fired the fatal shot. They had no ballistic evidence because the fatal bullet and spent cartridge from the rifle had never been located. Eyewitnesses told the jury they saw Ryan fire the gun, while others testified of smoke coming from the rifle he was holding and then seeing a recoil after the shot had been fired.

Ryan's incriminating comment made at the Ormond bank robbery was supported by two witnesses, as were verbal statements he made to police when extradited back to Melbourne. Detective Sergeant Bill Walters gave evidence that on the day after his arrest in Sydney, Ryan said to him:

'In the heat of the moment, you sometimes do an act without thinking...Hodson...had no need to interfere...told to keep away...he caused his own death. I didn't want to shoot him. I could have done a lot more.'[75]

---

75 *The Queen v Ryan and Walker* [1966] Unreported, Supreme Court of Victoria, Justice Starke,15-30 March 1966-Transcript of Proceedings. Also see The Hanged Man: The Life and Death of Ronald Ryan, Mike Richards, Melbourne, Scribe 2002.

This unsigned and unrecorded confession was further corroborated by Detective Senior Constable, Harry Morrison, who informed the jury that on the plane flight back to Melbourne, Ryan told him:

'The warder spoilt the whole show. If he had not poked his great head into it, he would not have got shot…'[76]

The defence put forward two main arguments that Ryan was not guilty of murder because, put simply, he didn't fire the shot. Renowned Queen's Counsel, Philip Opas, in support of such a contention said that the trajectory of the bullet indicated it was fired from a higher position. It then followed that it must have been discharged by a fellow prison officer, looking down on what was happening below. This was supported by Ryan who said the only reason he didn't dispose of the rifle was because he knew if and when he was caught, the testing of the spent bullet would show it didn't come from that rifle. As previously mentioned, the fatal bullet was never found.

Regarding the supposed unsigned statements made to police, Ryan's evidence was that he was being verballed as he never said anything of the sort. His concluding remark to the jury, professing his innocence was:

'At no time did I fire a shot. My freedom was the only objective. The rifle was taken in the first instance, so it could not be used against me.'[77]

On 30 March 1966, the jury, after listening over 12 days to all the evidence and the incriminating and sometimes inconsistent witness statements, returned a verdict of guilty of murder against Ryan. In respect of Walker, he was found

76 Ibid.

77 Ibid.

not guilty of murder, but guilty of manslaughter. Justice John Starke, although believed to be a harsh critic of capital punishment, had no choice but to sentence Ryan to death as he was bound by the mandatory sentencing legislation in place at the time.[78]

Prior to being led away to face his pending death by hanging, Ryan said:

'I still maintain my innocence. I will consult with my counsel with a view to appeal.'

Such an appeal would also include Walker, after he was sentenced on 29 April 1966 by Justice Starke to imprisonment for 12 years, without any minimum term and not to be served concurrently with the sentence he was serving, prior to the escape. In that regard, His Honour stated:

> *The plan to which the jury found you to be party was indeed a desperate and lawless one...In the result, a prison officer was killed while doing his duty and doing it with considerable courage...I regard your part in this killing as being extremely grave and deserving most severe punishment.*[79]

Walker was also convicted of the manslaughter of Arthur Henderson, who he shot dead in Middle Park on Christmas Day. Justice Starke found such death to be a particular gross case of manslaughter. On being urged to make this sentence concurrent with the Hodson manslaughter, understandably he declined to do so. In that regard, Walker was now facing

78 *Crimes Act 1958* (Vic) applied and included such a sentence for murder.

79 *R v Walker, Peter John* [1966] Unreported, VicSC 36, Justice Starke, 29 April 1966.

another 12 years with hard labour, with a minimum of seven years before being eligible for parole.[80]

The subsequent appeal by Ryan and Walker was heard by the Victorian Court of Criminal Appeal, mainly based on the ground that the weight of evidence did not support their conviction. In a unanimous decision by the court in June 1966, the three judges agreed the weight of evidence against both convicted men was supported by eleven eyewitnesses and there was no substantial miscarriage of justice.

As to the fatal shot fired by Ryan, it was:

> *...an intentional, voluntary, conscious and deliberate act. In respect of Walker, he was a party to the plan to escape from Pentridge Prison, with the use of violence to some degree, to commit a violent act.*[81]

By this stage, Ryan was starting to run out of time before he would be met by the hangman. Not only was his special leave to appeal to the High Court of Australia dismissed in October 1966,[82] but the Victorian Government, led by Henry Bolte, withdrew any further legal aid. In addition, they would also not fund any appeal to the Privy Council. Given that no person in Victoria had been hanged since 1951, Ryan still had a forlorn hope that his death sentence would be commuted to life imprisonment.

No such luck as the Bolte State Government announced

---

80 *R v Walker, Peter John* [1966] Unreported, VicSC 87, Justice Starke, 29 July 1966.

81 *R v Ryan and Walker* [1966] VR 553, Winneke, CJ, Hudson and Mc Inerney, JJ, 8 June 1966.

82 *Ryan v The Queen* [1966] HCA, 14 October 1966.

on 12 December 1966, that Ryan would definitely go to the gallows. This was despite numerous opposing views from many in the community. This was not just confined to academics and church leaders but also the federal opposition and even from some of the jury members in his original trial.

Ryan then tried for an order from the Supreme Court of Victoria, restraining the Victorian Government from carrying out the execution, until such time his planned special leave to appeal to the Privy Council had been heard. It failed as His Honour Justice Menhennitt determined on 23 December 1966, he had no power to make such an order.[83] It didn't matter though because on 23 January 1967, such an appeal was in any event refused by the Privy Council.

Ryan's execution was set for 8am on Friday, 3 February 1967, and in the absence of any unforeseen successful petition for mercy, he would be hanged. He tried for a second plea of appeal to the Full Court, which was rejected. A plea by his counsel, Philip Opas, to Justice Starke also failed, as did efforts to get Victoria's Governor General involved. It was all based on supposedly new evidence. One alleged former prisoner, even tried for a stay on the basis he submitted an affidavit saying he saw a warder shoot Hodson from a prison tower. All it achieved though was a charge of perjury as it was ascertained he wasn't even in prison at the time.

With a number of people silently gathered outside the walls of Pentridge Prison at 8am on the morning of 3 February 1967, Ryan met his maker. His last words in a calm manner to the hangman were:

'God bless you, please make it quick.'

---

83 *Ronald Joseph Ryan v A.G. for Victoria & O'Brien and I Grindlay*, [1966] VicSC, Justice Menhennitt, 23 December 1966.

His remains were buried in an unmarked grave within the prison walls but in 2007 the Victorian Government gave permission for his body to be exhumed. His ashes were then buried alongside his ex-wife at the Portland Cemetery.

As to his perceived innocence, I could write another chapter based on statements and comments, varying from ex-prison officers, former Pentridge prisoners, to leading academics. As far as they are all concerned, Ryan was an innocent man when he went to the gallows to meet his maker. In that regard, I will perhaps leave the final say to retired Pentridge Prison Governor, Ian Grindlay. He stated to media outlets that Ryan told him 'straight out' that he had not meant to kill Hodson when he shot him.

This was, in fact, corroborated by an ordained member of the Abbotsford Good Shepherd Convent. Justice Starke went to his grave in 1992, somewhat troubled that he had sent Ryan to the hangman. He believed he was guilty but he was a committed opponent of the death penalty.

After being released from prison in December 1984, Walker, for the next 30 or so years kept his silence, maintaining a life free of crime. In 2014, he was embroiled in a clandestine drug laboratory and was arrested in Perth for possession of $100,000 and a fake passport. Walker subsequently pleaded guilty to a number of charges, including trafficking a commercial quantity of drugs and firearms offences and was sentenced to a minimum of four years and four months.[84] He passed away in 2022 at the age of 80.

Ryan was the last man hanged in Victoria and it was interesting that some months later, in late May 1967, another murderer, Keith Ryrie, had his death sentence commuted by

84 *DPP v Walker* [2016] VCC 160.

the Victorian Executive Council to 50 years imprisonment, with a minimum of 40 years. Ryrie was the 38th murderer to be lucky enough to have such a death sentence commuted by the Victorian Bolte Government after taking office in 1955.85 Ryan, of course, was not as fortunate.

Perhaps Ryan was simply unlucky and went to the gallows as an innocent man. I will let you be the judge and jury in that regard.

---

85 Ryrie murdered 18-year-old Maureen Ferrari in December 1965 and 5-year-old Rhonda Irwin in April 1966. Also see *Regina v Keith Ryrie* [1966] Unreported, VicSC 160, 5 December 1966. He was initially sentenced to death but this was commuted in 1967 to 50 years imprisonment with a minimum of 40 years. After serving the minimum term he was released on parole and reportedly changed his name and moved to Queensland.

7
THE GHASTLY MUTILATOR

In early June 1961, the body of a nude man in his early 40s was found in a toilet block at Sydney's Domain Baths near a well-known hotel. A postmortem examination revealed that Albert Greenfield had been stabbed about 30 times, his genitals severed and later found floating in Sydney Harbour. Little did the public know, they were about to hear of a number of murders, similar to those carried out by "Jack the Ripper", in the East End of London in 1888.[86]

It was five months before the next mutilated body, that of Ernest Cobbin in his mid-30s, was found. In November 1961, again near a public toilet adjacent to the Bat and Ball Hotel, this victim had his neck's jugular vein severed, his genitals cut off

86 Jack the Ripper was the name given to a serial killer who murdered at least five 'ladies of the night' by cutting their throats and then removing various organs from their bodies.

but they were nowhere to be found. With police having no idea who was responsible for the two ghastly murders, the media began referring to the crazed individual as "the mutilator".

In late March 1962, the mutilator was at it again. This time the victim, last seen drinking at a local hotel, was still breathing when he was found by passers-by but, alas, not for long. When police arrived 40 minutes after being notified, it appeared Frank McLean, who had a number of stab wounds around the face and neck, had initially been moved. They secured the crime scene, thinking perhaps the killer had not finished his work and was interrupted by a young family on their way home.

No doubt, in their view, the murderer returned to finish his work. Once again, the defenceless victim's genitals had been sliced off and again taken away by the killer, perhaps as a trophy. Police increased their patrols, particularly around the streets of Darlinghurst and Surrey Hills, with undercover cops working after dark in known drinking establishments and public toilet areas used by various individuals for whatever reasons. Although quickly dismissed, one theory was that a medical practitioner, such as a surgeon, was responsible, as the method used in removing his victims' penises and testicles appeared to be very professional.

Around 20 November 1962, following reports of a putrid smell emanating from a now vacant mixed business shop in Burwood Road, Concord, police found a badly decomposed corpse, which initially could not be identified. A few weeks later, they concluded it must be the body of the missing shop owner, Alan William Brennan. At this point, they determined it was not connected to any crime and certainly nothing to do with the spate of mutilations. A death notice for Brennan was subsequently printed in a Sydney newspaper and his former workmates at a local post office even went to his burial. Little did they know that it was not the body of Brennan but another victim of the mutilator.

While the hunt for the serial killer still had police baffled, "Brennan" reappeared on a warm balmy day in late April 1963 near the Sydney Post Office. He happened to run into an old work colleague from the post office who couldn't believe he was still alive. With a wreath in hand, the workmate had attended Brennan's funeral to say, what he thought was, a last goodbye. Upon being recognised alive, Brennan told his identifier to leave him alone and, understandably, ran off in a panic.

Initially, police were not very interested in this event when told by the perplexed post office worker. However, it was not until a media article with the headline "Case of the Walking Corpse" sprung them into action. The deemed body of Brennan was exhumed and, believe it or not, it revealed the genitals had also been mutilated. Fingerprints determined the corpse was, in fact, a well-known crook by the name of Patrick Joseph Hackett, who had been released from prison early in June 1962. His name was certainly not Brennan, who they thought had been buried.

The next step was to have a composite identikit drawing made up of what Brennan actually looked like. After circulating it Australia-wide, a person of interest, working under a new alias at the Melbourne Railways, was quickly recognised, despite sporting a moustache and his hair dyed a different colour. In May 1963, 39-year-old William MacDonald, also known initially as Brennan and other aliases, was certainly very much alive and taken into custody.

New South Wales detectives thought they were in for a long, protracted interrogation to connect MacDonald to the murder of Hackett and, perhaps, also the other three murder mutilations. Little did they know, they were in for another surprise, as Macdonald didn't hold back in confessing what he had been up to.

In a 100-page statement to police, MacDonald set out his life history and went into vivid detail of his exploits, including an additional murder of which police were unaware. Being born in Liverpool, England, under a completely different name, to wealthy parents, his early history left no doubt he had a troubled childhood and his anti-social behaviour was believed to have stemmed from his parents' neglect.

An introverted MacDonald left to join the British Lancashire Fusiliers where he served during the Second World War. He was sexually abused during his army stint which, he would later suggest, was the reason he committed murder and enjoyed mutilating or removing his victims' genitals. After being discharged in 1947, his embarrassed parents didn't want anything to do with their strange, homosexual son who had also been diagnosed with schizophrenia.

Following a short stay in a mental hospital and keeping the name of William MacDonald, he moved to Australia in 1955, after spending time in Canada. His first brush with the law was for trying to fondle another person's penis and he was placed on a good behaviour bond. The "victim" happened to be an Adelaide police officer. MacDonald arrived in Sydney in early 1961 as a construction worker, spending many nights with his secretive, homosexual friends, before travelling to Brisbane for a short stay.

Police were somewhat taken aback when he set out his ghastly murders in explicit detail and telling them about his first murder in Brisbane in March 1961. The victim was a 63-year-old man with who he spent a night drinking, before going back to his apartment where they drank copious amounts of more alcohol. MacDonald initially hit his playmate around the head during a short struggle and strangled him before placing the now naked dead man in his bed. MacDonald then returned to Sydney. This murder was not known to police until now, as the initial postmortem listed the death as "heart failure", due to the body having clear signs of coronary disease.

The thrill of murder began to take over and MacDonald's next victim met his death in June 1961. In even more confronting detail, he described how he had met a dishevelled Alfred Greenfield, offered him alcohol and after he fell asleep, MacDonald severed his neck arteries, cut off his genitals and then disposed of them in a plastic bag. He stated that Greenfield reminded him of the soldier who had raped him during his army service and he needed to be murdered.

The same terrible death was waiting for his next three victims after initially befriending them, followed by the usual drinking sessions. MacDonald even described how he had to wear a raincoat so he wouldn't be covered in blood when it spurted everywhere. With the McLean murder, he confirmed he had been disturbed by a young family walking by so, after hiding from them, he returned to stab his victim a further six times, cut off the man's penis and testicles before placing them in a plastic bag for disposal.

The murder of Hackett, whose body was later identified by the victim's fingerprints, was of particular interest to police given that initially it was identified as Brennan, being the then alias used by MacDonald. He again went into some detail in his confession saying how they met on the night of 6 June 1962. Again, it was the usual "drinkathon" then, after returning to the shop that MacDonald was in under the name of Brennan, they continued drinking more alcohol. After Hackett fell asleep on the floor, he was abruptly woken up with Macdonald stabbing him in the neck.

In the melee that followed, MacDonald suffered a cut to his hand while Hackett faired much worse. The knife was so blunt, preventing his genitals from being completely cut off, so the weapon was plunged deep into his heart. Macdonald sought medical treatment for an 'accidental cut' after Hackett's body was placed under the shop with blood seeping through the floorboards. MacDonald then fled interstate. The rest is history as the putrid smell alerted neighbours and our man, Brennan alias MacDonald, was arrested in Melbourne.

It was not a pleasant time for the jury in the criminal trial of MacDonald in June 1963, with many jurists fainting after hearing the gruesome castration details. Despite MacDonald pleading not guilty, as he was totally insane and supported by psychiatric reports that he kept hearing voices encouraging him to carry out the killings, he was convicted of five murders, including the Brisbane strangulation. He was sentenced to life in prison with a recommendation that he never be released. It was obvious Judge McLennan also found the case before him rather confronting, saying at sentencing that this was one of, if not the most barbaric, murder cases to ever come before him in his court.

MacDonald served his time at Long Bail Jail, alongside the likes of Arthur "Neddy" Smith[87] and Bill, as he was now known, could apply for parole after serving 25 years but

87 Smith was a well-known Australian criminal with many priors for murder, rape, armed robbery and drug trafficking. He died in prison aged 76 in 2021.

reportedly chose not to pursue his release. He remained one of Australia's longest and oldest serving prisoners. The mutilator's life came to an end in May 2015, at the ripe old age of 90, after serving 52 years behind bars. I doubt he will be missed but may pundits believe he was in fact Australia's first renowned serial killer.

8
WAS HE AUSTRALIA'S MOST EVIL?

On 15 September 1948 in Strathfield, an inner suburb of Sydney in NSW, a young couple celebrated the birth of their first son, Derek Ernest Percy. He would become the eldest of four boys but, sadly, one passed away at the early age of only 10 months following a bout of diphtheria. Due to his work commitments, around 1958-9 their father decided to move his family to Mt Beauty in Victoria.

Percy attended the local state and secondary school where he failed year eleven, despite being regarded as quite intelligent. A further transfer in the employment of his father in 1966, resulted in him attending a school in Corryong where he repeated year 11. His family were totally unaware that one day, he would become Australia's most infamous murderer.

As early as 1964, the apple of their eye began to exhibit, what could be considered as, a deviate type of sexual behaviour, including the wearing of female underwear and dresses, which he had most likely stolen from the backyard clotheslines of local neighbourhood homes.[88] His conduct then accelerated into ripping up play dolls with knives and razor blades, even wearing stolen knickers and a negligee at a local swimming hole. This behaviour subsequently resulted in the assault of a young female primary school student in 1966.

Percy decided to leave halfway through his matriculation year in 1967 to join the Royal Australian Navy where he was accepted as an ordinary seaman in late November 1967. He undertook his initial training at HMAS Cerberus at Crib Point, Victoria and, on his days off, he drove his recently purchased cream-coloured Datsun Estate motor vehicle around the Mornington Peninsula. The rear window of the car prominently featured the insignia of the Royal Navy. His academic pursuits suddenly came to the fore and he graduated top of his class. In February 1968, Percy spent time at other naval postings, including the HMAS Melbourne and HMAS Sydney, before returning on a further posting to HMAS Cerberus in April 1969.

Some months later on 20 July 1969, despite a breezy cold day, two young school children, Yvonne Tuohy and her friend Shane Spiller, were enjoying the school holidays and what the seaside town of Warneet had on offer. This bustling City of Casey village is situated about 35 kilometres from Crib Point and southeast of the Melbourne CBD. It was not unusual in those carefree days for children to be out and about without parental supervision. As Yvonne and Shane wandered around, little did they know that a man, armed with a knife, was

88 'Snowdropping' is a term used for the stealing of women's underwear when it is hanging out to dry.

watching them closely from inside his motor vehicle. After enjoying snacks while they sat next to a small bonfire filled with driftwood, thanks to a small tomahawk that Shane had used, it was time to head home.

As they approached a dirt trail in the vicinity of the safety of home, the man appeared out of nowhere and tried to abduct both children. With Yvonne now in the stranger's grip and a knife pressed against her throat, Shane valiantly waved the tomahawk at the abductor but to no avail. As he ran through adjacent bushland to get help, he could hear Yvonne screaming in terror, clearly fearing for her safety. Shane safely made it to a roadway and the last thing he saw was a cream-coloured Datsun station wagon, with Yvonne, now wrapped in a blanket and still screaming from inside the car. Fortunately, he later recalled that the Datsun vehicle had a Royal Naval emblem on its rear window.

With Yvonne now firmly secured in the motor vehicle, the abductor drove to a remote and secluded area where he began to sexually interfere with her. Unsatisfied, he carried out other disgusting acts and, in an attempt to stop this poor, defenceless 12-year-old from screaming, he placed a gag down her throat. He then tried to strangle Yvonne before ripping her body to shreds, after cutting her throat. Yvonne's mutilated body would later be found concealed in scrub where he had discarded her.

Meanwhile, Shane informed his parents, who promptly called the police. After providing a detailed description of the motor vehicle and the Navy emblem, police immediately went to the HMAS Cerberus Naval Base. When driving through the car park, Shane spotted the vehicle in which he had seen Yvonne being driven away. On identifying the owner of the vehicle as Able Seaman Percy, police found him washing his clothes in the Navy barracks. Upon searching his vehicle, they found a knife with blood on it, drawings of children in naked poses and a series of handwritten notes setting out the abduction of children of similar ages to Yvonne, with explicit descriptions of their sexual assaults and murder.

Initially, Percy professed to having no knowledge of the kidnapping and disappearance of Yvonne but, following an identification line up and being told he had now been identified as Yvonne's abductor, he slowly changed his story. From first saying, 'I can't remember' to agreeing he was at Warneet, but had no knowledge of what he did, he finally admitted that he had abducted the young girl. In company with police, he took them to where he had concealed her remains.

Percy was found not guilty by reason of insanity in April 1970 and was detained indefinitely at the Governor's Pleasure for Yvonne's murder, first at Pentridge Prison and later at Ararat Prison. It is highly likely that his cell mates would have been double murderer, Keith Ryrie and also John Desmond David.[89]

Over a number of years, following the incarceration of Percy, police had suspicions that he may have been responsible for other similar murders of young children, including those who had simply disappeared and others whose bodies had been found badly mutilated. Between 1965 and the next four years, Percy's whereabouts, including family camping trips and various Naval postings, placed him near each crime police were investigating.

This was based on the fact he had some sexual obsession

89 David was a convicted triple murderer shooting to death Janice Freeman, Neil Bray and Linda Spinks in May 1965. His death penalty was also commuted to 40 years with a minimum to serve of 30 years.

with the assault and murder of young children. It was reinforced again when similar explicit handwritten notes and drawings of naked children were found in his prison cell at Pentridge in September 1971.

In 2004, the Victoria Police Homicide Squad reviewed the cold case of seven-year-old Linda Jane Stilwell and identified significant but circumstantial evidence, linking Percy to her disappearance, as well as to other unsolved cases from the 1960s. Around 1pm on Saturday, 10 August 1968, Linda's mother sent her to look for her siblings as it was time to come home for lunch. Two hours later, another daughter returned home to tell her mother that Linda was fishing with her brother off St Kilda Pier.

The last time she would be seen was near Little Luna Park and it was later that night that she was reported as missing. Despite an extensive search around St Kilda, including the beachfront, local football grounds and checking with Melbourne hospitals for any unidentified child admission, Linda could not be found.

Two days later, on 12 August 1968, local resident Mrs Edith Jamieson contacted police to report that she had observed a girl matching Linda's description, who had received considerable media attention, playing near a glassy slope on the Lower Esplanade adjacent to the St Kilda St Moritz ice skating rink. This witness also gave police a detailed description of a rather thin man with deep olive skin and sharp facial features, sitting nearby on a park bench.

However, given that there was no evidence of what had actually happened to Linda and, despite a five-thousand-dollar reward being offered for information regarding this missing child, police investigators were at a loss, even after questioning nearly 80 persons of interest. They had already formed the view that if Linda had been involved in some sort of accident, such as a drowning, then her body would have been located.

This cold case remained in the police archives until 2004, as mentioned previously, when it was then reviewed by Detective Senior Constable Wayne Newman of the Homicide Squad. He recorded a statement from a witness who, after viewing a media article featuring Linda's photograph, identified her as someone he had interacted with in the vicinity of Little Luna Park when they were similar in age, as well as having been present with Linda's siblings.

He did not remember the exact date but recalled an afternoon around 5pm when a man, estimated to be in his early twenties, approximately 5'10" tall with short, mousy brown hair and blue eyes, identified himself as Linda's uncle. He stated this after mentioning he was taking Linda home for tea, even though Linda appeared unfamiliar with him. He last saw this young lass in the front seat of a small, coloured car, with the so-called "uncle" pushing her down as they drove off toward Elwood on Beach Road.

Another witness, upon viewing Linda's missing photograph, reported seeing her at age 12, in the same area accompanied by a young man, estimated to be about 18 years old. Notably, this witness, along with Mrs Edith Jamieson, observed that following the publication of a photo of Derek Percy in the Herald Newspaper in 1969 (and its republication in the Herald Sun in February 2005), he appeared somewhat similar, though slightly older, to the individual they had seen near or with Linda.

A subsequent review of the Yvonne Tuohy archived file then led to an interview with an ex-police officer, Ronald

Anderson. He knew Percy from their old school days and had spoken with him when he was in custody in the City Watchhouse for her murder. During the conversation, Percy referenced the disappearance of the Beaumont children on Australia Day in January 1966, as well as the 1968 murder of Simon Brook in Glebe, NSW. These cases were later considered relevant during the inquest into Linda's death.

The conversation with Percy, regarding her disappearance, along with relevant notes, was provided to the Homicide Squad at that time:

> Police Officer: Well look, Derek, I'll ask you about some of the ones that I know about. You don't have to say anything. If you remember, I will jot it down and it could be used in court…
> Percy: I simply cannot remember.
> Police officer: What about Linda Stillwell? She went missing in St Kilda.
> Percy: Yes, I drove through St Kilda that day. I had been at Cerberus in the afternoon and was driving along the Esplanade on the way to the White Ensign Club for some drinks.
> Police officer: Did you kill Linda Stillwell?
> Percy: Possibly, I don't remember a thing about it.

Senior Detective Newman expressed heightened interest in the circumstances surrounding the disappearance of the Beaumont children, as well as the deaths of Simon Brook and six-year-old Allen Redston, whose body was discovered in 1966 in Curtin, Australian Capital Territory. The detective also found circumstantial evidence regarding Percy's possible involvement in the 1965 Wanda Beach murders near Cronulla, NSW. In that regard, two 15-year-old girls, Marianne Schmidt and Christine Sharrock, were last seen by their friends on Wanda Beach on 11 January 1965, in company with a teenage boy with distinctive blonde hair.

One of the children who witnessed this, confirmed by other witnesses, also told police that this youth, who had a knife tied around his waist and was in possession of a type of spear, was seen talking to two girls earlier that day. After the two girls had not returned home that evening, police were notified. Sadly, their mutilated bodies were found in the beach sand dunes the following day.

Newman's interest in Percy being involved in their horrific murders was heightened when the autopsy revealed they had both suffered stab wounds and lacerations similar to what Yvonne Tuohy had been subjected. The police file regarding Tuohy stated that it was not uncommon for Percy, who was known to have similar blonde hair as a teenager, also matched the identikit drawn at the time of the suspect in the double murder.

This was coupled with the knowledge that his family often visited their children's grandparents' home, which was within walking distance to where the two girls lived and also to Wanda Beach. Information contained on the police file confirmed that such a visit occurred during the summer vacation and at the January 1965 Yacht Club Regatta, which took place not far from the same beach front.

The two Beaumont girls and their brother, who varied in age from as young as four to the oldest being nine, had been missing since 26 January 1966 and remained a cold case for South Australia Police. This case had coexisting similarities with Percy as a suspect. Once again, with the three children playing in the sand at Glenelg Beach, they were observed with a thin, reasonably tall male in his late twenties, with surfie-coloured blonde hair. They were last seen just before midday at a local bakery buying lunch.

The Victorian Homicide detective reviewed several recorded facts, including that when Percy was interviewed at the City Watchhouse by police officer Anderson, his former schoolmate, he stated he had been at the same beach on the day the Beaumont children disappeared. His visit to Adelaide was also confirmed after checking airline flight records around that time.

The murder of Allen Redston was the next case to show a striking similarity. When his body was found in a Curtin creek bed with his hands and feet tied, it was very similar to how Yvonne's body had been tied up. This defenceless child had died by strangulation from a loop around his neck and, again, this was similar to the gagging of Yvonne. ACT police had also investigated reports of a teenager in the same location, with blonde hair and riding a dark push bike with handlebars looking like rams' horns. The youth had assaulted young boys around this time by tying them up, before placing a plastic bag over their head in an attempt to asphyxiate them.

What stood out in particular to Detective Newman was the bike the suspect was riding, which was very similar to one that Percy had owned around that time - same colour and with turned up handlebars. The identikit of the teenager ACT police was looking for was very similar to Percy, when compared to his photo in a high school magazine. As we know, every contact leaves a trace and this time it was a green and gold school tie found at the Redston crime scene. The school tie was the same colour and bore a striking similarity to Percy's Mt Beauty High School tie.

On 19 May 1968, the mutilated body of three-year-old Simon Brook was found in a construction site near his family home in Glebe. An autopsy revealed that he suffered a number of terrible injuries inflicted by a razor blade found near his body and his penis had been cut off. He had also been asphyxiated with wads of newspaper located in his throat. Once again, a witness enabled an identikit image to be drawn of a male with whom Simon held hands, as they walked along a street near Jubilee Park. The connection to Percy was again obvious, with not only the identikit, but the razor blades being identical to ones issued to Navy personnel.

His movements around the time of this murder also saw Percy stationed at a Naval Depot near Glebe, as well as visiting his father there in 1967. In his conversation at the City Watchhouse, Percy stated how he drove through Glebe on the day of the murder, not once but twice, near where the body was found. On being reinterviewed at a later date over Yvonne's murder, he said he couldn't remember if he killed Simon. What made him a definite suspect in Simon's murder was not only that all the injuries were similar to those inflicted on Yvonne but in Percy's writings, he described in detail how he had amputated a three-year-old boy's penis.

Now identified as a person of interest, Percy was brought in from Ararat prison for questioning in February 2005.[90] After being read his rights, he was questioned at length into the disappearance of Linda and also the other child abductions

90 A Melbourne Magistrates Court application was granted pursuant to section 464B of the *Crimes Act 1958*(Vic)-Questioning or investigation of person already held for another matter.

and deaths during the 1960s. Regarding Linda, he stated he was never in the St Kilda area on that day in August 1968, as he was on leave from the Navy and was staying with his parents in Newcastle, NSW.

A similar alibi of being on holidays at the time in early January 1965 and was most likely staying at Mt Beauty, was also offered by Percy regarding the Wanda Beach murders. As to the missing Beaumont children, he told Homicide Squad detectives that he was not in Adelaide on 26 January 1966. The only concession he made with the murder of Allen Redston, was that he spent time holidaying with his parents in Canberra around 1966.

The question of who murdered Simon Brook was another matter. Percy largely agreed with the conversation he had in the City Watchhouse but, this time, said he was travelling towards Newcastle on the day of the murder, which was about 170 kilometres from the Glebe crime scene. When questioned further during the February 2005 police interview, he again said he may well have carried out the mutilation murder but he simply had no memory of it.

Some months later in December 2005, the NSW Coroner, examined all the evidence, with Percy represented by legal counsel during the inquest. The coroner formed the view there was sufficient evidence with a reasonable prospect that would satisfy a jury that Percy had committed the murder of Simon Brook. However, on perusing the brief of evidence, the NSW Director of Public Prosecutions disagreed with the coroner, finding that, in fact, there was not sufficient evidence to satisfy a jury beyond reasonable doubt of Percy's guilt.

In April 2005, Senior Detective Newman perused an archived file in respect of Percy, which contained a number of his perverse handwritten notes and a quantity of Shell road maps. Other than maps of Sydney and the ACT, what stood out was a map showing the St Kilda foreshore and, more importantly, one with a pen mark over the local Esplanade.

In July 2007, the storage unit previously rented by Percy was combed through under a search warrant. A Road Touring Atlas was found in one of the 35 boxes and the page showing the St Kilda Pier and its adjoining pages had been highlighted in pencil. On being satisfied that Percy was responsible for the death of Linda Jane Stillwell, a comprehensive inquest brief of evidence was forwarded to the Victorian State Coroner for a finding to be determined into her death.

The brief relied on all the cold cases reviewed by Detective Newman in his thorough investigation: the similarity of injuries, identikit face fits and geographical locations, to further assist the coroner.[91] In addition, a number of expert reports were included, notably one from a renowned forensic psychologist and a director from the Victorian Institute of Forensic Mental Health. Amongst other conclusions, Professor James Ogloff came to the opinion that Percy had a tendency to commit the torture and complex mutilation of children and that Yvonne Touhy was unlikely to be his first victim, with her death occurring 11 months after Linda's disappearance.

In the first two weeks of December 2009, as part of his investigation into the death of Linda, Deputy State Coroner, Iain West, heard from a number of witnesses. Percy was called to give evidence by counsel assisting the coroner but this was objected to by his counsel on the basis that his evidence may lead to prove he had committed an offence, notably the disappearance and now

91 The inquest brief also included the attempted abduction of Linda Read in Bittern on the Mornington Peninsula in 1969 which bore a number of similarities incriminating Percy.

presumed death of Linda. The coroner upheld the objection on the basis of the mental state of Percy and the time of 42 years that had elapsed since the suspected murder of Linda. An application was then made to the Supreme Court in 'the interest of justice' that Percy be compelled to give evidence.[92]

However, in handing down his ruling that Percy would not have to provide evidence, Justice Iain Ross said:

> *In assessing the various factors, I am satisfied it would not be in the interest of justice to grant a certificate. While I have enormous sympathy for the family who waited a considerable time to hear from Mr Percy, as a matter of law it would be inappropriate for me to compel him to give evidence then give him a certificate granting him immunity in respect of that evidence.*[93]

Days prior to the passing of Percy from lung cancer, it was hoped he would make a death bed confession but he went to his grave on 23 July 2013, aged 64, still having made no admissions. Indeed, Deputy State Coroner West, at a bedside hearing, spoke with Percy three days earlier but he continued to deny any knowledge of or involvement into the disappearance of Linda. Even then, he continued stating he was in Newcastle at the time and not in St Kilda.

On 30 October 2014, the Deputy State Coroner handed down his finding of the circumstantial evidence implicating Percy, following an inquest into the death of Linda[94] and said:

92 *Coroners Act 2008*(Vic)-section 57(4).

93 *Priest v Deputy State Coroner & Anor* [2010] VSC 449.

94 Linda Jane Stilwell, Finding into Death with Inquest-Coroners Court Reference 2005/1489.

I accept the evidence of Mr Anderson regarding the conversation held in the police cell, with Derek Percy telling him that he was in St Kilda the day Linda disappeared. I prefer Mr Anderson's evidence for the reason that Derek Percy had the capacity to make false denials, as was demonstrated by the Yvonne Tuohy case. In addition, support for his presence, in the vicinity of where Linda was last seen, is found in the evidence given by a number of witnesses. I am satisfied the description given of a male observed loitering near her, or in her company, is consistent with Derek Percy's appearance at the time. As well, the description of the vehicle in which she was driven away is consistent with the vehicle owned by Derek Percy.[95]

In his findings, Deputy Corner West concluded that:

I formally find that Linda Stilwell is deceased, having met her death by foul play.[96] *I find that Derek Percy was at St Kilda when Linda was abducted on the afternoon of 10 August 1968*[97] *[and] I find that Derek Percy caused the death of Linda Jane Stilwell.*[98]

The question remains of whether Percy 'was the most evil offender in Australia's criminal history'. He was convicted of the murder of Yvonne Touhy and two coroners found sufficient circumstantial evidence that he was responsible for the deaths of Linda Stilwell and Simon Brook.

This leaves six other mutilated and deceased children who

95 Ibid-para 56.

96 Ibid-para 58.

97 Ibid-para 59.

98 Ibid-para 60.

may well have encountered Percy but, sadly, we will never know if he was responsible for their deaths. With Allen Redston, no one has come forward to this day to provide any evidence of who may be responsible for his death, leaving Percy still the most likely suspect predator.

With regard to the Wanda Beach murders, there was some suggestion in 2016 that a supposed loving husband and father, now convicted and imprisoned of sexually assaulting his daughter, had earlier confessed to his then girlfriend that he was the Wanda Beach murderer. This was later recanted but it is of interest that he had also attended the same school as Marianne Schmidt.

In respect to the missing Beaumont children, 60 years later, a now deceased company director remains a person of interest[99] and a further unsuccessful evacuation at the site of his former Adelaide business premises took place over the weekend of 22 February 2025, in the forlorn hope the remains of the children could be located.[100]

It still begs the question though, whether child murderer,

---

99 Initially one of his sons said he saw the Beaumont children at their family home, which was situated close to the Glenelg Beach, on the same day they disappeared. Three days later, his father arranged for a hole resembling a grave to be dug at his business premises, which is now the subject of a further but deeper dig. It was later determined that this now suspect was related to the father of the Beaumont children by marriage.

100 Another cold case with striking similarities was the August 1973 disappearance of Joanne Ratcliffe(11) and Kirste Gordon(4) believed to be abducted and murdered and known as the Adelaide Oval abductions. A similar site excavation was to take place in March 2025 in South Australia's mid-north where it is believed their bodies may be buried in barrels. A known child abuser has been nominated by his grandson as being responsible.

Derek Percy, was responsible for the deaths of a total of nine children. It remains to be seen but in the interim, the jury is still out in that regard.

9
TWO MODEL PRISONERS

On 6 September 1971, police received a frantic call of a probable mass shooting, from a local doctor, at a small farm in the country town of Hope Forest near Willunga, situated about 40 kilometres south of Adelaide in South Australia. After arriving at the farm around 7pm, what they found would remain with even hardened detectives for many years to come.

It was gruesome and gut wrenching. What made it even more confronting was, when police arrived at the now murder crime scene, they found 40-year-old abattoir slaughterman, Clifford Bartholomew, calmly sitting at his kitchen table enjoying a cold beer with an empty bottle of Bacardi lying next to him.

At approximately 1am, Bartholomew had murdered his wife, Heather and their seven children, aged from four to 19 years. They had been bludgeoned with a mallet before being shot with a .22 single shot rifle. The bodies, clad in their underwear and pyjamas, were located in and near their bedrooms and in the hallway of the seven-room rented farmhouse. He had also shot dead his sister-in-law, leaving her body lying outside the home. In addition, he killed her 19-month-old baby. The use of such a rifle meant that for each deadly shot he fired, he would have had to empty the spent cartridge and reload each time, given it was a single shot.

Immediately placed under arrest, he first stated to police he had only meant to kill his wife because he felt rejected and thought she was having an affair with a younger man, after finding a letter written to her. This man was staying at their farm. Bartholomew then showed police what he had written before carrying out the horrendous crimes. The note stated that he had snapped and there were *'screaming noises that was splitting me head wide open and that horrible look on my wife's face, I couldn't control my actions.'*

As the other soon-to-be victims each woke up from hearing gun shots, he said he then shot his eldest daughter and came to the conclusion that they all had to die. In his words, 'I couldn't leave any behind as I loved them too much.'

What was even harder to fathom was his shooting of his 19-month-old nephew. After having a few drinks at the kitchen table, he realised he had forgotten about him as he was still sleeping. Bartholomew stated he went to the baby's cot, put a gun against his head and pulled the trigger. The baby was found lying face down on his pillow with a dummy still in his mouth. He then covered all the bodies with blankets and telephoned his local doctor, confessing to what he had just done.

Bartholomew was charged the next evening at the City Watchhouse with only the murder of his wife. According to one now-retired police detective, there was nothing to be gained by charging him with all 10 murders because, if found guilty, he would still receive the same maximum sentence, namely the death penalty. In addition, the evidence in respect of her death was overwhelming, whereas with the remaining nine murders, there was some concern Bartholomew might rely on a defence of insanity. He was then remanded in custody after appearing at the Adelaide Magistrates Court.

In late November 1971, Bartholomew pleaded guilty before Supreme Court Judge Mitchell. He told of his suspicions that she was having an affair, which police found to be without any basis. He complained that when his wife washed and ironed his clothes, Bartholomew had to put them away but she would happily iron and fold the young man's freshly washed items before neatly putting them away. He then said his wife denied any wrongdoing on her behalf and he was simply imagining things but he believed she was involved in an illicit relationship with the boarder.

Bartholomew then said to the body of the court:

It got me that way in the end that it suddenly came in mind to kill her. At least the kiddies would be better off, even in a home or living with somebody else, who would take care of them, even if I couldn't.

He stated, after getting out of bed and putting on some clothes, he retrieved a rifle from his shed with the intention of rendering his wife unconscious from a blow to the head. Before he could take her out to the shed, she began screaming. In his court statement, he said:

My mind was in a state of madness and it seemed as though I couldn't stop myself from doing what I intended to do... I couldn't control my action... All of a sudden, things seemed to be dead quiet. By this time, I was in the kitchen with a rifle in my hand and I wondered what I was doing there with it. I started to tremble all over.

After hearing this self-serving rubbish from Bartholomew, Justice Mitchell sentenced him to death for the murder of his wife. Even the judge had some reservations as to whether he would be hanged, in view of rumblings of Government policy and that the death penalty was now under review.

The Don Dunstan-led Labor Government in South Australia was known for its progressive social policies, implementing several significant reforms. These included the decriminalisation of homosexuality, the relaxation of censorship and alcohol laws, the recognition of Aboriginal land rights and, in 1976, the abolition of the death penalty. This meant Bartholomew would not go to the gallows but would spend the rest of his life behind bars. Remarkably, that didn't happen.

In November 2002, a 71-year-old gentleman, known to his family as "Poppy Cliff" Palmer, passed away, leaving his loving and devout Christian wife of 22 years heartbroken. She likely missed him but lived another 10 years, passing away at 83. When Poppy Cliff's family began the sad task of cleaning out their mum's family home and its contents, they found Poppy's prison discharge papers.

His actual name was not Clifford Palmer but the despicable Clifford Bartholomew. To say they were in absolute shock was an understatement and they found it extremely difficult believing the kind, loving, hardworking man they'd known for over 22 years was capable of murder. Even his stepson-in-law was shocked, saying he never expected this gentle, elderly man to harm anyone, especially while watching his grandchildren.

This then 40-year-old man had committed familicide by killing 10 members of his family. Subsequently, he re-entered society under a new name, remarried, and appeared to resume an ordinary life. Bartholomew was released on parole in 1979 after serving eight years, which equated to approximately nine months for each of the 10 deaths.

Why was he paroled then?

The discharge papers included, in essence, that his crimes were carried out when he had mental issues and was also suffering from depression. A learned psychologist also stated that Bartholomew was not a danger to society, as he only murdered his own family and, on that basis, he was not a threat to any other person. The Parole Board was further enlightened that he was indeed a "model prisoner" and deserved to be released back into the community.

On his release from prison, Bartholomew initially thought it would be a great idea to reside in Port Adelaide but the local community had other ideas. After receiving a number of death threats, he changed his name to Clifford Palmer, moved to Victoria and then, after remarrying, retired to Queensland. His gravestone read:

In loving memory of Clifford Palmer–Dearly loved husband... Devoted to and sadly missed by children and grandchildren.

On remarrying, Poppy Cliff became a stepfather to seven children, all around the same ages of his children at the time he blatantly murdered them. It is likely that few people will visit his gravesite but then again, he was a model prisoner, so he obviously deserved to resume a normal life. But let's not forget about the 10 innocents who died far too early.

Another model prisoner must have been John Fairley, as he only served a paltry nine years for the murder of two innocent parents, Mick and Susan Lewis. In late September 1978, in the small country town of Jerilderie in NSW,[101] a telephone exchange operator, when checking a faulty phone line, spoke with a four-year-old girl who answered the phone:

> Hello?
> Hello there, is your mummy at home?
> She is but she is asleep.
> Well, is daddy there?
> Yeah but he's asleep too. He's sleeping on the kitchen floor.
> Oh. Could you go wake up mummy for me and tell her to come to the phone? I need to tell her something. Can you do that for me?
> No, no. I don't like mummy any more cause mummy's turning black.

This poor little girl had no idea that both her parents had been shot dead. After being notified by the operator, police found two young children alongside their parents' decomposing bodies at the secluded home. The mother had two gunshot wounds to the back of her head, so it was initially considered that the scene was one of murder-suicide. Her husband, Mick,

101 It is situated along the Newell Highway near the Victorian border and is largely know as an irrigated farming Centre. Ned Kelly also paid the town a visit in February 1879, locked up the local constabulary, kidnapped residents and then robbed the local bank

was known to police for sheep theft and was also a heavy drinker and gambler. He had a track record of coming home drunk and abusing his wife. On one occasion he pointed a gun at her.

Finding him shot dead in the kitchen, police assumed he was responsible for his wife's murder and then killed himself. The scene was quite confronting as the wife's body had not only turned black but she was unrecognisable as a female. The children were not only understandably frightened but looking very thin having survived solely on cans of dog food.

However, it was not all as it seemed and police would uncover several clues that led to the conclusion Mick wasn't responsible. Not only did they find evidence of his pockets being ransacked but when Susan's body was collected for removal, it was found she had been left lying on a heated blanket, with the dial turned up to the highest level. Police also found a .22 calibre bullet casing, the absence of any rifle on the property and evidence of a forced entry into the house. This was no murder-suicide but now a case of double murder.

To the credit of NSW homicide investigators, they launched a painstaking and complex inquiry and the first breakthrough was the identification of the make of rifle used. After examining the bullet casing, ballistics determined it came from an Australian-made rifle. Each owner of a Fieldman .22 rifle was identified and questioned about their movements round the time of the murders. No significant outcome was reported, so a command centre was established in Jerilderie, where rifle owners were required to attend for police inspection. In addition, investigators spoke with Mick's drinking mates, numerous friends and work colleagues trying to find any clue which may lead to further inquiries.

Two things happened that would lead to the killer's identity. A rumour had been circulating that Mick had intentionally smashed his car some months earlier with the sole reason of claiming insurance money. Detectives then spoke with the insurance agent involved in the suspicious transaction. They had already questioned John Fairley as part of their general enquiries but he was able to offer an alibi for his movements around the time of the murder. However, it was brought to the attention of police that Fairley had wanted to have a discussion with Mick regarding a money issue. On further questioning, he became evasive about his employment as an insurance broker and gave different alibis from those in his original statement to police.

The pivotal breakthrough occurred during the comprehensive review of Fieldman rifle owners. A set of cartridges provided by a local resident, Ray Rafferty, was found to be an exact match to the bullet casing recovered at the crime scene. Police first thought that Rafferty may be the person they were looking for, especially when he could initially only produce the matching .22 cartridges. On being asked again where the actual rifle was, he admitted it had been lent to his friend Fairley but was never returned.

Following questioning and presentation of the evidence, Fairley admitted responsibility for the murders of the Lewis couple. As to motive, it turned out that Mick had been involved in a legitimate car crash but, after receiving only an insurance payment of $1,000, Fairley kept the rest for himself. Mick then faked a further car smash to try and recover what the vehicle was worth. Fairley kept the insurance money but, fearing Mick might retaliate or contact the police about the theft, he decided to kill him. Unfortunately, Susan was a witness, so she too was eliminated. The children were left unscathed as, according to Fairley, he didn't know they were in the house at the time.

Not a lot is known about Fairley, other than he was from Shepparton in Victoria, was a local contract painter and part-time insurance agent. On 28 June 1979, 40-year-old Fairley pleaded guilty and was sentenced to life imprisonment. However, after only serving nine years behind bars, for reasons only known to the State Parole Authority of NSW, he was granted parole. This individual, convicted of double murder and described as a model prisoner, served only nine years and was released, leaving two children without parents.

Like Poppy Cliff, Fairley must have also been the true definition of a model prisoner.

10
SERIAL KILLER PAUL STEVEN HAIGH

In 1969, students at Swinburne Technical School on Burwood Road, Hawthorn, were unaware that one of their classmates, then approximately 12 years old, would later be responsible for seven homicides. Paul Steven Haigh was raised by adopted parents from the age of three months in what can only be described as a dysfunctional childhood.

For the following nine years, after dropping out of school, he lived a life of crime including acts of burglary, theft, unlicensed driving and assault. In 1978, after serving time at the Youth Training Centre at Malmsbury, where he was involved in an incident with a prison officer, Haigh was then paroled, following an earlier sentence in the County Court of five years imprisonment, with a minimum of three years. He would now raise the bar higher, from committing armed robberies to murder.

After entering a pizza shop in Prahran on 10 September 1978 and demanding money, he shot dead the man who was working behind the counter, Bruno Cingolani, a father of two young children. On 21 September 1978, Haigh robbed a Tattslotto agency in Prahran and fatally shot 58-year-old employee, Evelyn Abraham, after demanding cash at gunpoint. He did not stand trial for the two murders in the Supreme Court of Victoria until May 1986.

In June 1979, he continued his murderous rampage alongside his former prison mate Robert Lindsay Wright, who he first met in 1975 while serving time in the Young Offenders Division at Pentridge Prison. After taking up residence with one of Wright's older sisters, he met several people, some of who he would later kill.

On 27 June 1979, he shot dead a once trusted former associate of his and Wright by the name of Wayne Keith Smith. His weapon of choice was a .25 pistol placed against his victim's neck, followed by multiple gun shots into the body using a .22 rifle. Three weeks later on 22 July 1979, Haigh then killed Sheryle Gardner using a .22 rifle. Supposedly out of fear that her 10-year-old son, Danny Mitchell, would dob him into police. Haigh then shot him. Police would later find Gardner slumped behind the steering wheel of her car with a number of bullet holes in her head and her young son lying across the back seat.

The murders of all three were believed to be over their knowledge of the murder of Ivanka "Éva" Karlson. She was a girlfriend of escaped prisoner, Barrie "Barry" Robert Quinn,[102]

102 Quinn escaped from Fairfield Infectious Diseases Hospital on 16 November 1978 after being transferred from Pentridge Prison suffering from hepatitis. Gardner was also one of Quinn's numerous girlfriends.

who was known to be a good friend of both Wright and Smith, having helped him flee when serving a sentence for a 1974 double murder.[103] After being apprehended in Perth in 1979, Quinn and Wright would subsequently be acquitted in 1980 of the murder of Karlson.

Haigh committed his most heinous murder when he turned on his then girlfriend, Lisa Brearley. This was supposedly not only over her questionable infidelity but Haigh thought she had spoken to her mother about the .22 guns which had been purchased to kill Gardner and her son. In the words of Haigh, she was now 'a loose end that had to be gotten rid of.'

Her death was terrible, as Haigh didn't have a gun he could use, so he stabbed her 157 times. The murder was watched by Wright and another so called mate, Ernie Strachan. However, before being killed, she was raped by Strachan.

On 12 November 1980, after a jury trial lasting 10 weeks, Haigh was found guilty of the four murders and sentenced by Supreme Court Judge Anderson to be imprisoned for the term of his natural life with no minimum.[104] With regard to the September 1978 hold up murders, six years later, Haigh handed a nine page handwritten document to members of Victoria Police Homicide Squad confessing to both murders and unrelated offending, including armed robberies.

103 Quinn was serving a life sentence for the March 1974 double murder at the Car O Tel Motel in St. Kilda. His subsequent appeal against conviction was dismissed. See *The Queen v Barrie Robert Quinn* [1975] Unreported, Vic Court of Criminal Appeal, 3 April 1975. Also see chapter 11.

104 Wright was also found guilty of the murders of Smith, Gardner and Mitchell and received the mandatory life sentence. In 1983, he would escape from prison but after being recaptured, Wright was one of five prisoners who died in a fire in October 1987 in the high security division known as Jika Jika.

He then waived his right to a committal hearing, appeared unrepresented and pleaded guilty. On 17 June 1986, Haigh was again sentenced to a term of imprisonment for his natural life and various other terms for unrelated offending, all to be served concurrently. However, the matter did not conclude at that point.

According to Haigh's version of events, in 1991 fellow Pentridge prisoner, Donald Hatherley, who was convicted of a number of sex crimes, said he had enough of serving time behind bars and wanted to end it all. Haigh was only too happy to oblige and considered the best way would be to arrange his hanging and, if that didn't work, he could always strangle him. Finding a suitable nylon cord rope in the toilets of B Division, it was arranged for Hatherley to hang himself in his cell after the evening meal and prior to the 4.10pm lock up, naturally with Haigh's assistance.

Haigh then tied the rope to a plastic pipe in Hatherley's cell and, after determining it was strong enough to cope with the weight of the soon to be deceased victim, he tied his hands up. Haigh placed a noose around Hatherley's neck, told him to stand on a small cupboard and then kicked it from underneath him, leaving him dangling. The problem was Hatherley didn't die so Haigh finished the job by strangling him. Haigh tried to conceal his role by having Hatherley spit on the binding material, hoping to link him to his own death, but his efforts failed. He had even arranged for the cupboard to be positioned so it appeared that Hatherley was able to kick it out from under himself.

In May 1993, Haigh entered a plea of not guilty, however, the jury found him guilty, resulting in a sentence of life imprisonment with a minimum term of 15 years. This marked

Haigh's first murder conviction in which the court was able to set a non-parole period. In delivering Haigh's sentence, Justice Coldrey made several pertinent observations, with one comment in particular encapsulating the gravity of this most recent homicide.

> *It may be that your attitude towards Hatherley's death is the product of long years in prison which have brought with the development of moral perspectives designed to ensure your own physical and mental self-preservation...Certainly your personal approach to Donald Hatherley's death represents a morality which the general community would regard as quite distorted.*[105]

His Honour then went on to say:

> *Although I accept that you were to a degree, activated by sympathy for Hatherley's situation and that you did not believe your participation in his demise to be murder... you were ready and willing to utilise the death of an unstable and vulnerable man as a vehicle for self–fulfilment. A further and most disturbing aspect of this case, in your willingness, yet again, to involve yourself in the killing of another human being.*[106]

As to self–fulfilment, His Honour may well have been correct. There was some suggestion by Pentridge Prison warders that Haigh was annoyed his status as the most prolific serial

---

105 *R v Haigh* [1993] Unreported, Supreme Court of Victoria, Judge Coldrey, 26 May 1993, transcript sentencing remarks, page 173.

106 Ibid-page 174.

killer was now in jeopardy, thanks to Hoddle Street killer Julian Knight,[107]which Haigh would emphatically deny.

In May 2009, a judgment was handed down of an application for a minimum term[108] by Haigh before Justice King in the Supreme Court of Victoria, regarding the six terms of life imprisonment without parole. Haigh, represented by Patrick Tehan QC, made several submissions including the tendering of a book he wrote entitled, "The House of Blue Light". The ramblings contained a number of letters written by him setting out vivid details of the first six murders.

In refusing the application, Justice King did not discuss the contents of the book on the basis it was not particularly helpful, preferring to rely on other material. This included evidence from Haigh and his further handwritten letters to the Court expressing remorse and that he was a "changed man". His Honour was not impressed regardless and in refusing the application, said:

> *The circumstances of the separate murders of six members of the community, together with the callous and brutal manner in which they were murdered, would, in my opinion, make the fixing of such a period inappropriate…You are not the judge, jury and executor, who can determine who may live and*

107 On 9 August 1987, Knight committed one of the worst massacres in Australia's history firing over 100 rounds of ammunition shooting dead seven innocent people and injuring a further 19. (See chapter 26).

108 On 1 July 1986, section 18(a) was inserted into the *Penalties and Sentences Act 1985* (Vic) providing for such an application. Such Act was repealed on 22 April 1992, and the *Sentencing Act 1991*(Vic) came into operation allowing under section 13 the fixing of a non-parole period by the Supreme Court, unless it considers it not appropriate given the nature of the offending and past history of the applicant.

die...they were entitled to live as any other member of this community...[109]

Haigh, however, was given one last go at parole and hoped eventually to be released when the Supreme Court of Criminal Appeal in 2011 reversed the decision of Justice King.[110] A further application was heard by Judge Beach in the Supreme Court of Victoria in December 2012.[111] Haigh, now 55 years old, clutching rosary beads, appeared unrepresented due to a lack of legal aid funding and again relied on his book which contained a number of letters setting out what can only be described as pathetic excuses and a lack of remorse for the multiple murders.

In respect of the first two murders Haigh stated:

...were in separate armed robberies. In both hold ups I didn't prostrate myself and beg for a loan but made a gunpoint demand for money...In both cases an unknown criminal, who wasn't wielding an imitation handgun, gave pre-emptory instructions to the victims...In both cases they acted beyond the scope of instructions and the consequence was the loss of their lives...Though I was a lone gunman, in both cases firearms have triggers that don't take long to pull. The woman was shot once in the head [Evelyn Abraham], and the man was shot once in the abdomen [Bruno Cingolani].[112]

As to the murder of Smith, his lack of remorse was particularly evident when he wrote:

109 *R v Haigh* [2009] VSC 185-para 202.

110 *Haigh v The Queen* Unreported-Court of Appeal, Buchanan and Nettle JJA and Kyrou AJA, 19 April 2011.

111 *R v Haigh* [2012] VSC 617.

112 Ibid-para 17.

The day after he was murdered I went to give my false condolences to his loved ones. The real reasons was going to see them to find out what was being said and to make out as if my relationship with the deceased...was the same as it apparently was before the chap was shot...I also went to the victim's funeral...We stopped at the flower shop to get something appropriate...we went to the cemetery and saw the deceased lowered into the ground...I didn't tell the victim's girlfriend that she was lucky to be alive...I had her in my sights for badmouthing me and when she wasn't home I helped kill her boyfriend.[113]

Regarding victims three and four, the situation was further exacerbated when he noted in one of his letters:

It turned out that I was the one who killed them both but before doing so I made the woman[Sheryle Ann Gardner] think she wasn't going to be shot...I pulled the triggers on the sawn off .22 rifles that were aimed at the victims...I took the second gun from the bag I had and used that to finish the job...whilst consoling the boy[Danny Mitchell], I shot him with the second gun when his back was turned to me. I shot him three times in the back of the head and, after this, I turned the gun on his mother again, just to make sure she was dead.[114]

Haigh then described the sickening rape and murder of his then girlfriend, Lisa Brearley:

I invited my girlfriend to a party...however, the only thing that awaited her up in the dark forest track was rape and death...

113 Ibid-para 18.

114 Ibid-para 19.

one of my co-offenders asked if I was going to let others use my girlfriend for sex...I produced a knife and put it to her neck...I permitted the man to have sex with her, because if his semen was in her corpse, it was something he could reflect on if he later thought about telling the police of her murder...if the body were later discovered, semen in the corpse along with stab wounds, would be a deviation from our usual modus operandi...I experienced her as a kind-hearted and nice enough lass...when the fellow who wanted sex with her had finished using her body...I attacked her with the blade. Amazingly, it seems, I stabbed her one hundred and fifty-seven times...she fought amazingly hard...because of this when she was finally still, I decided to stab her more, in order to make sure she was dead.[115]

While Haigh maintained he had remorse for his first six victims, he told the court he had absolutely none for fellow prisoner Hatherley, describing his death as some sort of adventure and saw it as a challenge for his personal growth. Indeed, His Honour would comment, 'Each of the six murders... was a callous, brutal, disgraceful and entirely unjustified act.'[116]

There was also some suggestion that after the murder of Hatherley, he had been somewhat of a model prisoner for several years, apart from some isolated events, which included using drugs and sewing his lips together.[117]

The court was also assisted by a plethora of expert reports and in the one dated 11 April 1990, psychiatrist Dr Brian Hutchinson stated:

---

115 Ibid-para 20.

116 Ibid-para 21.

117 Ibid-para 45 and footnote 24.

I asked him how he compared himself to the Hoddle Street shooter. He declared he was totally different because he had killed for a reason. He admitted he might stuff up again if he was released. He might even kill but only with a good reason. Education and religion provided no answers but he had 'learned to play the game' and 'learned to manipulate people'. [118]

His Honour Judge Beach was certainly not going to be manipulated and he said:

…the applicant's continued willingness to attribute blame to others; his continued use of illicit drugs in prison; the murder of Donald Hatherley; his lack of remorse in respect of the murder of Donald Hatherley; the significant episodes of bad behaviour in prison up until the last several years and the future risk of him committing further offences of violence(as discussed in the evidence) are matters that do not tell in favour of the granting of a non-parole period.[119]

It was of no surprise then that on 13 December 2012,Judge Beach handed down a conclusion that it was inappropriate to grant parole to Haigh. This serial killer remains behind bars and the only way he will ever be released is in a pine box, perhaps being buried alongside his now deceased mate, Barry Robert Quinn[120] and also Alexander Tsakmais, alias "The BBQ King" at the Fawkner Memorial Park.

---

118 Ibid-para 60.

119 Ibid-para 64.

120 Memorial ID 140678019.

11
THE BBQ KING

After completing National Service in 1969, I resumed my public service career with Victoria Police. The use of public servants in police line ups had not changed, with the only difference being, the lines ups were now usually conducted on the vacant sixth floor of the new building at the rear of Russell Street Police Headquarters.

Prior to this relocation, they were held on the headquarters' ground floor auditorium facing La Trobe Street. One of the line ups in which I first participated was regarding armed robber, James "Iceman" Bazley. Litte did we know at the time, he would later be sentenced to life imprisonment for the 1979 murder of Isabel and Douglas Wilson, whose bodies were found buried in Rye, Victoria in May 1979.[121]

121 Bazley or sometimes referred to as 'machine gun' or 'iceman' was also convicted of conspiring to murder NSW anti-drugs campaigner Donald Mackay, who vanished from a NSW Griffith Hotel car park in 1977, being sentenced to a concurrent term of nine years jail. *R v Bazley, James Frederick* [1986] Unreported VicSC, 133, Judge Gray, 16 April 1986.

For unknown reasons, I was still being chosen to be part of line-ups and on Tuesday, 26 March 1974, I stood alongside two males in custody for armed robbery. The men were Barry "Barrie" Quinn and his alleged accomplice, Robin West.[122] Although Quinn was shorter than me, he was placed alongside me due to our similar build and hair style. Homicide detectives brought in a witness who was asked to look along the line of men, see if he could recognise the person or persons who robbed him at gunpoint, then walk up to him and tap him on the shoulder.

The witness was wearing a sling as, apparently, he had been wounded during the robbery allegedly committed by Quinn and West. The well-built male witness walked along the line, stopped in front of me, then took one step to my left and let go with a round-arm right hook, knocking Quinn to the floor. I stood there totally stunned before police quickly escorted the witness away.

As he was leaving, a bloody-faced Quinn screamed words to the effect:

'You think you were tough when you had a snooker cue in your hand, you fucking weak prick!'

I was later to ascertain, from investigating police, when Quinn and West attempted to rob a snooker parlour, they burst in, telling everyone to stop playing and hand over their wallets. Apparently, our witness just kept playing and told them both to piss off. Quinn or West then shot him in the arm as he was trying to hit them with the snooker cue. That witness was one tough cookie in my mind and I doubt police would have charged him with assault. As much as they were shocked with what took place, a couple had smirks on their faces.

---

122 West would subsequently give evidence on behalf of the Crown against Quinn in respect of the Car-O-Tel Motel double murder which was committed on the night of 25 March 1976.

West was subsequently charged with a number of armed robberies, including wounding with intent to murder, whereas Quinn was charged and convicted of the botched armed robbery and murder of two men at the Car–O-Tel Motel in St Kilda in March 1974.[123] Little did Quinn know then that at the age of 36, he would cop his right whack from fellow convicted murderer, Alexander "The BBQ King" Tsakmakis.[124] This moniker was awarded to him while a permanent resident in 'H Division' at Pentridge Prison.

Tsakmakis was not known to police as initially, he was a company director and dedicated family man residing in Ivanhoe, Victoria. Despite any hardships he may have faced, he was ultimately a cold-blooded murderer. His first brush with the law occurred in January 1978 when he murdered 25-year-old professional runner, Bruce Lindsay Walker, allegedly over a dispute regarding the ownership of a vintage motor vehicle. Not content in settling the dispute in court, he invited Walker on a fishing expedition in Port Phillip Bay but Tsakmakis was the only one to return to the pier. Walker's body, with his hands and feet tied up in chicken wire, eventually made it to shore at Point Lonsdale.

Police had no doubt that Tsakmakis was responsible and, after being charged with murder, he was able to obtain bail.[125] He needed funds to pay for his upcoming defence in his murder

123 Quinn appealed the conviction and sentence largely on the grounds that he denied he ever confessed to police that he was responsible for the two murders. The appeal was dismissed- *The Queen v Barrie Robert Quinn* [1975] Unreported, VCCA,3 April 1975.

124 Also known as Alekos Taikmaskis.

125 Bail was granted by Justice Kaye with a surety of 1,000 pounds and the surrender of his passport. See In the Matter of an Application for Bail by Alexander Tsakmakis, Unreported VicSC–Justice Kaye, 19 September 1978.

trial so, in June 1979, he shot the two owners of a Tattslotto agency in Hawthorn. After handing Tsakmakis $1500, they were told to lie on the floor where he then fired five bullets into their heads, with one lodging in a victim's brain. The man's wife was also shot in the face.

Somehow, they both survived and, in 1981, Tsakmakis was sentenced to 22 years to be served concurrently with his life term. Earlier that month, a Fitzroy North massage parlour prostitute, Margeret Clayton, didn't get to finish her shift as she was shot dead, also found lying face down on the floor.

After Tsakmakis was convicted of the murder of Bruce Walker and sentenced to life imprisonment in August 1979,[126] he then boasted he was also responsible for the shooting deaths of three Melbourne jewellers on St Patrick's Day in March 1978, following the theft of diamonds valued at $30,000. A .22 rifle had been used to shoot each victim in the back of the head and their bodies were found lying spreadeagled, face down on the floor.[127]

The State Coroner would later find that the men had been murdered by 'a person or persons unknown.' However, now retired Homicide Squad chief Paul Delianis said in 2013, he had no doubt that Tsakmakis was responsible for the Manchester Unity triple murder and also prostitute Margeret Clayton. They fitted his usual scenario, first making sure his victims were lying on the floor and then shooting them dead.

He was also believed to be responsible for the mysterious disappearance of celebrated chef and owner of the Olinda

---

126 His subsequent appeal against conviction was dismissed by the Court of Appeal. *The Queen v Alexander Tsakmakis* [1979] Unreported, VCCA, 24 October 1979.

127 This triple murder would later become known as the Manchester Unity murders.

Cuckoo restaurant, Willie Koeppen. In late February 1976, this wealthy restaurateur suddenly disappeared. According to the infamous Mark Brandon "Chopper" Read,[128] his cell mate, Tsakmakis, told him he was responsible. Interestingly, some years after the death of Tsakmakis, his daughter contacted the wife of Koeppen to apologise for the loss of her husband.

Read also said Tsakmakis had made admissions to other murders. This included the Clayton murder and that of Brian Finemore, who was found murdered in his East Melbourne apartment in October 1975. If Read was correct about Tsakmakis' actions, all up, he had allegedly committed seven murders by the time he was imprisoned for Bruce Walker's death, not just the one for which he was convicted.

In any event, Tsakmakis would turn out to be his ex-cell mate, given that Chopper later stabbed him with a pair of scissors over a jail power struggle, while he was reading of all things, *The Australian Financial Review*.

However, Tsakmakis would increase his overall tally to at least one more in July 1984, while watching the TV soap drama, *The Restless Years*, with Barry Robert Quinn. Being the double

---

128 Read, between the ages of 20 and 38, only spent 13 months not being locked up with convictions for armed robbery, assault, arson, kidnapping and various firearms offences. In Pentridge Prison's H Division, after a war over consuming too many sausages, he became the leader of the Overcoat Gang wearing long coats to conceal weapons to be used in attacks on fellow prisoners. Most of his gang cohorts would die violently but those who were lucky to survive included gunman, Amos Atkinson, murderer, Greg Brazel, armed robber, 'Sammy' Hutchinson and famed bareknuckle bash artist, Frankie Waghorn. Read had a fellow inmate chop off both his ears, but his nickname was from a cartoon character. Read was first released in 1991 and again in 1998. He died in 2013, aged 58.

murderous joker he was, Quinn thought he would torment Tsakmakis over the rape of one of his girlfriends. In an act of revenge, the BBQ King poured industrial glue over Quinn, then flicked lit matches at him until he went up in flames while running in circles in the day room. Tsakmakis tried unsuccessfully to stop prison officers from entering and putting out the flames with a blanket, after initially trying to use a fire extinguisher.

You have to give Quinn credit though for his "toughness" and "stubbornness" for not dobbing on his so-called mate. Even as he lay dying in his hospital bed with burns to 85 per cent of his body, he refused to comment when questioned by detectives as to who set him on fire. The following day, after the death of Quinn, a death notice appeared in one of the daily newspapers:

Barry, we always stuck together-Alex.

Tsakmakis was placed in solitary confinement after this unsavoury fatal assault but only received 10 years for manslaughter, to be served concurrently with the sentence he was already serving.[129]

He survived for another four years before Russell Street Bomber, Craig Minogue,[130] assaulted him with a pillowcase

129 The verdict of the jury negated any proved intention to kill Quinn and found that he wanted to only cause him grievous bodily harm. *R v Taikmaskis, Alexos* [1985] Unreported Vic SC 496, Justice Tadgell, 8 October 1985. An appeal by the Crown against sentence was dismissed-*The Queen v. Alekos Taikmaskis* [1986] Unreported Court of Criminal Appeal, 12 March 1986.

130 Minogue was convicted of the murder of Constable Angela Taylor who died in the Russell Street Police Headquarters bombing of March 1986. He was sentenced to life imprisonment with a minimum of 30 years and despite a High Court Appeal for release, he remains incarcerated. He will remain in prison and will not be granted parole unless he is in imminent danger of dying or is seriously incapacitated.

complete with gym weights in July 1988. He suffered a fractured skull and some brain damage, dying six days later at the age of 40.[131] Minogue tried a self-defence argument saying he feared Tsakmakis was going to kill him but was found guilty of murder with the court imposing a concurrent prison sentence of 27 years.[132]

Many of his now former cell mates joked Tsakmakis didn't die from brain damage as he didn't have one. In their view, the BBQ King was nothing but a power-hungry sociopath. Prior to his death, he reportedly was running money rackets from inside prison, making lucrative drug markets throughout Victoria and if you didn't do what he said, he would arrange for other inmates to be savagely bashed. But the last reflection following the murder was best left for Chopper Read when he said:

None of us saw Alex's death as anything other than an act of God.

---

131 Tsakmakis is buried at Fawkner Memorial Park-Memorial ID 142843372.

132 *R v Minogue, Craig William John* [1988] Unreported Vic SC 670, Justice Hampel, 14 December 1988.

12
COLD CASES–PART ONE

All Australian states and territories have been subjected to a number of baffling cases which, unfortunately, have never been solved. Following a criminal investigation, they are then typically referred to as a "cold case", usually when they have been inactive for a significant period and after all leads have been exhausted. Cold cases can also include not only homicides but a plethora of missing person cases and other serious types of crimes.

Cold case homicide units face the problem of being left with an old file in archives, some vague police witness statements and a coronial inquiry, finding that the death was indeed a murder committed by person or persons unknown. The passage of time then leads to any physical evidence not only lying dormant but gathering dust. Suspects and even witnesses, over a period of time, then become more difficult to locate and memories fade.

Despite these challenges, numerous cold cases ultimately

result in arrests, sometimes many years later and often due to new leads or information contributed by members of the public. Homicide investigators re-examine the evidence with fresh eyes and a new and different approach, even if they have not been blessed with a properly sealed-off crime scene, noting every contact leaves a trace. They are also now assisted by advanced fingerprint technology,[133] exhaustive phone records and global positioning systems (GPS) that can determine an exact location, time and velocity.

There is also the use of evolving DNA technology[134] to re-test old exhibits and, on many occasions, enhanced CCTV and dashcam footage, which allows a "face fit" image of the possible offender. Facial reconstruction technology is also available, particularly when assisting investigators in identifying the remains of any unidentified person suspected of meeting with foul play.[135] Looking at old crime scenes can also now be complimented by 3D imaging and virtual reality, which assists investigators in establishing crime scenes in a new and advanced way. The end result, hopefully, will then bring some closure and justice for the victims' families.

---

133 NSW Police unveiled in June 2025 new forensic technology that can print the whole finger and not just the fingertip. This means prints can be matched from the phalange area of the hand being the part between the tip and the palm.

134 Forensic DNA Phenotyping, still being developed, can identify almost with 100% accuracy a source's gender, likely hair and iris color and height. Police also have access to the National Criminal Investigation DNA Data Base

135 Facial reconstruction can be developed by drawing either a 2-D or 3-D face over a photograph of the skull, or by manually sculpting the face onto the skull using for example clay or wax.

Technological advancements, for instance, may facilitate the identification of "The Woman in Yellow" whose remains were discovered years later in bushland near Darwin, Northern Territory, following her unexplained disappearance around 1987. The woman, believed to be Aboriginal and about 25–27 years old, was likely wearing yellow clothing. A small piece was found near her body but, sadly, she has never been identified. Police were able to construct an image of her face, which they considered would result in someone coming forward to assist in this missing person case. It is hoped advances in such technology, together with modern DNA analysis, will not only identity this woman but hopefully assist in another 63 cases of unidentified human remains in the NT.

Detectives may review credit card records related to purchases made near the time or location of an incident, such as the acquisition of an accelerant or other relevant items.[136] There is also a crime analysis technique known as geographic profiling that compares the location of similar and possible connected crime scenes, to produce a probability map of either the home of a suspect or place of employment.

Although DNA analysis techniques have led to the successful resolution of some cold cases, by identifying responsible individuals, ageing and contamination of evidence often compromise exhibits, presenting significant challenges for investigators working on these cases. A cold case detective may still make progress if a DNA sample from a crime scene

136 Criminal investigators follow a process which is often referred to as 'basic101investigation methodology'. This is a progression of steps starting with gathering evidence from a properly sealed crime scene, followed by information analysis, then to theory development and validation, in order to form reasonable grounds to arrest and charge a suspect.

or human remains, leads to the identification of a suspect. A reward also provides motivation for new information, or if, over time, someone comes forward with relevant details about the case.

One prime example of modern DNA analysis techniques is when it is combined with Investigative Genetic Genealogy (ICG). It can create new avenues leading to identifying a suspect in a cold case.

This is what occurred when Kerryn Tate's body was discovered in 1979 in dense bushland in Karragullen, near the Canning Dam catchment area, approximately 40 kilometres from Perth's CBD. The 22-year-old woman was last seen alive around 11am on Saturday, 29 December 1979, enjoying what life had to offer with her friends the night before. The following morning, her remains were found and it would take another 45 years before a person of interest would be identified.

Police had recovered the DNA of an unknown male from the crime scene and such profile was then used by its ICG team. They uploaded the unidentified DNA sample to one or more commercial genetic genealogy databases[137] in an attempt

137 DNA testing entities, for example, Ancestry DNA, 23 and Me and MyHeritage, who do not permit access for comparison by law enforcement, have the genetic data of millions of people worldwide and as far back as the1700s. WA Police only have authorised access to public investigative genetic genealogy databases such as GEDMatch and FamilyTreeDNA which contain around 5-10 per cent of Australians on their databases. There is also Othram, which is a private DNA laboratory that specialises in the recovery, enrichment and further analysis of human DNA even from contaminated trace quantities of materials. It also plays a role in identifying human remains and solving missing person cases in collaboration with the National Missing and Unidentified Persons System known as NamUs and the AFP National DNA Program.

to identify any genetic relatives. After assembling a family tree, comprising over 10,000 individuals, including potential third and fourth cousins, cold case detectives were able to proceed further with their investigation. This enabled additional enquiries to be conducted and the pool of potential suspects was slowly narrowed down to location, age and physical description.

As a consequence, WA police announced in March 2025 that a person by the name of Terrence John Fisher, had been linked to the DNA profile from the crime scene of the murder of Kerryn. Fisher was not known to police other than for minor driving infringements. This, however, did not mean Fisher was definitely the person responsible for her murder but investigators, although quite confident, would still make further enquiries, including seeking assistance from the public. The problem they faced, however, is that Fisher would not be the subject of any arrest and police interview as he died in 2000. Investigators will put together a comprehensive timeline of his movements around this murder and they are also now interested regarding two other cold case murders.

The remains of missing mother of two, 38-year-old Barbara Anne Western, were found in 1991 and approximately 300 metres from where the body of Kerryn was located. Barbara had been reported missing after last being seen in June 1986. She was identified from not only the bones found by two people collecting wood but items of clothing and jewellery which confirmed it was her. Kerry Suzanne Turner was another woman who disappeared on Sunday 30 June 1991. Her fully clothed body was found a month later, hidden behind a log around Bedfordale about seven kilometres from the site from where the other deceased victims were found.

An additional reason WA detectives believed these three murders could be linked was the fact the girls were known to be hitchhiking at the time of their disappearance and all had been out drinking the night before. Although Fisher remains a person of interest, the families of the deceased victims may never know if he was responsible and what motivated such horrendous acts of violence.

Another recent development in a WA cold case involved the suspected murder of missing person, Lisa Mott. She was only 12 years old and last seen around 9pm on 30 October 1980, walking across a railway line in the outback town of Collie, approximately 200 kilometres south of Perth. Police were told that Lisa then hopped into a yellow panel van which looked like a 1970s Holden model.

In 1996, an abandoned vehicle of the same colour and make was located in bushland not far from the country town. Police planned to undertake a further and more thorough search of the same area looking for any vehicle identification clues, such as number plates, hoping to uncover the identity of its owner. Cold case detectives in announcing this new search in late March 2025, said it would include other areas around Collie, thanks to further information from members of the local community. Hopefully there will be a breakthrough in this unsolved murder mystery.

Dieter Pfennig, a convicted murderer serving a minimum sentence of 38 years in a South Australian prison, initially believed this would be the sole murder conviction against him. In 1992, he was jailed for the abduction and murder of 10-year-old Michael Black who disappeared from the country town of Murray Bridge. Trying to conceal what he had done, Pfennig placed the schoolboy's belongings in the river to make it appear that the boy had drowned. Although this young child's body has never been located, Pfennig was convicted of his murder.

The cold case mystery of the January 1983 abduction and murder of schoolgirl, Louise Bell, resulted in a massive search and would also become one of South Australia's most perplexing cases. However, in 2013 Pfennig had a knock on his prison door by cold case detectives. DNA analysis techniques once again had come to the fore. This time it was thanks to scientists in the Netherlands who were able to connect him to the DNA found on the missing girl's pyjamas. Her neatly folded top was located on the front lawn of a neighbour's house, together with her earrings nearby. That was not the only mistake Pfennig made, as he also admitted to prison cell mates that he was responsible for the murder.

In December 2016, he was sentenced to 35 years in prison and won't be eligible for parole until he is aged 103. Pfennig's subsequent appeal on the grounds the DNA evidence used to convict him was not sufficient to prove his guilt beyond reasonable doubt, was dismissed by the Court of Criminal Appeal in 2018.[138]

One cold case murder that SA Police thought they had solved, was in respect of Karen Michelle Williams. This 16-year-old girl disappeared from the northern outback town of Coober Pedy.[139] In the early hours of 4 August 1990, after a night of enjoyment, socialising with friends, Karen was last seen in a vehicle with an unknown male at a local Caltex service station. Despite a thorough search of surrounding mine

138 *R v Pfenning* [2018] SASCFC 27.

139 The town is situated on the Stuart Highway and is approximately 850 kilometres from Adelaide and is often referred to as the' opal capital of the world', thanks to the copious quantity of opals that are mined there.

shafts and along the Stuart Highway, police found no trace of her. Over two decades later, this now presumed murder may have been solved when 42-year-old Nikola Novakovich, who previously resided in Coober Pedy, was charged with Karen's murder.[140]

In the Supreme Court of South Australia, it was stated at his subsequent judge-alone trial in 2016[141], he had allegedly confessed to a few friends about his involvement in the murder of Karen. The fact that witnesses also said they saw him with her on the night of the disappearance, would form the basis of the Crown's case. As to motive, there were conflicting accounts, with one witness saying Novakovich killed her because she was a witness to an armed robbery in which he was involved. Another witness said the accused had admitted to raping and then strangling Karen and a principal prosecution witness also gave evidence assisting police in a covert operation in which Novakovich made certain admissions.

The problem the Crown faced was they only had circumstantial evidence. There was no direct evidence that proved beyond reasonable doubt that he had murdered Karen. Novakovich pleaded not guilty, elected not to give evidence or call witnesses and, by choice, he wanted the judge-alone trial. After a lengthy trial, the Crown was unable to prove to the requisite standard that Novakovich killed her in the early morning hours before dumping her body down a mineshaft.

140 *Criminal Law Consolidation Act 1935*(SA)-section 11 provides for a sentence of life imprisonment.

141 South Australia, Western Australia, Australian Capital Territory and New South Wales only have provision for judge alone trials. Victoria allowed it during the COVD pandemic under certain conditions but it has since been removed.

In a 56-page judgment, Justice Stanley, in returning a verdict of not guilty said:

> *Having considered all of the evidence in this matter, I am unable to be satisfied beyond doubt that the accused killed Karen Williams, let alone that he did so with the specific intent of killing her or inflicting grievous bodily harm. Accordingly, I am not satisfied that elements of the charge of murder have been proved beyond reasonable doubt...*[142]

In the end, the evidence, as presented, was impossible to make a finding of guilt beyond reasonable doubt, including for manslaughter.

One of Queensland's cold cases which remains on the books with 'further enquiries pending', was the strangulation and bashing of 22-year-old Commonwealth public servant, Betty Shanks. On 19 September 1952, she was innocently walking home from work in the suburb of Winston after alighting from a tram. Her body was found 20 minutes later, holding a bloodstained tram ticket in her hand, with her gold watch still on her wrist and stopped at 9.53pm. Despite an exhaustive criminal investigation, police could find no apparent motive and it remains a cold case to this day.

The same can also be said for the cold case rape and murder of Mima McKim-Hill. On a sunny day in March 1967, this sprightly 21-year old's motor vehicle was found the day after she went missing but her body would not be found until 16 days later. It was located 80 kilometres from her abandoned car in a waterhole at Collard Creek, southeast of Rockhampton in Queensland. At one stage, in late 2009, police did identify

142 *R v Novakovich* [2016] SASC 132-paras 211-212.

a possible suspect but he died from cancer before he could be interviewed. The investigation remains open with a $250,000 reward still on offer.

On 21 March 1972, teenager Marilyn Wallman was abducted while riding her bicycle in a suburb near Mackay, Qld. Following the reclassification of her disappearance as a homicide investigation, police were left without any suspects. To this day, her body has never been recovered.

The murder of hitchhiker, Robin Jeanne Hoinville-Bartram, also remains unsolved after being found in a shallow grave under a Flinders Highway bridge, southwest of Townsville in late 1972. Additionally, her girlfriend, Anita Cunningham, who was accompanying her while hitchhiking, was never seen again.

Six years later in October 1978, the bodies of three friends were found in bushland at Spear Creek,[143] not far from Mount Isa. Gordon Twaddle, Karen Edwards and Timothy Thompson had been travelling together on motorcycles from Alice Springs, across Queensland then were to head to Melbourne but they were found shot dead. A coronial inquest in 1980, determined they had been killed by a person or persons unknown. In 2019, Queensland Police thought they had solved the cold case with the arrest of 63-year-old male, Bruce John Preston. He admitted to stealing one of the deceased's motorbikes but, after being committed to stand trial for the triple murder, the changes against him were later withdrawn in 2023.[144]

143 It was later dubbed the 'Real Life Wolf Creek' murders due to similarities with the 2005 Australian film in which three backpackers were hunted by a serial killer.

144 Referred to as the filing of a 'nolle prosequi', a Latin term for 'unwilling to pursue'. This, however, doesn't mean the prosecution cannot bring the same charges at a later date.

However, this case may not remain unresolved, as the State Coroner is anticipated to conduct an additional inquest in late 2025. The new information now to be looked at, questions if they were in the company of a fourth rider, the time they had spent at a local caravan park together with the identity of a driver of a Toyota Camry. There is also a question for the coroner to address-was the initial and subsequent investigation carried out by Queensland Police as thorough as it should have been? Hopefully, there will be a positive outcome in solving this 45-year-old cold case mystery.

After a person was charged in 2009 with being an accessory with a male who had previously died of a drug overdose, Queensland detectives thought they were about to solve the 1987 stabbing murder of Bundaberg tax driver, Bryan Hodgkinson. However, the charge was never proceeded with, after a magistrate ruled there was insufficient evidence. Further evidence of a covert wiretap came to light in a 2018 coronial inquest, in which this person confessed to his de facto partner about his involvement in the murder. During the inquest, the suspect claimed privilege on the grounds of self-incrimination[145] which was his right. The inquest concluded that the available evidence remained insufficient.[146]

However, advances in DNA and forensic analysis of items from both the victim's taxi and clothing have now initiated a new line of investigation with the hope that Queensland police

---

145 A limited right at common law against making a statement that could lead to criminal prosecution is available in Australia. However, for example, there is no exemption to such a right in giving evidence before a number of Federal Government agencies.

146 Hodgkinson, Bryan (COR 2017/1744) [2018] Qld CorC (18 December 2018).

may still solve this cold case. In the interim, a $500k reward remains on offer, leading to the conviction of the person, or persons responsible.[147]

147 The reward also provides an indemnity against prosecution for any accomplice who first comes forward, such person not being the actual offender who carried out the murder.

13
COLD CASES-PART TWO

One Victorian cold case that is also still to be solved is the disappearance of 12-year-old Terry Floyd, last seen on the side of the Pyrenees Highway near Avoca, in country Victoria, June 1975. In 2001, a coroner concluded that he had been murdered but to date his remains have never been located. However, there soon might be a knock on someone's door by cold case detectives at 6am one morning.

Convicted paedophile, Raymond Kenneth Jones, has been a person of interest for some time, with the latest information that Terry was talking to him, where he was last seen. It seems Jones, at the time, was sitting in parked panel van having an earnest conversation with the young boy. The problem is though, after police interviewed him two weeks after Terry disappeared, they had misplaced seized stained, blue overalls found in the back of his panel van.

This means that any DNA, which could now be forensically examined leading to credible evidence against the culprit, won't happen. Another person of interest, who just happened to be a close mate of Jones, also wore similar type clothing. They gave each other alibis on the day of the disappearance but they have also now been brought into question.

The other compelling argument against Jones though is, when serving time in Pentridge Prison in August 1975, he allegedly admitted to a fellow prisoner that he was responsible for the then missing Terry. There has now been a further call for another coronial inquest, in view of the extra information that has now come to light. Victoria police have now submitted a brief of new evidence to the coroner, who will determine if a second inquest is required. In the interim, a million-dollar reward remains on the table leading to a conviction.

Librarian, Julie Garciaceley was only 19 when she disappeared from her North Melbourne apartment in July 1975. The only possible evidence that she may have met with foul play, was the discovery of a blood-soaked towel and her underwear on the floor of the apartment. Victoria police had three persons of interest, namely a former boxer, a crime journalist and well-known and violent criminal, John Joseph Powers. He just happened to be acquitted some three years earlier of the murder of a woman. He would later be convicted and sentenced to 30 years for a variety of offences, including armed robberies and the 1992 rape of a female, the same age as Julie.

When interviewed by detectives at Port Phillip Prison in 2003, he admitted that on the night of 1 July 1975, after drinking with two acquaintances who he refused to name, they visited Julie's apartment but departed after she had left to make a telephone call. A coronial inquest in 2018, determined that, despite her remains never being found and no evidence of the exact circumstances and cause of death, the coroner was satisfied she was deceased as the result of a homicide.[148]

Mary Anne Fagan, a mother of five children with the youngest only 17 months, to this day has left her family and friends grieving, trying to come to grips with what happened. Her children, on returning from school to a locked home in the Melbourne suburb of Armadale on the afternoon of 17 February 1978, were unable to gain entry but could hear their young baby sibling crying from inside.

The children called their father. He would leave work and found his much-loved, deceased wife bound and gagged in the front bedroom. She had been stabbed multiple times. No motive has ever been established and the personal items taken from the home have never been located. Her poor children and their father would be left to resume a life without their much-adored mother and loved wife.

A reward of $1 million remains on offer over the Ferntree Gully murder of 35-year-old nurse and law student, Margaret Tapp. Along with her young daughter, they both had been brutally murdered in August 1984. To make it even more confronting, not only had Margaret also been strangled but her daughter had been brutally raped. Police had a number of suspects, given that Margeret was a very attractive and socially popular young lady with several male acquaintances.

In 2008, it seemed detectives may have cracked the case when DNA taken from the crime scene matched a Queensland man. However, it then came to light that the DNA had been contaminated. This not only led to Victoria police being sued by the ex- suspect but they had to review over 6,000 other

148 Finding into Death With Inquest- Julie Ann Garciacelay, Coroners Court of Victoria- (COR 2001 2158).

criminal matters which may have also been tainted by a similar error. This double murder has, in fact, now been labelled as one of Australia's most infamous cold case murders.

The disappearance from Ringwood in Victoria on the night of 6 December 1994 of Elisabeth Francis Membrey, 22, appeared to be solved following a male acquaintance being charged with her murder in 2010. However, after a two-month trial in 2012, he was acquitted by a Supreme Court jury. Police, unperturbed, continued to investigate her apparent murder, given that significant blood stains were later found in her home.

A coronial inquest was first held in August 2000 with Coroner Heffey unable to determine who may have been responsible but new facts and forensic evidence led to a further inquest in early July 2025. This was based on DNA found in her vehicle, which matched that of a brother of her housemate. What may well have further implicated this person, who had a previous conviction for rape, was that he relocated to Queensland the day after Elisabeth disappeared. However, Coroner John Cain was not convinced, concluding that the evidence fell 'just short of the coronial standard of proof.'[149] Sadly, this gave no joy to her elderly mother who vehemently believed this suspect was responsible for the murder of her daughter.[150]

Another cold case murder mystery that remains unsolved has even been made more difficult as Victoria police have no idea who the victim is. On 1 May 1995, the body of a male,

---

149 Inquest into the death of Elisabeth Membrey, Coroners Court of Victoria (COR 1998 0682) 2nd July 2025.

150 Cold case detectives also forwarded a brief of evidence to the Office of Public Prosecution who had also determined there was no reasonable prospect of gaining a conviction.

believed to be aged between 25 and 35 and wearing a navy-blue jumper and shorts, was found in long grass in a business park in the outer northern suburb of Roxburgh Park. He had been badly beaten and also suffered a number of upper body stab wounds.

After exhaustive enquiries, which included searching Australian and international fingerprints and dental records, his identity to this day remains unknown. This was also despite computer generated face images being released in 1995 and again four years later. It is hoped that, thanks to modern technology, after a new colour generated image was created, someone will know who he is and contact the Homicide Squad.

The murder of Gianni "John" Furlan in Coburg North, around 8.35am on Monday, 3 August 1998, to this day still remains unsolved. This 48-year-old man was driving his white Subaru Liberty sedan, when he stopped at a local newsagency near Merlynston Railway Station to buy a paper and coffee. He returned to his vehicle and continued on to his Glenroy Auto wrecking business when commercial grade explosives attached to his vehicle caused a massive explosion, killing him instantly. The vehicle was catapulted some 15 metres down the road, shattering nearby shop windows, with debris being sprayed for a further 300 metres.

Notwithstanding a thorough police investigation by the Victoria Police Homicide Squad and the Arson and Explosives Squad, it remains an unsolved and open homicide case. In information provided to the coroner and detailed in the 2017 inquest,[151] Mr Furlan was known to be an aggressive businessman and had numerous disgruntled customers who

151 Finding into death with inquest of Gianni (John) Furlan, (COR 1998 2331) 31 August 2017.

had lodged claims against him with Victoria's Small Claims Tribunal. In addition, it was reported that Mr Furlan had made illegal motor car trading allegations to Consumer Affairs due to odometer readings being tampered with. An initial reward of $100,000 has since been increased to $1 million, to hopefully bring the person or persons responsible to justice.

Execution style killings also included the shooting death of Vincenzo Mannella, in Fitzroy North on the night of 9 January 1999. This was followed by the murder in the same suburb of his brother, Gerardo Mannella, on the evening of 20 October 1999. Two unknown males shot him, first in the legs and then while he was lying on the side of the road near his home, followed up with several bullets to his head. Information provided to the coroner in 2017,[152] disclosed that the brothers were known to be associated with the Italian Organised Crime Syndicate, known as "Ndrangheta" or "Honoured Society". Both deaths remain on Victoria's unsolved cold case list.

German tourist, Nancy Grunwaldt, on a trip of her lifetime suddenly disappeared in March 1993, while travelling along Tasmania's east coast. Police had no doubt she met with some sort of foul play but it would take them a further six weeks before they began any sort of investigation. No doubt this would have assisted the perpetrator to hide any evidence and, indeed, her body. There was some suggestion she may well have been involved in a hit and run accident, when she was pedalling along on her bicycle but no trace of the bike was ever found, let alone her clothes or remains.

There may have been a possible link though to the 1995

152 Finding into death with inquest of Vincenzo Mannella, (COR 1999 0094) 31 August 2017. Finding into death with inquest of Geraldo Mannella, (COR 1999 3198) 31 August 2017.

stabbing murder of 20-year-old Victoria Cafasso. Tasmanian Coroner, David Jones, while recognising police had devoted considerable time and resources, determined that some aspects of their investigation was, again, open to criticism. Victoria's body was found on a sunny day on 11 October 1995, lying on the scenic Beaumaris beach on Tasmania's east coast, with one of a number of stab wounds through the heart. The similarities included that her body was only a few kilometres from where Nancy was last seen, they were both of around the same young age and also just happened to be tourists from overseas.

An autopsy would later find Victoria had been stabbed a total of 21 times, including slashes to various parts of the body. There was also evidence of blunt force trauma to her upper jaw, with three teeth missing. The murder appeared not be related to any sort of sexual attack, with no obvious signs of penetration to her vagina and anus. Some witnesses indicated seeing a distinctive light-coloured Subaru station wagon driven by a male in his 20s, who was also observed near the beach area where Victoria's body was located.

Unfortunately, some questionable aspects of the initial investigation came to light, when Coroner Jones determined the non–attendance at the crime scene by the State Forensic Pathologist was not the only issue.[153] The crime scene had not been adequately cordoned off and the use of a tarpaulin to cover her body only led to potential contamination of any evidence. To make matters worse, there was an unexplained delay with the attendance of crime scene forensic science personnel. There was no crime scene video taken and only one

153 Cafasso, Victoria Anna Elizabeth, Record of Investigation into Death (2005) TASCD {2005] Tas CorC 2 (23 March 2005).

footprint of a potential suspect was cast in plaster.[154] This cold case also remains unsolved, with a reward now on offer of $1 million leading to the identity and conviction of whoever is responsible.

NSW Police also have several cold case murder murders, one being that of 15-year-old Jessica Small. This young lass was last seen on Sunday, 26 October 1997, after spending some time at an amusement parlour in the country town of Bathurst. In company with a girlfriend, they decided to hitchhike home and, after being picked up by a male driving a white Holden Commodore vehicle, he attacked them both. Her girlfriend was able to escape but the man drove off with Jessica inside.

In 2014, after the State Coroner ruled that she died at the hands of a person or persons unknown,[155] the State Government offered a $1 million reward. In May 2025, thanks to the reward with new witnesses coming forward, NSW Homicide Squad supported by the Crime Commission announced new lines of inquiry, particularly in respect to the kidnapper's motor vehicle. Hopefully, this will be one cold case murder that will eventually be solved, with the State Coroner determining a fresh inquest will also be held in due course.

NSW Police Strike Force Anthea may have achieved a breakthrough to the probable murder of Pauline Sowry, some 30 years ago. She was also known by her married name of Pauline Lawrence, last seen by her loved ones in December 1993 in the northern suburbs of Wollongong. The first clue to her most

154 Tasmanian Police have since addressed the issue of crime scene management, particularly in respect of training and forensic awareness following the introduction of Integrated Crime Management Strategy.

155 Inquest into the disappearance and suspected death of Jessica Beth Small, State Coroners Court of NSW, 2009/472901, 6 June 2014.

likely murder was when, in May 2023 and October 2024, the strike force located items of interest in bushland in Figtree, a 14-minute drive from Wollongong. The clothing discovered was a cream, button-down long sleeve blouse, together with black pants. However, there was no suggestion the items were those of Pauline but police said the clothing included a variety of hand stitching, which she was known to do when altering her children's clothes.

The clothing may well have proved crucial as in early June 2025, strike force detectives arrested a 64-year-old male, who has been charged with being an accessory to the fact of murder and conceal, a serous indictable offence.[156] There may well be further developments in this cold case, given the breakthrough to date. NSW Assistant Police Commissioner Cassar, in announcing it was indeed a 'good day' for both police and the Lawrence family, put out a warning in respect of cold cases, stating:

> *It's a clear message to officers out there who have committed these crimes and have gone undetected, that we never forget... We will continue to investigate. Whether it's this generation of police or a generation 20 years down the track, they never forget.*

Investigators can also, at times, uncover evidence of unrelated offending not related to cold case murders, resulting in the arrest of perpetrators to face their day in court. For example, Strike Force Arapaima was established by NSW Police

156 The maximum penalty for being an accessory to the fact of murder is 25 years imprisonment. *Crimes Act 1900*(NSW)-section 349. Also see section 316(1) in respect of concealing a serious indictable offence.

in 2019,[157] to have another look at the 1979 disappearance and suspected murders of 18-year-old Robyn Hickie and 14-year-old Amanda Robinson.

Both girls vanished separately in April 1979 from Lake Macquarie and, despite a $1 million reward, their bodies have never been found. As part of their investigations, strike force detectives uncovered information relating to the sexual abuse of two young males in the late 1980s and early 1990s. As a consequence, twin brothers, now aged 69, were both charged in late November 2021 with multiple offences.

Strike Force Arapaima is also actively involved the disappearance of Gordana Kotevski, who was last seen being forced into a white Toyota Hilux on the night of 24 November 1994. This 16-year-old was walking a short distance to her auntie's place in Charlestown, a suburb of Newcastle, after finishing some shopping. A 2003 coronial inquest determined that, in all likelihood, she was now deceased as a result of being abducted.[158]

Some other cases that still remain unsolved include missing university student, Leanne Goodall, who vanished in December 1978 after leaving the Newcastle Star Hotel. A cold case inquest in 2010, also looked at the circumstances surrounding the disappearance of 35-year-old, Susan Kiely, who was last seen in Bellingen on 1 December 1989. In handing down the findings into her presumed death, the Deputy State

157 Police Task Force Fenwick was initially set up in 1998 to investigate the disappearance of nearly 20 young people from the Newcastle region over a 20-year time frame. (Also see Chapter 31- Ivan 'The Rat' Milat).

158 In July 2025, a 26-metre-wide mural of Gordana was unveiled on a wall at the Cardiff Shopping Centre in NSW.

Coroner determined the police investigation was 'hopeless and below standard.'[159]

NSW Police also faced some criticism, following a landmark Special Commission of Inquiry into Hate Crimes,[160] of still to be solved homicide cases dating as far back as 1970. These included an estimated 88 gay men, who died in suspicious circumstances between 1976 and 2000.[161] Of these, the Commission determined that NSW Police had some sort of bias in, at least, 25 such cases.[162] Their report, which was released in December 2023, detailed major forensic issues which also included lost exhibits and incomplete police files. As a consequence, Taskforce Atlas was set up with 24 detectives appointed to systematically examine and audit hundreds of unsolved homicide cold cases.

One cold case, now under such scrutiny, was the

159 The Çoffs Harbour Coroner's Court heard that at the time Susan went missing, the local council had laid landfill near the property where she was last seen. However, for whatever reason only known to police, such site was never searched for human remains.

160 The Inquiry was established in April 2022 and led by Justice John Sackar, following a 2019 NSW parliamentary report and recommendation.

161 The wave of anti-gay crimes peaked during the AIDS epidemic of the 1980s. Despite homosexuality being decriminalised in NSW in 1984, homophobic attitudes still remained and also with certain NSW Police members.

162 For example, the death of 31-year-old John Russell, whose body was also found at the bottom of a cliff at Marks Park in November 1989, initially determined that he fell off the cliff. However, evidence led before the Inquiry said the fact his head and upper body were facing the cliff face, strongly indicated it was no accident and was linked to other numerous gay hate crimes, commonly referred to as 'poofter bashings'.

disappearance, later re-categorised as a homicide, of journalist Ross Warren. After a night out on 22 July 1989 with his gay friends in Oxford Street, Sydney, car keys belonging to Ross were found at the bottom of a cliff at nearby Marks Park. According to NSW police at the time, he somehow must have fallen into the ocean and, despite a search, his body was never found. In 2005, Deputy Coroner Jacqueline Milledge, in finding that he had been murdered, described the NSW Police investigation as nothing but 'grossly inadequate' and 'shameful'.

Another murder was that of Cyril Olsen, whose body in August 1992 was found floating in Rushcutters Bay, a harbourside inner-east suburb of Sydney. This location was a renowned pick-up location for gay men and, despite an autopsy revealing he had been bashed and then probably thrown into the sea, his death is still listed as an accidental drowning.

One cold case murder NSW Police thought they may have solved though, was the disappearance of 17-year-old Helen Harrison, who was found buried half naked in a shallow grave in 1968 near the northwest Sydney suburb of East Kurrajong. A person of some interest, Frank Abbott, would be arrested and charged by cold case detectives.

However, following two trials in the early 1990s in which the jury in his first trial were unable to reach a verdict, Abbott would be found not guilty of her murder. One of the possible mitigating factors in the accused's favour was medical evidence that Helen was an epileptic, which possibly meant she died of natural causes. On the other hand, she was found buried in a shallow grave.

Abbott would subsequently be imprisoned for child sex offences in 2020 and as a convicted paedophile, would become one of a number of persons of interest for Strike Force Rosann detectives in the disappearance of William Tyrell in September 2014. No one has never been charged to date in respect of the missing presumed dead, three-year-old William. An inquest finding in that respect should be handed down by the State Coroner in late 2025.

Success in solving some murders though, can mean it is only a matter of time before justice is finally seen to be done. As in all unsolved cold case murders, police will not only re-examine previous lines of enquiry but also new forensic possibilities that were certainly not available when these ghastly murders were committed.

Indeed, one cold case from 1982 that was solved 40 years later, leading to a conviction for murder, deserves a chapter on its own.

14
'JUSTICE FOR MY MUM'

On 17 March 2023, 72-year-old John Douglas Bowie learnt that, in all likelihood, he would spend the rest of his days behind bars. Bowie had just been sentenced for the murder of his first wife, Roxlyn, who disappeared some 40 years earlier on or about 5 June 1982. The much loved 31-year-old mother of a six-year-old daughter and a two-year-old son, left her children with no answers.

Following sentencing, the daughter said to waiting media on the steps of the Supreme Court of NSW:

'It's justice for my mum...Not closure for me because I still don't know what happened or where her remains are but it's definitely justice.'

Knowing the person he was, the family didn't hold any hope that their despised father would ever reveal exactly where or how she died. After marrying Roxlyn in August 1971, Bowie was known to indulge in the odd affair and heavy drinking. They were blessed with three children but, tragically, their second daughter passed away, nine days after she was born. This death had an untold impact on Roxlyn but it didn't seem to bother her husband.

After relocating to Walgett in March 1978, with Bowie appearing to be an esteemed member of NSW Ambulance, his favourite pastime was indulging in extra-marital affairs. On the other hand, Roxlyn became a doting mum to her two loved children and effectively became their full-time carer. Little did she know that in early June 1982, Bowie had other plans for her, in order to continue his affair with a woman who now lived in Sydney. According to his version of events, on Saturday, 5 June 1982, after finishing his ambulance shift, he told Roxlyn he was going to the hotel to have a few drinks. She allegedly said, 'If you do that, I won't be here when you get back.'

According to Bowie, she wasn't home when he returned around 11pm. Bowie's neighbour, who was helping him look for the missing Roxlyn, found a note under a sugar bowl in the dining room. Supposedly in the handwriting of Roxlyn, it said:

'Dear John, I am leaving you with the kids for good. I've thought about it for a long time and tonight I finally did it. I've packed a few things and you can have the rest. I don't want anything to remind me of you and the kids. Don't try and find me, because I will never come back to you. Bye Roxlyn'.

Three days later, another handwritten note surfaced but, this time, it was addressed to her parents and postmarked 7 June 1982 from the Coonamble Post Office, a town approximately 105 kilometres from Walgett. This "Dear Mum and Dad" letter stated:

'Just a short note to say that I have left John and the kids for good. I'm making my way to South Australia or Western Australia to start a new life. Please don't be hard on John because it wasn't his fault that I left. I will write again when I settle down. Love Roxlyn.'

At this point, Bowie wanted everyone to believe that the doting mother of two young children, who was in the process of planning their son's second birthday party, suddenly took off. People who knew her were suspicious of what was alleged to have taken place. They could not comprehend that Roxlyn would suddenly disappear without a trace but Bowie didn't waste any time grieving. On 11th June 1982, he applied for a transfer to Bankstown Ambulance Station to be near his lover. Just prior to that, he arranged with a family friend for the children to be picked up and placed in the care of Roxlyn's parents.

In August 1983, this same friend made a statement to police in which she said when Bowie phoned about the children, he stated that Roxlyn had left with her clothes in a blue suitcase. Some days later, after her husband had collected the children, Bowie stayed at their house with his clothes packed in a blue suitcase.

What was even more questionable though was his failure to make contact with her parents, not just for the care of their young children but also to advise them that Roxlyn had left him and the kids. She had a much loved and valued relationship with her parents and it beggared belief to think she would just write them a letter and never make contact again.

Towards the end of June 1982, a relative of Roxlyn had made enquiries into the circumstances surrounding her sudden disappearance, then reported her as missing to local police. An investigation was subsequently commenced, with the investigators being totally unaware at the time that this mystery would take 40 more years before Bowie was finally brought to justice.

The life and times of Bowie, however, slowly began to unravel, starting with his planned full-term relationship with his Sydney lover on 21 June 1982. He was abruptly rebuffed by her so, for the time being, he was on his own. She later made a statement to police, saying he arrived at her place in late June 1982 and asked if he could move in with her because his wife had left him. After refusing this request, his soon to be ex-lover went out with Bowie a few more times before she ended the relationship.

Two years later, in 1984, he married another woman but this relationship also fell apart. As was his usual demeanour, he continued having other domestic relationships and, no doubt, while he was still married. At the age of 34 years, Bowie came to the attention of police again but not for the mysterious and unsolved disappearance of Roxlyn.

He first forged her signature on divorce papers, then did it again on a block of land in order for it to be sold. He now had a conviction for forgery and clearly was still a person of police interest. In addition but unknown to police at the time, he also pawned a pendant, two wedding rings and a diamond ring at a Sydney pawn shop. These items were later alleged, at his criminal trial, as belonging to Roxlyn.

At this stage of the investigation, aside from a letter to her parents, there was no evidence that Roxlyn engaged in any daily activities after leaving Walgett in 1982 for an allegedly better life without her children. She had not used her bank account or

Medicare health card, her driver's licence was never renewed, and she had never been seen or heard of, since vanishing into thin air.

Roxlyn did not drive her own car so the only way of leaving what was then an isolated town, was by public transport which didn't operate on weekends. While the possibility exists that an unknown individual may have encountered her, Roxlyn's strong commitment to her children suggests her departure was likely due to other, less benign circumstances. Police really didn't have a lot to go on, hence she remained listed as a missing person.

It took another seven years before police interviewed Bowie again and it was due to information given to them by a Walgett local. When Bowie lived in the country town, he was known to be involved with a local commercial piggery, which was adjacent to a kangaroo abattoir. In 1991, police were told of comments he had made to the effect that the best way to dispose of a body was to feed it to the pigs, so it wouldn't leave any evidence.

In an eight-hour record of interview, consisting of a 170 questions and answers between Bowie and Detective Sergeant Russell Oxford, Bowie again denied any knowledge or involvement in the sudden disappearance of his then wife. Part of the record of interview included questions about the piggery comment namely:

> Q. Did you ever dispose of any carcasses at the kangaroo works?
> A. Yes.
> Q. Are you aware that animal carcasses, mainly kangaroos, were disposed of in the pits at the kangaroo works?
> A. I knew the pits were there. I used to get a few carcasses out of it. I used to get the carcasses out for the pigs.

The experienced detective had formed the view, if you wanted to dispose of a body, this would be an ideal location. However, the problem was, they had no forensic evidence to support such a possible theory. With regards to Roxlyn leaving her children to start a new life without her drunk and womanising husband, the police record of interview went along the following lines:

> Q. Do you seriously believe that Roxlyn would leave your home during the night, leaving the children alone?
> A. Deep down, I didn't think she would leave but apparently, according to the note she left and I haven't seen her since.
> Q. How can you explain that a person whom you have described as a devoted mother, would leave her children in the middle of the night?
> A. I don't know if she left in the middle of the night because I came home at approximately eleven o'clock.

Regarding the handwritten letters, police had given them to forensic handwriting experts for close examination. By looking at previous letters written by Roxlyn, the initial view was the handwriting was most likely to be Roxlyn's. However, what was of interest to police, the expert analysis had also come to the view that some of the letters and words in the handwritten note left at the house, including the one to her parents, were not consistent with her style of writing.

In addition, the two letters did not match Roxlyn's pattern of indentation, for example, a complete line break between paragraphs. Experts had also formed the view that the two letters were written on the same note pad, with one to her parents being sent from another country post office. It was feasible, of course, if Roxlyn did write the two letters, she may have done so from her home before leaving and possibly when under duress.

Bowie remained a person of interest, particularly after witnesses told police they had often seen Roxlyn with bruises and, on one occasion, a black eye, with force type grab marks on her arms. Investigators faced the challenge of lacking direct evidence to establish that Roxlyn had been murdered and there was nothing beyond suspicion to suggest Bowie's involvement in her disappearance.

Following his 1991 police record of interview, it wasn't long before Bowie was again under NSW police attention but it was not in respect of the missing Roxlyn. He pleaded guilty in 1992 to an offence of shoot with intent to murder.[163] Bowie was known to have a violent disposition, especially when he did not get his own way after a night of heavy drinking.

On this occasion, after becoming infatuated with another woman, he went after her partner. Bowie was sentenced to a term of imprisonment of four years and six months, however, he only served one year and six months before being paroled. It was possibly thanks to the sentencing judge's remarks that Bowie, 'was full of contrition and had excellent prospects for rehabilitation.'

After being released from prison, he did not come under public scrutiny again until a coronial inquest in 2014. The main point of contention put to Coroner Mary Jerram, was the authenticity of the two letters. By this stage, police had determined a lack of Roxlyn's DNA on the stamp and envelope

163 *Crimes Act 1900*(NSW)-section 27 with a maximum prison penalty of 25 years.

of the letter posted to her parents. Investigating police had also formed the definite view that the two letters had not been written voluntarily by her but it was still a point of contention.

Evidence was also obtained from Bowie's second wife who he had met within two months of the disappearance of Roxlyn. She confirmed they married in 1984 but divorced in 2008, thanks to his violence and relationships with other women. As to what had happened to Roxlyn, his now ex-wife told the inquest that whenever she brought up the topic, he would become very angry. At one point, he informed her she had allegedly left with a local bank manager.

Bowie also gave evidence under oath and made a point of telling the coroner he suffered from post-traumatic stress disorder, following his service in Vietnam. Allegedly, also according to his ex-wife during this deployment, Bowie said he had several wives while in South Vietnam and had killed two young boys when they tried to steal money from him.[164] As to his version of events on the night of of Roxlyn's disappearance, the coroner was not impressed, even asking him if he was making it up as he went along.

In regard to not trying to locate her, Bowie blamed that on a lack of money, the children and his work. He reiterated, she left because of his 'drinking, womanising and working'. Tearful evidence from his daughter, who was now 38 years of age, confirmed her mother was nothing but a loving, caring, devoted woman and when she disappeared, her life had changed forever.

On 18 September 2014, Coroner Jerram found that

---

164 According to evidence in mitigation against sentence at his murder trial, Bowie's service in Vietnam was only for a couple of months as an engineer on a supply ship.

Roxlyn was presumed dead and, in all likelihood, had met with foul play on or about, 5 June 1982. In respect of the evidence given by Bowie, the coroner summed it up perfectly when she said, 'I put little weight on it.'

As to the letters, they remained a puzzle and, indeed, a stumbling block as there was no direct evidence they were not in Roxlyn's handwriting. In referring the cold case to the Unsolved Homicide Unit, the coroner recommended that a further forensic analysis and report should be obtained.

If Bowie thought he could now resume his usual dubious lifestyle, he needed to think again. Old habits are difficult to break and in 2017, Queensland police charged him with sexual offences against his stepdaughter and domestic violence related offending. In late November 2018, while in custody on remand, NSW Robbery and Serious Crime Squad detectives, under Strike Force Maluka, announced, after receiving information, they would resume a search for evidence using groundbreaking radar technology in the suspected murder of Roxlyn.

Tip-off leads from members of the public were possibly due to a $1 million reward, which had been offered earlier that month. Two locations, which included a large dam on private property and some concrete slabs in an industrial site, were now of interest. These had been laid around the time of her disappearance and situated not far from the then Bowie family home.

In early 2019, Bowie was sentenced for his sexual offending in the Toowoomba District Court to a term of imprisonment of three years but to be suspended after only 10 months. It is likely that around 5 October 2019, he believed his period of incarceration was nearing completion. No such luck for Bowie because he was placed under arrest as he was about to walk out of the Woodford Correctional Centre on Queensland's Sunshine Coast.

In late March 2019, police had uncovered a number of items at the site close to the family home and, after forensic testing, determined they were certainly of much interest. Not only had they uncovered a metal wrapper, two facemasks and a Swann-Morton surgical blade, which Bowie would have had access to as an ambulance officer, but also a silver dress ring with the letter 'R' on it. A friend of Roxlyn's identified the ring had belonged to Roxlyn. They were also now aware of similar items of her jewellery that Bowie had previously sold to the Sydney pawn shop.

Bowie still vehemently maintained his innocence and, after being extradited from Queensland, he faced Parramatta Local Court on Sunday, 6 October 2019. On one count of the murder of Roxlyn Margaret Bowie on or about 5 June 1982, at Walgett or elsewhere in the state of New South Wales',[165] bail was refused and he was remanded in custody.

The jury trial of Bowie in the Supreme Court of NSW commenced on 20 September 2022 and was hotly contested with him pleading not guilty. It was the Crown's contention that Bowie committed a deliberate premeditated act or acts with the sole intention to kill Roxlyn, supported by a plethora of circumstantial evidence from witnesses. This included the finding of certain property belonging to the deceased mother of two children and the pawned jewellery which the Crown alleged belonged to Roxlyn.

Further, the accused's sole motivation was to continue

---

165 As at the date of the murder in 1982, a standard non-parole period did not apply to this offence and carried a maximum of life imprisonment. *Crimes Act 1900* (NSW)–section 18(1)(a).

an unfettered relationship with another woman and that he 'directed or coerced' Roxlyn to write the two letters. The expert evidence relied on by the Crown was that they were written differently to the normal handwriting of Roxlyn. This was part of his ruse that she had left their relationship and her children in search of a better life.

As to the disposal of her body, Bowie's sole plan was to ensure it would never be found and, therefore, subject to forensic investigation. In that regard, although evidence was heard from witnesses regarding the "feed it to the pigs" scenario, the Crown conceded that as there was no forensic evidence to support such a contention, it would not press for such a finding.

The jury also heard from another Crown witness who said he saw a person, strongly resembling Bowie, burying clothes on a golf course around the time of Roxlyn's disappearance. The witness, who was only 12 at the time, checked what had been buried and said the items were pantyhose and a bra, which he and his mate quickly reburied.

His defence counsel argued that the case against Bowie was indeed circumstantial and there was no direct evidence, particularly with the alleged coercion to write the two letters. As to the buried items, the Crown had contended they were most likely those of Roxlyn. Under cross-examination, it was put to the witness that his story was made up as he was hoping to get the $1 million reward after seeing Bowie on TV in 2019.

It was agreed that Bowie was a low life and certainly not perfect, what with his adultery and behaviour towards Roxlyn, but this did not make him a murderer. It was further argued by counsel that Bowie had cooperated with police from day one and had made statements, including a record of interview. So much was his cooperation, according to his counsel, he had been subjected in the witness box in the coronial inquest to a lengthy cross-examination.

A number of directions were given to the jury by Justice Dina Yehia,[166] which included that a manslaughter verdict could also be the subject of their deliberations. This was because the Crown's case was wholly circumstantial, meaning if they failed to establish the requisite state of mind, that Bowie had carried out a deliberate act or acts intending to murder his victim, they could bring in a verdict of manslaughter. This would be on the basis that Roxlyn's death was by way of an unlawful and dangerous act.[167]

On 31 October 2022, after a four-week trial, the jury retired to consider its verdict. It only took them just over four hours to find that Bowie was guilty of murder and on 17 March 2023, 72-year-old Bowie faced Justice Yehia for sentencing.

Her Honour, right from the outset, was mindful of the impact the loss inflicted on Roxlyn's loved ones, saying:

> *...It is apt to commence with an acknowledgement of the life lost. The overwhelming evidence was to the effect that Roxlyn was a loving and devoted mother to her two children and had a good relationship with her parents. She was a somewhat quiet and unassuming person. She took on her responsibilities as a wife and mother, living in an isolated county town, doing the*

166 On 6 July 2022, Justice Yehia became the first person of Greek Egyptian descent to be sworn into the NSW Supreme Court. Her Honour arrived in Australia from Egypt in 1970 at the age of seven and did not speak English. This was then later followed by a career first as a solicitor, then barrister prior to being a District Court judge.

167 Manslaughter carries a maximum penalty of 25 years in prison. *Crimes Act 1900*(NSW)- section 18(1)(b)

best she could in a relationship with a man who was a self-admitted womaniser, who often drank too much.[168]

As for Bowie, it was of no surprise he didn't have a lot going in his favour. He was not only a habitual drunkard but in view of his overall criminal offending, prospects of rehabilitation were considered to be poor. Indeed, in that regard, expert evidence tendered to the court suggested there was a high to moderate risk of Bowie reoffending within five years of his release from prison. Bowie showed no remorse and tried to rely, in mitigation, on the fact he had a history of trying to commit suicide on two occasions, followed by a nervous breakdown in 2007. His "questionable" Vietnam service also came to the fore, as did his age and pending further onerous prison conditions.

Her Honour, in considering all the factors in mitigation, was also mindful to impose a sentence that was not only adequate punishment in holding Bowie to account but also seen as public condemnation of his offending. Bowie was sentenced to a minimum non-parole period of 18 years, with an additional term of six years imprisonment.

This meant his total term of imprisonment was 24 years, expiring on 4 October 2043. His earliest release date, if he became eligible for parole, would be 4 October 2037 at the ripe old age of 86 years, if he survives that long in prison. The problem also for Bowie was, in October 2022, the NSW Government introduced legislation which meant "no body-no parole". This legislation applies retrospectively, regardless of when the homicide offence or conviction occurred.[169]

---

168 *R v Bowie* [2023] NSWSC 207-para 5.

169 *Crimes (Administration of Sentences) Amendment (No Body, No Parole) Act 2022* (NSW). Also see chapter 50.

Retired NSW Police Detective, Russel Oxford, who interviewed Bowie back in 1991 and was involved in investigating what happened to Roxlyn for 34 years, stated to waiting media after sentencing, it was 'satisfying but somewhat hollow', but 'I think he got his just deserts today'.

You never know, though. Bowie might find some compassion for his daughter who, sadly, is the last one left in her family after losing her brother. The fact remains though, he may never reveal how Roxlyn died, let alone where her remains are.

15
THE MCCULKIN FAMILY MURDERS

Queensland Police would be baffled by the sudden disappearance of 34-year-old mother, Barbara McCulkin, and her two daughters, Vicki, aged 13 and Leanne, aged 11. They were originally reported missing on 18 January 1974 by her estranged husband and father of the two girls, known criminal identity, Billy McCulkin.

Police would then determine the two girls had been attending a friend's 10th birthday at a house across from where they lived in Highgate Hill. Barbara, apparently, had stayed at home and reportedly was sharing a few drinks with two unknown men, who had parked a distinctive Valiant charger, two-door motor vehicle, painted bright orange with black racing stripes, in her driveway.

The investigation somewhat stalled as Queensland Police had other significant crimes to look at. In particular, there was the firebombing of Torino's Nightclub in February 1973.[170] This was followed a month later, on 8 March 1973, with the death of 15 innocent victims after the bombing of the Whiskey Au Go Go nightclub.[171]

Underworld violence was also running rampant, even with one group, "The Clockwork Orange Gang", named after a 1970s movie of British gangs, carrying out repeated acts of criminal violence and money-making escapades. Little did police know that Peter Hall, one of the local gang members,[172] would become a crucial Crown witness over 40 years later in the McCulkin cold case.

The code of silence[173] had remained steadfast, due to the mantra that if you give up one of your criminal associates, then expect significant consequences, including an unpleasant death, as you are nothing but a "dog". Hall had stuck to such code, that you don't dob on your criminal mates but what would also stay to haunt him, was his knowledge of the death of the two little girls. Investigators obviously had some suspicions of his criminal exploits, as in early 2014, Hall was called to

---

170 The bombing of Torino's nightclub is still deemed an 'unsolved arson case' and fortunately there was no loss of life.

171 John Stuart and James Finch were both convicted in October 1973 and sentenced to life in prison. See *R v Stuart and Finch* [1974] QD R 297.

172 Hall had served terms of imprisonment in both Queensland and New South Wales including being jailed for 10 years six months for malicious wounding with intent to do grievous bodily harm.

173 A well-known example of such a code is the omerta, which is the Sicilian Mafia code of silence.

give evidence before the Queensland Crime and Corruption Commission.[174]

If you are called before the QCCC, you don't have a right to silence when required to give evidence and you can also be required to produce documents. If you decline on the basis of privilege against self-incrimination, then you can be sentenced to an indefinite term of imprisonment. These powers are not normally available to other government bodies, including police, and the coercive hearings in seeking what would normally be unobtainable evidence, are paramount in their investigation into major crime, such as drug trafficking, fraud and murder.

At the QCCC hearing, Hall broke the code to a point when he admitted to his involvement in the firebombing of Torino's nightclub in February 1973 for a measly $500, shared with his three cohorts, one being Garry Reginald "Shorty" Dubois. Hall understood it to be an insurance job and, after they forced entry into the unoccupied premises, they doused it with petrol leading out towards the back door and then set fire to it, resulting in a massive explosion.

He also dobbed in some of his playmates from the Clockwork Orange Gang, in respect of a number of burglaries and other lesser crimes. When pressed further on the disappearance of the McCulkin girls and, in particular, what role if any, Shorty may have played, he simply denied any knowledge. However, what Hall did let loose, which was missed at the time, was a throwaway comment that Dubois 'went missing' the day after they were reported missing.

When cold case investigators listened back to his evidence,

---

174 The Commission has special powers as an anti-corruption body that affects the state's public sector under the *Crime and Corruption Act 2001*(Qld) and the *Police Powers and Responsibilities Act 2000*(Qld).

it suddenly hit them that Hall obviously knew more about the McCulkins than what he was letting on. Most likely, thanks to the code of silence. It would now take some painstaking months to finally get Hall to own up to exactly what he knew. What did help detectives, though, was Hall had not only let the murders play on his mind for some 40 years but after having to revisit it during the CCC hearing, it had now come back to haunt him. Hall had the support of his family members and it was now time to 'tell the truth, the whole truth and nothing but the truth'. What also helped him to break the code was the offer of indemnity from prosecution in respect to the Torino nightclub firebombing.

The crucial evidence of Hall, which criminal juries would later hear, was that Dubois and Vincent "Mad Dog" O'Dempsey had some concerns that Barbara had inside knowledge of the two nightclub firebombings. In addition, her estranged husband just happened to be a close associate of one of those eventually convicted for the Whiskey Au Go Go bombing, namely John Stuart. Barbara possibly also knew that O'Dempsey was believed to be the main instigator of the Torino firebombing, along with Hall, Dubois and other Clockwork Gang associates, so she had to be taken care of.

Hall was given an invitation to join them when they paid Barbara a visit on the basis that there would be "sex", so why not come along? Barbara was well known to O'Dempsey, as he had occasionally visited her home and was seen paying a visit on a number of occasions by other family members. Luckily for Hall, he decided not to join in as he may well have got caught up with what would take place. Two days after the McCulkin abduction, Dubois would have great pleasure in telling his gang mates, including Hall, exactly what happened on that fateful night.

O'Dempsey and Dubois conned Barbara and the two girls into coming with them for a short, fun-filled drive. Barbara, after being separated from her daughters with their hands tied, was then taken into some bushland, most likely somewhere near Warwick, which also happened to be the hometown of O'Dempsey. He then strangled her but the problem was, the two girls knew what was happening to their mother, with gurgling sounds being heard as she slowly died. The girls were next and allegedly, after they were both raped, the murderous O'Dempsey also killed them the same way - by strangulation. The men would then dig holes to bury the woman and her children and, in the words of Dubois, he was glad to get away from their lifeless bodies as dawn broke.

Both Dubois and O'Dempsey were charged in 2015 with murder, rape and kidnapping[175] but the rape charges against O'Dempsey were not proceeded with, due to lack of evidence.[176] Dubois was offered a full indemnity against prosecution on the basis he disclosed where the bodies were buried but he chose the code of silence. The evidence of Hall would be crucial, as would that of another protégé of O'Dempsey, Warren McDonald. They both managed a large drug crop southwest of Brisbane and one conversation McDonald had with his mentor was a critical piece of evidence.

O'Dempsey told him in the late 1990s that he had murdered the McCulkins and dobbed "Shorty" in for being nothing but a rapist. He also said the bodies would never be found so he would get away with it. Like Hall, McDonald chose to stay silent and maintain the criminal code and not

175 *Criminal Code Act 1899* (Qld)-section 355-deprivation of liberty.

176 See pre-trial rulings on admissibility-*R v O'Dempsey (No 1)* [2017] QSC 100. *R v O'Dempsey (No2)* [2017] QSC 101.

dob on his mates. However, when police suggested they would charge him over the drug crop and he would do time in prison, he immediately turned Crown witness.[177]

Another key witness was the girlfriend of O'Dempsey, who was also told, around 2011- 2012, about his glee at murdering the mother and her two young daughters. He also told her that he had been having a sexual relationship with Barbara for some time. She even suggested to police that her now ex-boyfriend had actually bragged to her about the notches on his gun, suggesting, all up, he had a total of 33 such notches. Indeed, if such questionable bravado was correct, O'Dempsey would have to be the worst mass murderer in Australia's history.[178]

The next-door neighbour to the McCulkin girls would also give evidence, as in the early hours of the morning of their disappearance, he became concerned for the girls' safety. He saw the colourful Valiant charger parked in their driveway and, on checking they were okay, he was introduced to O'Dempsey and his companion whose name he could not remember. Barbara had also previously told him, the two men convicted of the Whiskey Au Go Go arson were not the only ones involved and, if police asked the right questions, they would discover who the primary movers in the bombing were.

After separate jury trials,[179] O'Dempsey would be found guilty in May 2017 for the McCulkin murders and deprivation

177 McDonald would plead guilty to the crop drug charges but did not serve any time in prison in exchange for his evidence against O'Dempsey.

178 As to the suggestion that O'Dempsey played a part in the Whiskey Au Go Go nightclub bombing, he was never charged for that or any other murders.

179 See reasons for separate trial-*R v Dubois & O'Dempsey* [2016] QSC176.

of liberty. Dubois, now 70, had earlier being found guilty in November 2016 of two counts of murder, one of manslaughter and one count of rape. On 1 June 2017, they were both sentenced to life in prison.

Supreme Court Judge, Peter Applegarth[180] didn't hold back when he said, regarding 78-year-old O'Dempsey, who had shown absolutely no remorse, he was nothing but a 'cold blooded killer' and the claim he was innocent was completely without foundation. As to Dubois, he was simply a coward and did what he was told to do out of fear, including raping one of the girls and noting the last hours of their lives would have been absolutely terrifying.

His Honour had no problem in further telling them he expected them to both die in prison and said:

> *At least three things have ensured justice at last. First, the dedication of police. Second, the testimony of dozens of witnesses. Third, the conscience and courage of some key witnesses at each of your trials…You can have no expectation of early parole. If you maintain your silence over where the bodies are buried, you could not reasonably expect ever to be granted parole.*[181]

Both Dubois and O'Dempsey would subsequently file applications in the Supreme Court of Appeal, seeking a new trial on the grounds of improper admission or rejection of evidence. Both appeals were dismissed.[182]

---

180 Prior to being appointed to the Supreme Court in 2008, His Honour acted in defence of freedom of speech at the Fitgerald Inquiry during 1987 – 89 in respect of Queensland Police corruption.

181 *R v Dubois & O'Dempsey*, Unreported, Supreme Court of Queensland, Justice Applegarth, 1 June 2017.

182 *R v Dubois* [2018] QCA 363; *R v O'Dempsey* [2018] QCA 364.

Justice Applegarth was certainly spot on in all counts. In respect of Queensland Police, the exhaustive painstaking investigation was led by Detective Sergeant Virginia Gray, in particular, recognising what Hall said before the QCCC about Shorty Dubois going missing the day after the family disappeared. The three main witnesses were obviously crucial and, no doubt they will be looking over their shoulder, keeping an eye out, fearing some sort of payback and most likely a death sentence, for turning against the criminal code of silence and giving evidence against them. Macdonald certainly was worried and understandably so, as another Crown witness, who was a prison mate of O'Dempsey, suggested that he was plotting from his jail cell to murder Macdonald.

Both convicted murderers have maintained their silence on the location of the bodies and, as His Honour said, 'no body, no parole'[183] and they will most likely die in prison. The learned judge was certainly correct about Shorty Dubois who, by his own hand, was found dead in his prison cell on 7 June 2021. As for O'Dempsey, he would now be almost 86 years old, so hopefully he won't have much longer to brag about his murderous exploits.

183 In August 2017, the Queensland Government enacted the *Corrective Services (No Body, No Parole) Amendment Act 2017*(Qld) which means the Parole Board must refuse any application for parole by any prisoner serving time for murder, manslaughter, conspiracy to murder, accessory after the fact to murder and unlawful striking causing death. Also see chapter 50.

16
THE QUESTIONABLE LIFE AND TIMES OF 'MR STINKY'

Law enforcement investigators always have hope, sometimes a forlorn one, that something will give them a desperately needed clue in order to solve a murder. Victoria police, for example, have well in excess of 200 cold case investigations still sitting in their archives, with the earliest going back to 1951. Their cold case homicide unit usually pick out six cases at any one time and then carry out a reinvestigation. Sometimes it leads to an arrest and conviction but, in many cases, it obviously doesn't.

One cold case that touched the hearts of the Victorian community was the disappearance of eight-year-old Eloise Worledge. This young girl attended Beaumaris Primary School and was about to commence grade four. Her parents and two siblings woke up on the morning of 13 January 1976 to find her missing. A crime scene examination determined a flyscreen of her window had been cut from the inside and although the window was open, it was unlikely she was abducted from her bedroom.

Police came to the conclusion that, in all probability, Eloise was abducted from somewhere in the house but it was left to appear it was from her open window. Despite a massive search of parks, the local beach foreshores and even golf courses, to this day no one knows what happened to her. Then again, maybe someone does hold the key to her disappearance and, most likely, her murder.

Although State Coroner, Frank Hender, following an inquest, determined he was unable to identify the person responsible for her disappearance, one who may well know what happened to Eloise was serial killer, Raymond "Mr Stinky" Edmunds. This individual would eventually be awarded such moniker by the media, after foul body odour was reported by some of his victims.[184]

It seems he had a rather comfortable childhood and was educated to Form 3 standard at Wangaratta Technical School. He would then work on his father's farm and later as a share farmer at Ardmona, which is about 10 kilometres from Shepparton. In 1962, aged 18, he married his first wife and, after being blessed with two daughters and a son, who later died in a diving accident, their relationship ended after some seven years. There was some suggestion that during this marriage he had raped and bashed his wife and also sexually assaulted his then three-year-old daughter. Little did anyone know though, what else Edmonds had been up to during that period.

Police were unable to connect him to the disappearance of

184 The body odour was suspected as a result of his occupation from working on various dairy properties and believed to be a mixture milk, manure and chemicals.

Eloise but, for almost 20 years, he escaped punishment for the 1966 rape and murder of 16-year-old Abina Margaret Madill and the murder of her workmate, 18-year-old panel beater, Garry Charles Heywood. Abina and Garry just happened to be at a Shepparton Civic Centre concert on the night of 10 February 1966 when, after enjoying the music, they innocently left together and drove around surrounding streets in Gary's distinctive FJ Holden, waiting for Abina's boyfriend to join them after he finished work. That would be the last anyone saw them until their bodies were found in a paddock 16 days later on 26 February 1966, some 37 kilometres south of Shepparton, near Murchison East.

Their families would have been already bracing for the worst possible outcome as, three days after they disappeared, Abina's white handbag had been found in a dry creek bed adjacent to the Goulburn Valley Highway. Garry's car was also found near Lake Victoria on the outskirts of Shepparton. Over two weeks later, they were found 300 metres apart lying on their backs. Abina had no clothes on from the waist down, with the small pile of her clothes neatly folded and placed together.

An autopsy would find she had been raped and then bashed to death, suffering a fractured skull. Garry had been shot through the head, which would later be determined, using a distinctive .22-calibre Mossberg self-loading rifle. A crime scene and forensic examination would later conclude that his legs had also been tied with Abina's stockings. Two spent cartridges and one removed from the skull of Garry, confirmed they were from the same make of rifle.

Police had to start somewhere and focused their attention mainly on Abina's boyfriend as the culprit. All to no avail as he was not the perpetrator. There were even some suggestions that after he was hauled in for repeated interviews, when he failed to confess, he was repeatedly bashed by police. In those days, it was not uncommon for the local constabulary to give a suspect a belt around the ears, to ensure complete cooperation. Sadly, it all got a bit too much for Abina's boyfriend and he moved interstate and then to Singapore, where he was killed in a car crash, of all things, on the sixth anniversary of her death.

One of their other failings was, investigators didn't bother to check out who owned such a distinctive type of rifle. If they took the time by checking gun licenses and statewide gun dealer books, they might have uncovered one such rifle was indeed purchased by a local, who just happened to be the father of Mr Stinky.[185] Edmunds had, in the meantime, in the early 1970s, remarried and moved to Melbourne, ostensibly working in a factory. What he would then get up to during the late evening, however, was another question.

Mr Stinky would certainly live up to his name and would also become known as "The Donvale Rapist". While working as a security guard, he carried out the rape of several women in the eastern suburbs of Melbourne, during the period 1971 to 1984. In early 1985, Edmunds was routinely fingerprinted for offending in Albury, NSW,[186] which involved flashing his penis and masturbating while parked in his station wagon.

He would plead guilty and was fined $400 but it would lead to him finally being brought to justice. The prints were

185 In 1976, a piece of wood was found in a shed on the share farm where he had worked. This would, many years later, be found to have been sawn from the wooden stock of a Mossberg.22 rifle.

186 At the time, NSW had in place mandatory fingerprinting, which was introduced in Victoria three years later in May 1988 either by consent or court order- See *Crimes (Fingerprinting) Act 1988*(Vic).

subsequently matched in a national database to, not only one of the Donvale rapes, but also with unidentified partial composite prints found on Garry Heywood's motor vehicle.

The days of committing horrendous crimes was now all over for Mr Stinky after he was taken into custody on 22 March 1985. Following his arrest, a search of the garden around the home of Edmunds found several spent cartridges which matched those found near the bodies of Abina and Garry. He readily admitted to police, after he first spoke with a priest, that he was responsible and agreed to accompany them to the murder scene and complete a re-enactment.

In 1986, for the 1966 double murder and three counts of rape and two counts of attempted rape, committed between July 1971 and February 1977, after pleading guilty, Edmunds was convicted and sentenced to life imprisonment without parole. Supreme Court Judge, Alistair Nicholson, did not fix a minimum term, in view of the two life sentences imposed for the murders. As to the five other counts, Edmunds was sentenced to a total effective term of 30 years and, again, set no parole period.

His Honour was satisfied that the then 21-year-old Edmunds had carried out his murderous conduct by first abducting both Abina and Garry at gunpoint and then made them drive them to Murchison East. Around midnight on 10 February 1966 near the Goulburn River, he first shot Garry dead and then raped Abina, before she was bashed to death. An expert report was compiled by forensic psychologist, Ian Joblin, and probably best summed up what everyone knew. Edmunds suffered from a personality disorder but with no apparent cognitive functioning issues, was hypersexual with a higher than normal sexual drive.

The matching fingerprints of Edmonds certainly left no doubt with Justice Nicholson saying:

> *Those fingerprints...pointed to [Mr Edmunds] as the killer of two innocent young people 20 years before... on the driver's door of Mr Heywood's car found by the lake on that Friday morning there were two fingerprints. They matched the right middle and right ring fingerprints of [Mr Edmunds] taken by police...*[187]

Edmunds tried to escape from Pentridge Prison in 1992 and, thankfully, he didn't, because who knows what he might have got up to. Luckily, an alert prison dog by the name of "Sarge", alerted his handler at the last prison check point to the presence of Edmunds in the rear of a semi-trailer, which had already passed through one security point without him being detected.[188]

'Good boy, good boy Sarge'.

In April 1993, Edmunds appealed his sentence, which he later abandoned. However, the Court of Appeal did set a non-parole period regarding the sex offence convictions, to 16 years and 8 months. Regardless, not for one moment did that mean he would be released on parole, as his murder convictions meant he would remain in prison for the term of his natural life.

187 *R v Edmunds* [1986] Unreported, Supreme Court of Victoria, Judge Nicholson, 28 October 1986.

188 In 2006, new high-tech equipment known as MicroSearch Human Presence Detection Systems, also known as heartbeat scanners, were introduced into Victorian Prisons to assist in preventing these types of escapes. The scanners are attached to vehicles leaving a prison and by the use of seismic sensors, it can detect the presence of a heartbeat of anyone hiding inside the vehicle.

The Appeal Court, however, did comment in that his crimes constituted:

> *A blow at the very foundations of a civilised society. Each involved an attack at night on a woman in her own home and in the absence of her partner...Each victim had a child in the home with her...Particularly exacerbating is that on two occasions there was a young, terrified child in the same bed in which his mother was attacked and defiled...On all but one occasion, the applicant was armed with a long knife and entry to the homes were gained either by breaking in or by stealth...*[189]

The life and times of Mr Stinky, although his incarceration in prison meant he probably would no longer be called that, would see him back before the County Court of Victoria in September 1998. On this occasion, he was sentenced for offences of carnal knowledge and incest committed against his stepdaughter over a seven-year period commencing in January 1972, for which he received a further culminative term of imprisonment.[190]

Edmunds was held in H Division at Pentridge Prison in Coburg until 1997 and thereafter in protective custody and then, I wonder why, later at Barwon and Port Phillip Prison. From all reports, he was deemed as a "prisoner listener",[191] working in the kitchen and was somewhat a compliant prisoner.

---

189 *Edmunds v R* [1993] Unreported, Supreme Court of Victora, Court of Criminal Appeal, 13 December 1993.

190 *R v Edmunds* [1998] Unreported, County Court of Victoria, Judge White, 30 September 1998.

191 Listeners are prisoners who are part of a scheme to provide confidential emotional support to fellow inmates who are not coping with life in prison. How Edmunds qualified for such a role is somewhat perplexing.

His second marriage had ended following his incarceration in 1986 but he still had a few grandchildren and by 2019, even great-grandchildren. It was a pity he didn't give both Abina Madill and Garry Heywood the opportunity to be blessed with the same.

In 2019, the now 75-year-old Edmunds pleaded guilty to a further nine rapes. After obtaining legal advice, he willingly came forward and made admissions to police of his further sexual offending, during his reign as the Donvale rapist. He would be armed with a butcher's knife and, wearing a mask with the eyes cut out, stealthily either breaking into homes or entering through unlocked doors late at night or in the early hours around 2-3am.

On one occasion, he entered his chosen victim's house by first drilling a large hole in a back door and then reached through to unlock the door, so he could gain entry. His confessions to police included, not only the 1971 rape of a woman at Donvale, but also the rapes of women at Edithvale, Clayton and Wheelers Hill during the period from 1977 to 1984.

In sentencing Edmunds to a further 23 years and five months, to be served concurrently with his life sentence, Her Honour, Justice Sue Pullen, was horrified by his crimes stating:

> *It is difficult to find words to describe your horrific offending which I have no doubt was a traumatic and frightening experience for all the victims of it. In particular, the victims who likely feared their children might be harmed in some way if they did not comply with your demands…*[192]

---

192 *DPP v Edmunds* [2019] VCC 1581-para 101.

Edmunds was represented by Peter Chadwick, QC, who told the court he had asked his client why he had waited so long to confess to these additional crimes. Edmunds responded by first saying that he didn't have any reason and then said, he thought it was about time to bring 'some sort of peace of mind to not only himself but to his victims.'

This comment raises an interesting point of contention. On the one hand, if it was all about looking after oneself and the victims, then you would think he would have also admitted to other crimes, including murder, in which Edmunds was considered to be a very strong suspect.

On the other hand, given his age and the fact he was a marked man, only perhaps being saved by being in protective custody, maybe he thought better of it and didn't want to make himself even more of a target for other prisoners, who do not take too kindly to fellow cellmates like him. I will let you be the judge as I now turn to other cold case murders that Edmunds is perhaps not just a person of interest but also a clear suspect.

Camping during the Christmas-New Year period at Tocumwal town beach caravan park in NSW, was always something to look forward to for the Box Hill, Victorian family of 39-year-old Elaine Jones. They had been doing this for the past 18 years but all that was sadly about to change on 3 January 1980. Around 9.30pm the night before, Elaine left her husband and their 15 and 7-year-old daughters and walked from their cosy tent down to the shops to purchase some cigarettes and chocolate. Elaine, after leaving the shop, never came home.

The following morning, after reporting Elaine missing, her husband and youngest daughter, in a dinghy during a frantic search, would find a leg snagged on a log protruding out of the water. They quickly realised it was Elaine from a shoe she had been wearing the night before. On pulling her body onto the dinghy, what they witnessed was simply horrific, as the much-loved wife and mother had had her throat slit from ear to ear. It was so deep, it exposed her spinal column.

What followed next would leave their daughters without parents as Mr Jones, who had a history of heart issues, after covering her body with life jackets, suffered a massive heart attack and died. Fortunately, their daughter was able to stop the dinghy motor and swim to shore, much to the horror of people on the shoreline, who were able to remove the now two bodies from the dinghy.

A postmortem would reveal that Elaine had been murdered, suffering extensive head and body injuries by the use of a blunt object, which also fractured her skull. She had also been sexually assaulted and her throat savagely cut.

The problem police had was they didn't have a lot to go on and, to make matters worse, the local population of around 1300 people had grown to well over 10,000 during the holiday period. This also included a number of fruit pickers working in the area and, of all things, a nudist convention. Police were able to ascertain from the shopkeeper that Elaine was served by him about 10pm and around 15 minutes later, several campers said they heard a scream and then saw headlights driving away from a water supply pump.

Other issues detectives had was the absence of a proper crime scene, given the body of Elaine had been in the water for a few hours. There was little forensic evidence that could be obtained and relied on, to assist in leading to whoever was responsible for this ghastly rape and murder. They formed the view that Elaine was abducted by an unknown suspect, or suspects, being dragged into a vehicle and bludgeoned to stop her screaming, before being driven away.

A week later on 10 January 1980, a police picture, drawn by an artist, was released showing a male they believed could assist in their enquiries. Several witnesses, mainly women, told police about a man who had been harassing them around Town Beach, which was two kilometres from Tocumwal, and also in the town centre. The composite drawing and description of this male had him aged between 30-35 years old, quite tall and believed to be 192 centimetres (6ft 4in), sun bleached hair in a fringe and with a prominent nose. This rather tall male was also described as having an athletic build and with a tanned complexion.

Despite an extensive investigation, it would not be until 20 years later, when NSW police, in early 2000, announced a person of interest, namely Raymond Edmunds. He became a suspect after investigators were able to ascertain this now convicted double murderer had been living and working in Tocumwal during the month of January 1980. What was of particular interest was Edmunds, to a degree, fitted the description of the male suspect in the artist's drawing, being around the same age, as he would have been nearly 36 years old. Edmunds also had a slightly distinctive nose and wore his hair with the same sort of fringe. Edmunds, though, was not that tall and, when arrested in 1985, looked somewhat pudgy in his police mug shot.

The other interesting fact was, in respect of the murders of which he was convicted, Edmunds, after abducting his victims, drove off to secluded locations. In addition, both women had been raped and then bashed to death, each suffering a fractured skull. Police attempted to interview Edmunds but he refused to cooperate and most likely would have made a no comment record of interview in any event. On legal advice, of course.

In 2011, with the case of Elaine now gathering dust in the police archives, the NSW Government offered a $100,000 reward for any information, all to no avail. In early 2015, Detective Inspector John Lehmann again confirmed that Edmunds was very much a person of interest but, at the same time, did emphasis there were several other suspects. As to Edmunds, Lehmann said 'we can't rule him out,' but again added, '…we can't diminish the possibility that a number of other suspects who have come across our books over the years were involved either.'

Of course, it would later be revealed that the Donvale Rapist, alias Edmunds, carried a rather large knife with him, when committing his reign of terror during the 1970s-1980s. This knife was believed to be one he kept, after he had a short stint working in an abattoir. Now, in the case of Elaine, her throat had also been slashed from ear to ear, so the similarities continued to mount that perhaps Edmunds was more than just a suspect. I will let you be the judge and jury in that regard, as the murder of Elaine, to this day, remains a cold case.

There was also a reign of terror in various suburbs of Melbourne during May 1980 to October 1981, which resulted in the murder of six females of varying ages. They would later be found in 1980 and 1983, with four bodies at Tynong North and two in Frankston and, to this day, still remain unsolved. Were their murders as a result of the handiwork of Raymond Edmunds? I will again let you take time to reach a verdict, after considering all the facts.

The first Frankston victim was 59-year-old Allison Rooke, who was last observed by a neighbour leaving her home in Frankston North to catch a bus in Hannah Street and Frankston-Dandenong Road, to head to the main shopping area of Frankston. The next time she would be seen was some five weeks later on 5 July 1980, when a man out walking his dogs stumbled across her partially hidden decomposed naked body, in a shallow grave in McClelland Drive, Frankston.

A similar scenario, catching a bus to do some shopping, would also result in the disappearance and murder of 55-year-old Joy Summers, who was last seen at a bus stop in Chile Street and Frankston-Dandenong Road, Frankston around 1.20pm on 9 October 1981. This was in close proximity to where Allison had been waiting for the bus. The other similarity was that the partially covered naked body of Joy would be found in scrubland on 22 November 1981. This was only a short distance from where the body of Allison had been located.

The other interesting fact was both bus drivers told police they could not remember picking up either of these women, so they may well have been abducted, either waiting at the bus stop or walking along the street. Once again, due to the state of decomposition of Joy's body, the cause of death could not be ascertained.

Despite the usual reward being offered for information, the Frankston murders would remain unsolved, as would, what would become known as, the "Tynong murders". The first to suddenly disappear was Bertha Miller, who lived in Glen Iris and, at 73 years of age, was very much an active member of the local Spring Wesleyan Church in Prahran. This sprightly lady also just happened to be an aunty of the Chief Commissioner of Police at the time, Mick Miller. On 10 August 1980, Bertha was supposed to catch the 10.47am tram to meet a church friend along the same route but she was never on the tram.

Police, at the time, believed she was most likely abducted, either waiting at the tram stop or walking along High Street to catch the tram.

The next to disappear, just over two weeks later, was Catherine Headland. She was a teenager of only 14 years of age and was meant to catch a bus to start her casual shift at Coles in Fountain Gate. Catherine was last seen around 11.20am on 28 August 1980 at a bus stop in Berwick. This was despite the bus driver saying he did pick up a young lass matching her description. However, police came to the conclusion she never boarded the bus and was probably abducted within the 10 minutes of leaving home and arriving at the bus stop.

Just over a month later, on 6 October 1980, a young girl known to prefer hitchhiking against catching public transport, was thought to have obtained a lift from Cranbourne to travel to Dandenong. Anne-Marie Sargent, at 18 years of age, would last be seen at the Centrelink Office in Dandenong. Her disappearance was then quickly followed by a 34-year-old woman, in the early hours of 30 November 1980. Narumol Stephenson was with her husband visiting friends but she stayed in their motor vehicle, allegedly after they had some sort of argument. When he came out later around 6am to check on her, she had disappeared.

I think it would fair to say, at the time of these reports of the four missing persons, police, understandably, would not have connected them as possibly being linked, let alone in any way connected to the Frankston murders. Other than the missing Narumol Stephenson, the only similarity at the time was the other three women were last seen between 9am to midday, with two waiting for, or using public transport. The main difference though, was the different suburbs they were last seen at.

However, the finding together of the bodies of Bertha, Catherine and Anne–Marie on 6 December 1980 in a sand quarry, off a secluded bush track in Tynong North, confirmed these three murders were obviously carried out by the same person or persons. Bertha was fully clothed but, due the state of her remains, identification could only be confirmed by dental records and no cause of death could be established. Catherine was found naked but, once again, her cause of death could not be determined. Anne-Marie was also found naked and, again, was only identified from dental records and also from a plastic shunt, previously installed in her skull due to medical issues.

The missing Narumol Stephenson would then be linked, when her badly decomposed body was found by a man about to change his flat tyre on the Princes Highway in Tynong North. He noticed a bone sticking out of the ground from a short distance away and took it to Warragul police station. After the bone was confirmed as human, the remains of Narumol would then be found. Although it was not in the same location as the other three bodies, it was also located in Tynong North, leaving no doubt the four murders were connected. One scenario police considered was the same perpetrator(s) was going to partially bury her with the other three victims but was interrupted before doing so.

At this point, police would now have two separate investigations on foot, namely one for the two Frankston murders and one separate enquiry for Tynong North, but that would subsequently change. The first problem police had was the causes of death, in respect of each of the victims, could not be established. There were no personal possessions found with or near their bodies, or any other items that could lead to fingerprints or even DNA. This meant, whoever carried out the grisly murders either took the items, in order to conceal their victims' identities or, as is the common practice of serial killers, took them as some sort of trophy and to remind them of whatever experience they supposedly had at the time.

The six female victims were aged as young as 14, with the oldest being 73, meaning half were under 35 and the balance over 35 years. All, apart from Narumol, who was of Thai nationality, were Caucasian. The two older women were found fully dressed, while the remaining four were left naked, suggesting most likely a sexual motive for each these murders.

The similarities though that also started to slowly lead to a conclusion that the six murders were all linked, was they were all women, all were abducted near public transport and/or from the streets of Melbourne suburbs in broad daylight, apart from the abduction of Narumol. It was interesting that police confirmed no witnesses saw or heard anything untoward, or any evidence of these women being forcibly abducted, meaning they were most likely taken quickly and without putting up any sort of a struggle.

By 1985, the initial homicide investigators first came to the view that the six murders were carried out by three separate individuals. Following the establishment of a task force and assistance from both Canadian and US profilers, after interviewing over 2,000 people and following coronial inquests, police then determined they were now only looking for one suspect in respect of the six murders. One of three main suspects in the initial investigations was local 48-year-old Frankston man, Harold Janman, who was known to offer women lifts along the same road that Allison and Joy were last seen.

Janman, although quite religious, was also, according to some, a 'serial pest and gutter crawler', having a criminal record for soliciting sex workers. In 2018, he appeared on Channel

Nine's, A Current Affair, professing his innocence, even though there was some suggestion he failed two lie detection tests, which he again vehemently denied. He passed away in 2020, aged 88, and like the two other main suspects, was never charged as there was no credible evidence to connect him.

Convicted murderer, Bandali Debs, also came under the spotlight, not just from his shooting death of two Victorian Police officers.[193] His usual modus operandi, when in his late 20s, was after killing two sex workers. After he picked them up from highways,[194] he then dumped their bodies in a manner very similar to the Tynong North murders. He obviously had a penchant for sexual violence and, what also attracted police interest was, at one time he lived in an area near Tynong North. Debs remains incarcerated and will die behind bars but the likelihood he carried out the unsolved six murders is remote.

I have left Raymund Edmunds to last as a person of interest in the Tynong North and Frankston murders but, then again, maybe more than just a person of interest. Or is that just pure speculation on my part? Edmunds carried out a double murder in 1966, followed by a series of rapes between July 1971 and February 1984. Police believed he was involved in more rapes than he admitted to and was also likely to be involved in other murders. It is difficult to accept that Edmunds would simply stop at the 1966 murders and then put his killer instincts away and just be content with satisfying his sexual urges.

193 Debs is serving consecutive life sentences without parole for the murders of two Victorian Police officers in August 1998, *DPP v Debs & Roberts* [2003] VSC 30.

194 The 1997 murder of a Victorian teenager *R v Debs* [2007] VCC 220 and the NSW April 1995 murder also of a sex worker *R v Debs* [2012] NSWSC 119.

Edmunds was very much a suspect in the 1980 NSW murder of Elaine Jones. One of the reasons Victoria Police ruled him out as a person of interest for the Tynong North and Frankston murders in the same year, including the October 1981 murder of Joy Summers, was based on the fact that Edmunds was residing in NSW. With respect, Tocumwal is only a three-hour drive to Melbourne, being around 267 kilometres by road. There is every possibility that Edmunds came back to Melbourne during the period in question, so that can't be ruled out. Police were also of the view that Edmunds was somewhat lacking in charm and interpersonal skills, to encourage women to get into his vehicle without a significant struggle.

Again, on the one hand, as evidenced by the 1966 murders, he forced two people to drive him to bushland or to his own vehicle, when armed with a rifle. Given that, he wouldn't need to have any charm to get them to do what he said. On that basis, it makes some sense that when the six women were abducted, it was by force and they simply did what they were told in fear of suffering the consequences.

On the other hand, the fact that no witnesses heard any screams of anguish around the time each were abducted, it may well be due to the charm and interpersonal skills of their would-be abductor. By encouraging them to get into his vehicle, under some sort of pretext and looking like a nice and innocent person, they may well have obliged. Police, though, said Edmunds lacked that. Although, you only have to look at some of his rape admissions to police in 2019, which demonstrated that he indeed had some sort of calmness and convincing manner about him, albeit armed with a knife.

For example, he told one victim to quieten down and then, quite calmly, used her phone to make two calls. Another victim was told by Edmunds she was very beautiful and not to scream as she might wake the children, including nudging one on the arm very gently, telling her to go to another room. All this points to a person who knows placidly what he is doing, even with a raised knife in his hand. Edmunds repeatedly told his victims he wanted to 'make love to them and wasn't going to hurt them.'[195] Another interesting fact is Edmunds was quite selective in who he was going to rape. As we have read, one of the older women, being 73 years of age, in the Tynong North and Frankston murders, although found dead, was fully clothed. The younger ones were all naked, suggesting they may well have been sexually assaulted before being murdered.

In a 1973 rape, Edmunds told his victim, who was 57 years of age, to take her clothes off and then said, 'I'm going to have sex with you.'[196] For reasons only known to him, after pulling her clothes apart, he then said, 'Sorry, we have made a mistake…don't move until the next ad comes on TV.'[197] He then abruptly left, so it is apparent, Edmunds picks and chooses his victims to sexually assault, which is a further consideration to take into account to determine if he is the Tynong North and Frankston serial killer.

I will let you be the judge and jury, noting you have to be convinced, beyond reasonable doubt, and not simply on a balance of probabilities.[198] In other words, you can't reach a

---

195 *DPP v Edmunds* [2019] VCC 1581-see paras 46,47,53,54

196 Ibid-para 23.

197 Ibid-para 29

198 Beyond reasonable doubt is the criminal standard based on the evidence presented to a jury which leaves no doubt of guilt. Balance of probabilities applies in civil cases in that the evidence demonstrates in the matter before the court, it was more likely than not to have occurred.

criminal verdict of guilty on mere circumstantial evidence, gut feeling, certain odd behaviour and just a mere coincidence.

In the case of Edmunds, did he abduct each victim either armed with a gun or knife, or did he suavely persuade them to get into his vehicle? With Anne-Marie Sargent, did he simply offer her a ride when she was hitchhiking? Then again, Edmunds may, in fact, be totally innocent of these crimes but only he knows that.

The six murders have never been solved to this day, despite extensive media coverage. There remains a reward of $1 million, announced in 2017, for each unsolved cold case, for any information that may result in a conviction.

Meanwhile, Edmunds is believed to be one of a number of prisoners, including Hoddle Street killer, Julian Knight,[199] that, in due course, will most likely be relocated to a medium-security prison. These downgrades are as a consequence of the Victorian Government still dithering and fumbling, while the state remains subject to a record crime wave. Finally, after amending the bail laws and, in their words now the 'toughest in the country',[200] it seems the prisons are going to need more space, considering the pending closure of Port Philip Prison, to accommodate an anticipated increase of remand prisoners.

---

199 Knight was responsible for one of the worst massacres in the history of Australia, in which, armed with three weapons, he fired over 100 rounds of ammunition in Hoddle Street, Clifton Hill on 9 August 1987. Seven people died with 19 injured and it was fortunate there were not many more victims. (See chapter 26).

200 Remand in custody of youth offenders will no longer be viewed as a last resort and stricter bail tests will apply, especially for those committing offences while on bail. See *Bail Act 1977*(Vic)–amendments effective from 26 March 2025.

This means, prisoners like Edmunds will suddenly go down from a high security rating in protective custody, to two lower rungs on the ladder, being classified under less restriction in medium security. If he behaves himself and I am sure he will, and I say that with "tongue in cheek", Edmunds may even finish up at the lowest classification, being minimum security.[201]

Edmunds will, in any event, die in jail, unless someone gets to him first, but the chances of that are now lessened if he is relocated under a medium classification. Will this free him up to, once again, contact police and admit to what else he had been up to? We can only hope that, if he has any more confessions to make, he will come clean as time is quickly running out, as he is now 81 years old.

201 Security ratings are managed by Corrections Victoria with the aim to ensure that prisoners are managed in the least restrictive way, based on their level of security risk. See further Corrections Victoria Security Management Manual.

17
A QUESTION OF DOUBLE JEOPARDY

The question of double jeopardy raises the issue of whether a person who has been tried for a criminal offence and, either convicted or acquitted by a jury or a judge sitting alone, can be re-tried if new evidence emerges? Before I answer that question, it is useful to first look at the origins of the concept of "double jeopardy".

This is a principle that evolved as far back as ancient Greece and Rome[202] where, in effect, a person could not be tried twice for committing the same crime on the same set of facts. Indeed, a double jeopardy reference was even included in the US Constitution's Fifth Amendment which states, 'No

202 The doctrine, in all likelihood, emanated in ancient Rome and known as 'non bis in idem' meaning not twice against the same. It also has a similar concept in civil litigation known as res judicata. Also known as 'autrefois acquit' which is French term for 'previously acquitted'.

person shall…be subject to the same offence to be twice put in jeopardy of life or limb.' If under such provisions a person was to be charged again for the same offence, lawyers for the accused would raise a defence of double jeopardy and the fresh, but effectively same charge, would then be dismissed.

The same concept, in respect of double jeopardy, existed in English law for over 800 years. It was also perfectly articulated by Sir William Blackstone as a legal principle in that it had the effect of protecting individuals from being tried again for the same offence, following an acquittal.[203]

In Australia, this term was historically reserved for criminal proceedings and was formally incorporated into legislation. Specifically, Australian law stipulated that an individual cannot be prosecuted or penalised more than once for the same legal act.[204] This was to also ensure that any person in such a situation could not be taken into custody by police, face a lengthy and stressful interview and be charged once again, for the same criminal act.

However, following a crime that could only be categorised as one of the worst of the worst, Australia, like a number of other overseas countries, started to re-evaluate the legal principle of double jeopardy. This was particularly evident when the High Court of Australia even extended such a principle to dismiss a charge and conviction for perjury, or lying under oath, because

203 Blackstone's commentaries on the laws of England as published in 1765-69, unequivocally states that once a person has been acquitted of an offence, they cannot be tried again for the same offence.

204 For example, section 17 of the *Criminal Code Act 1899* (Qld) provided a defence by showing that the again accused person had already been tried, convicted, or acquitted on the same indictment. Section 16 provided that a person cannot be punished twice for the same act or omission.

it contradicted the acquittal of the same person on a charge of murder. That led to understandable widespread unrest within the community as, in effect, it now undermined the principle of double jeopardy, seen at the time as a cornerstone of Australia's criminal justice system but certainly in need of reform.

This considered outcry, to the principle of double jeopardy, came about as result of the April 1973 murder of 17-month-old baby, Deidre Kennedy. Her body was found lying on the roof of a toilet block near her parents' home in Ipswich, Queensland. It appeared she had died after being strangled, with evidence that she had been sexually assaulted. Her clothing had also been removed as she was found dressed in an adult slip and panties.

These items were later found to have been taken by the culprit from a clothesline next door to her parents' home. A postmortem confirmed the baby's death was by strangulation, with bruises on the lower part of her left thigh. These marks were confirmed by both medical and dental experts as caused by human teeth. In addition, there was evidence of extensive bruising to the head and neck, with abrasions adjacent to one eye and on her upper lip.

Police conducted an extensive investigation over many months but failed to identify who was responsible. It would take a further 10 years before they made some headway with their investigation when, on 11 October 1983, Raymond John Carroll was first interviewed by police. He denied any knowledge of the death of Deidre, let alone any involvement, maintaining that in April 1983, he attended a RAAF course at the Edinburgh base in South Australia. On that basis, given he was in another state, he had a firm alibi of his movements.

Police were obviously not convinced and further investigations would reveal that he was, in fact, not at the Edinburgh base at the time of the murder. Investigators had also obtained forensic evidence from odontologists, who specialise in the study of structure and abnormalities of teeth, that the bite mark on the baby's thigh was most likely a match to the teeth of Carroll. What made him more than just a suspect was his former wife, who would later give evidence at his trial on the charge of murder, that during their marriage, Carroll had a propensity for biting their baby daughter. This also included biting their child on her thighs, on more than one occasion.

On 24 February 1984, Carroll was arrested and charged with the baby's murder and his trial took place in the Supreme Court on 18 February 1985. Carroll pleaded not guilty and gave evidence under oath in which, when asked, 'Did you kill Deidre Kennedy?' he replied, 'I did not.' All to no avail, as the jury, satisfied with the evidence presented by the Crown, returned a verdict of guilty as charged.

An appeal against conviction and sentence then proceeded in the Queensland Full Court of the Supreme Court. On 27 November 1985, Carroll's conviction was quashed with a unanimous decision by the three appellant justices that a verdict of acquittal be entered. This, in effect, meant Carroll was now a free man, as the ruling was the same as a jury returning a verdict of not guilty.

In broad terms, the successful appeal determined that a jury acting reasonable could not have been satisfied beyond reasonable doubt of two main planks: (i) there was no direct evidence led that Carroll was anywhere near Ipswich at the time and (ii) the forensic odontology evidence was inconclusive, again placing a reasonable doubt to his guilt. On that basis, overall, there was no reasonable evidence led by the prosecution in which they clearly identified Carroll as the murderer.[205]

Carroll would resume a normal life in society for the next 14 years but that all changed in February 1999. Police were now in possession of further incriminating evidence, namely that Carroll was indeed in Ipswich at the time of the murder. In addition, it seemed Carroll had confessed to another prison inmate that he was responsible for killing Diedre. The Crown also had obtained further evidence, thanks to advances in forensic analysis, that the bite mark on the baby's thigh was definitely caused by Carroll's teeth.

The problem the Crown had though, was the principle of double jeopardy. This meant he could not be tried again for murder, so he was charged with perjury.[206] This was on the basis that he knowingly gave false evidence in respect of the murder for which he denied he was responsible.

Before Carroll was arraigned before the court, an application was made seeking the quashing of the indictment of perjury. This was on the ground that it was without foundation, contravening the doctrine of double jeopardy. Justice Muir had no hesitation in dismissing the application, as he concluded it did not prevent the laying of the perjury charge.[207] On 3 November 2000, a jury convicted Carroll of perjury, so he was now back behind bars. It didn't take long though before the

205 The overall evidence of the forensic odontologists was that it was inconclusive to establish with any degree of certainty, as to who was responsible for the bite marks on the dead child. See *Carroll v R* (1985) 19A Crim R 410, 410, 417, 435.

206 See section 123 of the *Criminal Code Act 1899* (Qld) which provides for a standard penalty of up to 14 years imprisonment.

207 *R v Carroll* [2000] QSC 308.

appeal process was again put in motion, noting the outcome would eventually lead to a complete review of "autrefois acquit" or, in layman's terms, double jeopardy.

The Court of Appeal on 21 September 2001 had no hesitation in accepting that the perjury trial, as put to the jury, was in effect a re-trial for murder. This was based on the incriminating new evidence, which had not been led at the earlier murder trial. In particular, the alleged confession Carroll made to a fellow inmate, regardless of its reliability, the now conclusive odonatological bite-mark evidence and the fact he was in Ipswich at the time of the murder. The problem was, none of this new compelling evidence was led at his murder trial, noting he had only subsequently been convicted of perjury.

Once again but now setting aside the conviction, this time for perjury, and entering a verdict of acquittal, Justice Williams, with the other two appeal judges concurring, said:

> *In my view, the trial should have been stayed as an abuse of process. But, in any event, when the evidence is carefully considered, I am of the view that the verdict returned by the jury was unsafe and unsatisfactory. On either ground, the verdict should be set aside and an acquittal entered.*[208]

The question of double jeopardy didn't end there though, first with an appeal by the Crown to the High Court of Australia. This was on the basis of whether the perjury charge undermined Carroll's acquittal of the earlier charge of murder and then, did his conviction infringe the common law rule against double jeopardy? Was it, in fact, an abuse of process? The High Court would have the final say in that regard.

208 *R v Carroll* [2001] QCA 394.

On 5 December 2002, in dismissing the appeal, Justice Michael McHugh best summed up the doctrine of double jeopardy in Carroll's case when he said:

It is an abuse of process for the Crown to charge a person with an office of perjury when proof of the charge necessarily contradicts or tends to undermine an acquittal of the accused in respect of another criminal charge. A perjury charge that has that effect is an abuse of process even if the evidence supporting the charge is different from the evidence that supported the prosecution case in respect of the charge on which the accused was acquitted. The long-established policy of the law is that an acquittal is not to be contradicted or undermined by a subsequent charge that raises the same ultimate issue or issues as was or were involved in the acquittal...[209]

His Honour then went on to say:

...the evidence supporting the charge of perjury put in issue the very fact that was in issue on the charge of murder, a charge of which Carroll was acquitted. By finding that he was guilty of perjury, the jury's verdict necessarily proved that he had murdered Deidre Kennedy. It contradicted the acquittal of Carroll in respect of the charge of murdering her. So, the issue is whether it was open to the Crown to charge Carroll with perjury when the resultant verdict on the perjury charge necessarily contradicted or, at all events, had a tendency to undermine the acquittal of the accused on a charge of murder. I

209 *R v Carroll* [2002] HCA 55; 213 CLR 635;184 ALR 1; 77 ALJR 157-para 117.

do not think that there is any doubt that this was a course that the common law does not tolerate...[210]

The High Court, in effectively throwing out the Crown appeal, finally brought an end to the long, drawn-out conclusion of the legal redress for Carroll. He had escaped the claws of justice, not once, but on two separate occasions, despite conclusive evidence that he was indeed the perpetrator.

However, this did lead, in due course, to a watering down of the consequences of the double jeopardy principle in Australia. In view of the horrific crime carried out of the murder of a defenceless 17-month-old baby and the complete failure to convict Carroll, despite the overall compelling evidence against him, the Australian public were not happy. The then Queensland Premier, Peter Beattie, was the first to come out commenting that, in the case of Carroll, 'it was an injustice.'

Other state premiers would follow. The call for reform was such that in 2007, the Council of Australian Governments known as COAG, ultimately would release details to amend the law and effectively water down the principle of double jeopardy.

What followed were significant legal reforms in most Australian jurisdictions in order to try and put in place a balance between protecting, not only the rights of the accused, but to ensure that justice was seen to be done. In essence, what has now been adopted provides a general exception to the rule of double jeopardy, largely based on the concept of 'fresh and compelling evidence' against the acquitted person concept.

It must, however, be in the interests of justice to make such an order. The new evidence must be reliable and substantial and not have been presented in the original trial. It does vary though

210 Ibid-para 127.

in its application in each Australian jurisdiction that has now changed the law. The general exception rule is, it cannot be used where a person, for example, was charged with murder but was convicted of the lesser offence of manslaughter.

In October 2006, New South Wales enacted legislation for such a further prosecution, again based on the new and fresh compelling evidence rule, in respect of life sentence offences and not only for murder.[211] In 2007, Queensland followed suit, rightly dubbed "Deidrie's Law" for such a retrial in the case of murder, like NSW, in respect of a tainted acquittal for any crime carrying imprisonment of 25 years.[212] In South Australia, it must be a category A offence[213] and in Western Australia, it must be for a minimum imprisonment of 14 years.[214]

In 2011, the Victorian Government passed similar legislation, based on fresh and compelling DNA evidence, in situations where key witnesses gave false evidence and also in respect of any person acquitted, who subsequently admits to a crime. It will also apply to a tainted original acquittal and even in situations where jurors were bribed or subject to intimidation in handing down a not guilty verdict. Criminal offences, now subject to such a re-trial, are for serious crimes including murder,

211 *Criminal Code (Double Jeopardy) Amendment Act 2007*(NSW). Also refer to the *Crimes (Appeal and Review) Act 2001*(NSW)- section 102(2). In order for such evidence to be 'fresh' it must not have previously been 'tendered 'or 'brought forward'.

212 *Criminal Code (Double Jeopardy) Amendment Act 2007*(Qld). Also see *Criminal Code and Other Legislation (Double Jeopardy Exception and Subsequent Appeals) Amendment Act 2024*(Qld).

213 *Criminal Law Consolidation (Double Jeopardy) Amendment Act 2008*(SA).

214 *Criminal Appeals Amendment (Double Jeopardy) Act 2012*(WA).

manslaughter, a number of terrorism offences, commercial drug trafficking, armed robbery and aggravated rape.[215]

The new laws are generally not retrospective, meaning the double jeopardy exception will only apply for any applicable offence, following the enactment of the legislation. Interesting though, the Queensland government, in 2014, amended its legislation to make it retrospective. This resulted in a Queensland man, who had been acquitted of a stabbing murder in 1987, the subject of an order sought by the Director of Public Prosecutions to be re-tried.

This was as a result of fresh evidence which brought into question his original acquittal. In that murder trial, he was acquitted by a jury when in evidence, the testing techniques, at the time, determined the blood on the pillow near the victim's body was consistent with not only him but also about one in 1000 Australians. The DPP now had fresh and compelling evidence, thanks to new forensic testing techniques that matched his DNA profile on the bloody pillowcase.

However, the Court of Appeal dismissed the application, seeking such order for a re-trial, on the basis the new evidence wasn't reliable due to the expert witness, who collected the original blood sample, not available to testify. The other issue, also raised by the judges, was even if the DNA profiles did match the suspect, there was no evidence of how it came to be on the pillow.[216]

The NSW Government also failed, based on fresh and compelling evidence, in its attempt to bring a male to justice for the murder of an Aboriginal child and two indigenous

215 *Criminal Procedure Amendment (Double Jeopardy and Other Matters) Act 2011* (Vic).

216 Director of *Public Prosecutions v TAL* [2019] QCA 279.

teenagers. The now 52-year-old, who for legal reasons can now only be referred to as "XX", had been previously found not guilty at a 1994 trial for the murder of 16-year-old Clinton Speedy-Duroux. His body was found dumped in bushland in late January 1991.

In what would become known as the Bowraville murders, which is a northern NSW town, XX was also charged with the murder of Evelyn Greenup, who was only four at the time of her disappearance in early October 1990. After her body was located in April 1991, the same male would eventually stand trial for her murder in March 2006 but, again, was found not guilty.

In May 2016, NSW Police obtained fresh and compelling evidence in respect of another missing teenager by the name of Colleen Walker-Craig. She had disappeared in September 1990, which was also during the same five-month period, from Bowraville. The same male would then be charged again with the murders of Clinton and Evelyn and now Colleen. It was noted these three children had all disappeared from houses on the same street in Bowraville. Police were confident the person now charged with all three murders was responsible, thanks to a lengthy brief of evidence.

However, whether such a re-trial would proceed depended on an application to the NSW Court of Criminal Appeal for an order, based on the now fresh and compelling evidence. This evidence, which was in respect of the murder of Colleen, was alleged to be also fresh and compelling for the murders of Clinton and Evelyn. The purpose of the application was for an order for the respondent XX to be retried again for those two murders and also for the murder of Colleen at a single trial on the same indictment.

The Court of Appeal determined that the evidence in relation to Colleen had, in fact, been previously available but not admitted at either of the earlier two trials. On that basis, it could not be deemed as 'fresh and compelling' evidence in relation to the murders of the first two children. In dismissing the application, the learned justices said it had, therefore, not been properly raised for determination by the Court.[217]

What all this demonstrates is, despite the intent behind the watering down of Australia's double jeopardy laws, it will still not be an easy road, in view of the strict guidelines, to bring anyone to justice who has already been acquitted, to be tried again for the same crime.

217 *Attorney General for New South Wales v XX* [2018] NSWCCA 198.

18
REMAINS LEFT IN A DRUM

It was never a cold case but, on reflection, maybe given the strange disappearance of Edwina Boyle with her remains, many years later, found in a drum, it should have been listed as one. Sorrow for the family would come to the fore when the wife of Frederick "Fred" Boyle and mother to two young children, suddenly was nowhere to be seen, after allegedly leaving a handwritten note for him when he woke up on the morning of 7 October 1983.

Boyle would tell his children and all who would listen, that the note said she was leaving him to live with a person by the name of Ray, who she had been having an affair with for some time and she was moving interstate. He had shown the note Edwina had left him on the kitchen table to his brother-in-law and also the children. The note even said she no longer loved him, that he was to look after the children and ensure their eldest daughter kept up her skating at the Frankston Ice Skating Rink.

Boyle and his wife had moved to Australia from Wales in 1972 and their two children were then born, supported by both parents who worked hard, with their father as a carpet layer. Edwina worked at a chicken farm and, to everyone that knew them, they had a loving and harmonious 11 years of marriage. Underneath though, Edwina, from around October 1982 knew of an affair her husband was having and their relationship had deteriorated to a point they would be heard arguing over his infidelity by their children, late into the night.

It's fair to say that even those close to the family had some suspicions of why 30-old Edwina would suddenly take off, never to been heard of again, leaving behind her two dearly loved children. Then again, according to Fred, she had left with another man, so why couldn't he also find someone to have a loving relationship with. The problem was, his alleged newfound lover moved in with her children, some three days after Edwina supposedly took off.

This blended family, now consisting of a total of five children, would, for the next five years, appear to live happily together, with Boyle telling relatives, friends and acquaintances the same story about Edwina and the new man of her dreams, Ray.

When his second relationship ended in 1988, Boyle would raise his two children on his own in Carrum Downs, a south-east suburb of Melbourne, Victoria, continuing with sub-contract work as a carpet layer and also as a courier. He, of course, would say he hoped Edwina was now happy and, even when he was interviewed by police a month after her disappearance, he also said that she took with her most of her clothing and around $400 in cash.

It was obvious, at this point, police still had some suspicions and Boyle was again interviewed in March 1992 by a detective-sergeant. However, in the absence of any evidence, particularly a body, they were really going nowhere. Boyle stuck to the same story and a note that he had sent to his sister-in-law in Wales in December 1983 supported his version of events of what had transpired. The note said:

> *Edwina took off with another guy, she has been planning this for some time…a well thought out plan…she told me she didn't love me anymore and hasn't for a long time…she also said that she was leaving the kids with me as they were better off with me…the part that really gets to me the most is the two kids, it's been a month now since they have seen or heard from their mother…How do you explain to two kids that not only does their mother not only no longer love their dad, but she doesn't give a stuff for them either…she could be overseas by now…if you have already heard from her, please ask her to write to the kids.*[218]

Boyle would get away with this story of fiction until August 2006, when it started to unravel. His son-in law, Michael, and eldest daughter, Careesa, had moved in with him, with Michael having some suspicions about a 44-gallon drum. He uncovered that the drum had accompanied Boyle on each of his house moves that had taken place since 1983. Michael initially made some off-the-cuff remarks that his wife's mother was locked in the drum. What he did notice, though, every time they would have visitors to the home, Boyle would become somewhat uneasy if they came close to the barrel, let alone touch it, with Boyle saying it contained toxic glue.

218 This letter would subsequently be exhibit P8 in the trial of Boyle in 2008.

During September 2006, Michael, while cleaning up the backyard, cut open the drum and found some women's clothing and a hessian bag but was then called in for lunch. It would not be until 13 October 2006 that he would uncover decomposed remains in the hessian sack in a wheelie bin, which included some bones and a skull. His suspicions that it was Edwina were confirmed after a forensic pathologist, using dental records, confirmed it was indeed her.

Boyle was immediately charged with murder but still professed his innocence, pleading not guilty before a Supreme Court of Victoria jury during a 10-day trial in early February 2008. The Crown would lead evidence, supported by a post-mortem examination of the remains, that Boyle first strangled his wife and then, after shooting her in the right side of her skull with a single shot from a .22 rifle, placed the body in a hessian bag, covertly sealing it in cement in the 44-gallon drum.

Boyle, not to be outdone, had now changed his story and, as he told police when he was arrested and charged, said in his evidence that on the night of 6 October 1983, on returning home from work, he thought Edwina was asleep in bed. However, on finding her dead shot in the head with one of his neck ties tightly wound around her neck, he panicked thinking police would blame him and he would be charged with murder. He then placed her body inside the barrel with cement to stop any smell and forged the note she allegedly left behind.

In a sobbing explanation to the jury, he then said:

I thought, I'm knackered now. No one's going to believe I didn't do it…I'm having an affair with another woman and I come home and find my wife shot in the head…

Well Boyle was right on this occasion, in respect of two comments. He was having an affair, which fizzled out some five years after the murder and yes, no one believed he didn't do it, with the jury finding him guilty as charged.

On 18 March 2008, 58-year-old Boyle appeared for sentencing before His Honour Judge Forrest, who took into account that Boyle had no prior convictions and given he was diabetic, would need ongoing medical attention whilst in gaol. His two daughters provided victim impact statements and, as was their right, said, with plenty of emotion, they still loved their father and attested to his caring and devoted fatherly nature. Boyle's sister-in-law's statement was not as glowing, telling the court of the family's devastation, coupled by the fact that her much loved sister's remains lay in a metal drum for 23 years.

Judge Forrest acknowledged Boyle may well have been a caring and devoted father to his two girls. Nonetheless, taking their mother from them was difficult to comprehend, particularly the fictional story that she had deserted them, which would have erased their memory of her.

In sentencing Boyle to 21 years imprisonment with a fixed non parole period of 17 years, His Honour said:

> *Despite your evidence that you still love your wife, your actions demonstrate the falsity of this position. You have shown no remorse whatsoever; you have sought to live a lie, with the sole aim of avoiding apprehension for your dastardly actions. Your letter in December 1983 to you sister-in-law contradicts any love and affection for your wife, as does your false statement to the police in 1992 about her asserted infidelity. These statements were anything but a profession of love; they were a denigration*

of the character of a faithful and devoted wife and loving mother who met her death at your hands. I do not accept that you have any remorse for the murder of the deceased…[219]

The only consolation the family would get, was Edwina had finally been found and laid to a dignified rest. Believing that justice had now been done, her sister walked out of court to tell the waiting media:

…I just feel so sorry for my nieces. They've lived a life, for all these years, believing their mother deserted them and now to hear this kind of verdict, is going to devastate them.

With time already served on pre-sentence detention of 522 days,[220] this meant Boyle would have been eligible for release around 2023. No doubt he will get to spend the rest of his days with his daughters and grandchildren, a pleasure he never allowed Edwina.

---

219 *R v Boyle* [2008] VSC 71-para 30. A subsequent appeal against conviction and sentence was dismissed by the Court of Appeal. See *R v Boyle* [2009] VSCA 289.

220 *Sentencing Act 1991*(Vic)-section 18(4).

19
'I KILLED A GIRL LAST NIGHT'

This time it would not be the discovery of a body in a drum, but a family member's conscience, no longer coping with keeping silent, of what he knew. The cold case of 16-year-old Michelle Buckingham had remained on police files for some 30 years, following her savage murder in late October 1983.

Michelle was found lying dead by a farmer, on the side of a road in Shepparton, Victoria, some two weeks after she had been reported as missing. She had been stabbed at least 19 times[221] and, as her mother would later say in a victim impact statement, read out by her other daughter to the court, she was left 'lying there like a dog.' The further sad episode for the family was that Michelle's mother would pass away from a heart attack, five days before the trial of her murderer, Stephen James Bradley.

221 Part of Michelle's body was decomposed but the woolen jumper she was wearing had a total of 24 cuts in it.

While the cold case unit of Victoria Police never gave up, this was one murder they were determined to solve but they still had their doubts in bringing the offender to justice. When it was reopened in 2012, cold case investigators enlisted the assistance of the Shepparton News, who gave the unsolved murder further publicity and much needed media attention to the local population, causing several potential witnesses to come forward. One in particular was the brother-in-law of Bradley, by the name of Norman Gribble.

He had kept a secret for many years, fearing family repercussions, about the murder of Michelle. After seeing the press article, Gribble finally came forward and told well-renowned homicide detective, Senior Sergeant Ron Iddles, what he knew. Gribble said he was approached by Bradley on the morning of 22 October 1983 in a distressed and agitated state. Gribble observed that Bradley also had a cut on his hand and, after placing a bandage around it, drove him to a local hospital. On the way, Bradley confessed to him that he and two of his mates, who he named, had killed a girl the night. He then admitted on two separate occasions it was him saying, 'I've killed someone.'

His differing version of events was, after they picked Michelle up from a local caravan park, she refused to have sex with them. The trio then decided they would all participate in stabbing her, which took place in a car park behind the Pines Hotel in Shepparton. The body was then placed in the back of Bradley's green HQ Holden sedan and dumped by the side of a rural road, a few kilometres from the main town centre. Gribble then advised Bradley to immediately tell police but he sold his motor vehicle and quickly moved interstate.

When first interviewed by Detective Ron Iddles in

November 2013, Bradley said he never made any sort of confession to Gribble. He admitted, however, that he had owned a distinctive HQ Holden sedan around 1983 but didn't know why he sold it. Police had already established that a similar-looking vehicle was seen in the area some days earlier before Michelle's body was found. He also said he was friends with the two mates Gribble had identified to police.

A second and third interview, some months later in January and again in March 2014, saw him admit he, in fact, knew of Michelle but had never met her. Bradley then went into detail of the persistent nightmares he had been having about a girl with long dark hair, who sometimes sat on his bed.

When pressed further about Michelle and whether he had stabbed her, Bradley first said he could not recall. But then he made some sort of admission with the comment 'we had to…we had…we all have to do it.'

He also now said that on the night of 21 October 1983, he had a vague recollection that he was at the Pines Hotel in Shepparton but still had no memory of what happened later that night.

Bradley was charged with murder and, after hearing the evidence against him at the committal hearing in March 2015, he again changed his story about his involvement in the stabbing of Michelle. This time, in further speaking with police, he implicated his two mates, in particular one who he said first killed her. After Bradley and the other mate then saw her dead in the back seat of his vehicle, they were told to also stab her. On being handed a fishing knife, they were then told by who Bradley now alleged was the killer, 'I go down for it, well youse'll all go down for it.'

At the subsequent jury trial of 54-year-old Bradley in

December 2015, he would again implicate his two mates, who were never charged and had denied any involvement on oath at the trial. The Crown had, indeed, put the case against Bradley as either one of murder by joint criminal enterprise or, alternatively, one of straight-out murder. His fourth version of events was told to police after the committal hearing was totally rejected by the jury, being satisfied beyond reasonable doubt of the evidence of Norman Gribble and that Bradley was guilty of murder.

On 18 December 2015, Bradley appeared for sentencing before Justice Osborn in the Supreme Court of Victoria, sitting at Shepparton. His Honour was indeed satisfied that the compelling evidence of Gribble was truthful and substantiality accurate, particularly what Bradley told him about the morning after the murder. In that regard, the judge said:

> *...you confessed to the murder of Michelle...in a state of emotional distress and consciousness of guilt* [222]*...In that confession, you first stated the terrible fact that you had killed someone. This was a true statement and that someone was Michelle Buckingham.*[223]

The judge was, however, satisfied beyond reasonable doubt that the killing was carried out jointly, after Michelle refused to have sex with at least one of them. Regardless, taking into account the lies Bradley told in the first three interviews with police and then disposing of his vehicle not long after the murder, demonstrating his guilt, His Honour stated:

---

222 *The Queen v Bradley* [2015] VSC 768- para 1.

223 Ibid-para 2.

There is a nightmare quality to the cruel brutality of your offending which comes from the combination of the following aggravated features:(a) the heartless and predatory nature of your attack upon a teenage girl who had all her life ahead of her;(b) the brutality of stabbing her at least 19 times in the back and (c) the callousness with which her body was dumped.[224]

His Honour was also mindful that Bradley had shown no remorse, let alone accept any responsibility for his ghastly conduct and even referred to a decade earlier of a Victorian murder, that brought further shock and grief to the Victorian community.[225] Bradley was no clean skin though, with priors, including for an armed robbery he carried out in 1984, and aggravated burglary offending involving a threat to kill a former partner in 1996. He had spent time behind bars in Pentridge Prison, so he knew what was waiting for him when sentenced to an extensive further term of imprisonment.

Indeed, Judge Osborn, despite considering that at the time of the murder Bradley was only 22 years of age and had good prospects of rehabilitation, a substantial prison term for this serious violent offender[226] was warranted. In that respect,

224 Ibid-para 25.

225 Christopher Lowery and Charles Ian King were both convicted of the 1971 brutal murder of 15-year-old, Rosalyn Nolte. Detectives had a fair idea who was responsible for the vicious murder which was confirmed when the fingerprint of Lowery was identified from a beer can left at the crime scene. Their death sentence was commuted in 1973 and after new minimum terms of 20 years were set by the Supreme Court, both were released on parole in 1992. Lowery died in 2007 while King lives a quiet life with his children in the northern suburbs.

226 *Sentencing Act 1991*(Vic)-section 6F.

Bradley was sentenced to a maximum of 27 years with a minimum non-parole period of 21 years. He was also credited with pre-sentence detention of 650 days.[227]

Bradley then appealed against his sentence as manifestly excessive, on the basis that Judge Osborn did not give sufficient weight to his immature and young age at the time of the murder. Victoria Legal Aid decided not to act for him as such appeal was unlikely to succeed.[228] How right they were, as the Court of Appeal refused leave to appeal and even questioned legal counsel for Bradley as to why any mercy should be shown. This was in respect why the applicant, who evaded culpability for such an horrendous crime for decades, should be given any leniency with the sentencing principles that may have applied in the 1980s.[229]

In refusing such leave, their Honours summed up the offending succinctly:

> *...to stab a defenceless teenage girl to death, inflicting multiple knife wounds, without having been offered the slightest provocation and merely in response to her refusal to engage in sexual intercourse, must merit the description that the judge applied to this crime, namely 'brutal and cowardly'...It was... an aggravating factor that her body was dumped by the side of the road. In addition, it must not be forgotten that the applicant*

227 Ibid-section 18(4).

228 Bradley was represented by a barrister acting pro- bono-in other words for no fee.

229 His counsel argued the concept of equal justice' in that in the 1980's, murderers were sentenced to life imprisonment but were released earlier on parole, as against what applied when he was sentenced in 2015.

pleaded not guilty and showed no remorse, thereby disentitling him to mitigation sometimes available in such cases.[230]

Bradley will be eligible for parole around 2034 and I think, it's fair to say that, providing he survives his time in prison, he won't be returning to live in Shepparton on his release.

230 *Bradley v The Queen* [2017] VSCA 69-para134.

20
POISON MY LOVE

As far back as nineteenth century Britain, arsenic was readily available for different purposes, including used to kill rats. It was odourless, tasteless and could easily be confused with cooking essentials such as flour and sugar. Arsenic also has the by-product as a medication to treat asthma, skin-related issues and even reduced libido problems. Being cheap and easy to buy, it would leave a trail of death and associated illnesses by the 1830s.

This was due to its prolific use in commercial goods, such as fabric dyes and wallpapers. There was also a suggestion that some of the fatalities, due to arsenic poisoning, were because of accidental use, after being placed in food as a sweetener. If you wanted to get rid of someone though, arsenic was readily available. In those early days, chemical methods of detection were simply not available.

If you wished to kill, you could give someone a single large dose or use repeated small doses over a designated period of time, known as chronic poisoning[231]. Doing it the latter way could result in escaping the claws of justice and that is what any poisoner would hope for. Like arsenic, strychnine can also be deadly, causing severe and painful muscle spasms, resulting in a slow lingering death as the victim struggled to breathe. High doses could cause instant death but was also used by early Australian colonial farmers to poison dingoes and other wildlife seen as a threat to their livestock.

Martha "The Black Widow of Richmond" Needle, was Australia's first notable case involving arsenic poisoning. The first to die was her daughter in 1885, followed by her husband in 1889 and then her two remaining young daughters in 1890. While doctors were somewhat baffled by what was behind their sudden deaths, Needle collected their life insurance policy monies after each family member passed. To make her motive more confusing, she then paid for an elaborate gravesite in their memory and would visit it regularly.

Now a single woman, she began a relationship with a saddler businessman which was frowned upon by his two brothers, one in particular. After visiting Needle in 1894, she served him a meal and he became ill with painful stomach cramps and again, the following morning, after she served him breakfast. He was treated by doctors but they had their suspicions, thinking he may have been poisoned. On taking a sample of his vomit, it was analysed at a government laboratory

231 Acute poisoning results in vomiting, severe burning of the mouth together with intense abdominal pain. The body's circulation collapses followed by a quick and painful death. Chronic poisoning takes its time with slow damage to red blood cells, kidneys and a gradual decline in strength and bodily functions. It can also result in pigmentation and skin rash, confusion and fingernail streaks.

which found the sample contained arsenic. It was all over for 31-year-old Needle, being convicted on four counts of murder and sent to the gallows at Old Melbourne Gaol on 22 October 1894.[232]

It's a pity Lorraine Whyte didn't do some research on Needle, before venturing down a similar path. Maybe she did but was hoping to be more successful in getting away with it.

In 1966, at the tender age of 18, Lorraine married the man of her life, Leonard John Moss. Over the next four years, this happily married couple were blessed with two daughters and a son. Leonard, a slaughterman in Bendigo, was well liked by his work colleagues and he enjoyed a beer. He drank most days of the week and on the odd occasion, would consume too many beers. Being a keen gardener, he grew vegetables and fruit trees, therefore, he was well aware of how to be careful when using poisons. His children adored him and he was seen as a very loving husband and father.

At first glance, Lorraine appeared to be a home body but, aside from her family, she enjoyed tenpin bowling. She also worked part time in domestic and home help and to all and sundry, appeared to be in a happy marriage. However, things started to change around November 1978, when Lorraine was faced with a very ill husband. He was admitted to Bendigo Hospital with a fever which quickly developed into lethargy and sore muscles, coupled with severe bouts of diarrhoea and

232 Needle was one of four women hanged at Old Melbourne Goal from 1863 to 1895. It must have run in her family as in July 1920, the son of Needle's older sister, Alexander Lee, went to the gallows in Adelaide Gaol after being convicted of the April Fool's Day murder of his wife and three of his children by the use of strychnine poison.

vomiting. The diagnosis was gastroenteritis and, after a few days in hospital, he recovered and was discharged.

Their lives appeared to be well and happy for the next few years but, in 1982, Leonard began to suffer from regular patterns of illness. Obviously concerned, Lorraine made sure he had nutritious lunches, which he took to work each day, but they didn't seem to help. Leonard often complained about the distasteful lunches to his workmates and threw them into a garbage bin. On a few occasions, two of his work colleagues saw the home-cooked meals about to be discarded, so they helped themselves. The only problem was, they became nauseous, which then continued for several weeks. It was nearly eight months before one worker fully recovered.

In September 1982, Leonard became chronically ill and, following a few medical tests over the next month, the consensus medical opinion was he may have been suffering from leptospirosis. Given that he worked in an abattoir slaughtering pigs, it was believed the contamination from their urine was what was causing his illness. His symptoms of stomach cramping, fever with cold sweats at night, headaches and attacks on his bodily organs, continued on a regular basis into early 1983.

Initially, Leonard still attended work but would then suffer a number of relapses, so he'd go home and rest and then return to work the next day. Despite several absences from work due to this illness, he was elected by his 50 workmates to the position of union representative. By May 1983, Leonard described his life as 'like a living hell.' He was slurring his words, his right eye was rolling in his head and his tongue was hanging out of his now blue face. Extremely concerned, doctors once again admitted him to Bendigo Hospital.

The medical professionals had absolutely no idea what was causing his near death-like symptoms, noting he couldn't even hold a knife and fork when eating a meal. After he had slowly recovered, he was discharged from hospital but, upon returning home, his symptoms reappeared. By this stage, Lorraine was obviously concerned, so with her 14-year-old daughter, Colleen, she went to the Bendigo Library to look for a cure.

Being the loving wife she was, her aim was to find a cure for her much loved but very ill husband, something the medical profession were unable to do. It was later revealed by Colleen that her mother had carried out extensive research at the library regarding poisons, their effect and how many doses were needed to obviously say goodbye to Leonard.

On 20 June 1983, Leonard was admitted to Austin Hospital as he was thought to be suffering from glandular fever. However, doctors were unable to find any infection and no evidence of any malignant tumour. His bone marrow was not functioning as it should and he was suffering on-going delusions and a confused state of mind. Like his other hospital admissions, Leonard recovered after 11 days and was then released to return home. Once again, it was still a mystery as to what was causing his serious health issues.

On 7 July 1983, he was again admitted to hospital with similar symptoms but, this time, he remained there for a total of six weeks. Again, the medical profession was at a loss, having no idea what was causing his on-going illness. By late July 1983, Leonard had deteriorated to a point where he could only walk assisted by a frame but was dragging his feet.

In August 1983, sadly he was confined to a wheelchair. At first glance, it appeared the cause of his illness had been found as doctors, after carrying out numerous tests, discovered significant levels of arsenic and lead throughout his body. For reasons only known to the Austin Hospital, the results of these tests were not immediately added to his file and no one was the wiser until it was too late for Leonard.

Towards the end of August 1983, Leonard was almost a complete invalid, becoming worse with each passing day. Bless her kind and loving soul, Lorraine was now his full-time nurse because Leonard could only move his hands, despite having no feeling in them. Much of his days were spent in his much-loved garden, lying on a mattress while Lorraine devoted her life to looking after him. She fed, bathed, shaved and groomed her ailing husband. Occasionally, Leonard was able to get out of his wheelchair, aided by his loved wife, who ensured his walking frame or crutches were close by. At this point in time, no one knew that Lorraine was, in fact, nursing him to death.

Fortunately for Leonard, his torturous life as he now knew it, ended on 13 January 1984. He had been admitted to the Austin Hospital in a terrible state with the usual stomach cramps, confusion, disorientation and hallucinations. It was highly likely seen as a relief to his family and friends that Leonard was no longer suffering. The impact of his death on his three children, Tracey 17, Colleen 15 and Timonthy 13, would have been devastating.

Now aged 35 years, Lorraine moved on with a new and exciting lifestyle. She dyed her hair, wore revealing and expensive clothes and quickly brought out into the open, her new "friendship" with a fellow workmate of her now deceased husband. Little did she know at the time that her devious efforts in poisoning Leonard would come to light but it would take another 18 years before justice was finally served.

Not long after Leonard passed away, his test results,

clearly indicating arsenic poisoning, came to the attention of medical staff at the Austin Hospital. As a result, a hair sample was removed from Leonard's head and was subjected to extensive tests, which included scanning and an electronic microscopy using a nuclear reactor-type tool. What this showed to analytical chemists was, during the last two weeks of his agonising life, Leonard had received a dose of arsenic to a level of 189 parts per million. Further analysis then showed, in the lead up to January 1984, over the previous two months, such levels of dosage varied from 131 parts per million, to massive doses of 247 parts per million in November 1983.

In addition, there was clear evidence of his fingernails inflicted with what is known as Mees lines.[233] It was later collaborated by another analytical chemist that Leonard had received substantial and varying amounts of arsenic over a period of time from about 1982. Their report, to put all this into perspective, indicated that the level of arsenic naturally occurring on average in the human body is usually in the range of four parts per million, to a high of 10. In other words, anything above the top range of 10 is not only potentially dangerous, but as evidenced could and did result in death.

In July 1986, the Homicide Squad visited the family home of Lorraine as they had sufficient evidence, albeit circumstantial, that Lorraine had murdered Leonard by poisoning him. During a lengthy police record of interview, Lorraine maintained her innocence and continually proclaimed her on-going love and support, further demonstrated by her full-time care as Leonard

---

233 These lines are horizontal white bands on fingernails which can indicate persistent health issues often related to systematic conditions, or indeed exposure to toxins.

had become progressively more ill. Regardless, Lorraine was charged with murder and placed in custody on remand.

At this point in time, two of her children, Tracey and Timothy, wanted nothing more to do with their mother but Colleen still supported her in the belief that it was not possible she had murdered their adored father. Following a coronial inquest in late 1986, luck was on Lorraine's side when she was released from custody with the charge of murder withdrawn. This was because the coroner had concluded there was insufficient evidence to commit Lorraine for trial. She would also now progress her so-called friendship with Leonard's workmate, marrying him some months after the coronial inquest.

In late March 2000, Lorraine may have started to feel guilty or was it because she thought she couldn't be prosecuted after 15 years?[234] Tracey, her eldest daughter, contacted the Homicide Squad telling them her mother had apparently confessed some details to her sister, Colleen. In a conversation, which allegedly took place on 31 March 2000, Lorraine told Colleen her father had died from an accidental overdose of poison. This was then elaborated on in a lengthy admission to not only Colleen but also her partner, that it was not accidental as she had deliberately set out to kill him with arsenic.

In trying to justify why she would do such horrific acts over a period of two years, Lorraine said she couldn't take any more of his violent outbursts, especially after he had been drinking. She also told her new husband the same thing but

234 The law relating to a statute of limitations sets time for commencing legal proceedings such as in civil matters. For criminal offences, some summary and indictable offences have a strict time limit but serious crimes such as murder, there is no statute of limitations, meaning such a charge can be brought at any time.

now included the reason was to get Leonard's superannuation pay out. It must have become extremely stressful for Lorraine because she took an overdose of tablets and was admitted to the Bendigo Hospital psychiatric ward. During her time there, Lorraine also told one of the medical staff she had killed her first husband. Following a diagnosis of financial and work-related stress the reason behind her overdose, Lorraine was discharged.

After being made aware of what had transpired, in December 2000 homicide detectives arranged for a listening device to be worn by Colleen, hoping to obtain a recording of such confessions. She met with her mother in the Malmsbury Botanical Gardens and, despite Colleen's best efforts, Lorraine denied she had ever killed Leonard. On 17 January 2001, police, on deciding they had sufficient evidence, took Lorraine into custody. After being read her rights and confirming her name, date of birth and address, Lorraine then refused to answer any more questions. On being charged with murder and refused bail, after a contested committal hearing, the trial proceeded before a judge and jury on 2 April 2002 in the Supreme Court of Victoria sitting at Bendigo.

Over two weeks, with Lorraine Alice Whyte pleading not guilty, evidence led by the Crown from expert witnesses put to the jury, in no uncertain terms, that Leonard received increasing doses of arsenic from October 1983 to his final dose just before he passed away in January 1984. The chemical analyst evidence clearly supported the Crown's position of the level of dangerous toxicity ingested by her victim. Also called to give evidence, her daughters were subjected to exhaustive cross- examination, particularly in respect to the confessions. They also left no doubt in the minds of the jurors that Leonard was nothing but a loving and devoted husband and father and was clearly respected by his friends and workmates.

Whyte chose not to give evidence or call any witnesses and the final address by her defence counsel set out what she said took place. In that respect, he submitted the death was due to accidental poisoning and not at the hands of the accused. As to the so-called confessions alleged to have been made by her, they were either not made or, if she did indeed make such a statement, it was either misinterpreted or made at a time when she was mourning her deceased husband.

The jury handed down its unanimous verdict of guilty on 19 April 2002. On sentencing Whyte on 3 May 2002, Justice Gillard stated:

> *The verdict establishes that the jury found you killed the deceased, who died from arsenic poisoning. You caused his death by acts which were conscious, voluntary and deliberate and were done either with the intention to kill or with the intention to cause the deceased really serious injury....*[235]*...your conduct over a period of about 15 months, ensured the progressive destruction of the father of your children in in the most excruciating, distressing circumstances...your wickedness knew no bounds*[236]*...your lack of concern for your children's well-being and your determination to kill your husband in the most painful way. You truly tortured him to death.*[237]

His Honour, who was also critical of the Austin Hospital

235 *R v Whyte* [2002] VSC146-para 5.

236 Ibid-para 52.

237 Ibid-para 53.

for misplacing the medical report of August 1983, then turned to a sobbing Whyte saying:

> *This gross negligence played into your hands; you were able to continue your callous, heartless activities, unchecked and undetected.*[238]

In respect of a possible motive, Judge Gillard formed the view that it was possibly for financial advantage as she received around $14,000 from Leonard's superannuation. Other than what appeared to be a deep ongoing level of hatred she had for him, what drove her over 15 months was still shrouded in mystery. His Honour made mention that perhaps it was partly to do with the early relationship with her present husband and that was why she committed what would be the final acts.

Whyte didn't have a lot in her favour as to mitigation in sentencing as there was very little, if anything, of remorse. Indeed, a report tendered from a psychiatrist found it difficult to comment on why she killed Leonard which in part said:

> *...given Mrs Whyte's lack of recall and sketchy nature of the information available to me...most unfortunately my capacity to assess Mrs Whyte is limited by the lack of corroborative information.*[239]

His Honour did accept that Whyte was now suffering her

238 Ibid-para 40.

239 Ibid-para 66. Whyte did say that Leonard had beaten her, shot her dog in front of her and had forced her to have sex with him while he was having sex with another man. These claims were totally rejected by Justice Gillard.

own punishment by losing the love and support of her children, including having no contact with them. She would also be deprived of a relationship with grandchildren and her husband, with whom she had a close and loving relationship. The only other factor that Justice Gillard could take into account was the initial confession Whyte made to daughter Colleen, which led to the investigation being re-opened.

Regarding such a domestic type of murder, His Honour was mindful to put the following on record:

> *Occasionally, a partner in a relationship decides to remove the other partner by killing him or her. History has shown examples of alleged accidental shootings, so called accidental drownings and the disappearance of spouses. There has never been an open season on spouses and partners and there never will be. The Court must send a clear message to those who wish to rid themselves of a troublesome partner. If a person does so, the punishment will be very severe and result in a very long period of imprisonment. Invariably, the crime is committed with premeditation, as indeed was the case here.*[240]

To a degree, the sentence of 22 years imprisonment imposed on Lorraine Whyte, with a minimum of 18 years before being eligible for parole could, on one hand, be seen as not sending such a clear message. Then again, Whyte aged 53 years at the time of sentencing, will be around 71 years old, when she becomes eligible for parole.

An appeal against conviction was always going to happen but the Supreme Court of Appeal on 13 February 2004 had no hesitation in dismissing such application. The grounds of

240 Ibid-para 97.

appeal included that Justice Gillard erred in his findings that Whyte showed 'little or no remorse.' In that respect, Justice Bongiorno stated:

> *...In my view, with his Honour's conclusion that her "pricked conscience" had brought her to a short-lived point of repentance, followed by a renewed resolution to 'tough it out'. She was given credit... for the consequences of the 'point of repentance' ...the fact she would have to live with...what she had done for the rest of her life. It was those factors which became relevant to the sentencing process and not the remorse which is now claimed. She was quite content to put her daughters through the ordeal of the trial; to the point where their evidence was strongly challenged by counsel.*[241]

In rejecting another argument of the sentence being manifestly excessive, His Honour, again supported by the other two Court of Appeal justices, said:

> *...I am conscious that a significant part of the appellant's useful life will be gone by the time she is eligible for parole... his Honour was entitled to impose a sentence of the order which he did without it being labelled as "crushing". In my opinion, the sentence was proportionate to the nature of the crime committed...*[242]

For the rest of her days regardless, Leonard may be looking down asking, 'Why did you poison me, my love?'

---

241 *R v Whyte* [2004] VSCA 5- para 22.

242 Ibid-para 31.

21
KIND DEFENCELESS AND INNOCENT WOMEN

Victoria Police Homicide Squad detectives would continue to have a number of cold case investigations that would remain unsolved. Any success, of course, would depend on whether exhibits from the case still existed and had not been contaminated, whether the main witnesses and suspects were still alive and a question, if there was the DNA of an unidentified suspect that had yet to be processed.

One that has brought untold family grief to this day, was the death of Mandy Lee Yodgee, whose body was found on 8 May 1984, lying alongside the Mountain Highway in Sassafras, near the Dandenong Ranges. Police considered her death suspicious as, when she was found, her favourite pink suede boots she was wearing when last seen, were missing.

Mandy had previously told a friend that when she left home on Sunday, 29 April 1984, she would be spending the night at her boyfriend's flat. She was about to turn 18 years old and, during that evening, she socialised, drinking at a number of hotels around South Yarra and Windsor. Interesting though, the person she was last seen with was not her boyfriend. According to his version of events, Mandy left his Prahran flat around 1.30am heavily intoxicated and, sadly, was never seen again, until her remains were found.

This perplexing case can also be compared to the disappearance of Michele Brown, who's badly decomposing, naked body, alongside her clothes, was located in a shed behind a gun shop in Frankston North on 14 March 1992. Her cause of death could also not be determined due to the state of her remains but investigators believed she had been murdered by a person or persons unknown. Michelle was known to use drugs and associate with undesirables and was last seen some 13 days earlier on her 25th birthday, walking around Frankston at about 7.15pm. A reward of up to a $1 million remains for information leading to the arrest and conviction of those responsible for her death.

Another cold case murder that occurred only two days later on 16 March 1992, would take nearly three decades before it was finally solved. The body of 29-year-old Geelong West woman, Annette Steward, a mother of two children, aged 13 and 10, would be found lying naked on 18 March 1992, with her legs spread, in the bedroom of her Hope Street home. Annette was known as a lovely, kind woman, caring very much for her children who resided with their maternal grandparents. Annette worked full time at a local ammunition factory and was in a relationship but lived on her own in Hope Street. Her boyfriend, after visiting her two days earlier in company with his two friends, would then find her body after he hadn't heard from her and he immediately informed police.

After a crime scene was established, police would find an electric iron lying on the floor nearby, with latent fingerprints also taken from various items throughout the house. In addition, loose hairs would be found on her body which would also prove crucial many years later in bringing the suspect to justice. A post-mortem examination of her body noted a ligature impression around the neck, confirming strangulation and a number of injuries to the head, arms and back, indicating she had also been viciously assaulted.

One set of fingerprints from an ashtray was identified as belonging to Darren John Chalmers, who police knew had been at the home two days earlier in company with her boyfriend. The boyfriend had given them a full account of the visit on 16 March 1992, saying they stayed for about 45 minutes. Police then spoke with his mate Chalmers, who confirmed what police already knew about the visit.

Despite an intensive investigation over many months after the murder, including a reward of $1 million being offered in 2015, it remained a cold case until further developments in 2019. Chalmers apparently couldn't keep his mouth shut and around 2002, 10 years after the murder, he allegedly told his brother that he had killed a woman in Geelong in 1992. The brother, obviously due to family loyalty, didn't go to police but he made the mistake of telling an acquaintance what he knew.

This person also knew Chalmers and was well aware of the Hope Street murder but didn't want to get involved. He kept quiet, thinking if he told police, Chalmers would know he was the source of their information. It eventually became too much for him and in 2019, he told Homicide Squad cold case detectives what he knew. Chalmers, who was now residing in

Western Australia after moving there in 2012, was now deemed to be a person of interest.

He would become a very firm suspect after a check was carried out on the National Criminal Investigation DNA Database (NCIDD), which had his DNA listed in WA.[243] The DNA database profile of Chalmers that Victoria Police obtained, was then linked to DNA from the original hair fibres found on Annette's remains. This DNA analysis led to the conclusion that if it wasn't from Chalmers, in all probability, it was connected to a close relative of his.

What was also of interest to Victorian cold case detectives was their colleagues in WA advised them that Chalmers was a suspect in a missing person case for Dianne Barrett. This lovely 60-year-old woman, who lived in the suburb of Medina in WA, suddenly disappeared in May 2019. Her house was found vacant with the television still on, her much-loved dog inside and a locked car in the driveway. Chalmers became a suspect, as he was known to Dianne and lived close by and would be often seen chatting with this caring and friendly neighbour. On being interviewed by WA police, he denied any knowledge of why she suddenly was a missing person.

Chalmers, who was made a ward of the state as a teenager, had a long criminal history with 29 separate convictions for not only dishonesty, offending with a history of drug abuse, but numerous breaches of community-based orders. What was particularly noted was also his history of violence, including repeated breaches of intervention orders in both Victoria and

243 The NCIDD retains over 1.7 million DNA profiles that are uploaded by Australian Law Enforcement taken from crime scenes, convicted offenders, suspects and various other items including from unidentified human remains.

WA. Whilst he had no prior convictions for violent offending prior to the 1992 murder, he had also breached bail and escaped from custody and had been detained in a youth training centre on several occasions.

It was now time to have a very close look at Chalmers and investigating detectives from both states put in place a covert undercover operation in September 2019. For the next four months, undercover operatives would get very close to Chalmers and offered him various financial incentives. Chalmers, thinking he was in for some sort of payday, disclosed to his new mates, albeit the covert police, what he knew about the 1992 murder of Annette Steward. Little did he know but his confession was being recorded and would later be transcribed for his December 2023 Supreme Court of Victoria trial.

Regarding the 1992 murder, Chalmers gleefully said that after visiting her home for the first time on the night of 16 March 1992, in company with her boyfriend and another mate, to help fix a television set, he then later returned alone. This was on the pretext it was his birthday, which it wasn't, as it was the day before. He was invited back in for a drink to celebrate and, after being told he could stay the night and sleep in the lounge room, Annette then went to bed. Chalmers said he found her bedroom door wide open and she was lying asleep, butt-naked.

For whatever reason and, only he knows why, wearing gloves he then struck Annette over the head a few times with an iron, with her waking up and crying out in pain. Chalmers then wrapped either the iron cord or one from a lamp around her neck and strangled this poor defenceless woman. He even tied the cord under the bed to keep it tight before he left the house. After washing blood off his hands, he quietly left, disposing of the gloves in a rubbish bin, went back to his brother's home and washed his blood-stained clothes. According to Chalmers, he never told anyone about the murder and just resumed his treacherous life.

Chalmers then admitted to the same undercover operatives, again no doubt hoping for some sort of financial reward, details of the murder of Dianne Barrett. So confident was he of taking them into his confidence, on 4 January 2020 he even took them to her body covered under vegetation in Byford, WA. This innocent woman had been left lying there since her murder on 12 May 2019, with her body now badly decomposed.

According to Chalmers, Dianne invited him in for a meal and then they went to his home for a cup of tea. Again, without any sort of explained motive, other than being in a meth-induced rage, he simply bashed her, followed by placing an iron bar across her throat for nearly three minutes, until she stopped breathing. Making sure she was covered up with a towel and blanket, with a plastic bag over her head to stop any blood being spread in his home, he then drove the deceased woman to Byford and disposed of the body. He said he meticulously cleaned his house and disposed of several items of furniture, making sure there was no evidence that might implicate him in this horrific murder.

It was now all over for Chalmers, being arrested by WA police on 5 January 2020 and charged with the murder of Dianne Barrett. Chalmers, obviously knowing the damning evidence against him, pleaded guilty in the Supreme Court of Western Australia. On 28 January 2021, Judge Hall sentenced him to life imprisonment with a non–parole period of 20 years.[244]

244 *The State of Western Australia v Chalmers* [2021] WASC 3.

Chalmers had also been interviewed by Victorian detectives while in custody at the WA Homicide office and, again, repeated what he had told undercover police of the 1992 murder of Annette Steward. He reiterated it was not over wanting to have sex with her, as that was never discussed, and they had not been involved in any sort of argument. When pressed on motive, he didn't have one and all he would then say was:

'It just happened...stupid, unlawful killing that shouldn't have happened.'

In March 2023, an inter-jurisdictional order[245] was put in place and Chalmers was then transferred to Melbourne. He pleaded guilty to the murder of Annette Steward and on 18 December 2023 appeared for sentencing before Justice Tinney. His Honour had no hesitation in describing 56-year-old Chalmers as a grave danger to the community and any rehabilitation prospects for him were in fact non-existent. In that respect and regarding the two murders, Justice Tinney said, in his view:

> *...your subsequent criminal history after your commission of the current crime and, in particular, your murder of Dianne Barrett in Perth 27 years ago after you first committed murder, are important matters which cast clear light on your prospects of rehabilitation...The later murder of Dianne Barrett...removes any doubt...even 27 years after the murder of Ms Steward and, with all of that time to ponder your crime, you had failed to gain any insight into the enormity of your conduct. You were*

245 *Prisoners (Interstate Transfer) Act 1983*(Vic) regulates the transfer of prisoners between participating states.

perfectly content to repeat that depraved conduct against another defenceless and innocent woman.[246]

A psychological report, which set out the mental history of Chalmers, in all likelihood provides a vivid and telling description of him. In his own words, he told the psychologist:

...I'm a monster, only a monster would do what I did. I need to live with what I did. I will suffer(from) the consequences. I'm ashamed. For the family that I destroyed. I should get as much time as possible...[247]

His Honour would carefully consider the terribly sad, joint victim impact statement from the children of Annette Steward, who lost their mother at such a young age. The enormity of losing their mother would come home to all that sat in court and, hopefully, Chalmers, when they spoke about the overwhelming grief and anxiety they continue to suffer, especially as they approach her death anniversary every March.

His Honour, in imposing a life sentence to be served concurrently with the sentence imposed for the murder of Dianne Barrett, also fixed a new non-parole period. regarding both murders. of 36 years. The new non-parole period would commence as of 18 December 2023 as no pre-sentence detention applied. In summing up the offending and the sentence handed down, Justice Tinney succinctly stated:

...the sentence of this Court must unambiguously demonstrate this Court's condemnations and abhorrence, on behalf of the

246 *DPP v Chalmers (Sentence)*[2023] VSC 764-para 51.

247 Ibid-para 54.

> *community, of the type of violent criminality in which you engaged in this case...you cut short the life of an innocent and defenceless young woman who had done you no harm and shown you nothing but kindness. Male violence towards females is at the heart of so many crimes which come before this Court and is a very disturbing part of the fabric of our society. An important purpose of this sentence is to strongly condemn your conduct.*[248]

If it had not been for the plea of guilty by Chalmers, the Court would have imposed a life sentence without parole.[249] In any event, I don't think he will see the light of day from prison, as he will be 92 years old if he becomes eligible to be released. Not that anyone has any sympathy for this monster.

248 Ibid-para 121.

249 *Sentencing Act 1991*(Vic)–section 6AAA.

22
THE FAMILY COURT BOMBER

In late February 1980, a man's body, weighted down with eleven house bricks, secured by a fireman's pocket line, was found lying adjacent to Cowan Creek on the Hawkesbury River, situated around 50 kilometres from Sydney, NSW. It was apparent that Stephen Blanchard had been shot dead at point blank range and little did police know then what connection this would ultimately have, regarding events that took place over the next five years.

Although NSW police were carrying out an intensive investigation over the murder of Blanchard, their resources would be somewhat stretched with the murder of Justice David Opas, on the evening of 23 June 1980. His Honour was a judge of the Family Court of Australia, sitting at Parramatta, and no doubt at various times, he would have upset litigants with a particular ruling. In other words, the life of a being a judge was not easy, but to be murdered by a person or persons unknown was something totally unexpected.

Justice David Opas was enjoying an evening meal with his family when he left the table to answer the front doorbell. This indicated that either someone was at the front door or their front gate. After he had been absent for some five minutes, his wife became concerned only to find him lying in the front yard with a bullet wound to his stomach. He would subsequently pass away that evening in hospital. Detectives had looked at a possible motive for the Opas murder and immediately focused their attention on disgruntled litigants that had previously appeared before His Honour.

While there were a number of possible suspects, one did stand out, namely 33-year-old fireman, Leonard John Warwick. He had appeared before Justice Opas at the Parramatta Family Court over a full-time custody dispute that he was having with his estranged wife. They had separated in 1979, after being married for a turbulent violent-filled five years and were now involved in a costly legal dispute over full-time custody of their infant daughter. Justice Opas had recently made adverse findings against Warwick and investigators also located a witness who stated that he had seen a man running away from the Opas home, looking very similar to their suspect.

What they were also to find was that Warwick's wife was the sister of Blanchard, in other words, his brother-in-law. The fact that Blanchard had assisted his sister and her baby daughter in the custody dispute, including to move in with him in their father's home, was also an incriminating factor to be taken into account. However, all this was simply circumstantial evidence, including the fact that Warwick was off duty when Blanchard and Opas were murdered. What was also not known, at the time of both murders was, it would still take police over 30 years to bring the perpetrator to justice, not just for this chilling murder, but also the wave of violence that would continue unabated.

Although it would be nearly four years later, the next in line was another Family Court Judge, Justice Gee. In the early hours of 6 March 1984, the Gee family, other than his wife who was in hospital, were asleep in bed when a bomb, equivalent to 50 sticks of gelignite, was placed on the front doorstep, adjacent to where his Honour slept, and then detonated. The explosion completely demolished the front of their Belrose house and caused extensive damage throughout. Fortunately, Justice Gee and his two school-aged children escaped with minor injuries.

The possible link to Warwick was that the judge had taken over the duties of the deceased Justice Opas and, lo and behold, had also made adverse findings against him around June 1983 that Warwick was not happy with. In addition, Justice Gee was due to appear that same day of the bombing in the on-going Warwick custody battle. Other than this attack may also be related to the two murders four years earlier, there was nothing that would provide police with sufficient evidence to lay criminal charges. I would suggest, however, that they would have placed Warwick under close covert surveillance by now, or did they? This latest attempted murder of a Family Court judge would become just another cold case to gather dust in their archives.

One month later, the culprit would strike again and now was given the moniker of the Family Court bomber. This is what happened when on Sunday, 15 April 1984, a pipe bomb was placed against a pillar outside the front of the Family Court building in Parramatta. It didn't detonate until later that evening and, most likely, when the building was vacated.

However, luckily no one was walking past or nearby as the consequences could have been fatal, given the court building was extensively damaged.

Once again, Warwick was the main suspect, particularly as his matter was listed for hearing the day after the latest bombing. Police, again, questioned Warwick at length but as was his right and usual practice, he remained silent, no doubt, on legal advice[250].

As a former lawyer, if I was contacted by a client in custody and prior to being interviewed by police, my advice, until I obtained proper instructions, was always provide a no comment record of interview, other than confirming name, date of birth, address and occupation. Following that, the response would be 'on legal advice I make no further comment.'

It would only take a couple of months before the bomber would strike again, this time on 4 July 1984, targeting Justice Ray Watson. Yes, you guessed it, the learned judge was also from the Family Court of Australia sitting at Parramatta. He had also taken on some of the case files but, this time, they were the ones being handled by Justice Gee, who was still recovering from his injuries in the earlier blast.

The bomb, which police would ascertain, from the extent of the damage, consisted of a number of kilograms of high explosives. It was also believed to be made with a set of individual components and designed to be what is known as "victim activated". This meant it would only detonate when

250 Suspects have a fundamental right to silence regarded by Australian Courts as a fundamental privilege against self-incrimination. There are, however, some exclusions including appearing before an Independent Commission Against Corruption where a person can be compelled to give evidence.

the front door of their Greenwich apartment was opened, not unlike a booby trap.

After placing the device at the front door, the offender must have thought it would not be opened until the next morning when the judge left for work. The only problem was, it was opened by his wife, killing her instantly with the body thrown so hard backwards, it was stuck against some brickwork. To make matters more confronting for the emergency responders, her legs were blown off and half her face was missing.

Once again, there was no physical evidence that could link Warwick to this confronting murder, other than the usual nexus to a Family Court judge. Police would find, this time, that Justice Watson had ruled against Warwick by restricting his access to their infant daughter, after on-going access breaches.

No doubt, police examined each crime scene very thoroughly and, after forensically examining each exhibit, carefully ensured it was properly stored to be relied on as and when needed. This would include the clothing of victims killed in each blast, blood samples, fingerprints and anything else of relevance, noting that 'every contact leaves a trace.'[251] Lack of poorly secured exhibits, however, would later prove to be somewhat compelling, in the time it took to finally identify the serial killer who was, in fact, responsible.

Following the latest bombing murder, additional security measures were put on for all Family Courts, judges and associates, together with the formation of Special Joint Taskforce Redden,

251 Forensic science pioneer Dr Edwin Locard, in the early 20th century, devised the principle that when two objects come into contact with each other, there will be an exchange of materials between them thereby leaving a trace. Became known as Locard's Exchange Principle and now forms the basis for modern forensic investigation.

consisting of detectives from both state and federal police. They would focus their investigation on all Family Court cases heard by Justices Opas, Gee and Watson and the common link, not surprisingly, was our man Warwick. But, once again, in the view of very experienced detectives, there was insufficient evidence to bring him to trial, let alone ensure they could prove his guilt beyond reasonable doubt. In the interim, a $500,000 reward was on offer for information about the attacks.

The bomber was at it again and this time it was a Family Court lawyer, with a bomb secured under a car bonnet of a vehicle parked outside his Northmead home. Luckily, on the morning of 10 February 1985, the owner opened the bonnet to do some work on his car and found an explosive device secured by a detonator attached to the battery terminals. It was set up to detonate once the car ignition was turned on.

The other problem the would-be murderer had was, the lawyer being targeted no longer lived at this address, even though he was still listed as being there in the phone book, having moved out months earlier. Regardless, if the bomb, consisting of four kilos of Molanite explosive had been detonated, it would have caused at least one fatality and maybe even more.

It just so happened that Warwick had been previously advised by his ex-wife that this lawyer had been acting for her for two years in her matrimonial litigation, including giving certain further advice on their custody dispute. Obviously, Warwick was not happy with what she told him and, once again, bashed her but her lawyer was now next on the list. Police were still no closer to bringing him to justice, so all they could do was suggest she move out of town as she feared for her life.

Her next step was then to enlist the assistance of her sister's

Jehovah's Witness congregation and moved to Forster, a coastal town in the mid-north coast area of NSW. It is approximately 308 kilometres from Sydney, so hopefully, Warwick wouldn't know where she was and leave her and their daughter in peace and safety. It wasn't long after she relocated, that an unknown male made threatening telephone calls to selected members of the congregation, demanding to know her whereabouts. On or about the weekend of 13 July 1985, the Jehovah's Witness Kingdom Hall in Casula, situated in the south-west of Sydney, was forcibly entered on two separate occasions but nothing was taken.

On Sunday, 21 July 1985, worshippers attended at the Kingdom Hall to enjoy a religious service with their Lurnea congregation faithful. Little did they know, a bomb with a timing device was planted under the hall platform, either on the evening before or during the break-ins a week earlier. It had been secured so it could not be seen by those meeting in the hall.

At 10.05 am, there was a massive explosion which, not only destroyed the hall, but killed one of their worshippers sitting in the front row with his family, who were also severely injured, instantly. The person offering a bible discourse from the pulpit, was blown through the roof and landed outside the hall on a pile of debris, with critical injuries, including two broken legs. Of the 71 people taken to hospital, 16 were children and five were babies.

What crime scene detectives uncovered though, was blood on some carpet between a broken south-eastern window and the platform and also on a cardboard box retrieved from the south-eastern storage area. This blood, which was most likely from the previous week's break-ins, tested O-positive, which would later become a somewhat incriminating piece of evidence. What police didn't know at the time after the bombing, Warwick was seen by his friends and associates with cuts on his face.

The hall attack motive remained "questionable" but, given what police knew at that point, it was most likely related to the Family Court bombings and their main suspect. Fearing more repercussions, Warwick's daughter, who was now seven years of age, was handed over to him and suddenly there were no more bombings and deaths of innocent people.

By this stage, the task force had determined that their number one suspect had a motive on each occasion to carry out his reign of terror. They found that for each incident he was off duty as a fireman and, as far as they could ascertain, he had no alibi of his whereabouts. Warwick, of course, maintained his right to silence and, in the absence of any direct compelling evidence linking him to the atrocities, they would not charge him.

In April 2006, a coronial inquest was held in the Glebe Coroner's Court in respect to the death of the Jehovah's Witness speaker. In opening submissions by counsel assisting the coroner, it was submitted that Warwick was the only possible link between all the bombings and the shooting deaths. The court also heard evidence from the ex-wife of Warwick, who didn't hold back and blamed him for the bombings, including that he had made verbal threats against Justice Opas saying, 'he won't be here much longer.'

Warwick refused to give any evidence but was legally represented. The lawyer put to the ex-wife that she had only made such accusations to assist in their then custody battle. The head of the Police Taskforce told the court that, at this stage, there was no direct evidence to link Warwick to the bombings.

In 1987, Coroner Waller conducted an inquest into the July 1985 death of the wife of Family Court Judge Watson.

While His Honour recorded an open verdict, he was obviously extremely frustrated and somewhat disappointed at what was, apparently, insufficient evidence to charge the main suspect, Warwick. The coroner stated the evidence clearly connected him to each of the victims saying:

In Warwick's case, the coincidence of motive and opportunity, as regards all the events, is quite extraordinary.

Nonetheless, the NSW Director of Public Prosecutions thought otherwise on the basis there was not a skerrick of evidence that the so-called main suspect had been to any of the crime sites. In addition, he never had access to explosives, let alone was ever in possession of them or had the ability, in any event, to construct a bomb. In the words of his defence barrister, the police case had more gaps in it than a fisherman's net. Perhaps he should have said "a fireman's net"!!

The investigation would lay dormant for another 15 years and, given that their main suspect was now behaving himself, in some eyes there was 'no need to worry'. It was not until 2012 that the NSW Police Crime Command's Homicide Squad had another look at this very cold case, albeit multiple crimes of murder. One of the problems detectives had though, were several other cold cases that were unsolved, coupled with the mishandling of crime scene exhibits, even to a degree that some had, in fact, been lost.[252]

---

252 The 2001 cold case of 23-year-old Rachelle Childs, who was found murdered after being set alight, was overlooked for reinvestigation thanks to a series of case exhibit blunders, including and not limited to, misplacing CCTV footage from service stations, contamination of the crime scene by a police officer and a failure to properly forensically examine her remains and motor vehicle. It was finally reopened by NSW police in March 2025 with a call for fresh DNA testing of the cold case exhibits.

This included eight pallets of exhibit evidence that had been incorrectly stored, making it very difficult to tie them in with each murder crime scene. This led to investigators finding such exhibits, including those, not just from murder scenes, being somewhere in NSW police stations throughout the state. Coupled with this, DNA analysis on such items as murder victims' clothing, postmortem and crime scene specimen swabs were so poorly secured, it could only be described as a complete mess.[253]

As luck would have it, detectives in 2013, who were specifically looking at the Family Court bombing cold case, came across numerous exhibits in the basement at the Sydney Police Centre. Among them were the blood sample exhibits taken from the Jehovah's Witness Hall following the bombing. When first tested in 1985, they were found to be O-positive, which was the same blood group as Warwick but that was not enough to charge him. It was not until 2013, thanks now to advanced technology, when it was firmly established that the samples taken from these bloodstains indeed came from the blood and matched the DNA profile of Leonard John Warwick.[254]

Although NSW police now had more than just circumstantial evidence to charge Warwick, they had to compile an exhaustive brief of evidence before they could lay charges. Finally, around 6am on the morning of Wednesday, 29

---

253 Prior to the Warwick trial, in 2016, NSW Detective Chief Inspector John Lehmann wrote a report criticising the improper storage of exhibits saying new opportunities utilising forensic technologies to identify an offender or suspect were lost and needed an urgent review.

254 Forensic experts at the trial of Warwick would say that there was one in 100 billion chance that the profile didn't belong to him.

July 2015, Strike Force detectives, together with officers from the tactical operations unit took Warwick into custody. He was subsequently charged with multiple offences, including four counts of murder[255] and various counts of using an explosive device which damaged or destroyed buildings.[256] Warwick pleaded not guilty to a total of 24 charges which occurred between 21 February 1980 and 21 July 1985 and was refused bail, pending his criminal trial.

Notwithstanding the incriminating evidence police had meticulously put together in proving Warwick was guilty beyond reasonable doubt, little did anyone know when he was charged in 2015, it would take almost another five years to the day before he would be convicted. A total of 92 interlocutory applications were made by the parties and generally by his lawyers, seeking procedural or practical court orders. One such application by Warwick, which was granted, was an order seeking a trial by a judge alone, which was also agreed to by the NSW Director of Public Prosecutions.[257]

The Supreme Court of NSW criminal trial commenced on 15 May 2018 before Justice Peter Garling and would involve a total of 155 witnesses for the Crown. It was initially estimated the duration of such trial would only be six months but it dragged on for just over two years, finally concluding on 6 April 2020. This was despite the Crown's compelling argument that Warwick was not only inextricably connected, due to his retaliation in respect of the on-going custody battle, but the

255 *Crimes Act 1900*(NSW)- section 18(1)(a).

256 Ibid- sections 30,46, and 204.

257 In view of consent by the DPP to such an application, the court was obliged to agree to trial by judge alone pursuant to section 132 of the *Criminal Procedure Act 1986*(NSW). See *R v Warwick (No 21)* [2018] NSWSC 654.

DNA was the final piece of compelling evidence. They also submitted that he had the knowledge and skill to put together the improvised explosive devices.

His defence argued the former firefighter had no such skills to put together any sort of bomb, let alone the ones used in the Family Court-related bombings and certainly not in respect of the massive Jehovah's Witness Kingdom Hall explosion. As to his Family Court proceedings battle with his ex-wife, it was submitted they, in fact, had a somewhat cordial relationship, so the accused simply had no such motive.

This was despite evidence from her totally to the contrary, citing his violent and intimidating conduct that left no choice but to end their marriage in March 1979. As to motive, the defence suggested such bombings were carried out by others, who had some sort of hatred or retaliatory axe to grind with the Family Court and its judges.

After final submissions were made to Justice Garling over four days in early April 2020, His Honour retired to consider the verdict. On 23 July 2020, with 73-year-old Warwick intently waiting for his fate on an audio link, the judge, in a 203-page judgment, found him guilty on all counts, except the alleged shooting murder of his brother-in-law, Stephen Blanchard. This finding, amongst other things, determined there was no ill-will between him and Warwick.[258]

Warwick appeared before Justice Garling for sentencing on 3 September 2020 and received three life terms of imprisonment without parole for the murders, and varying other prison terms, ranging from 10 to 25 years in respect of the malicious use of an explosive substance. As to motive, the judge stated:

---

258 *R v Warwick (No 93)* [2020] NSWSC 926.

Each of the offences involved sophisticated planning, preparation and careful conduct. They were part of a sustained course of conduct by the Offender against anyone whom he concluded to be acting contrary to his interests in maintaining access to his daughter and preserving his own financial position–both of which were under threat in his ongoing Family Court proceedings.[259]

In respect of the murderous bombing of the Lurnea congregation, His Honour said further:

...members of...the Jehovah's Witness faith were also targeted because some members of the congregation assisted the Offender's ex–wife to escape Sydney, which had the effect of hindering the exercise of the Offender's right of access to his daughter.[260]

As to the violent offending involving the Family Court, His Honour didn't mince his words when he said:

These offences could only have engendered sheer terror in the hearts and minds of all judges and staff of the Family Court of Australia, judges of other superior courts and the lawyers who practiced in those courts. They must have felt absolute fear at the prospect that any one of them might have been the next target for simply doing what all Australians expected and wanted them to do in the course of their public duty.[261]

Justice Garling also rightly pointed out that Warwick

259 *R v Warwick (No 94)* [2020] NSWSC 1168-para 91.

260 Ibid-para 92.

261 Ibid-para 100.

was simply not content with these mindless attacks, by then unleashing such further evil saying:

> *...then sought to wreak revenge on innocent members of the Lumea (sic) congregation...meeting in an expression of their faith by setting a bomb timed to explode when their meeting hall (which was a place of sanctuary) was full and members of that congregation were doing nothing other than contemplating features of their faith. This was an entirely unjustified and cruel attack on innocent people by the use of extreme violence. Such flagitious conduct has no place in Australia.*[262]

You would like to think that Warwick would spend many difficult years in jail but it was not to be. He died in the Long Bay prison hospital in February 2025, less than 10 years since his arrest in July 2015. His death will be reported to the State Coroner and may be the subject of a coronial inquest, but then again does anyone really care.

---

262 Ibid-para 104.

23
ONE EVIL PREDATOR

After finishing school on the afternoon of 19 August 1986, nine-year-old Samantha Knight quickly walked to her home situated in a block of flats in Bondi, NSW. After changing out of her school uniform, Samantha then told her mother she would be home by 6pm and was most like going to enjoy some time at the local beach. This young girl was last seen on Bondi Road around 5.30pm, with a number of witnesses later saying she was in the company of an adult male. Despite police conducting extensive inquiries and various searches, including distributing missing person posters throughout NSW, Samantha was never found.

In early 1996, police, after being advised by the mother of two young girls that they had been molested by a male, they took 45-year-old Michael Anthony Guider into custody. He was known to police, having been involved in setting fire to a shop premises owned by his now ex-girlfriend and new boyfriend some years earlier.[263] In addition, Guider, who worked as a gardener at the Royal North Shore Hospital, had other prior matters such as being fined for stealing and false pretences.

Police then carried out a search of both his work and home and would find literally thousands of slides and photographs, the majority of which depicted what he had no doubt been up to. This included evidence of young children being indecently assaulted by Guider and they would also find children's underwear, cameras and various articles to do with child abuse and incest.

On 6 February 1996, detectives conducted a lengthy interview with him in respect of indecently assaulting the two seven-year-old girls, which he admitted to. Guider made a comment to police that he was obsessed with young children and, in particular, liked to photograph them, as well as collect their underwear. In two further records of interviews some weeks later, he named some of the children depicted in the photographs taken by him but only admitted to the indecent assault of one young child.

He also said he had met Samantha Knight on no more than two occasions. He stated he had an attraction to keeping scrap books with photographs, which he said he no longer had, of a number of missing children. These articles included not only Samantha but also the disappearance of the Beaumont children. Other than that, he vehemently denied any knowledge of what had ever happened to Samantha. NSW police then set up Operation Jadite to have a much closer look at Guilder, including further cases

263 For that offence his sentence was deferred in 1979 with the condition that he enter into a good behavior bond of five years.

involving young children,[264] and notably the disappearance of Samantha Knight.

Further interviews then took place in early July 1996 with Guider now in custody, in which he made, what could only be described as, bizarre, rambling confessions. After telling detectives he may well have taken some photographs of Samantha, they were in no way of a sexual nature. As to her disappearance, in his view, she was most likely kidnapped by either, aliens or white slave traders. He then even suggested that police should undertake a search for her remains at Cooper Park, which is in the Sydney suburb of Bellevue Hill.

His reasoning was that he had developed a passion for Aboriginal culture and particularly their sites around Sydney. He then had visited the park looking for a connection to his passion, thinking perhaps Samantha was also buried there. Guider, once again, said he had no knowledge of her whereabouts but, this time, suggested Satanists may have kidnapped her.

Guider was charged with, not just the sexual offending of three children he had admitted to but, a total of 60 counts for another 11 children aged between two and 16 years, which included two young boys. The charges would set out his offending over a period of almost 6 years, first commencing in January 1980 through to January 1986. These included 18 counts of indecent assault,[265] 15 counts of sexual intercourse

264 Guilder was also looked at as a possible suspect in the February 1984 disappearance of five-year-old Renee Aitken. It was believed she was abducted from her home at Narooma on the south coast of NSW. Police, however, subsequently believed another person with the nickname 'the Spider' was involved who died in a motor vehicle accident some weeks before the coronial inquest into her death.

265 *Crimes Act 1900* (NSW)-section 61M (2).

without consent[266] and notably 16 counts of administer a stupefying drug, called Normison.[267]

The comprehensive brief of evidence, which would leave Guider with no choice but to plead guilty, set out his modus operandi in which his victims would unfortunately meet him, after he became friends with their mothers. Guilder would then regularly visit their homes, bringing gifts and taking the children on supposed outings. On gaining the trust of the parents, he would baby sit them in the absence of any parent, followed by drugging a child with the Normison drug mixed with Coca Cola. Once the child was in a drug-induced sleep, he would then carry out his offending, taking explicit photographs which included their genitals and sexually interfering with them.

Guider appeared before His Honour Judge Flannery in the District Court of New South Wales on 12 September 1996. The judge noted that although Guider showed some remorse for what he had done, he had no excuse for his incorrigible and uncontrolled behaviour. He was sentenced to a total of 16 years imprisonment with a fixed minimum term of 10 years, which meant he would be eligible for parole on 27 February 2006, taking into account time served on pre-sentence detention.[268]

Almost two years later, in May 1998, to their credit and not convinced Guilder had not committed other offences, NSW Police set up Strike Force Harrisville. This was particularly also relevant to the disappearance of Samantha Knight. Officers

266 Ibid-section 61D (1).

267 Ibid-section 38. Guilder was also charged with other indecency offences pursuant to the *Crimes Act*.

268 *R v Guider* [1996] Unreported, District Court of New South Wales, Justice Flannery, 12 September 1996.

from Operation Jadite had, in 1996, obtained information from a prison inmate, in which he had discussed the sexual offending with Guider, for which he had been sentenced by Justice Flannery.

According to this prisoner, Guilder made mention of Samantha and allegedly told him he hadn't meant to kill her. In that regard, Guider referred to the use of the drug Normison in her glass of coke, saying he must have used too much as he couldn't wake her. Guider also referred to several photographs of Samantha he had stored with his Aboriginal artefacts in a factory storage unit. The prisoner then asked Guider what had happened to her body and Cooper Park was again mentioned, with him saying that if police had a close look there, they might find her in some salt bushes.[269]

Pursuant to a search warrant in June 1998, Strike Force officers searched a storage unit belonging to Guider located at Girraween. Once again, they would uncover incriminating evidence, which included the usual obscene photographs of drugged young girls, two of which police would later identify Guider had not previously been charged. Importantly, they would also locate three scrap books which contained numerous newspaper cuttings concerning the disappearance of Samantha Knight. This was particularly relevant as Guider had previously told police these scrap books were no longer in his possession, as he had thrown them away.

Guider was again interviewed by the Strike Force Team on 19 July 1999 and made certain admissions to his further offending. These acts took place between January 1983 and

269 NSW Police had already searched Cooper Park and also other areas that Guider was known to frequent but were unable to locate any trace of Samantha Knight.

May 1985, with girls aged between five and eight years old. This involved his usual practice of first befriending the mother of one of the infants, again visiting their home and then, under the pretext of babysitting, would indecently assault them and take numerous explicit photographs.

The only thing Guider did not admit to, in respect of this offending, was the use of the Normison drug but, no doubt, police knew it was all part of his usual practice. Regarding Samantha Knight, he first denied any knowledge of, not only her disappearance but also carrying out indecent assaults and taking photographs of her.

The only issue Guider had was, when shown the scrapbooks police had found in the storage shed, the photographs which were taken around May 1985, demonstrated otherwise. They were not only explicit photographs of the two young girls but also of Samantha with one photo of her genitals. When presented with this evidence, Guider now admitted Samantha was present and then responded in his usual fashion, first saying he thought the scrap books had been destroyed.

He then stated he had, in fact, retained such books as they held some sort of interest, no doubt, of a sexual nature. Again, he denied any knowledge of what happened to Samantha and that he had ever sexually assaulted her. Despite saying this, he would then ramble on once again about her mysterious disappearance and that police were not looking in the right areas to find the body.

Guider would subsequently plead guilty to his further sexual offending[270] regarding the two young girls, appearing

270 The eight counts included three of indecent assault and five of sexual intercourse with a victim under the age of 16 years. He was not charged in respect of administer a stupefying drug as he made no admissions in that regard.

before Justice O'Reilly in the District Court of NSW on 11 February 2000. The judge was quite correct when he labelled Guider nothing but a "compulsive paedophile" and effectively imposed concurrent fixed terms of imprisonment with the sentence imposed in September 1996, which only extended his parole eligibility by six months.[271]

What was considered though, by Judge O'Reilly, was the fact Guider would continue to serve such custodial sentence in protective custody, noting other prisoners do not take kindly to child molesters. Overall, this meant the earliest date Guider could be released would now be 10 August 2006, when he would be nearly 56 years old. Little did he know, at the time though, what lay in store for him regarding Samantha Knight.

Strike Force detectives unperturbed, continued to carry out their enquiries and would put together a large body of circumstantial evidence against Guider. They already had evidence from one prisoner of the conversation about Samantha with their suspect in 1996. Another cell mate of Guider had also told them of a discussion he had with him in 1998. The conservation went along the lines that Guider admitted he had in fact drugged Samantha at his storage shed and then found her dead.

Guilder then said in company with another acquaintance, they buried her body in a shallow grave. Sometime later, according to Guider, he returned and, after digging up her body, placed her remains in a refuse dumpster at his then place of work as a gardener with the Royal Yacht Squadron at Kirribilli. The remains would have then been removed when the dumpster, also full of garden refuse, was emptied at a local garbage depot.

271 *R v Guider* [2000] Unreported, District Court of NSW, Justice Flannery, 11 February 2000.

This conversation varied compared to what he first said some two years earlier on the probable location of her body. However, along with other evidence, which included the fact that Samantha had been with Guider on more than just the one occasion back in 1985, it was sufficient to charge him with her murder. Following his arrest on 22 February 2001 and with Guider still not making admissions, he was committed to stand trial in the Supreme Court of NSW in April 2002.

The problem the Crown had though, in the absence of, not only her remains but any other direct evidence let alone an admission by Guider, it would be unable to prove beyond reasonable doubt that he murdered Samantha. To prove the elements of such an offence, it would have been necessary for the Crown to prove that such act of murder was committed with an intent to inflict grievous bodily harm or an intent to kill. Such reckless indifference to her life meant, even with him using the drug, that did not mean he knew the likelihood would be her death.

The other option open to the Crown was to withdraw the murder indictment but only on the agreement with Guider that he would plead guilty to the lesser charge of manslaughter.[272] In that respect, such a criminal act was carried out by an unlawful and dangerous act or he was criminally negligent.

Guider, who had concealed his guilt for 16 years, had already indicated at his arraignment on 7 June 2002 that he would plead guilty to manslaughter, as he would only face a maximum of 25 years imprisonment, not life imprisonment. Such a plea to the lesser charge was accepted by the Crown and on 28 August 2002, Guider appeared before His Honour, Chief Justice James Wood, for sentencing.

272 *Crimes Act 1900* (NSW)-section 18(1)(b).

Regarding the circumstantial evidence to the guilt of Guider, the Crown submitted that on the late afternoon of 19 August 1986, Guider took Samantha to an undisclosed location. He then gave her the drug Normison so he could take indecent photographs or interfere with her, while she lay drugged. Sadly, she stopped breathing and died with Guider disposing of her body in an undetermined location.

His Honour noted, although he pleaded guilty to manslaughter, specific details of what had taken place were indeed lacking. In that regard, Chief Justice Wood said:

> *The prisoner has not since his arrest provided any specific information to the police or to the Court, in relation to the details of the offence, nor has he provided any firm information concerning the whereabouts of Samantha's body. In particular, he has not disclosed whether his meeting with her was a chance meeting or something which he had planned. While he had, by his plea, admitted to having killed her, the details of the contact and what followed remain unknown…I find this particularly disturbing.*[273]

Psychiatric assessments of Guider were submitted to the Court to assist in sentencing and if he had any insight of the offending. He did give some insight, however, as to what may have taken place, saying:

> *I never physically harmed the girl. I intended to take her home. It's a very sad thing. It caught me by surprise that the drug had any effect like that. Naturally I panicked…I knew I was in trouble and the other side of me took over, the protective side*

273 *R v Guider* [2002] NSWSC 756- para 37.

which tried to find some way out of the problem, disposing of the evidence, I guess. I've blanked all this out of my mind. I can't be much more specific...[274]

The fact he now had, supposedly, no recollection of the whereabouts of the remains of Samantha certainly did not give any comfort to her parents. Guider, who was now nearly 52 years of age, had significant personality disorders and clearly was a committed and compulsive paedophile, left His Honour with no doubt that 'he remains a serious danger to the community.'[275]

On that basis, Guider, for the manslaughter of Samantha was sentenced to a 17-year term of imprisonment to apply from 7 June 2002 and to expire on 6 June 2014. The non–parole period was 12 years, meaning the earliest date he would be eligible to apply for parole would be 7 June 2014.

In March 2003, the parents of Samantha were given some hope that at long last they may be able to at least give Samantha a decent burial. Guider now told police her body was, in fact, buried in the grounds of the Royal Sydney Yacht Club, contrary to what he originally said in 1998 to a fellow prisoner. Despite a police sniffer dog reacting very favourably to the site of the dig, her remains were not located, once again leaving her parents with their untold grief. Guider, of course, applied for parole in June 2014, which was denied by the State Parole Authority as it was on two further occasions, meaning he would have to serve his full term to June 2019.

The NSW Attorney General was then approached by the mother of Samantha, with a 130,000 signed petition

274 Ibid-para 58.

275 Ibid para 90.

calling on him to bring in "no body, no parole" legislation,[276] to be known as "Knight's Law". On 5 September 2019, a government application to the Supreme Court to keep Guider in jail for at least a further 12 months failed. Despite being a high-risk offender, he was released on an extended supervision order (ESO) for a period of five years,[277] together with strict monitoring conditions, including being fitted with a Buddi Insight Smart Tag.[278]

Despite the rigorous supervision under the ESO, Guider couldn't help himself and, in September 2022, following a random search of his home, police found child abuse and pornography material on his mobile phone. After receiving a further sentence for breach of the ESO, this evil predator would remain in prison until he died, aged 73, on 7 September 2024. Sadly, he would never reveal where Samantha was buried.

---

276 Such legislation was finally passed in October 2022 in response to the much-publicised murder carried out by Chris Dawson, who was convicted of killing his wife Lynn, some 40 years earlier. See *Crimes (Administration of Sentences) Amendment (No Body, No Parole) Act 2022*(NSW). Also see chapter 50.

277 *State of NSW v Guider (No 2)* [2019] NSWSC 1145.

278 This cutting-edge technology is a tamper proof ankle device that allows constant location tracking and was developed in consultation with police and local governments, to provide enhanced community safety and support offender rehabilitation.

24
ONLY A MATTER OF TIME

Back in the 1980s, police were not blessed with DNA testing, despite every contact leaving a trace, meaning an offender could leave behind, for example, their own blood stains or semen. It could not be forensically tested to connect them to the crime but, what offenders didn't know was, it would always remain on file, pending further enquiries.

Such a cold case DNA sample would ultimately lead to the killer of six-year-old Kylie Maybury. This innocent child was abducted, raped and then murdered on Melbourne Cup Day, 6 November 1984.

After watching the cup, won by Western Australian bred gelding, Black Night, Kylie's mother sent her to the local Food Plus store in Plenty Road, East Preston in Victoria to purchase a bag of sugar. The store was only 140 metres from their home and, in those days, it was always considered safe to send your young child on a shop errand.

Kylie, although bare foot, was wearing a red skivvy with a white singlet and matching pants, carrying with her green and red handbag. She was last seen around 5.30pm after buying the sugar, first leaving through the store car park and then obviously heading back home, happily walking along the footpath.

After being reported missing by her now fearful mother, Kylie would not be found until around 12.45am the following morning, with her body lying in a gutter in Tyler Street, which ran just off the top of Plenty Road, near its tram terminus. She was still wearing the same clothes but it was obvious she had been murdered with numerous bruises over her body and particularly her neck region. It would not be until the post-mortem that would reveal Kylie had suffered an horrific sexual attack.[279] It would also reveal that she had ingested Valium and the cause of death was by suffocation.

A further examination of swabs taken would determine the presence of semen on her clothing, her vagina and externally from her anus. A DNA profile was taken from such swabs which, at the time of the murder such testing didn't exist, would later prove crucial some 30 years later in bringing the perpetrator to justice.

Homicide detectives had several suspects to look at, including Robert Arthur Selby Lowe, who they found had been interviewed some days earlier before the murder regarding offensive behaviour involving three young Preston girls. Such offending was committed within a kilometre of where Kylie

279 There was evidence of tearing to her vaginal walls, a torn hymen with penetration by either a penis or some other similar object.

was found. Lowe was not prosecuted due to lack of evidence,[280] so police focused their attention on three other persons of interest,[281] one of which was 42-year-old Gregory Keith Davies.

He had a rather long criminal history as far back as 1968, with convictions for larceny and forgery. In 1971, he was acquitted of charges of attempted murder and wounding with intent to commit grievous bodily harm to a 14-year-old girl. Such acquittal was on the grounds of insanity but to be detained at the Governor's pleasure.[282] This unprovoked attack took place in September 1970, when a teenage high school student, after finishing lessons for the day, was travelling home on a train along the Hurstbridge line towards Diamond Creek.

Davies snuck up behind her and then struck her several times around the head. His plan was then to rape her but, in some way, luckily for his victim, a copious amount of blood led to him fleeing. He did, however, return to the train carriage a few minutes later and struck the dazed girl again. Davies, thanks to a Diamond Creek police officer noticing how agitated he was and on seeing a blood stained hammer he was carrying in a bag, placed him under arrest.

---

280 Lowe was subsequently convicted in 1994 of the murder of Sheree Beasley and in 2003 DNA profiling excluded him in respect of the murder of Kylie. See chapter 29.

281 Two relatives of Kylie were considered suspects at the time but both committed suicide two years apart in 1985 and 1987, not knowing they would later both be deemed innocent.

282 *The Indeterminate Sentences Act 1907*(Vic) provided for habitual criminals to be detained at the Governor' pleasure. The *Crimes (Mental Impairment and Fitness to Stand Trial) Act 1997* (Vic) abolished Governor's pleasure and established new procedures for the detention and management of persons found unfit to stand trial or not guilty on the grounds of insanity.

As for the young girl, her prognosis was not good with her parents being told to prepare for the worst. However, she recovered a month later but, no doubt, has never properly healed. Davies would remain in custody and at Ararat Prison, until he was released in 1982. Based on his offending, this was a warning to police that they must keep a close watch on him, given he may well strike again.

What was of further interest to investigators was the fact that Davies owned a white holden station wagon, which was similar to the vehicle seen being driven away with a young girl, who looked a lot like Kylie. Davies also lived in East Preston with his mother and sister and within walking distance to the Food Plus store, where Kylie's body was eventually found. He was interviewed two days after her body was located but denied any involvement and offered a good alibi as he had attended a barbecue on Cup Day, then spent the night alone at home, with his mother and sister away for the night.

He did say though, he had driven home around 5.30pm, which was about the same time Kylie was on her family errand. However, whilst somewhat suspicious, given the fact he lived near where Kylie was murdered, had a similar vehicle and a prior questionable criminal history, it was not enough to prove he had committed the murder. Davis couldn't help himself though and in 1993 was convicted of offences of burglary, theft and numerous other offences of dishonesty and would serve a further custodial sentence.

In late December 2014, Victoria police announced the formation of a further elite squad that was now looking at a total of 63 unsolved homicides, some as far back as 1975. This new cold case Homicide Squad would replace its informal cold case unit, now consisting of a total of 28 officers supported by three intelligence operatives. The cold cases they would now re-examine included the abduction and murder of 13-year-old Denise Gail McGregor, in March 1978.

This case would later have striking similarities to both Kylie Maybury and also the 1991 Sheree Beasley murder, as Denise was also out buying some food and soft drink from a local hamburger shop in Bell Street, Pascoe Vale. Her partially-clothed body would be found a day later on 21 March 1978 in Wallan East, which is approximately 45 kilometres from Pascoe Vale. It was obvious she had been sexually assaulted and then beaten to death with police describing the crime scene as absolute sickening.[283]

The 1994 murder also now being looked at was that of Williamstown grandmother, Leah Buck, who was bashed and left to die after the offender stole her handbag and purse and, despite a substantial reward for information, this murder still remains unsolved.[284] The 1997 murder of 34-year-old mother of three children, Jane Thurgood-Dove, who was shot dead in the front of her driveway while her three children watched on in absolute horror, would also be the subject of a cold case review.[285] Another cold case now under review was the June 1999 murder of Bendigo mother, Vicki Jacobs, in what was described as an execution killing. She was shot six times in the

283 In September 2021, Victoria Police announced a $1 million reward in an effort to solve her brutal murder.

284 In December 2014 a reward of $1 million was offered for information in relation to her murder.

285 Detectives ultimately formed the view this murder was a case of mistaken identity and despite interviewing a number of persons of interest, it still remains unsolved.

head, face and chest as she lay asleep beside her six-year-old son.[286]

Despite these unsolved cold cases, success was now about to come to fruition. When homicide detectives had another look at the cold case of Kylie Maybury, Davies once again became a firm person of interest. Coupled with his close proximity to where the body of Kylie was found, and, notwithstanding he owned a similar car, they found that in 1996 he had again been convicted of further numerous offences. These included indecent assault and gross indecency, being sentenced to a lengthy term of imprisonment.

After then being advised by one of his family members of their suspicions that Davies was involved in the murder of Kylie and with advances now in forensic technology, it was time at long last to obtain a DNA sample from him. It was now only a matter of time before this now-retiree would be brought to justice.

The Waterford Park Retirement Village, situated in the quiet outer eastern suburb of Knoxfield, offers peaceful living for those over 50 years of age looking at a contemporary retirement lifestyle. It's blessed with its own bowling green and tennis court and sits opposite the Waterford Valley Golf Course. By this time, 73-year-old Davies thought he would be enjoying its

286 Vicki Jacobs had previously given evidence in a murder trial against her former husband, who also happened to be an associate of an outlaw motorcycle gang. Police believe her murder was on the instructions of his former bikie group and, despite an offer to enter a witness protection program, Vicki chose to change her name and then move to Bendigo. In 2004, Victorian Coroner Phil Byrne delivered an open finding as the evidence before him was not sufficient to implicate anyone in her murder.

facilities and leading a life of leisure after he finished travelling around the state as a country music performer.

It was all about to change when homicide detectives knocked on the door of his unit on 9 June 2016 and requested, he provide a voluntary biological DNA sample in the form of a buccal swab.[287] Being the uneducated gentlemen he was, Davies immediately obliged, thinking he had nothing to worry about. I have no doubt that if he refused, police would have immediately obtained a court order giving them the power to obtain such DNA.[288]

His DNA profile was then entered and further analysed by comparing it to the DNA found on Kylie's clothing and from the semen detected from the vaginal and anal swabs. Finally, after 32 years of anguish, Davies was identified on a probability factor finding, that it was 100 billion times more probable he was the contributor to the DNA, rather than any other person selected at random. As a consequence, he was arrested and interviewed, where he still denied any involvement, again providing the barbecue alibi reunion, allegedly attended by his brother and friends who had served in Vietnam.

When faced with the fact his DNA was detected on Kylie, combined with other circumstantial evidence, he now claimed

---

287 Also known as a buccal smear which involves the swabbing of the inside of a person's cheek in order to collect a DNA cell sample.

288 In March 2019 following the rape and murder of an international student committed by Codey Herrmann some two months earlier, the Victorian Government passed the *Justice Legislation Amendment (Police and other matters) Act 2019*(Vic). This act provided police with the power to take DNA samples for adult and juvenile suspects in indictable matters without a court order and when the suspect does not consent to such sample being taken.

he had no memory and exercised his right to seek legal advice. Davies, on 12 June 2016 was then charged with her murder,[289] which carried a maximum penalty of life imprisonment, and also with rape.[290] Davies was remanded in custody and, on 29 May 2017 on the first day of a committal proceeding at the Melbourne Magistrates' Court, he indicated he would plead guilty to both charges.

Following his guilty plea, it was apparent this child rapist and killer was now reviled by his fellow Port Phillip Prison inmates and they didn't muck around. Just over one month later, on 23 July 2017, Davies was attacked in his cell and had boiling water poured over his neck and groin. He was immediately transferred to the Austin Hospital with burns to 15 per cent of his body and his injures included a fractured cheekbone.

I don't think anybody would have had much sympathy for him and, no doubt, these injuries would be a subsequent reminder to him of his murderous escapade. In addition, he would be seeing out his days in protective custody. In early September 2017, his defence counsel requested an extension of time before the plea hearing and sentence, advising the court Davies had only just resumed being able to walk and was still in considerable pain and discomfort.

On 21 December 2017, Davies, now 75 years old, appeared for sentencing before Justice Lasry in the Supreme Court of Victoria. His Honour had some difficulty in accepting that he, although pleading guilty, still had no remorse whatsoever and continued to claim an apparent lack of memory to committing such a horrific crime.

In that respect, Justice Lasry said:

289 *Crimes Act 1958*(Vic)–section 3.

290 *Crimes (Sexual Offences) Act 1980*(Vic)-section 45(1).

The murder you have committed is extremely serious because you killed a defenceless child after raping her. You probably committed the offence of rape for some kind of sexual gratification. Having committed these offences, you lied to police at the time and kept what you had done to yourself for 33 years. I wonder how you were able to do that. As well, I am confronted with you now asserting that you have no memory of committing these offences.... particularly in view of your record of interview, I find that impossible to believe and reject the genuineness of your claimed lack of memory. You may not wish to recall what you have done but your claimed lack of memory is, I think, more about that than not being able to...[291]

His Honour accepted that Davies had a very bleak future, now having to spend the bulk of his prison sentence in protective custody. A psychiatric report, although suggesting a diagnosis of non–exclusive paedophilia, found no evidence of any mental illness to somehow explain his horrendous offending. Victim impact statements really demonstrated the effect on the family of Kylie, in particular her mother and sister.

Judge Lasry, in taking that impact into account when determining the sentence to be imposed, highlighted such suffering saying:

These people have had to endure, not only the death of this child but the extended time since while you kept your secret. The fact that the person who killed Kylie was still at large, obviously a matter of concern and fear for them. There is nothing the Court can say that will lessen the suffering of these people. The victim impact statements highlight the catastrophe that is a case like

291 *The Queen v Davies* [2017] VSC 800-para 20.

this. They show that the effect of your fatal and violent actions will last a lifetime for these people and highlight the suffering they have already endured. They illustrate that the sentence to be passed on you can never repair the damage they have suffered, which you caused. For the members of the families, who have lived without Kylie since 1984, the wounds of your violent conduct have developed into sadness and trauma that detracts from every aspect of their lives…[292]

His Honour, in in sentencing Davies to life imprisonment, with a minimum of 28 years before for being eligible for parole, said further:

Though these crimes happened 33 years ago, they were terrible offences. You were 42 years of age at the time and in the prime of your life. This child did nothing except walk to a shop and, at age six years, she then lost her life in the process. You saw her and chose her at random for the very worst of motives and then ended her life. Your conduct was simply disgusting…[293]

If it was not for his guilty plea, His Honour would have declined to fix a minimum term saying further:

…I have come to the conclusion that given your history, age and plea of guilty I should not exclude some slight element of mercy and hope from your sentence, however remote that may seem to you.[294]

---

292 Ibid-para 22.

293 Ibid-para 45.

294 Ibid-para 51.

It was a pity that Davies didn't show the young child he murdered any element of mercy, but as Justice Lasry said, his future was now very bleak indeed and this marked man will remain incarcerated, until he meets his maker.

25
THE NOT SO LOVABLE BIRNIES

When Perth-born David John Birnie and Catherine Margert Harrison came into this world some three months apart in 1951, little did they know, or anyone for that matter, what they would get up to years later. Then again, David did initially display some evidence of what can only be described as perverted behaviour in his teenage days and into adulthood.

However, in the early 1960s, David met 12-year-old Catherine and for two years they had a rather strong romantic relationship. Catherine, on the other hand, brought up by her maternal grandparents, by the time she was 21 years old, would be married and go on to have seven children, with her first born dying as an infant after being struck by a car. This all changed, of course, when in 1985 aged 34, she left her husband and got back together with her romantic teenager lover, David. She changed her maiden name to Birnie even though they never married. Catherine was obviously besotted with him and now known as the Birnies, would soon go on their murderous crime spree.

David was a real piece of work, as was his family, which included four younger siblings. His upbringing was somewhat dysfunctional and marred by both his parents and probably the whole family enjoying a drink or three. There were also some persistent rumours that the family was a tad promiscuous, with even suggestions of conduct involving incest.

Around 1966, Birnie left a local Perth school, planning to become an apprentice jockey but, of all things, this now known exhibitionist was also physically abusing horses in the stables.[295] There was even an incident where he attempted to rape an elderly lady, wearing a stocking over his head. He would spend time in prison also for other misdemeanours and would then marry his first wife, being blessed with a daughter.

Little did Perth police initially know what had happened to four females, aged as young as 15 with the eldest being 31, when they suddenly disappeared over five weeks with the first being reported missing on 6 October 1986. The only possible lead they had at the time, was with 22-year-old university student Mary Neilson, after her motor vehicle was found parked near police headquarters. Two weeks later, 15-year-old high school student, Susannah Candy, went missing but supposedly was okay when her parents received a letter, allegedly written by their much-loved daughter.

On 1 November 1986, 31-year-old Noelene Patterson, was nowhere to be seen and neither was Denise Brown four

295 Birnie was later considered to have some sort of paraphilic disorder which is a mental health condition that results in recurring and intense sexual arousal.

days later. The only possible link in this latest mystery was she was last seen at the bus stop on the Stirling Highway, as was Susannah Candy, who police ascertained had been hitchhiking along the same main road. On Monday, 10 November 1986, investigators would suddenly achieve a major breakthrough, not due to exhaustive and painstaking police work, but thanks to 17-year-old Kate Moir.

Her statement to police would be quite compelling and lead to the arrest and subsequent conviction of the Birnies. What Kate did not know at the time when she was picked up after accepting a ride offered by them, as far as the Birnies were concerned, she was going to be victim number five and not just solely to be sexually abused. Kate had just finished a night out with her friends on Sunday, 9 November 1986.

It's fair to say she'd had a few drinks and the offer of a ride home was something she didn't hesitate to accept. As they got near her family house, this harmless-looking couple would suddenly show their true colours. David pulled out a knife from his Ugg boot and held it against her throat. Kate tried to get out of the vehicle but there was no interior car door, so she was now at their mercy.

They arrived at the Birnie home in Moorhouse Street in Willagee, a suburb of Perth. For the first couple hours, they played all sorts of games with Kate. First, they made her watch the movie "Rambo" and then, after quizzing Kate about her background, the Birnies told her to take a shower. By this stage, Kate knew what was about to happen and, as she danced before them to the Dire Straits song, "Romeo & Juliet", she told police there were tears streaming down her face.

David then raped her around midnight while Catherine watched on, taking copious notes, followed by another shower and again being raped. At this point, Kate, knowing she would most likely be murdered, asked for a pen and paper, so she could write a goodbye letter to her parents. They happily obliged and then, after she was led screaming into the master bedroom, Kate was raped once more by David wearing a distinctive mustard coloured robe.

He then handcuffed her foot to his bed and offered her sleeping pills, so she could supposedly have a good night's sleep. Kate knew she would be killed if she fell asleep, so she placed the pills in her mouth but under her tongue. When the Birnies weren't looking, she then put the pills under the mattress. Kate certainly had her wits about her as she also placed her lipstick and a note with her phone number written on it, under the couch. As she later detailed this to police, it was obvious in their mind, they had a very brave woman who, knowing she might not survive, was trying to make sure her soon-to-be killers would later be identified.

Kate survived the night by staying awake. She was told to call her parents and explain that due to her bout of heavy drinking, she had stayed overnight with friends. She was soon to escape the clutches of her so called "friends", after David left for work. Catherine was distracted following a knock on the front door and forgot to ensure Kate was chained to the bed. Kate took a chance when she broke the lock on the bedroom door, escaped through a window and into a shop close by. After screaming she had been raped, Kate was quickly driven down to the nearest police station.

This very important witness would not only detail what had taken place but also, the evidence she left behind at the Birnie house under the couch, would be proof of her ordeal. Not only did she know the home address but told police her rapist was David Birnie. This was despite the Birnies telling her an alias. Kate had noticed a bottle of medicine at the home which had David's name on it. The Birnies were quicky taken into custody later that morning and Catherine initially denied any knowledge. David, however, first gave some sort of rambling excuse that Kate had willingly gone to their home for consensual sex.

The problem he had, of course, if it was indeed consensual, then how did he explain what was found at the home under the couch. If it was consensual, how could he also explain a barefoot, screaming Kate running from the house into a store wearing only black leggings and a singlet. It was all over for David and, no doubt, after some gentle persuasion, he not only confessed to each brutal rape and murder, but also the location of the remains of each of the four victims.

When Catherine was told her much-loved partner had now confessed, her excuse was she only became involved in the murders due to her obsession with him. This included taking part in the sexual assaults on some of the victims, to further show her love.

With the Birnies in handcuffs, on the evening of 10 November 1986, they took police to a shallow grave near the Wanneroo Pine Forest, which was situated about 25 kilometres north of Perth. There they would find the naked body of Denise Brown and, according to David, they abducted her at knifepoint from a Sterling Highway bus stop on 5 November 1986 and drove back to their Moorhouse street home, where she was subjected to repeated sexual assaults.

Late the following day, after taking Denise to the pine plantation, David raped her again and then stabbed her in the neck. The body was then placed in the shallow grave but Densie was still alive and sat up from the grave, only to be struck and killed with an axe wielded by David.

Early the following morning, police were then taken by the Birnies to a forest area in Glen Eagle, located 60 kilometres from Perth, near the Albany Highway. David indicated to detectives they would find three more bodies buried along a bush track and, after a short dig, police would uncover the remains of both Mary Neilson and Susannah Candy.

According to David, Mary was given his phone number to buy some car tyres from him and when she attended at the Moorhouse Street property, she was gagged and then chained to a bed. As he raped her, Catherine looked on, no doubt taking notes. Mary was taken to Glen Eagle after being raped again and then strangled with a nylon cord. David stabbed her a number of times, telling police he thought it might help with the decomposition of her remains.

The next body to be found in the same area, was that of Noeleen Patterson, who was also buried in a shallow grave but not with the other two victims. This 31-year-old victim fell into their clutches when her vehicle ran out of petrol on the Canning Highway and she was offered a lift by the Birnies. The same scenario took place, being taken back to their house and subjected to repeated rapes.

This time though, David became somewhat obsessed with her and kept her tightly bound for three days until Catherine, in a jealous rage, said either you kill her or I will kill myself. They buried her body after she was forced to consume a few sleeping pills and while she slept, was strangled. Police would later say that Catherine was certainly jealous of this poor victim as when they found her body, she said she had thrown sand over her face as they buried her. What was also more demeaning, as the body was being removed, Catherine, again showing her jealousy, spat on the remains.

On Wednesday, 12 November 1986, the Birnies were each charged with four counts of deprivation of liberty, rape and murder and, in respect of Kate Moir, two counts of rape, aggravated assault and deprivation of liberty. In February 1987, both appeared before Justice Wallace in the Supreme Court of Western Australia for sentencing, after pleading guilty to all counts. David Birnie was sentenced to life behind bars without the possibility of parole and His Honour said:

> *...Each of these horrible crimes were premeditated, planned and carried out cruelly and relentlessly over a comparatively short period. He should never be let out of prison...*[296]

As for Catherine Birnie, she also received four life sentences but with a minimum term of 20 years, meaning she would be eligible for parole in 2007. His Honour, however, determined that she needed to be placed under strict security, as she was dragged out of court to serve her sentence, not only kicking and screaming but with her usual spitting antics as she was led to the prison van. David, on the other hand, simply blew kisses to those in the public gallery screaming at him as he was led away from the dock.

David Birnie knew, as did Corrective Services, what would be waiting for him at Fremantle Prison so he was held in protective custody, then relocated to Casuarina Prison. He still could not help himself though, as in early 2005 he was suspected of sexual assault of another prisoner and in possession

296 *R v David Birnie & Catherine Birnie* [1987] Unreported, Supreme Court of Western Australia, Justice Wallace, February 1987.

of pornography on his computer. On 7 October 2005, at the age of 54, he hung himself by using a length of cord tied around an air vent. No one claimed his body, with a subsequent burial in an unmarked pauper's grave, not that his victims' families would have any sympathy for him.

A coronial inquest later determined that a bungle over his anti-depressant medication not being provided may have led to his suicide. These tablets were apparently required, following a breakdown in his relationship with Catherine, albeit up to then only by love letter correspondence, as she was serving her prison time at Bandyup Women's Prison.

However, this so-called model prisoner would apply for parole in 2007, which was rejected, which it would be on several more occasions after being reviewed every three years under WA legislation. She had many enemies, including her youngest son who, under an alias, said his mother should only be released following her execution.

In 2018, the WA Attorney General was afforded the power to determine the parole eligibility of certain mass murderers and to overrule any parole decision by the Prisoners Review Board.[297] In November 2024, Attorney General John Quigley determined that three serial killers,[298] one being Catherine Birnie, would not be considered for parole again until 2030. She will by then be 79 years old, so we wait to see whether she will ever be released. In the meantime, she spends her time,

---

297 *The Sentence Administration Act 2003*(WA) (as amended) is the main source of law for parole in WA and also governs the Prisoners Review Board.

298 Peter John Maloney was jailed in 1980 for the murder of Caroline Fountain in 1978 and Catherine Burden in 1979. William Patrick Mitchell killed a mother and her three children with an axe in 1993-see chapter 35.

most likely, not thinking about her despicable crimes as she continues painting and working in the prison library.

26
THE HODDLE STREET MASSACRE

After being discharged from the Royal Military College at Duntroon, due to his unsatisfactory conduct, 29-year-old Julian Knight carried out a mass shooting in August 1987 in Clifton Hill, Victoria. It became known as the Hoddle Street Massacre. Days earlier, upon returning from Canberra to Melbourne, following his not so honourable discharge, Knight discovered that his girlfriend had moved on and his mother had converted his former bedroom into a living room.

Since his early childhood and after being adopted, Knight struggled throughout his schooling but finally completed his higher education certificate at Melbourne High School in 1985. He tried to undertake a degree at La Trobe University but that went nowhere and by 1986 was unemployed. His fascination with the military, in particular battle scenes and heroic deaths, also led to an obsession with guns. He owned his first rifle at the tender age of 12 and then, after joining the army cadets, massed together a number of firearms, including a .22 rifle, a 12-gauge shotgun and a lethal high-powered M14 rifle.

His daily alcohol intake was not helping and he was on bail, following the incident that led to him being booted out of the Royal Military College Duntroon, where he was training to become an army officer. With no money and no ability to earn any, he spent the early evening on Sunday, 9 August 1987 drinking at a local hotel in Clifton Hill. Following flashbacks of soldiers being ambushed, no doubt, thanks to the amount of beer he had drank, he staggered back home to his mother's house nearby. Adding to his depression was the fact his car, being literally his only worldly possession, had broken down. So, it's fair to say his mood wasn't great.

Unbeknown to his mother, Knight had stored, under her bed, many weapons for which he had held applicable licences. These included a Ruger rifle, a Mossberg pump action shotgun and the 7.62 mm M14 semi-automatic rifle. He also had significant rounds of ammunition from which he extracted a number and stuffed his pockets full, to no doubt use in what he had now planned to carry out. No doubt, looking like the combat soldier he always wanted to be, he left the house at around 9.20pm, with the M14 rifle slung over his shoulder. He was also carrying in each hand the Mossberg and Ruger, with a black combat knife stuck down the back of his jeans.

Knight then took out his frustrations around 9.30pm on Sunday, 9 August 1987, first firing rapid bursts at cars as they drove along Hoddle Street, Clifton Hill. Over a 30-minute period, he had shot dead seven innocent civilians and wounded 19 others, some seriously. After the Ruger ran out of ammunition, he kept firing with the Mossberg shotgun and at

9.35pm, an urgent call was put out for any police in the vicinity to attend. By the time numerous police units arrived, which was only a matter of minutes, Knight was now using his M14 rifle. Ambulances were also directed to park at a nearby Mobil service station, which had been deemed safe as a rendezvous point.

As Head of the Victorian Education Department Security Services Group, I recall being on patrol that evening when our control room issued a warning to our officers over our radio network to stay away from Hoddle Street, due to the mayhem that was unfolding. A Police Dog Squad unit and the Air Wing headquarters at Essendon had advised our control room what was transpiring and said many police were responding, including Air 495 and the dog squad.

Knight was subsequently arrested 45 minutes later but not before he had fired three shots at Air 495, piercing the main fuel tank and causing the chopper to do a forced emergency landing on a sports field nearby. His arrest was not without its own drama though, as Knight, on seeing one police car, let go several shots. The two police officers escaped injury after they abandoned their vehicle at the first opportunity. Another police officer was slightly wounded in his right side, as Knight, at around 10.15pm, was heading back to what would be later determined as his ex-girlfriend's Fitzroy North house.

After firing his last few rounds at two police officers, with one receiving minor shrapnel wounds to his face and left hand, their pistols were aimed at Knight and it was all over. On being called to surrender, Knight dropped his now empty M14 rifle onto the ground and, after having another shot fired at him by police, he put his hands up and yelled out, 'Don't shoot, I'm coming out.'

The 45 minutes of mayhem was now at an end and, as one police officer would say, Hoddle Street was, uneasily, very quiet.

The mayhem and what had transpired would forever remain with many police and victims, particularly the sight of abandoned shot up cars lying at odd angles along Hoddle Street. Some of Knight's victims were lying in the middle of the road, shot dead by a blast to their head or chest and others to various parts of their body.

One grieving victim who survived, would later tell police he saw his wife fatally shot with his young son receiving minor fragment glass wounds as he sat on her lap below the car windowsill. Another victim was seen to be shot, first only wounded as she tried to run away along the footpath. When Knight saw her fall over, he fired a further two shots, killing her.

Knight, now in handcuffs, was taken back to the St Kilda Road Police Complex and now cooperating with police, was returned to Hoddle Street the following day for a crime scene re-enactment. By this stage, police had estimated he had fired over 100 rounds of ammunition from his three weapons at, not only passing motorists, but police as they tried to place him under arrest. Regarding the wounded woman who fell over on the road, the chilling police video re-enactment was somewhat confronting:

> Knight: The first one fell onto the road and then the second one. I don't know where, where he came from, but I dropped him as well.
> Police: Now, did they appear to be dead, when you…?
> Knight: The one that fell back on the road wasn't.
> Police: What happened then?
> Knight: Oh, I let off another two rounds.

Police: For what purpose?
Knight: Finish her off.

On 10 November 1988, Knight appeared before Supreme Court Justice George Hampel for sentencing, after pleading guilty to seven counts of murder and 46 counts of attempted murder. Now you would think, given what had transpired, Knight would be sentenced to life behind bars without any possibility of parole. Well, think again. Then it may be because he had a very experienced barrister, Robert Richter, acting for him.

While Knight was sentenced to a life maximum, in the mind of the learned judge, he was considering if it was appropriate to impose a minimum term of 27 years, before Knight would be eligible for parole. This meant that Knight, after callously murdering seven innocent people and wounding countless others, would be eligible for release in May 2014.

In that regard, His Honour first said:

> *There are, in your case, a number of significant mitigatory factors, such as your age, the absence of prior convictions, your abnormal mental state, your co-operation and plea of guilty, and the fact that, from one point of view, the killing and attempted killing of so many people can be seen as part of one continuous course of conduct. It is also significant that these killings were not motivated by gain or revenge and were not occupied by acts of torture or cruelty. However, they were random and particularly 'public' crimes, which caused, not only deaths and injury, but also a great amount of suffering to many people.*[299]

299 *R v Knight* [1989] VicRp 62; [1989] VR 705-page 4.

Now at this point in the sentencing process, I think it's fair to say no one really knew where this was heading. Perhaps Knight would get life without any possibility of parole but that was not to be. Justice Hampel then stated:

> *In my view, the fixing of a minimum term in this case is appropriate because of your age and your prospects of rehabilitation as well as other mitigatory factors I have already mentioned, which justify some amelioration of your sentence, not only in your interests but in the interests of the community.*[300]

On that basis and if the judge was correct, was it appropriate in the interests of our community that if Knight behaved himself in prison, on release he would, in fact, have posed no danger to the community? Knight then would have been around 56 years of age with a life still ahead of him. What you perhaps need to balance with Justice Hampel's reasoning, was that an unduly high minimum term would be in direct opposition to the rehabilitation of Knight. This would defeat his eventual release, enabling him to be able to adjust back in the community. I will let you be the judge of that.

However, the Crown must have been satisfied with the sentence imposed, as there appeared to be no evidence of any appeal being lodged of it being manifestly inadequate. The same couldn't be said for Knight though, as he would ultimately become known as a vexatious litigant. While waiting on his 2014 possible release date, he instigated a plethora of court applications. For example, in October 2001 he sought an injunction in the Supreme Court against prison authorities, all over the return of some documents relating to a prisoner who

300 Ibid- page 5.

had hanged himself. This was followed by a complaint then filed in the Victorian Civil and Administrative Tribunal in July 2002, over certain items relating to Adolf Hitler being seized from him. Both applications, in part, were dismissed.

Knight was back in the Supreme Court in August 2002 again seeking an injunction over mail being withheld from him. He then made a further application to the Victorian Civil and Administrative Tribunal a month later purportedly over access to prison documents. The list was endless[301] with most being dismissed and, by October 2004, Supreme Court Justice Tim Smith's patience was tested one last time. This time he declared Knight to be a vexatious litigant.

This was as a result of an application by Victoria's Attorney-General, Rob Hull, in an effort to prevent Knight continuing to bring whatever pitiful grievance he could think of before the court. The ruling by the court meant Knight was unable to bring any further legal proceedings, including both civil and criminal, for the next 10 years unless he first obtained permission from the Supreme Court.[302]

Knight, in preparation for his pending release in 2014, made an application to the Supreme Court for access to rehabilitation as part of a sentence management plan. He also sought permission, of all things, to write letters of apology, with an explanation, to his Hoddle Street victims. His 2007 application not only saw outrage from his angry victims, but the

---

301 For example, see *Knight v Minister for Corrections* [2003] VSC 412; *Knight v State of Victoria* [2003] VSC 459.

302 On 30 August 2016 the Victorian Supreme Court granted an indefinite litigation restraint order against Knight pursuant to the *Vexatious Proceedings Act 2014*(Vic). See *Attorney-General for the State of Victoria v Knight* [2016] VSC 488.

Victorian Government quickly amended applicable legislation, creating a new offence for prisoners attempting to send letters of contrition to their victims.[303]

With Knight's potential release on parole fast approaching, on 2 April 2014 the State Government made further legislative amendments to ensure he remained behind bars. The amending Act put in place would prevent the Adult Parole Board from ordering Knight be released on parole, unless they were satisfied, amongst other factors, that he was in imminent danger of dying, or was so seriously incapacitated, he posed no risk to the community if released.[304]

The final legal bid for freedom by Knight all came crashing down when the High Court of Australia, in August 2017, dismissed his appeal, which was based on the grounds that the amendments to the legislation were unconstitutional and also interfered with his original sentence.[305]

Knight, however, kept complaining that he should be allowed to spend his days in a more accommodating prison other than Port Phillip, where he had been since 2005. One of his claims was he was continually targeted by other prisoners, who certainly had no compassion for him, given the notoriety of his mass shootings. In early October 2025, the High Risk

---

303 As the Supreme Court had ruled that Knight was eligible to fight such legal case as to his right to contact his victims, the *Corrections Act 1986*(Vic) was amended to not only create the new offence but also to give power to Victorian prison governors to seize mail sent by inmates in respect of such distressing victim contact.

304 *The Corrections Amendment (Parole) Act 2014*(Vic) inserted a new s.74AA into the Corrections Act 1986(Vic).

305 *Knight v Victoria* [2017] HCA 29.

Management Advisory Panel[306] considered his leniency plea and, after reviewing his security classification, determined he could be transferred to Loddon, which was better known as a 'campus style' medium security prison.

Knight will still spend the rest of his days behind bars, never to be released, but will now have the pleasure of Loddon's modern style housing and its landscaped grounds, which clearly makes life for him a lot more comfortable, compared to Port Phillip Prison. Apart from his usual nonsensical court applications,[307] hopefully he will become a distant memory to us all. Sadly though and understandably, the loved ones and friends of his victims will never forgive, let alone forget him. Perhaps the other legacy he left behind was the Queen Street mass shooting, which would take place one day shy of four months after Hoddle Street.

---

306 The panel in conjunction with Corrections Victoria comprises Australian Federal Police, Victoria Police and a former Supreme Court Judge.

307 For example, in June 2020, it was reported that Knight made another application to the Supreme Court of Victoria over wanting access to the confronting Hoddle Street crime scene and autopsy images as part of a further anticipated appeal. Other reports also suggest Knight made a separate complaint to the United Nations Human Rights Committee. An application to the Federal Court of Australia in which Knight was alleging abuse while at the Royal Military College Duntroon was dismissed in September 2025.

27
THE QUEEN STREET MASSACRE

On the sunny afternoon of 8 December 1987, around 4pm, city commuters walking along Queen Street in Melbourne's CBD, thought they could hear a motor vehicle backfiring a number of times. These sounds though were being confused with many gunshots fired indiscriminately by 22-year-old Frank Vitkovic, after he entered the building at 191 Queen Street.

Vitkovic was armed with a sawn off M1 carbine, which he was carrying in a brown paper bag. He first caught the ground floor lift, after telling security he wanted to visit his mate Con on the 5th floor, where he worked for the Telecom Employees Credit Co-Operative. For reasons only known to Vitkovic, he held some sort of grudge against Con who, on welcoming him at the front counter, was suddenly staring at the gun, after Vitkovic took it out of the bag.

Fortunately for Con, the weapon initially jammed as he

ducked behind a counter. However, a young female employee was not so lucky and was shot dead by Vitkovic. Another worker, seeing the mayhem that was unfolding, triggered an alarm that notified a Wormald security control room that something was not quite right at the Queen Street office complex.

Some Australia Post workers also in the building, had no idea what was happening below them but, after Vitkovic took the lift to the 12th floor, they were unfortunately soon to find out. He burst through the security doors firing his gun at random and, by the time he had finished, three staff members had been shot dead with two others severely wounded.

Vitkovic, not satisfied with his killing spree, then went down to the floor below and again fired indiscriminately at the petrified employees, killing and wounding many. One of his victims was a 38-year-old father, who was standing at a coffee machine looking forward to going home shortly to celebrate his son's fifth birthday. Sadly, he was denied any such joyous occasion, shot dead at point blank range.

Other victims would also be killed but several others would survive, when they hid behind their desks. Thanks also to three brave but wounded male office workers,[308] who tackled Vitkovic and were fortunate to grab the rifle from him. It beggars belief that one of these heroic men had been shot four times in the back but was still able to disarm him. Another brave female employee, on seeing the rifle lying on the floor, was able to quickly hide it, of all places, in a refrigerator.

A further struggle ensued but Vitkovic escaped from their clutches, first smashing his way through a shadow glass

308 Two brave employees would subsequently be awarded Australia's second highest bravery decoration, namely the Star of Courage. Two other employees received bravery commendations.

window. Despite one brave employee holding this mass killer by the ankles to prevent him from getting away, Vitkovic was able to climb out onto an external ledge. Waiting below, with the complex surrounded, were heavily armed police. At 4.27pm, Vitkovic met his fate, jumping from 11 storeys high to his death.

The crime scene was now a grisly sight, with ambulance members and police attending to what Vitkovic had left behind. A total of eight of his victims were dead, with another five lucky to survive from their gunshot wounds. The internal complex, where the shootings took place, was riddled with bullets, not just in the walls and doors but also in posters wishing everyone a happy and joyful Christmas.

Another stark reminder were the bloodstains throughout, leaving no doubt of what had transpired. This included stains on the outside of the building, which traced Vitkovic to his remains splattered on the pavement below. It was later revealed that approximately 1,000 employees had been in the building at the time of the mayhem.

Police would visit the home of Vitkovic and, on searching his room, located press clippings of the escapades of Julian Knight, not that they needed to be reminded of that, given it only occurred some months earlier. The thought did cross everyone's mind though, that Vitkovic may have seen Knight as some sort of hero. He had underlined in red, specific parts of the Hoddle Street massacre media reports, so perhaps he saw himself in the same light as Knight. What police also found was a suicide note addressed to his parents, written by Vitkovic, which would be tendered in evidence at a subsequent coronial enquiry.

Regarding the weapon in his possession, Vitkovic had

obtained a shooting permit in the middle of September 1987 and in his application stating that he wanted to go hunting. Of course, no one at the time suspected what, in fact, he would go hunting after. The rifle was bought on 21 October 1987, after he paid it off by lay-by. At some point, prior to his exploits on that fateful day, he removed the gun barrel and handle.

Vitkovic's background was closely looked at, to see if there were any possible motives or mental issues behind what he had done. Vitkovic was the son of a Croatian father and an Italian mother. He attended local schools in Preston and was known to love playing tennis. He then attempted a law degree at Melbourne University in 1984 but, after poor grades over the next three years, he opted out.

The friends and neighbours of the Vitkovic family, although obviously in shock, suggested to investigators that he was always friendly. One witness did, however, say that Vitkovic was known to throw the odd tantrum if things didn't go his way on the tennis court. There were also some suggestions that after his tennis playing days came to an end, due to a knee injury, he became rather isolated and depressed.

A coronial enquiry, which commenced in September 1988, before Coroner Hal Hallenstein, to a degree, shed some light on what led to that terrible day in December 1987.[309] A postmortem of Vitkovic determined he had died instantly from multiple injuries as a result of the fall to the pavement but there was no evidence of any drugs or alcohol in his system. Witnesses, no doubt, still traumatised, would give evidence at how Vitkovic ran from victim to victim, again shooting the already wounded.

309 Queen Street Massacre: Record of Investigation into Deaths; State Coroner's Office of Victoria, September 1988.

Diary entries by Vitkovic set out his concerns over, of all things, his penis not being circumcised and then being picked on in the school locker room, when he was forced to undress. One entry even said, 'I am the odd man out, there's no doubting that.'

Just prior to the shooting, he wrote, 'As Rambo said in *First Blood*: once you accept a problem, it's no longer there.'

Perhaps he did see himself as some sort of Rambo but there was no evidence found that he had any ill-will to his friend Con, who he had known for a few years and first spoke to on the 5th floor at Queen Street. Interesting though, forensic psychologist, Dr Alan Bartholmew, in his report to the coroner concluded, after carefully going over the diary entries of Vitkovic, that he was a paranoid schizophrenic and was, most likely, criminally insane.

This was also based on a disheartening personality test Vitkovic had undergone in early October 1987, which may have also contributed to his depressed state of mind. A signed suicide note certainly supported such a diagnosis, which was tendered to the enquiry in which Vitkovic wrote:

> *'...I hope you can forgive me for what I've done but even if you don't, I'll understand it.... I don't understand why I ~~fell~~ feel such violent impulses, they run through my whole body. I've kept them reasonably under control until now, though you've seen flashes of it in my rages. But now, it's just reached the point of no return. These rages have been so bad the last month, they've caused me terrible headaches. I just can't go on...'*

There were a number of victims and emergency responders, understandably, who would continue to suffer for many years to come. However, Coroner Hallenstein still allowed confronting photographs, taken from a 5th floor security video, to be released to the public at the end of the inquest.

Perhaps at the time, the only potential positive outcome from this mass murder was the Victorian Government announced they would consider amending the regulations to prevent the purchase of the type of semi-automatic rifle used in this latest massacre by Vitkovic.

The Australian Government, however, in its usual fashion, advocated for tougher gun laws, but said that was an issue for each individual state and territory. Little did anyone know, of course, what would take place in 1996 at Port Arthur, Tasmania, that finally led to some action on easy access to firearms.[310]

---

310 See chapter 51.

28
NO MORE GRANNIES

Australia is renowned for its love of humble meat pies, especially the Four' N Twenty brand, which began baking delicious pies as early as 1947. History suggests the brand name originated from the nursery rhyme, 'Sing A Song of Sixpence', and it has also left an indelible mark on AFL footy fans. You will often see supporters enjoying the game of Australian Rules Football, munching away on their favourite meat pie.

Indeed, John Robert Glover enjoyed the meat pie delicacy, even to a degree he became one of their salesmen. He worked as one of their representatives and, at the age of 56, seemed to be nothing other than a loving husband with two daughters. Glover had been married for 20 years, was considered by all who knew him as a lovely man and even gave some of his time as a volunteer with a Senior Citizens Society.

But, unbeknown even to his family, Glover had a dark past, dating back in England to 1947, for the theft of clothing and handbags. On leaving school at the age of 14, he joined the British Army but that quickly came to an end with a dishonourable discharge. On emigrating to Australia, around late 1956, Glover, after being naturalised as an Australian citizen would get up to his old tricks, mainly through larceny, indecently assaulting women and a 'peeping tom offence.'[311] However, he would only be sentenced to lengthy good behaviour bonds. He moved to Sydney in 1968, to supposedly live a carefree married life and working for Four' N Twenty.

In January 1989, an 84-year-old woman was slowly walking down a road in the NSW suburb of Mosman, when she was punched in the face by a male and the contents of her purse, amounting to just over $200, was stolen. Police quickly formed the view it was a typical street mugging and they, most likely, would never be able to identify who was responsible. Little did they know at the time though, what else was about to take place and certainly a lot more sinister.

Two months later, on 1 March 1989, again in Mosman, a badly beaten elderly woman by the name of Gwendolin Mitchelhill was hit over her head and body with what appeared to be a hammer and her purse had been stolen. Sadly, for this 82-year-old, she would pass away, not long after emergency services arrived at the now murder crime scene.

The problem for police, though, was no one had witnessed what had taken place and, thanks to well-meaning neighbours of the deceased lady, they had scrubbed and washed the front of her apartment of blood before police were called. It seems, they

311 A peeping tom typifies a person and usually a male who obtains sexual gratification from observing others looking through bedroom windows at night. There was also a 1960 psychological thriller of the same name about a serial killer who murdered women recording their dying on a portable film camera.

thought she must have fallen, so police were now left with no forensic evidence to assist in their enquiries. Again, this crime, albeit one of murder, was considered to be another mugging that went horribly wrong.

It didn't take long for another ghastly Mosman murder to take place, this time on 9 May 1989. The body of Lady Winifreda Ashton, the 84-year-old widow of famed English Australian impressionist artist, Sir John Ashton, was found on a pavement near a small bin alcove, after being bashed. Crime scene detectives would also find her pantyhose had been placed tightly around her neck, with blood running from her mouth.

A post-mortem examination later ascertained that Lady Ashton also had a number of bruises to her body but there was no evidence of any sexual assault. The other perplexing issue was, she was still wearing her diamond ring, so robbery may have not been the reason why she was murdered. Police would later ascertain though that her purse was missing.

Police, on connecting all the dots, now started to think of the possibility of a serial killer roaming the streets. Each of the three victims, two of which had been murdered, were all elderly woman and the attacks occurred in the same suburb. All suffered similar wounds and had their purses, most likely containing cash, stolen. Their serial killer theory then started to gain more weight when an elderly woman was assaulted in August 1989 in a back street of nearby Lindfield. This was followed then by another bashing of an 86-year-old widow, near a retirement village in Mosman. Luckily, both victims survived, but they could not provide a definitive description of their attacker, also not helped by one of the women suffering from an advanced stage of dementia.

Such fears were reinforced when on 2 November 1989,

Lane Cove resident, Margaret Pahud, on her way home from shopping, was murdered due to blunt instrument strikes on the back of the head. This suburb is about a 10-kilometre drive from Mosman and, given she was also frail and elderly at the age of 85 years, a serial "granny killer" was definitely on the loose. Before police had time to organise a task force, within 24 hours of this latest murder, the perpetrator struck again.

This time, 84-year-old Olive Clevland became the fourth victim, after she was found on 3 November 1989 lying in a secluded side lane, adjacent to a retirement village, in the suburb of Belrose. Once again, this suburb was in close proximity to the other murder locations and this latest victim suffered similar head injuries, with her neck being tied tightly with pantyhose. The vicious attack had not been seen by any witnesses and, for some unexplained reason, the crime scene was hosed down before a proper forensic examination could take place.

A task force was now in operation, with over 70 detectives assigned to investigate what clearly were serial murders. In addition, the NSW State Government was concerned about what was taking place and doubled the reward for information to $200,000. Investigators were then faced with victim number five, as on 23 November 1989, another elderly Mosman resident suffered the same fate.

Muriel Falconer, at the age of 93, had little chance to defend herself and not just because of her age. She was also partially deaf and blind and it didn't take long for the granny killer to go about his work. She was found that afternoon by a next-door neighbour and, again, the victim had been bashed and strangled. A crime scene was immediately set up and bloody footprints were photographed and bagged as potential evidence. In addition, a door knock revealed one of the neighbours recalled seeing a middle aged and overweight grey-haired man in the vicinity of Muriel's home the day of her murder.

At this point of the investigation, the task force had a staggering 700 potential suspects to locate and speak to. In addition, literally thousands of pages of witness statements were mounting up but, hopefully, they would get the breakthrough so urgently needed.

On the one hand, that's what happened on 11 January 1990 when Glover indecently assaulted an elderly woman in palliative care. He visited the Greenwich Hospital as part of his pie selling round, dressed in his usual Four' N Twenty work uniform and carrying a clipboard. He then proceeded into the palliative care ward and asked an 82-year-old woman suffering from advanced cancer, if she was losing any "body heat".

Before this, now confused, very ill lady could respond and, perhaps thinking he was one of the nurses, Glover then pulled up her nightie and indecently poked and prodded her. On being assaulted, she called out and buzzed for help, with Glover running off after being confronted by a nurse. Fortunately, this quick-thinking nurse was able to obtain his car registration details then notified local police.

Now this is where NSW Police could be criticised for the way this incident was handled. Two young local police officers first attended the hospital, with Glover now identified and not just from his vehicle registration plates. He was well known to the hospital staff as their favourite pie man and police had no doubt who they were now looking for.

The problem here was, even on checking his police record and finding he had previous convictions for similar offending, local police still didn't think of, or even consider, Glover to be a possible person of interest in the granny murders. Not only was his prior offending of some interest but the description given by one of the witnesses, regarding the Falconer murder, clearly resembled Glover.

Apart from not passing on this incident and information to the task force, police didn't think to at least obtain a search warrant for his home and vehicle. They, instead, just called his home and left a message with his wife, that Glover was required to report to Chatswood Police Station on 13 January 1990, to be interviewed in respect of an indecent assault. Glover didn't show up, as police would be told by his wife it was because he had now tried to kill himself. No doubt, the reason for his admission to the North Shore Hospital was because he knew why police wanted to speak with him and not just over the patient assault.

Local police then attended the hospital where Glover was recovering and he denied he carried out the hospital assault, despite what witnesses had told police. He allowed them to take a polaroid photo of him, which would also be confirmed by hospital staff as the person who assaulted the elderly patient. Police also recovered a handwritten suicide note and on the middle of the page with the Four' N Twenty logo at the top, Glover had written, not only the name of the investigating Chatswood police officer, but the words 'No more grannies-Essie started it.'

Finally, on 5 February 1990, which was just over three weeks following the patient assault, local police notified the task force. On being presented with a plethora of evidence, which included his previous convictions, a murder witness identification of a middle-aged grey to white haired man, which clearly resembled Glover, and the suicide note, you would like to think the task force would bring him in for questioning. Such record of interview would, of course, be not only over the hospital assault but the granny murders. For reasons only known to task force detectives, they erred on the side of caution, deciding to just place him under covert surveillance.

Around 10am on 19 March 1990, with two plain clothes undercover police watching intently, they saw Glover enter a home in the suburb of Beauty Point. When Glover knocked on the door, it was opened by a middle-aged woman who police later ascertained was 60-year-old divorcee, Joan Sinclair, an acquaintance of Glover, with who he played bridge. Some hours later, with no sign of Glover or the woman, the police operatives entered the house to be faced with an horrendous scene.

Sinclair was naked from the waist down with a hammer lying next to her body. Her head was wrapped in blood-soaked towels, pantyhose wrapped around her neck and evidence that she may have been sexually assaulted. As for the confirmed granny killer, he was located unconscious in the house bathtub but he would survive to face his day in court.

During the police interview, Glover confessed to the six granny murders in addition to several other matters, including the attempted murder. With Joan Sinclair, thankfully being his last victim, Glover said they had been in a relationship for a period of time. This murder was similar to the other five murders, with the use of a claw hammer, which he hid under his shirt. He would also strike their head on concrete or a brick wall, then strangle his victim, chosen at random, with their pantyhose.

As to motive, Glover said he had a gambling addiction and, after stealing whatever money he could find, would usually go to the Mosman RSL Club and lose it on the poker machines. As to his murderous attacks, they were not sexually motivated, as he had no interest in sex. He just wanted their money. With remorse, he really didn't show any but his two suicide attempts suggested otherwise or was it a fear of getting caught. Glover was remanded in custody on 28 March 1990, with an order that he be kept in the psychiatric ward at Long Bay Prison.

In November 1991, Glover appeared before a jury in the Supreme Court of NSW on the six counts of murder, one of attempted murder and over the 14-month period, counts of robbery with wounding and indecent assault. He pleaded not guilty on the basis of diminished responsibility, which meant he was impaired by some sort of mental disorder.[312]

The Crown contended that Glover was more than aware of his offending, all over the theft of money to feed his addiction and even taking the time to clean his hammer to destroy any forensic evidence. As to psychiatric evidence submitted on his behalf, Glover was deemed to be sane but did have some sort of anger towards his mother, and particularly Essie, his mother-in-law, as expressed in one of his suicide notes.

The jury had no hesitation in finding him, not only sane, but guilty after deliberating for just over two hours. Justice Wood, in imposing a life sentence without parole said:

> *...The period since January 1989 has been one of intense and serious crime involving extreme violence inflicted on elderly women, accompanied by theft or robbery...On any view, the*

312 A partial defence to murder is based on a substantial mental health or cognitive impairment. See section 23A of the *Crimes Act 1900* (NSW) Also see *Mental Health and Cognitive Impairment Forensic Provisions Act 2020*(NSW).

prisoner has shown himself to be an exceedingly dangerous person...I have no alternative other than to impose the maximum sentence available...he is never to be released.[313]

As Glover was led away from the dock in handcuffs to spend the rest of his life in prison, there still remained a burning question. How many more grannies had suffered the same fate? Detectives had no doubt his total tally was not just six murders and, following his conviction, would pay him numerous visits at Long Bay Prison. One of the task force investigators had nominated Glover for the murder of two other elderly women, one in August 1984, followed by another one in November 1986.[314] Both had been bashed to death in similar circumstances inside their homes and in suburbs about 90 minutes travelling distance from Mosman. On asking Glover if he had anything he wanted to say about these two murders, Glover asked what evidence he had and if it was good, he might tell him.

Victoria Police also had their suspicions but, unfortunately, it was reported they had misplaced a number of crime scene exhibits for each murder. Glover was living in Melbourne before he moved to Sydney in late 1968, when four murders took place between June 1957 and April 1968. Again, they were middle-aged to elderly women and were killed in suburbs

---

313 *Regina v John Wayne Glover* [1990] Unreported, NSWSC. Justice Wood, November 1991.

314 Josephine McDonald was aged 73 and was killed in her home in Ettalong. Wanda Amundsen lost her life at the age of 83 found dead in her Umina residence. There was also a similar murder in 1977 when 78-year-old Florence Broadhurst was murdered in Paddington.

close to where Glover was residing at the time.[315] Two were killed suffering similar injuries to his NSW victims for which he was convicted, so it was again reasonable to consider him a very firm person of interest.

Unfortunately for their families, they would never know if, indeed, Glover was responsible for these still unsolved and very much cold cases. Glover, now aged 72, took his own life by hanging himself on 10 September 2005, being found dead in his cell at Lithgow maximum security prison. I'm sure he won't be missed and there will not be anyone visiting his grave to pay their respects.

To make it even more sinister, some days before he killed himself, he drew a sketch of a park with two pine trees. However, the main focus in the drawing was the number "nine" situated in the middle of the two trees. Did this mean his total number of murder victims were nine or does that reflect the total ones unsolved to this day? We will never know.

---

315 Emmie May Anderson lived in East Melbourne and died aged 78 in October 1961. Irene Kiddle was 63 years old living in St Kilda when she was murdered in March 1963. These two victims were stabbed to death, which was not the usual method of Glover. The only connection was they lived in close proximity to him. Elsie Boyes, 63, resided at Prahran and in June 1957 was strangled in a toilet block just a short distance from where Glover lived. Albert Park resident Christina Yankos lost her life in April 1968 aged 63 and was also strangled, this time with a cord from her nightgown, both being very similar acts to some of Glover's NSW victims.

29
A CHURCH ELDER

On a warm and sunny afternoon on 29 June 1991, in the sleepy beachside town of Rosebud in Victoria, little did the locals know what was about to unfold.[316] Six-year-old Sheree Beasley, after riding her bicycle down the road to the local milk bar on an errand for her mother, would suddenly disappear.

Sheree had spent the day at her primary school and thought nothing of helping her much-loved mother buying some milk, a bottle of lemonade and a couple of Four and Twenty pies. For her help, she was also given some money to buy some sweets. The last thing she said to her mum was, 'I'll be back in a couple of minutes, love you.'

That was the last time her mother would see Sheree until the badly decomposed body of a child was found by two horse riders on 24 September 1991, 10 kilometres away in a Red Hill stormwater drain. It was readily assumed the body was Sheree,

316 At the time it bore similar chilling circumstances to the 1984 Kylie Maybury murder.

as clothing located at the crime scene was very similar to what she was wearing on the afternoon of her disappearance. It would take police some weeks, however, to finally determine it was definitely the little girl, after they used a much-publicised method of genetic profiling.[317] Such DNA from the deceased person's muscle tissue is then compared to a family member's blood sample, which was taken from her mother.

Police now had a murder to investigate, including the abduction and rape of three schoolgirls, who luckily survived.[318] Detectives seconded from various crime squads, together with local police, under the direction of Detective Inspector Laurie Ratz,[319] started to make some headway. A young boy had earlier told police he had seen a girl, who resembled Sheree, being forced into a small, blue hatchback car, which then sped off towards the Nepean Highway in Rosebud. This was then followed by a woman confirming with investigators that on the afternoon Sheree went missing, she saw a similar vehicle with a young girl sitting in the front seat, wearing a pink helmet,

---

317 Such profiling is known as Polymerase Chain Reaction (PCR) in which minute quantities of DNA samples is replicated over and over again to reproduce selected sections of DNA for better analysis.

318 Karmein Chan (13) was abducted at knifepoint from her Templestowe home on the night of 13 April 1991, with her remains found in April 1992. Her murder and the abduction and sexual assault of three other schoolgirls in the northern and eastern suburbs of Melbourne in the late 1980s and early 1990s are all believed to be linked to an unidentified serial child rapist known as 'Mr Cruel'.

319 In my book titled 'From Vietnam Nasho to Catching School Crooks', I devoted a chapter to Laurie in recognition of his career as a dedicated police officer.

looking very distressed. The male driving the motor vehicle was middle-aged and appeared to be clean shaven.

Detectives had already started looking at a number of local known males of a similar age and with convictions for indecent behaviour, particularly with offences involving young children. One male who immediately came under suspicion was 55-year-old Robert Arthur Selby Lowe who not only had prior convictions for indecent exposure involving young girls but also had a holiday home on the Mornington Peninsula.

A closer look at Lowe revealed that by day he was a travelling salesman and on a Sunday was a respected church elder, even taking classes teaching children about the Christian faith. However, his criminal history went as far back between 1959 and 1965 in New Zealand, committing offences of indecent assault on a male, wilful and obscene exposure and had been imprisoned serving a six-month sentence.

Lowe then relocated to Australia, after the NZ justice system labelled him nothing but a 'rogue and vagabond', where he met the love of his life. He married this extremely religious woman in the early 1970s but would still get up to his old tricks, appearing in court on numerous occasions for similar offending. This included loitering for sexual purposes, theft and his usual wilful and obscene exposures.

Police then interviewed Lowe over the disappearance of Sheree and he denied any knowledge but said he knew of it as he saw it on the news. He did admit though, to being a regular customer at the same milk bar. When shown her photo, he denied he had ever seen this girl before. Interesting though, he also owned a motor vehicle that just happened to be blue in colour and resembled the one that witnesses had seen driving towards the Nepean Highway, with a visibly upset young girl in the front seat. What also stood out for police was an earlier telephone conversation they had had with Lowe in that, when asked where he was on the day she vanished, he quickly replied he was at home with his wife and two children.

The suspicions by police, that Lowe was involved in the abduction and murder of Sheree, were then confirmed. They had secretly recorded several of his psychotherapy sessions and telephone calls with his therapist in early November 1991. Detectives were aware he had been receiving counselling sessions from the therapist at various times over several years, after being referred following charges of wilful exposure. In addition, not long after Sheree disappeared, Lowe attended for further counselling, initially saying he was having marital problems.

These taped sessions then quickly turned to Lowe talking about the missing child and he knew police were closely watching him. He then discussed what prison sentence he might receive for an accidental death, if he pleaded guilty to manslaughter, hoping if he did, it might save his marriage. After asking the therapist to show him where Sheree's body was found, she produced a road map and Lowe quickly marked the exact spot. In late November 1991, with his psychotherapist now concerned about Lowe's involvement in the abduction and murder, she consented to enable police to secretly tape conversations during his therapy sessions.

In March 1992 with police covertly listening, Lowe then suggested the therapist accompany him to Red Hill, to jog his memory and he could then confide in her. This was followed in early April 1992 where Lowe was taped admitting he took Sheree for a ride in his car. He then said she began coughing and, for some reason, became hysterical, then stopped breathing.

Lowe then said he called on God to forgive him as he pushed her body down into the stormwater drain.

You would think this was enough for police to place him under arrest but it was not to be. Obviously, detectives needed to put a thorough brief of evidence together and it would be another 14 months before they arrested Lowe. After being charged in late May 1993 with the murder of Sheree, two counts of kidnapping and one count of false imprisonment, he was subsequently remanded in protective custody. Understandably, his defence lawyer said there were concerns for his safety and, as we know, fellow cell mates don't take kindly to this type of offending involving children.

In October 1994, Lowe pleaded not guilty before Justice Cummins and a jury in the Supreme Court of Victoria. The evidence before the jury was overwhelming with his ex-wife stating that on the day of Sheree's disappearance, Lowe was absent and when he came home, he washed his clothes and vacuumed his motor vehicle, which was a first time ever for him. When he was initially interviewed by police, she said he couldn't stop crying telling her he was very sorry, despite saying he was innocent of any wrongdoing.

While the evidence on tape of all the secretly recorded conversations with his therapist and her compelling evidence in support, what Lowe didn't expect was also testimony from a fellow prisoner. The jury had already heard from a forensic pathologist, who quickly rejected the theory from Lowe that Sheree suddenly died from pure fright or stress. Now it was time for inmate Peter Reid[320] to testify.

320 Reid was originally sentenced to life in respect of the 1982 murder of Victorian police officer, Stephen Henry. Following the enactment of fixed minimum terms, he would only serve 21 years and was released in 2004.

He had had a conversation with Lowe under the pretext of assisting him with his defence. Reid was told Sheree had choked to death when spitting out blood, as he forced to her commit "dirty acts". Reid would also tell, by now, a very distressed jury, that Lowe admitted he had first seen Sheree a couple of times before he abducted her, on the pretext he would drive her home as her mother was ill. When she got into his car, all she could say was, 'Take me home to mummy. I want my mummy.'

Reid then said Lowe told him he got sperm all over her clothes, so he undressed her and, with his feet, forced Sheree into what would be her final resting place.

There was no doubt to the guilt of this so-called church elder. In early December 1994, a visibly upset Justice Cummins said this had been the most harrowing trial he ever faced and sentenced Lowe to life imprisonment without any chance of parole.

In the words of His Honour: 'And Mr Lowe, life means life.'[321]

Lowe appealed the decision and, in particular, it was based on a psychotherapist's obligations of privilege and confidence respecting their client. This was also raised at the initial trial in that a court should reject confessional evidence obtained under a relationship of trust and confidence. The Court of Appeal clearly ruled that such client privilege does not apply, particularly with a client's involvement in a serious crime.[322]

---

321 *R v Lowe, Robert Arthur Selby* [1994] Unreported Vic SC 756, Justice Cummins, 2 December 1994.

322 *R v Lowe* [1997] 98 ACrim R 300. The Court of Appeal also stated that there was no general common law or statutory privilege in any event between a client and a psychotherapist.

In 2010, Lowe couldn't help himself and was believed to be involved in smuggling pornographic material involving children into the Ararat Hopkins Correctional Centre. In 2014, Lowe tried unsuccessfully to launch a bid for freedom when he concocted an illogical story where he was a scapegoat and drug addicts must have killed Sheree. Her grandfather had the final say though and summed it up perfectly when he said, 'Go straight to hell, Robert Lowe.'

Hopefully, that was his final destination after he died behind bars in November 2021, aged 84.

30
LIFE MEANS LIFE

One despicable murderer who won't see the light of day is Andrew Peter Garforth. This follows his conviction and sentence for the sexual assault and murder of nine-year-old, Ebony Jane Simpson. On 19 August 1992, Ebony was on her way home from Bargo Primary School in NSW, when she was abducted, brutally raped, thrown into a dam and left to drown.

What happened to Ebony was an unthinkable tragedy, never experienced before in the town of Bargo in the state's southern highlands. Upon receiving the report of her disappearance, a request for assistance was issued and the local community promptly participated to conduct an extensive search of the surrounding area. Numerous parents from the local primary school collaborated with other concerned community members, alongside more than 100 police officers. This included the Air Wing and Dog Squad, as well as State Emergency Service personnel and Rural Fire Service volunteers.

Police were able to ascertain that the bright, bubbly grade

four student caught the school bus, which would then always drop her off, approximately 400 metres from her home. On this particular day, her 14-year-old brother was to meet her at the bus stop so they could walk home together. His school bus was delayed so Ebony began the short distance walk to home. Sadly, that was the last time she would be seen.

Following missing person flyers distributed throughout the local community, one eagle-eyed person told police he had seen a short, thin male, around the age of 18-19 years, with shoulder length brown hair carrying out repairs under the bonnet of his motor vehicle. The vehicle, described as being a dirty white or cream colour and looked to be in very poor condition, was situated on the same road Ebony would have walked down.

While this would give police at least one line of enquiry, it quickly escalated to a definite person of interest. Police also became aware that a similar vehicle had been seen driving slowly past both the primary and high schools, including Ebony's, over the past few months. Police were, however, sceptical that this was the same car as earlier reported until Ebony's distraught mother gave police a similar description of the male seen repairing his vehicle.

After informing police she had also seen him days before her daughter's disappearance, she assisted in putting together a composite image drawing of his face. After the image was circulated to the public on the basis of 'do you know this man?', many calls were received nominating the sketch as remarkedly similar to 29-year-old Garforth.

This individual was known to police with a number of prior convictions, mainly for burglary, theft and the usual traffic infringements. He was also a married father of two young children and resided within three kilometres from Ebony's home. Given he had only just moved to Bargo and was wanted by Western Australian police after skipping bail, it gave police even more reason to bring him in for a little chat. However, they did not foresee that he would willingly provide admissions regarding the events that transpired on that significant day.

In a video–taped confession and in some detail, he confirmed he was, indeed, under the pretence of working on his motor vehicle while waiting for Ebony to walk past. Garforth stated, after grabbing her, he placed the petrified and now screaming young girl into the boot of his car and quickly drove off. With music blaring from the car, no doubt to drown out her calls for help, he went to an isolated dirt track where he would not be seen. When Garforth described the repeated sexual assaults, brutal rape and murder in casual and relaxed detail, even the more experienced detectives had to take deep breaths and turn away.

With Ebony pleading for her life and begging to be freed, he threw her into the Wirrimbirra wildlife sanctuary dam, located nearby. Despite being a good swimmer, Ebony had no way of saving herself, due to both her hands and feet being tied with wire. After throwing her pink school bag full of rocks into the dam to further dispose of any evidence, Garforth simply walked away as she slowly drowned.

To make his conduct even more appalling, he told police he even joined the massive search, agreeing with all and sundry of where she could possibly be. On 21 August 1992, two days after Ebony disappeared, her body was found in the dam where Garforth had left her to die. Life for the callous and brutal murderer became very difficult after he was charged with her murder and remanded in custody because his fellow cell mates turned on him.

After two separate incidents in which Garforth was assaulted, including one that occurred while he was in his locked cell, prison authorities decided to place him in protective custody. Given the hatred that other prisoners had for child abusers of this type, it was surprising Garforth wasn't already under such protection.

After pleading guilty and offering no defence, no explanation and no remorse, Garforth appeared for sentencing in the Supreme Court of NSW before Justice Peter Newman on 9 July 1993. His Honour made a somewhat surprising decision not to call for any family victim impact statements because he believed it would only bring further grief to her family.

In that regard, given the cruelty and coldness of the actions of Garforth, Judge Newman said:

> *… Plainly enough, the effects of these events upon the victim's family would be horrific… [the crime] was chilling to the extreme…It's my duty to make the sentence a deterrent to other offenders who commit crimes against young girls…*[323]

His Honour certainly didn't have any issue in sentencing Garforth to life imprisonment, with his papers marked "never to be released".[324] This meant such a despicable offender, given the danger he posed to the community, would never have any possibility of parole and would remain in prison for the term of his natural life. Although a sentence of life imprisonment was

---

323 *Regina v Garforth* [1993] Unreported, NSWSC, Justice Newman, 9 July 1993.

324 *Crimes Act 1900*(NSW)-section 19A. Also see *Sentencing Act 1989*(NSW) in which being sentenced to life meant life and no possibility of parole.

imposed, it did not satisfy many members of the community. Notably, there were 200,000 signatures advocating for the death penalty, particularly in relation to this individual convicted of child murder.

His fellow inmates, once again, didn't take too kindly to Garforth, belting the living daylights out of him. The 10 prisoners involved, some who were also in protective custody for varying reasons, bashed their marked man, known as a "rock spider",[325] when they were being relocated into new prison cells. While Garforth was being treated in the prison hospital for minor injuries sustained in the bashing, which included a cut to one of his eyes and bruises by kicks to his back and legs, a spokesperson for the Department of Corrective Services commented that:

> *The code has always been that, if it's a child molester, then the prisoners seem to think they've got some right to bash those prisoners once they get their hands on them...Never mind what they've done, an offence against a child is unforgivable as far as they are concerned...*

A truer word could not be spoken but I digress. What was interesting though, he also denied the prison officers simply turned a "blind eye" to the attack on Garforth. Life in prison wasn't going to get any better for him, following a failed appeal against his life sentence, all the way to the High Court of Australia. The court ruled there was no error in sentencing as it fell into the worst type of case to attract the maximum penalty.[326]

325 This term is commonly used in Australian prison slang for a child molester or paedophile 'lurking in wait like a spider'.

326 This was the first life sentence under section 19A to be considered by the Court of Criminal Appeal in NSW.

Garforth's lawyers then tried, in 1994, to convince the High Court that he should be given the opportunity to apply for parole. Given that even in situations where he no longer posed a risk to the community, due to an advanced state of ill health, life meant life behind bars. The only way Garforth could have been released was under a Royal Prerogative of Mercy and that simply was not going to happen. In any event, the High Court found there was no error of principle saying the Court of Criminal Appeal was, 'fully alive to the gravity of the sentence.'[327]

Garforth didn't give up though, as the following year in 1995, he felt so aggrieved by being bashed in prison, he lodged several victims of crime compensation claims. Following an uproar, once again from the community, the claims were subsequently withdrawn. The public would hear nothing more about Garforth until early July 2015, when the Serious Offenders Review Council had a closer look at the so-called plight of this life term prisoner.

The council is tasked with the management of security classifications, placement and case management of prisoners who are classified as serious offenders,[328] which make up around seven per cent of the NSW prison population. They also provide reports to the State Parole Authority, Supreme Court and to government ministers, such as the Attorney General and Minister for Corrections.

With inmate security classification, the council can also, without government approval, downgrade any prisoner classification, particularly if it recognises the potential to

327 *Garforth v The Queen* S98/1994[1994] HCA Trans 149.

328 See serious offender classification under the *Crimes (Administration of Sentences) Act 1999*(NSW).

rehabilitate the inmate. The NSW prisoner classification has a total of seven categories, with the category AA as the highest, down to the lowest, labelled C3.

If you are deemed to be at an AA level, then you are considered to be a prisoner who poses a special risk and needs to be confined at all times and under constant surveillance monitoring. At the other end of the scale, if you are a C3, you are low risk and do not need any sort of supervision.[329]

In the case of Garforth, he was serving his life sentence in maximum security at Goulburn as a serious offender and was deemed to be a category A2, which is still at the highest level. However, the council determined that he should now be downgraded to a category B, which meant he would be now incarcerated in medium security, making him eligible for work and rehabilitation courses. This decision was then rubber stamped by the Corrective Services Commissioner, so Garforth was now looking at perhaps a more comfortable and relaxed prison lifestyle.

That lasted only two days because on 14 July 2015, a furious Corrective Services Minister, David Elliott, reversed the council's decision and even announced he was considering taking away any privileges Garforth may still have at Goulburn Prison. In that respect, Elliott said:

> *This guy gets nothing. He will die in jail. I've taken personal responsibility for this matter and I will today be writing to*

329 All offenders when sentenced to prison are classified in accordance with the security levels set out in sections 12-14A of the *Crimes (Administration and Sentences) Regulations 2014*(NSW). The Corrections Commissioner may also designate an inmate at High Security, Extreme High Security to even High Risk Restricted, particular in respect of prisoners who are considered a threat to the peaceful stability of a prison.

Mrs Simpson and offering a heartfelt apology on behalf of the people of NSW for the way she has been treated... I have today instructed the Commissioner that Garforth gets zip. And I have asked for a list of everything he had prior to reclassification so I can see if I can take anything away from him...it's certainly not what the people of NSW expect out of the judicial system.

Following community outrage, regarding what was first ordered by the council but then thankfully overruled, it was summed up best by Ebony's mother, Christine Simpson. On Channel Nine's "A Current Affair", she stated what was needed for her daughter's killer:

...lock him up, throw away the key...He needs a plate of beans kicked under that door of his cell and a glass of water, that's all he needs...

Garforth is now nearly 62 years of age, so it's fair to say he still has many more years left before he leaves prison but, when he eventually does, it will be in a pine box. One positive outcome from all this, was the setting up of Homicide Victims Support Group (HVSG) founded in 1993. This was thanks to Ebony Simpson's parents in collaboration with the family of 26-year-old Anita Cobby, who was sexually assaulted and murdered by a gang of five men in February 1986, when walking home from Blacktown railway station. Each of her attackers were sentenced to life imprisonment, also without the possibility of parole.[330]

330 John Travers was deemed the leader of the gang together with Michael Murdoch and the Murphy brothers, Michael, Gary and Les. Other than Michael Murphy, who died in Long Bay Hospital in 2019, the rest remain incarcerated never to be released.

The HSVG offers counselling, support and provides information to families and friends of homicide victims in NSW. It is funded by the Western Sydney Health District and donations from corporate sponsors and members of the community.[331] This would be considered the only positive outcome regarding Garforth, other than his life sentence of never to be released.

331 The HVSG can be contacted on (02) 8833 8400 for general enquiries and also has a hotline available 24 hours a day, seven days a week(1800 191 777).

31
IVAN 'THE RAT' MILAT

Ivan Robert Marko Milat came into this world on 27 December 1944 and was one of 14 children. Milat would die in prison 74 years later on 27 October 2019, at the Long Bay Correctional Centre in NSW, where he was serving seven life sentences without the possibility of parole. He left this world with several nicknames but was probably better known as the "Backpacker Murderer".

Although Milat and his 10 brothers had a decent upbringing, attending the local Bossley Park and Liverpool Catholic schools, the Milat clan soon became well known to police. Their alcoholic father didn't help in discouraging their life of crime, which included possessing weapons of choice, such as knives and firearms. The local neighbourhood would know when the "Milat Rat Pack" boys were at home, often hearing copious rounds of ammunition being fired when they practiced target shooting in their backyard.

Milat would progress to being described, by some who

knew him quite well at the young age of 17, as nothing but a psychopath. He experienced his first stint in a detention centre, following a conviction for theft. He would then progress to carrying out numerous burglaries and, in 1964, after serving another prison sentence, he couldn't help himself with further time, which included two years with hard labour for theft of a motor vehicle.

After being released for further offending involving, once again, theft in 1971, Milat's penchant for abducting and raping young attractive female hitchhikers would come to the attention of police. After then disappearing, while on bail on two counts of armed robbery and one of rape when armed with a knife, Milat was finally brought before the court in 1974. This was after returning from spending two years in New Zealand, where he also came under the attention of their police, but somehow and perhaps because he had a decent lawyer, he was acquitted on all counts.[332] It would be hoped that this truck driver, working at various times for the Roads and Traffic Authority, would mend his ways but, alas, that was wishful thinking.

During the period from December 1989 to April 1992, seven backpackers aged between 19 and 22 years, five being female, would suddenly disappear. After leaving the Sydney CBD, three individual groups had all separately hitchhiked south along the Hume Highway from around Liverpool. These

332 John Marsden, his lawyer accused both girls at the trial that they were lesbians, receiving psychiatric treatment and were taking prescription drugs. There was also some suggestion that one of the girls had, in fact, agreed to have sex with Milat. In those days, according to Marsden, juries had some sort of prejudice against gays and lesbians. For further insight see 'I am what I am' by John Marsden – published 2004.

soon-to-be victims included a young couple from Victoria, three from Germany and two from the United Kingdom.[333]

Their sudden disappearances remained a mystery, until over a period between September 1992 and November 1993, their bodies would be found, covered separately with branches and other forest litter, in the Belanglo State Forest,[334] each in an advanced state of decomposition. Some of the bodies were located within walking distance of each other but one was about five kilometres away from the other victims.

It was evident they had all been attacked with some brutality. Two of the victims were shot a number of times with extensive head wounds from bullets fired from a Ruger 10/22 semi-automatic rifle. One female victim had been decapitated by a type of sword, with no sign of her skull. Three had suffered stab wounds, which included two having their spines completely severed. Forensic evidence and post-mortem examinations also suggested all but one had suffered from sexual assault, which may have also been carried out after they were killed.

Three of the bodies had gags placed around their mouths and at some of the crime scenes, forensic investigators would

---

333 On 30 December 1989, Australians Deborah Everist and James Gibson left Melbourne and were last seen planning to hitchhike to Albury. On 20 January 1991, German girl Simone Schmidt left Sydney to join her mother for a camping holiday. German backpackers Gabor Neugebauer and Anja Habschied left Kings Cross on 26 December 1991 to travel to Adelaide and then Darwin. British tourists Joanne Walters and Caroline Clarke also left the Cross on 18 April 1992 heading to Victoria, hoping to do some fruit picking.

334 This state forest is located near the Hume Highway south of Berrima in the Southern Highlands of NSW and consists of a total area of approximately 3,800 hectares.

find and tag Winchester and Eley spent cartridge cases, some found in the skulls of some of the victims. In addition to locating respective ammunition boxes of the same brand, police also came across a distinct blue and yellow piece of Telecom rope and black electrical tape. At two of the crime scenes, rather strange-looking brick fireplaces had also been built, not far from where the remains were found.

In October 1993, NSW Police had by now established Task Force Air, consisting of around 20 detectives supported by analysts. After the three bodies were found in early November 1993, the NSW Government had increased a reward from $100,000 to $500,000, for information about who may have been responsible. Police by this stage had not considered the seven murders as all being connected to one single suspect, given that the victims, other than one, had been traveling in pairs and most likely the murders were carried out by more than just one killer.

One incident they had not yet connected to the seven murders, was the attempted armed robbery of 24-year-old English tourist, Paul Onions. On 25 January 1980, after travelling to Liverpool by train, he was hitchhiking along the Hume Highway. After failing to obtain a lift, he stopped at a shop in the town of Casula to quench his thirst. He was then approached by a male, around 30 years of age, who said his name was Bill. He told his soon-to-be, new-found friend that he worked for the Roads and Traffic Authority at Liverpool and was currently on holidays, of Yugoslavian descent and divorced. After offering him a lift, Paul happily accepted until things turned somewhat nasty.

When they came within a short distance of the Belanglo State Forest, Bill, armed with a camouflage knife, suddenly produced a revolver and demanded the young man to hand over his possessions. Onions quickly jumped out of the vehicle with Bill firing a shot at him but he, fortunately, escaped after stopping another motorist.

This incident was immediately reported to Bowral police, with a detailed description of Bill, including his height, build and the fact he also had what was described as a very bushy distinctive moustache[335] of black straggly hair. The vehicle driven by Bill was said to be a white or silver Nissan 4WD and when he was able to get way, Onions had left behind in the vehicle his rucksack, containing all his belongings, in particular a distinctive type of Next brand shirt and his passport.

This important and, in due course, Crown witness, Onions, would then contact task force detectives in late November 1993. This was after extensive media publicity, particularly in British newspapers, following the finding of the three latest bodies on 1 and 4 November 1993. The reward would be increased by the government. What was of importance now to police, was this witness had previously provided a distinct physical description of his Belanglo Forest attacker, the silver Nissan 4WD and the personal background offered by Bill.

After the initial report was made to Bowral Police, for some unexplained reason, it was never followed up and lay dormant in their files. However, task force detectives would later obtain a statement from the woman motorist who picked Onions up and took him to Bowral Police Station, in which she corroborated his version of what had transpired.

During the on-going investigation, another witness had

335 This witness told police the moustache reminded him of Merv Hughes, an Australian Test Cricketer who was well known for his large handlebar moustache.

also come forward and told police about an attempted abduction in 1977, after she and a girlfriend accepted a lift from a man, very similar looking to Bill and aged in his early thirties. They were able to escape and hide in the bushes for several hours. When shown photographs of two of the Milat brothers, one of the girls suggested that Milat's brother looked very similar to the person who tried to abduct them. Another caller to the police 24-hour hotline also told police of her suspicions of Ivan Milat, who drove a 4WD and was often seen with his guns and known to like shooting.

Task Force Air, by February 1994, thanks to exhaustive work by its investigators, led by Superintendent Clive Small, clearly by this stage had the Milat brothers as persons of definite interest, in particular, Ivan. They had information that he was in possession of a similar 4WD vehicle, that he indeed sometimes went under the moniker of Bill, notwithstanding, he also had one of his numerous brothers with the same name. The criminal history of Milat carried some weight and what was also of interest was a red-light camera device which had detected Milat driving his vehicle in the area at the day and time when one of the backpackers had most likely been abducted.

What, of course, also stood out was Milat was of Yugoslavian heritage, was indeed divorced and, lo and behold, had a very distinctive handlebar moustache. If he wasn't involved in the seven murders, either acting alone or just him, he certainly was in respect of the armed robbery and attempted abduction of British tourist, Onions. The fact he had previously been charged with and put on trial for the alleged rape of two hitchhikers, notwithstanding, he was acquitted after the prosecution had put together a somewhat weak case, it was still another link in the suspicion chain. Milat was also known to be an active hunter with an obsession for guns.

It would also later be revealed that one of the Milat neighbours was approached by Ivan, after the disappearance of one of the backpackers, to see if he was able to repair a bullet hole in his Nissan 4WD. Interesting though, this vehicle would also be sold by Bill, not long after another two backpackers suddenly went missing. What also stood out to police was that a search of the work records of Ivan Milat uncovered that he was indeed absent from work on the days of the known abductions and murders.

On 26 February 1993, Task Force Air decided to place the Milats, in particular Ivan, under covert surveillance. At this point, they didn't have enough evidence to obtain a warrant for telephone intercepts and to place listening devices in his southwest of Sydney Eagle Vale home that he shared with his sister. The other problem would be gaining access to the premises, which police now knew was fitted with a very elaborate security system and Ivan always turned it on when he left the house. Police, anyway, were about to find out whether he had something to hide.

The lucky Onions, who managed to escape from being abducted, returned to Australia in early May 1994, to further speak with police. Onions was able to identify Milat from a series of photographs shown to him by police. Police, at this point, now had enough evidence to, not only place an intercept on Ivan's phone, but to also take him into custody to charge him initially with the attempted abduction and armed robbery, pending further enquiries into the backpacker murders. Detectives from Task Force Air then made a very wise decision knowing the only way to connect Ivan to the murders, was to obtain a warrant and search his house and any other properties belonging to the Milats.

Around 6.35am on 22 May 1994, after the Milat house was surrounded by heavily armed police, the suspect was taken into custody. When read his rights and told that police were investigating the January 1980 attempted abduction and armed robbery, Milat, in his usual belligerent manner, played along with police as though they had the wrong man and he had nothing to worry about. However, after searching his house and that of his mother and some of his brothers, police would uncover a large amount of property and other incriminating evidence, clearly linking him to the backpacker murders and the attempted Onions abduction.

The first item of interest was a New Zealand postcard with greetings of 'Hi Bill' and, although Milat had a brother of the same name, the card wanted to know when he would be returning to NZ. Police would later identify the sender of the post card as a good mate of their suspect, Ivan. Indonesian currency was also located in one of the bedrooms and, notably, he had never travelled to that country but two of the murder victims had spent time there, just prior to coming to Australia. What would then be found was numerous articles of clothing and equipment, which clearly belonged to some of the seven deceased victims, together with a distinct map of the southern NSW highlands.

Some other items located and linked to the seven murdered backpackers included a green water bottle and pouch, black electrical tape, a green sleeping bag of a Salewa brand used by two of his victims and also a camouflage knife, as previously described to police by Onions. A blood stained cord was later DNA tested and linked to the blood of one of those who died.

They even found an album with photos of Ivan's then girlfriend, wearing a very distinctive green and white Benetton top, which police knew was very similar to clothing worn by one of the female victims. Remarkably, the caption on the photo was 1992, which just happened to be the same year this victim had disappeared. They also located, amongst Ivan's belongings, the distinctive Next brand shirt, left behind by Onions during his attempted abduction.

A search of a hall cupboard would again find incriminating evidence, which included a broken Ruger 10.22 rifle used in two of the murders, Winchester ammunition with the same batch numbers used in one killing, together with other similar cartridges found at one of the murder scenes. Also stacked in a corner of the cupboard was a camera with cooking utensils, owned by a murdered female tourist who had been found with a severed spine.

When detectives asked a now-handcuffed Ivan to explain some of the items, he nonchalantly replied he had no knowledge of them, sitting there as though he was completely innocent. Interesting though, when questioned about whether he had ever been to Belanglo State Forest, he confirmed he had at one point driven along its dirt track back in the 1980s.

Well, he now did have a problem, because he was remanded in custody on 23 May 1994, after the searches of his home and that of his mother and five of his brothers were completed, being charged with the offence of detain for advantage in respect of Onions.[336] A week later, he was also presented with

---

336 Offences of kidnapping are pursuant to section 86(1) of the *Crimes Act 1900*(NSW). The Crown has the burden to prove that the taking or detaining was without consent.

seven counts for the murders of the backpackers, with bail, of course, being refused.

Following his committal hearing, which lasted nearly two months, with over 200 witnesses giving evidence, on 12 December 1994 the soon-to-be 50 years of age, Ivan Milat, was committed to stand trial in the Supreme Court of New South Wales. No doubt, he would continue to maintain his arrogant not guilty persona.

Although the trial of Milat was set down for June 1995, it was delayed over his representation being paid for by NSW Legal Aid but would finally commence on 25 March 1996. He, of course, pleaded not guilty to all eight counts and following the Crown witnesses giving evidence, which included copious exhibits and crime scene photographs, defence counsel would make a startling admission in his final address to the jury. Milat had given evidence that he was in no way connected to any of the counts as charged, particularly regarding the seven murders. His supposed innocence was also supported by various family members who offered gratuitous alibis for him at various times around each backpacker disappearance.

However, his learned defence counsel, in his closing summation, admitted that the evidence was so overwhelming, he agreed the Crown had demonstrated, beyond reasonable doubt, that the murders were carried out. However, they were not by the accused but a member or members of the Milat family. In that regard, counsel nominated two of Milat's brothers as the most likely perpetrators, either acting alone or in concert with others. Certainly not his client, Ivan Milat, though, as this was all a family set up trying to blame him.

During the 15-week trial, Justice Hunt went to great lengths, not only at the start and during the trial, but also in his jury summation. He said the 12 jurors needed to determine their verdict dispassionately and only on the evidence before them and not be swayed in anyway by the extensive media coverage of the case, not only prior, but during the trial. On 27 July 1996, the jury, after deliberating for three days, finally returned its verdict that Milat was guilty as charged on all eight counts. In respect of the seven counts of murder, Milat was sentenced to penal servitude for life without parole and six years for the detain for advantage count.[337]

It didn't take long for Milat to be dealt with by another Maitland prisoner, being bashed the day after he was sentenced. He then put together, in May 1997, an elaborate escape plan with fellow cell mate, George Savvas[338] but, luckily, that was foiled by Maitland jail prison authorities and Milat was then transferred to the maximum-security section at the Goulburn Correctional Centre.

It was only a matter of time before Milat lodged an appeal, being one of a number, which was heard and ruled on by the NSW Court of Criminal Appeal in February 1998. His main grounds of appeal were that certain photographic evidence should have been excluded on the grounds it was unreliable and that he was not afforded a fair trial, due to the ongoing and exhaustive media coverage.

In the first instance, their Honours, in a 22-page judgment, concluded that Justice Hunt was not in error to exclude such

337 *Regina v Milat* [1996] Unreported, Supreme Court of NSW, Hunt CJ, 27 July 1996.

338 Savvas had previously escaped from prison and would not see out his 30-year sentence for importing a large shipment of heroin in 1994. The day after this next escape plan was uncovered, he was found dead hanging from a rope in his cell.

evidence of photographic identification. As to the fairness of the trial, it was succinctly summed up by the Court of Appeal:

> *In our criminal justice, jurors are put in a position of high responsibility. We ought to give them due credit for being able to discharge that responsibility. There is no reason to doubt that, in the present case, the jury observed the clear and emphatic warnings they were given by the trial judge and decided the case conscientiously, by reference only to the evidence and arguments they heard in court, influenced by extraneous considerations.*[339]

Milat was obviously not happy his appeal failed as he went on a further rampage, this time harming himself by swallowing razor blades and all sorts of metal objects. In 2004 he tried again, this time to the High Court of Australia seeking special leave to appeal.[340] His application was dismissed, as was a further summons and application for an inquiry into his convictions to the Supreme Court of NSW in late 2005.[341]

In the interim, earlier in 2001, he was subpoenaed to give evidence in a coronial inquest into the disappearance of three other females, who had disappeared during the period December 1978 through to April 1979. The only evidence connecting Milat was the fact he was known to be working and staying in the area at the time they vanished. Police Task Force Fenwick had initially been set up in 1998 to look at their disappearances, as well as around 20 other young people in the

339 *Regina v Milat Matter* No CCA 60438/96[1998] NSWSC 795- page 20.

340 *Milat v R* [2004] HCA 17; (2004) 205 ALR 338; (2004) 78 ALJR 672.

341 *Regina v Ivan Robert Marko Milat* [2005] NSWSC 920.- Inquiry for such an order- see section 474D of the Crimes Act 1900(NSW).

Greater Newcastle area since 1978, including victims who were subsequently determined to have been murdered.[342]

The bottom line is, the only person who knows how many murders he was actually involved in is, indeed, Milat himself, and perhaps other members of his family, in particular his siblings, who also may have some idea. In the 2001 inquest, Milat, in a fit of anger, denied any involvement in the disappearance of the three women.[343]

The State Coroner, however, was somewhat critical of police and their "handling" of the initial investigations for the three missing women. He was perplexed at why it had taken 23 years for the presumed murders to be referred for a coronial inquest. In addition, he failed to accept that police never followed up on leads and, in effect, their investigations were "shut down" within a year of the women disappearing.

In August 2001, Milat was then identified by police as the person most likely to have murdered 18-year-old Berowra schoolgirl, Michelle Pope, and her 21-year-old boyfriend, Stephen Lapthorne. They both mysteriously disappeared, as did their distinctive Bedford green van from northern Sydney in August 1978. Milat, of course, played dumb, denying he was responsible and, to this day, their bodies nor the vehicle have been found. In August 2005, a coronial inquest ruled they had both died, however, such cause and time of their deaths was undetermined.

Milat, regardless, continued on his merry way in prison

342 This also included the murder of 20-year-old expectant mother, Keren Rowland, whose remains were found in a pine plantation near Canberra in May 1971. Milat was known to travel from Liverpool to Canberra as part of his work requirements.

343 This was in respect of Leanne Goodall (December1978), Robyn Hickie and Amanda Robinson (April 1979).

harming himself, this time in January 2009, cutting off his little finger, allegedly on the basis he was going to mail it to the High Court of Australia to try for another appeal. This was followed by a hunger strike in 2011, all over him wanting a PlayStation to pass the time away, in addition to the toaster and television set he already had in his cell.

In April 2019, NSW Police set up another task force, this time called "Arapaima", to have a further look at the cold cases involving the missing three girls.[344] Police would later say they had visited Milat on at least eight separate occasions, including when he was hospitalised due to terminal cancer, but no confessions were forthcoming.[345]

The problem is we will never know the full extent of his murderous exploits. Milat "The Rat", took all his secrets to the grave, dying from oesophagus and stomach cancer at the Long Bay Correction Centre Hospital Wing on 27 October 2019. He was 74 years of age and certainly lived a lot longer than his seven known victims.

---

344 This re-investigation was not only in respect of Hickie and Robinson but included a closer look at the 1994 Newcastle kidnapping and suspected murder of 16-year-old Gordana Kotevski. The NSW Government also announced in October 2025 a new state parliamentary inquiry into unsolved murders that took place between 1965 and 2010.

345 NSW police said they put in place a number of strategies, which included different combinations of detectives and even used recorded interviews with some of his victims' families to try and elicit any confession in respect of other attacks and murders. Milat well may have also been involved in the disappearance of Italian backpacker, Anna Liva, who was last seen in Coober Pedy in South Australia in 1991. Two other missing females include Lorraine Kessy and Pauline Walter, who disappeared in Western Australia in 1977 and 1980 respectively and may well have been thanks to Milat.

32
THE GATE-CRASHER

Over time, we have seen many incidents of gate-crashers storming into a party or celebration, uninvited and unwelcome. A sensible outcome is they are asked to leave without causing any trouble, but this was not the case at a party in late March 1992 in Kinglake,[346] a quiet Victorian town approximately 55 kilometres northeast of Melbourne.

On the night of 28 March 1992, hostess, Kayleen McDonald, was mingling with her 30-35 invited guests celebrating her new home. They had been well fed, thanks to a barbeque and at about midnight, most guests were congregating around the barbecue fire in the small backyard. Sadly, they were unaware of what a 30-year-old gate crasher would do.

John William Lindrea was well known to police with a long criminal rap sheet dating back to 1978 when he was aged 16 and sentenced to a two-year term of detention in a Youth

346 The town now has a population of around 1,800 and was one of the worst affected by the 2009 Black Saturday bushfires.

Training Centre. This was thanks to three counts of burglary, other theft offences as well as escaping custody. Lindrea continued with similar criminal escapades from 1980 to 1985 but upped the ante to conspiracy to commit armed robbery at banks in Oakleigh and Williamstown, for which he would be sentenced to a term of eight years.

Following his release on parole in December 1991, after serving six years and now with about 54 convictions from nine court appearances, it didn't take long for Lindrea to, once again, make his presence known, but this time resulting in the death of two innocent party-goers.

It was evident that Lindrea regularly consumed alcoholic beverages and on 28 March 1992, he and his associate, Shane Foley, began drinking at the Kinglake National Park Hotel from the late afternoon. Unknown at the time but he was armed with a small handgun. At approximately 12:30am, the next morning, Lindrea and Foley, both under the influence of alcohol, went to the housewarming party after learning about it, despite not knowing the hostess or having received an invitation.

What transpired next defies imagination. When asked to leave by one of Kayleen McDonald's friends, Foley re-entered via the back yard with Lindrea staying next to the side gate. At that point, two males and a female friend of Kayleen's asked them again to leave, to no avail. So, two of the partygoers used minimal force to evict Foley, even stating they didn't want any further trouble.

Lindrea returned to the yard and would later say at his Supreme Court trial, he didn't know what had transpired at this point. Nonetheless, he fired a shot into the air with his pistol, which understandably resulted in many people panicking and trying to get away.

On being challenged by one of the same men, David James, who had earlier tried to assist in their eviction, Lindrea shot him at almost point-blank range. This victim didn't realise he had been shot, even though the bullet had gone through his chest. James informed Lindrea that he possessed a dummy firearm, to which Lindrea responded by indicating he would demonstrate otherwise. He fired the gun into the back yard where many people were still standing and aimed at Kayleen and her friend Andrew Johns. Lindrea only stopped when he ran out of bullets.

Lindrea and Foley quickly left the yard, which, by this time, could only be described as a devastating sight. Kayleen McDonald and Andrew Johns were dead but James would survive. The bullet had punctured his lung but his injuries were not fatal, thanks to expert medical attention. Police knew who they were looking for and quickly took both into custody, charging Lindrea with two counts of murder and one count of attempted murder.

While on remand in Pentridge Prison, some months prior to his pending trial, Lindea escaped and was on the run for two months. For this offence, he was sentenced in June 1993 in the Magistrates Court at Melbourne to two years imprisonment. On appeal to the County Court, it was reduced to a period of 18 months.

In September 1993, he was found guilty by a Supreme Court jury on two counts of murder and one of intention to cause serious injury. This was despite Lindrea pleading not guilty and arguing that his actions at the Kinglake property were carried out in lawful self-defence, trying to defend his mate. I think the jury would have thought such a defence was laughable, given his actions were voluntary and clearly accompanied by the necessary criminal intent.[347]

In addition, Crown witnesses told the jurors he kept shooting around, pointing his gun at the victims after he shot James and continued firing randomly. Regarding the wounding of James, the jury acquitted Lindrea of attempted murder as they were not satisfied that he intended to kill him but found him guilty of the lesser charge of intentionally cause serious injury.

As to the circumstances surrounding what took place, Justice McDonald summed up the offending of Lindrea succinctly when he said:

> *Knowing that you were not invited to the party and not welcome to it, you invaded the home and security of Kayleen McDonald with a gun where she and her friends were enjoying a party. You killed the hostess (and) a young man who was seeking to go to her assistance to peacefully remove Foley and you seriously injured a third who also went to the assistance of Kayleen Mc Donald when she endeavoured to have Foley leave the party. Your purposes of entering the rear yard when the hostess and other persons objected to the presence of Foley was, as I have said, to get him out, and you were prepared to use a gun to do so. The fact that you entered someone else's home and did what you did, not only deprived two people of their lives and seriously injured a third but clearly caused many innocent persons to be terror stricken, as one can readily expect.*[348]

347 Two essential elements are the guilty act known in Latin as 'actus reus' coupled with the criminal intent or guilty mind, the Latin term which is 'mens rea'.

348 *The Queen v John William Lindrea* [1993] Unreported VSC 475 , Justice McDonald, 10 September 1993- Transcript of Proceedings, page no 1540

Taking into account Lindrea's past criminal history, His Honour was mindful of his conduct in respect of robbing banks, and that he had little or no regard for anyone's safety. Justice McDonald was particularly concerned that Lindrea would use a gun at any opportunity to achieve what he wanted. It was also noted that despite Lindrea expressing a degree of remorse, when he said to his counsel he couldn't believe he was responsible, the judge agreed with the jury that such remorse was fanciful.[349]

Overall, Lindrea didn't have much going in his favour for mitigation, even the fact that, given his past record of escaping from custody, he would spend his sentence in more stricter security conditions than even his present confinement in H Division at Pentridge. As to both counts of murder, Lindrea was sentenced to 22 years and for the wounding of James, a term of seven years. In total, his head sentence was fixed at 25 years, with a minimum of 20 years before becoming eligible for parole[350].

The fact he shot dead two people and not even considering he seriously wounded another, it effectively would mean, if he was freed on parole after 20 years, he would only serve 10 years for each murder. On that basis, I think it is fair to say the sentence was lenient, although Lindrea considered it otherwise and lodged an appeal against sentence, which was, in any event, dismissed.[351]

It didn't take long for Lindrea to test his stricter security confinement, despite being transferred from Pentridge to

---

349 Ibid- page no 1545.

350 Ibid-page 1548. This sentence also took into account the 474 days he had already served on remand.

351 *The Queen v John William Lindrea* [1994] Unreported VSCA 432.

Barwon Prison, a high risk and maximum-security prison located near the township of Lara. Despite being held as a high-risk prisoner in the Acacia unit, Lindrea literally continued with his mayhem. Not only did he confront a few warders but he also attempted to escape with notorious criminal, Christopher "Badness" Binse.[352] That didn't go well as they only got as far as cutting through a high security fence from their cells and were found some hours later, hiding under building materials.

Lindrea, along with four others, would again face court in September 2000, this time accused of the prison bashing of triple murderer, Gregory Brazel, but he was acquitted.[353] After being transferred to Loddon Prison and then returned back to Barwon, he was granted parole in May of 2012 after serving just over 20 years for the Kinglake fracas.

Lindrea breached his parole in September 2013 and again, after being paroled in March 2016, he cut off his ankle bracelet. He was arrested by police six weeks later and remained in jail until December 2017. By this stage, you would think he would have learned his lesson but on 2 March 2020 he was at it again. On this occasion, carrying a double-barrel shotgun, Lindrea committed a robbery at a pub located in Westmeadows, in the northern region of Melbourne. Together, with an unnamed accomplice, they entered through the roof in the early hours of the morning and waited patiently for two hours for the tavern's

352 'Badness ' was once described by the media as Australia's 'weirdest criminal' with a history of armed robberies and shooting at police to avoid capture, for which he was sentenced to a minimum of 14 years. See *The Queen v Binse* [2014] VSC 253.

353 One of those also charged and found guilty was Mathew Johnson who would be sentenced in 2011 to the prison murder of fellow gangster, Carl Williams. See *R v Johnson* [2011] VSC 633.

assistant manager to arrive for work. She was then forced to open an ATM machine in the gaming area and also three safes.

A siege followed, with police surrounding the venue but they couldn't find Lindrea and his mate, who were secretly hiding in the walls of the complex. After police left, thinking both offenders had got away, Lindrea removed his balaclava and gloves and, as he was leaving, he inadvertently looked in the direction of a security camera. He didn't get to spend the $176,000 he had hoped to take from the venue because, in their panic, it was left behind. Police now knew who they were looking for, given that his face was captured by the security camera and his DNA was found on other items from the crime scene, including his balaclava and gloves.

Knowing the game was up, he pled guilty before Justice Lex Lasry in the County Court of Victoria. On 4 October 2021, 59-year-old Lindrea was sentenced to a total effective term of imprisonment of 11 years and six months with a minimum of eight years and nine months.

It is highly likely Lindrea will be released on parole at some point in time, but he will be in his late 60s. We wait with "bated breath" to see what Lindrea may get up to on his eventual release. Then again, perhaps this gate crasher, armed robber, double murderer and prison escapee has finally learnt a salutary lesson. One can only hope.

33
'CAPTAIN BATHTUB'

On 29 July 1992, two university students, aged 22, were looking for a tenant to share their rented premises in the eastern suburb of Burwood, Victoria. That evening, after their advertisement had been placed in the Herald Newspaper, there was a knock on the door. They quickly opened it thinking they were about to meet their new housemate but it wasn't to be.

The following morning, a mother of one of the victims went to visit her daughter but, after getting no answer to the knock on the door and obviously worried, forced her way into the house. She found the iron had not been switched off, nor had the TV and there were still unwashed dishes waiting to be done. What would be found next was her daughter Kerryn Henstridge, lying dead in a bedroom with her flatmate, Anne Smerdon, also suffering the same fate, found nearby in the hallway and naked from the waist down.

Police, on attending, would also find the brother-in-law of Anne, Peter Dempsey, who was only staying for one night, had also been shot in the head and, like the other two victims, had been bound with plastic cable ties. Each of the victims also had a towel or dressing gown placed over their heads.

The only evidence left behind was the three .22 bullet casings and the long cream plastic cable ties, used by the killer to gag and bind each of the deceased. What police didn't know at the time was the person they would be looking for, Ashley Mervyn Coulston, just happened to be about an hour's drive away, living at the Westernport Marina in Hastings.

Coulston, aged 36, had come to the attention of police in 1971 as a juvenile when he was 14 years old, after abducting two women and wanting them to drive him to Sydney. Luckily, they escaped from his clutches at a Gundagai roadhouse, resulting in Coulston being sentenced to spend three months at the Turana Youth Training Centre. During his stay, he supposedly told another detainee about his dream of abducting females, followed by raping them in a cave. Other than his short time in detention, it appeared Coulston had not been involved in any other criminal pursuits. However, he would come to the attention of the media, around early 1988, thanks to his would-be sailing adventures.

This wanna-be sailor had built his own 2.4 metre sailing vessel known as "G'Day 88" and tried to sail from Port Stephens in NSW to New Zealand. However, thanks to a cyclone, then again, it may well have been a poorly designed boat, after spending 46 days at sea, he was rescued by a passing tanker.

Many months later, what was left of his now unseaworthy vessel was washed up on the shores of New Zealand. At least the boat made it but Coulston would be dubbed "Captain Bathtub" by the media, despite being able to repair the damaged boat and sail it back to Brisbane after many months at sea, debarking in early January 1989.

However, unperturbed and obviously encouraged, he continued his sailing exploits, delivering yachts to wealthy clients and enjoying what the coastal town of Hastings in Victoria had to offer. He was residing at the marina with his girlfriend in his yacht named "Gulliver", most likely named after the satirical novel.[354]

For reasons only known to Coulston at the time, in January 1992 he purchased a .22 rifle and proceeded to cut off part of the barrel and stock. In addition, some months later, around June, he made some alterations to an oil filter and was able to fit it to the muzzle of the sawn-off rifle as a makeshift type of silencer. On the night of Wednesday 29 July 1992, after visiting his girlfriend in hospital after she had surgery, Coulston would carry out his murderous rampage.

He had collected from the marina a bag which contained the sawn-off rifle, complete with silencer, ammunition and some plastic cable ties. He needed a Melways street directory to find the advertised address of those looking for another tenant. He then carried out the three murders and left the scene. There appeared to be no motive or robbery and it could only be classified as some sort of thrill killing. The crime scene really left no clue of who was responsible as, in those days, it was before DNA and, in any event, the murderer's fingerprints were not on any police file.

Around five weeks later, on 1 September 1992, he would once again get up to his old tricks, so he thought. Armed, this time with the same kit but complemented by a knife, handcuffs and balaclava, a gloved-up Coulston, after parking

354 Gulliver's Travels written by Jonathan Swift in 1726, provides the satirical tales of Lemuel Gulliver who embarked on four voyages to fantasy type locations.

near Government House Drive not far from St Kilda Road, was on the lookout for another victim. A young married couple just happened to be walking to their vehicle near the Botanic Gardens, when Coulston pointed his rifle at them. They immediately handed over some cash, thinking that was all their assailant was after. Coulston had other ideas though and forced them both away from their car, making them lie down near a tree close by.

As he took out one of the cream-coloured plastic cable ties to first hogtie the young woman, he made a costly mistake. He placed the rifle down on the ground so he could fasten her hands behind her back. The husband saw his chance and jumped on Coulston from behind yelling at his wife to run, followed by him as they took off down St Kilda Road.

What followed next was something out of the Wild West when two-armed security guards, after being told by the petrified couple what had just happened, became involved in a gun fight with their abductor. One security guard was shot by Coulston in the hip, with another luckily escaping a bullet fired close to his head. After chasing Coulston through the Botanic Gardens with him trying to hijack a vehicle, police arrived with one officer having a gun pointed at her head by Coulston. Thanks to the heroic efforts of one of the security guards, he was able to disarm him by side-kicking Coulston in the head. He was now in custody and taken back to St Kilda police station for questioning.

As far as police were concerned, Coulston had some explaining to do over the attempted armed robbery and what followed, before he was placed in handcuffs. Coulston stuck to the story that it was all a robbery on the spur of the moment, which all went wrong and he only planned it on the way to see his partner, who worked at the National Gallery. During the police interview, a rather laid back Coulston also said he had purchased the rifle when last in Devonport, Tasmania in August 1992. He said it was because he needed it to shoot sharks when sailing, having a fear of them.

He tried to explain the silencer which he said he just put together with an oil filter and then cut a thread on the barrel, so he could attach it and use in any robbery. As to the plastic ties, they were bought by him, at least 12 months prior, as they were used all the time on boats.

What arresting police were quick to ascertain though was, after a forensic firearms and tool examiner tested the bullets from the sawn-off rifle, lo and behold, they matched those removed from two of the deceased Burwood victims. The bullet removed from the third victim though, was too badly damaged so it could not be compared. Further, one of plastic cable ties used in the attempted St Kilda Road abduction, was identical to those used at the Burwood murders.

A close examination of his gun and one of the dressing gowns, recovered from the head of a victim, found both contained a high velocity blood splatter. The splatter on the dressing gown was consistent with the blood stains on the rifle oil filter, with it being fired at close range giving off the source of the splatter. In addition, it was noted there was no gunshot residue on the material used to cover each of the victim's heads, which was further evidence that a silencer had been employed.

What it did show on the material though, was evidence of propellant grain patterns, which was overall totally consistent with those produced by the same sawn-off rifle, after it was tested by being fired at extremely close range. When all this incriminating evidence was put to Coulston, regarding the

Burwood murders of 29 July 1992, he simply answered, 'No comment' to each question put to him. His chances of getting bail were zero and he would be remanded in custody. However, some days later on 4 September 1992, Coulston requested a further interview with homicide detectives.

In the presence of his lawyer, he now gave a version of events surrounding the sawn-off rifle. Coulston said he was approached around 20 to 24 July 1992, by a person well known in the sailing fraternity, asking if he could borrow his rifle. Part of the deal was for Coulston to shorten the barrel and he would be paid $250. He then did what he was asked and told the lender, when he was finished with the now sawn-off rifle, to place it back in Coulston's car boot and he said he gave him a car key so he could do that. Some days later after 29 July 1992, he observed that it had in fact been returned. Police interviewed the person named, who was adamant he did not even know Coulston, let alone be involved in some sort of sinister and mysterious borrowing of a rifle.

In early September 1993, Coulston appeared before a jury in the Supreme Court of Victoria charged with a total of 14 counts, which included three counts of murder and two of armed robbery.[355] Coulston chose to remain silent, which was his right, as it was not for him to prove his innocence. That onus remained solely with the Crown to prove him guilty. He also called no evidence but, alas for him, after a 15-day hearing he was found guilty on 12 counts, which included the three Burwood murders.

355 Coulston was also charged with two of false imprisonment, two of recklessly endangering life, one of intentionally cause injury, one of assault, one of using a firearm to prevent arrest.

Justice Teague, on sentencing Coulston to three life terms with a non-parole period of 30 years, said:

As to the events in St Kilda Road, you were co-operative. As to the events at Burwood, you have, for the most part, exercised your right to remain silent. To the extent that you have chosen to speak of matters relevant to the Burwood events, I consider that the verdict of the jury reflected their assessment that you lied.[356]

As to motive and the horrendous nature of the crimes, His Honour said further:

It is not possible for me to provide any reasonably satisfactory explanation for your having acted as you did…a specialist… examined you and that the examination revealed that you are of normal intelligence, and that there is no evidence of psychological disturbance or personality disorder…The crimes for which I sentence you are unfathomable. They are also chilling, because they were so calculating, so suggestive of cold blood planning, so indiscriminate.[357]

Justice Teague certainly had some sympathy for, not only the families of the three victims, but those who suffered at the hands of Coulston saying further:

At Burwood, you snuffed out the lives of three people in their prime. Untroubled by number, you showed an extraordinary contempt for human life…The seasons of life left to you will

356 *The Queen v Ashley Mervyn Coulston* [1993], VSC 21 September 1993-page 7.

357 Ibid.

scarce allow for more feats of fame or notoriety. But you have made for the beloved of the three you killed, an enduring winter. And for the three, there are no more seasons.[358]

For "Captain Bathtub", as he was led away from the dock in handcuffs, there would be no more sailing the high seas but, then again, maybe he thought different. His lawyers ran an appeal against conviction in the Supreme Court Appeal Division, based on the grounds that Justice Teague erred in allowing the Crown to rely on what took place at St Kilda Road as "similar fact evidence".[359] They submitted that such similar fact evidence should not have been allowed, in support of its case for the three counts of murder.

Such evidence was the murder weapon and plastic ties, similar to those found at the Burwood crime scene and used in the St Kilda Road incident. It was their firm contention that the attempted armed robbery, by the use of the murder weapon, forcing the couple to lie face down on the ground at gunpoint and, although the plastic cable ties were identical to those used at Burwood, all up, could not in any way be characterised as evidence of similar facts.

It is interesting that similar fact evidence has not been without some controversy and is largely not admissible at trial. This issue, time and time again, has raised its ugly head and is somewhat limited in its admissibility as evidence.[360] The Crown,

358 Ibid-page 8.

359 This is evidence of past misconduct to demonstrate a nexus to the current alleged criminal act.

360 In *Pfennig v R* (1995) HCA 127 ALR 99, the High Court of Australia again reviewed similar fact evidence admissibility, however, there still remained a dilemma in respect of its practical application.

of course, was faced with the choice to either have a joint trial, thereby facing a risk of prejudice to Coulston, or two separate trials, one for the Burwood murders and one for the St Kilda Road events. The Crown chose a joint trial, notwithstanding at the appeal, it conceded such joint trial did result in a risk of prejudice to Coulston, albeit in their counsel's view it did not result in a miscarriage of justice.[361]

Their Honours did not agree, finding that most of the evidence for the events at St Kilda Road were wrongly admitted in respect of the three counts of murder against Coulston and were only relevant to the remaining eleven counts. What should only have been led as evidence from the St Kilda Road criminal events, was that which was plainly relevant to the Burwood murders and nothing else.

It followed:

> *We remain of the view that there was a miscarriage and that such miscarriage could effectively be avoided only by the severance of the counts. The miscarriage was not avoided by the directions given to the jury about the use of the St Kilda Road incident. The appeal must be allowed. The convictions on counts 1,2 and 3 must be set aside and a new trial had in respect of them.*[362]

361 From the outset, Counsel for Coulston in his first trial, made an application for two separate trials, which was refused. The Court does have a discretion to order severance if in the interests of justice. See further in that regard - *Sutton v The Queen* [1984] HCA 5; (1984) 152 CLR 528.

362 *R v Ashley Mervyn Coulston* [1995] VSC 97; [1995] Vic SC 97 (12 April 1995). The Appeal judges did affirm the remaining convictions in respect of the St Kilda Road counts, which was the effective sentence of Justice Teague of four and a half years, which was later increased on appeal to seven years.

At this point, perhaps Coulston might be thinking he may be able to once again enjoy his "Captain Bathtub" moniker by getting out of jail in due course, if found not guilty of the Burwood murders. Wishful thinking on his part because, in a second trial in September 1995, he was again found guilty by a jury. Coulston had the opportunity to give sworn evidence for any possible alibi about his movements on the night of the triple murders. He could also explain how he came into possession of the rifle, noting at one point, he blamed it on the alleged sailing colleague. However, Coulston again chose to remain mute and, in that regard, Judge O'Bryan said:

> *...for the second time you stood mute. You were not prepared to give sworn evidence as to your movements on the evening the murders were committed, nor as to your possession of the murder weapon. I infer you remained mute out of fear of self-incrimination.* [363]

His Honour was also somewhat scathing that Coulston chose the right not to incriminate himself, when he said further:

> *...In my opinion, the time has arrived when a trial judge should be empowered to comment to the jury upon the failure of an accused to give evidence on oath...A jury should not be left to speculate in the jury room why the accused stood mute...* [364]

---

363 *R v Coulston, Ashley Mervyn* [1995] Vic SC 493(11 September 1995)-page 2.

364 Ibid. Section 41 of the *Juries Directions Act 2015*(Vic) now provides that when an accused has chosen not to give evidence, defence counsel may request the judge to provide a direction to the jury about the right to silence and such choice cannot be considered as an admission of the accused.

Regardless, it didn't matter, as Coulston was sentenced to three consecutive life sentences, without parole. In that respect, His Honour said:

> *Your motivation is obscure but the evidence points most obviously to robbery and sexual gratification as your motives.*[365] *You know that for these murders, life sentences will be imposed. No less a sentence would be appropriate...In my opinion, you have forfeited forever your entitlement to live outside the confines of a prison. I am of the opinion that you should never be released... The fixing of a non-parole period is mandatory unless the nature of the offence or the past history of the offending make the fixing of such a period inappropriate. In my opinion, the wicked nature of these offences alone empowers this court not to fix a non-parole period in this case... Taking into account the wicked nature of these crimes and the absence of remorse of any kind on your part, I shall not fix a non-parole period.*[366]

While Coulston wiles away time in prison waiting for his release, which will only take place when he is buried in probably a pauper's grave, it does beg the question though, was he involved in other crimes? It is hard to accept that after the abduction of the two young women in 1971, he waited another 21 years before he would carry out more chilling crimes. What is of interest is when he was released from the Turana Youth Training Centre in Melbourne, his family moved to Kyogle in

365 Ibid- page 1. Motive is not an element in order to prove murder- must only be proven beyond reasonable doubt the accused, with intent, killed the victim.

366 Ibid- page 3.

Northern New South Wales around 1979, situated inland from Byron Bay.

A series of brutal rapes and armed robberies ending in a murder would then take place from around mid-December 1979 to February 1980 on the Gold Coast and nearby at Tweed Heads, with the unknown offender becoming known as the "Balaclava Rapist". This lone young offender, wearing a balaclava and armed with a rifle, usually riding a motorcycle, would find couples embracing in a typical, quiet type of lover's lane location. After tying up the male and making him watch what was about to happen, he then raped the female with one victim even being left in a car boot.

All up, there were three rapes and two armed robberies but worse was to follow. In the early hours of 2 February 1980, after leaving the Twin Towns Services Club in Tweed Heads, a couple were about to collect their vehicle from a park nearby, when the armed rapist struck. The 29-year-old woman managed to escape after her boyfriend grabbed the gun but, sadly, he was shot dead.

Not for one moment am I saying it was Captain Bathtub, alias perhaps the Balaclava Rapist, but Coulston just happened to still be living around this time at the family farm in Kyogle, only 100 kilometres away, or about a one-hour drive. There was also a suggestion he had, in fact, moved closer to Tweed Heads. The other telling factor is, not long after this murder, Coulston moved to Sutherland, a southern suburb of Sydney and about 30 kilometres from the CBD. This is also about a nine-hour drive south from Tweed Heads but, thereafter, the Balaclava Rapist was no more to be seen.

Five years later though, in 1985 in this sleepy town, a very similar type of crime suddenly reared its ugly head, once again with the culprit wearing a balaclava and carrying a sawn-off rifle. There were at least five vicious attacks on women and couples, with the females being raped. This time, the culprit was awarded the moniker of the "Sutherland Rapist". Following his yachting expeditions and, after being terminated from his employment, allegedly for stealing from his employer, Coulston then moved to Hastings in Victoria around 1989.

Once again, the only connection to Coulston possibly being the Sutherland Rapist was the similar modus operandi, in the commission of the offending, similar to his attempted St Kilda Road abduction, three years later in September 1992. Again, coincidentally, the Sutherland Rapist exploits suddenly came to an end when Coulston moved interstate back to Victoria.

In 2000, Coulston, who had now served eight years at Barwon Prison, was the subject of a court order to force him to provide to police a DNA sample. At this point, he was considered to be a number one suspect for the Balaclava rapes, the murder and also the Sutherland crimes. However, for reasons never explained, it was not uploaded to the National DNA database. The next issue was that the male shot dead in Tweed Heads had blood samples taken from his fingernails, believed to be linked to his person responsible. However, this potential crime scene evidence, which could have led to the identity of his attacker, was lost by local police.

It couldn't get much worse but it did. One of the police investigators, since retired, later revealed that he removed from the Coulston property in Kyogle, two bullets to be compared to those retrieved from the body of the Tweed Head victim. The jury is still out in that regard as, when examined by a police firearms examiner, the verdict was he was "unsure" and said it needed to be examined further and perhaps under a scanning electron microscope.[367] The only problem was, no such closer examination was believed to have ever been carried out. It goes without saying that the balaclava rapes and murder in Queensland and the Sutherland rapes in Sydney, to this day, remain unsolved.

As for Coulston, he is not likely to put his hand up and confirm that he was indeed responsible for these unsolved crimes. Justice O'Bryan was on the money when he said Coulston gained some sort of sexual gratification, tying up and killing his three Burwood victims. This was reinforced in February 2005, when pictures of a fully-clothed woman being beaten were found on Coulston's computer in his cell.

Despite only losing 14 days of privileges, the now 68-year-old is on the short list of Australia's worst of the worst, spending his days in Barwon Prison, alongside the likes of other mass murderer psychopaths, such as Raymond "Mr Stinky" Edmunds, Paul Haigh and Peter Dupas.[368] He, like his cell mates, will never be released.

---

367 Such type of microscope provides detailed surface structure images enhancing their clarity and perspective.

368 Serial killer Dupas is currently serving three life sentences without parole for two murders that took place in Melbourne in 1997 and one in 1999.

34
ANOTHER WORST OF THE WORST

A mass murderer who was also destined to die behind bars, aged 76, was Malcolm George Baker. In October 1992, Baker, not only killed his former partner but, in a fit of rage which lasted over an hour, his son and four other innocents, including a heavily pregnant woman, became his victims. What was difficult to comprehend, let alone understand at what took place, was the then 45-year-old motor mechanic had no previous record of violence, so what triggered his murderous rampage?

Baker's early life saw him educated, along with his two sisters, in Penrith, NSW and an expert report, later tendered in court, suggested their upbringing was marred by fits of anger and violence from their war veteran father. A constant state of anxiety would prevail over their young lives, witnessing frequent beatings of their mother, with Baker even being subjected to whippings from his father using a "cat-o-nine tails". His mother also didn't escape criticism, as Baker suggested she never showed any love towards her children and even broke his nose on one occasion, albeit accidentally, by throwing a can at him.

He was well aware of the effect of guns as, at the young age of seven, his father threatened to shoot the family after lining them up in the back yard of their Penrith home. On another occasion, he also fired off a shot which just missed his mother's head. All this obviously became a bit too much for Baker as he left home in 1964, aged 17, relocating to Terrigal on the NSW Central Coast.

Although he had left school some two years earlier, he was still able to obtain employment, eventually becoming qualified as a motor mechanic and even obtained a qualification as a panel beater. He was quite industrious, even renting out caravans he had purchased, to anyone who was in need.

Baker certainly wasn't lonely, fathering nine children, thanks to a number of relationships but he was also known to police. His first conviction was in August 1968 for theft and by 1980, he had a racked up a total of eight convictions, which included theft of a motor vehicle, larceny and traffic offences. It must be noted though, he had no convictions for any sort of assault or other violent acts. Overall, he was seen by others, including his close friends and children, as a person you could rely on in times of need. So, what went wrong, leading to the horrible events on the evening of 27 October 1992?

In the weeks prior to his murderous rampage, Baker, now unemployed due to a back injury, was also subject to a domestic violence intervention order (DVIO) taken out by his 23-year-old ex-partner, Kerryann Gannan. They had previously lived together for seven years but around late September 1992, they separated. Baker obviously not happy with the separation, then allegedly assaulted Kerry, inflicting on her a black eye, so she was left with no choice but to seek the intervention order. It certainly wasn't an amicable spit, with Baker blaming her friends and relatives that he believed had, in some way, influenced her to separate from him.

He also alleged, in a meeting with his doctor, that he formed the view one of his sons, David Baker, was in an intimate relationship with Kerryann and most likely supplied her with drugs. Although he expressed untold hatred for all those connected with Kerry, his doctor only saw it as anger and frustration. It was noted that, although he had been prescribed anti-depressant medication, he had stopped taking it at least two weeks prior to his murderous rampage.

On the night of 27 October 1992, he decided to pay Kerryann a visit at her Terrigal apartment. After first visiting her and covertly hearing a conversation she was having with a 22-year-old family friend, by the name of Christopher Gall, he then returned armed with a fully loaded sawn-off 12-gauge shotgun and an ammunition belt.

Although a condition of the DVIO was that he hand over to police all firearms in his possession, somehow, he retained the shotgun after his weapons permit had been revoked. Police had seized, what they believed to be, all his weapons. This was even though it was a known fact on the permit, he had a total of six weapons in his possession.

Around 9.12pm, the first to be shot and badly wounded but would survive was Gall, with the shotgun pellets hitting the right side of his face. Baker then shot Kerry dead and, as he moved through the apartment, he located her father,

Thomas Gannan, who had been visiting his two daughters. After a short struggle, no doubt in an attempt to disarm him, Baker shot Thomas twice and he would later be found dead in the driveway nearby. The heavily pregnant 18-year-old Lisa Gannan, who shared the premises with her sister, Kerryann, was also shot dead and later efforts to save her unborn child sadly failed.

At this point, Baker had killed three of the Gannans but his anger had not waived and next in line would be one of his children, 27-year-old David Baker. When his father arrived at his home in Bateau Bay, a 10-minute drive from Terrigal, this happily married young man, with a month-old baby, was shot dead, with his body later found in the back yard.

Baker then proceeded to the North Wyong home of Ross Smith, who he had some business dispute with, albeit two years earlier. On entering the premises, Baker found him soaking in a bath, which would soon turn red with blood after he was shot dead. The other innocent victim who would also lose his life was Smith's house mate, Leslie Reid. He unfortunately happened to be home at the time and later died in hospital.

Baker would then go to his friend's home but he was not his next victim. After a lengthy discussion, with Baker telling him about his murderous exploits, his friend convinced the murderer he had to hand himself in at the closest police station.

During an interview later that night with homicide detectives, Baker went into some detail of what was behind the six murders. Apparently, when he first attended Kerryann's home, he believed he could hear a conservation about sex she was having with Gall. In a fit of rage, he then said:

'I just seen red. I just shouldn't have gone around there and done what I did.'

Regarding the murder of his son, he also believed he was having an affair with Kerryann. With Smith and like his other defenceless unsuspecting innocent victims, Baker said he went up to them, including one person he didn't know, being Reid and, without saying anything, shot them all dead at close range.

On 6 August 1993, Baker appeared before Supreme Court Justice Newman for sentencing, after pleading guilty to six counts of murder and one of attempted murder. His Honour was presented with two psychiatric reports, which confirmed that Baker committed the crimes in a tempestuous rage. It could only be described as a psychiatric state. It was, however, somewhat surprising both expert reports determined Baker could not be considered, in the future, any sort of danger to the community, noting he still had the support of his close family and friends.

In other words, the experts had come to the conclusion his psychotic state, at the time was only temporary and the events that led to the horrific murders, were only a short blight at the time to his mental state.

His Honour had little sympathy for Baker and had the discretion to sentence him to life without parole. In describing the callous murders in the worst type of category as a 'vengeful and bloody odyssey', Justice Newman said:

It is a necessary part of the sentencing exercise for the judge to form an appreciation of the gravity of the particular crime viewed as part of a spectrum of offences of murder of which it can be postulated that some are so serious as to fall within the category of the worst type of case and thus attract a life sentence.[369]

Baker would appeal his life sentence all the way to the High Court of Australia, on the contentious argument that he did not pose a risk to society. If he was to be released, after serving a lengthy non-parole period, that also meant his prospects of rehabilitation had indeed improved. However, their Honours, in taking into account the gravity of the crimes and the expectations of the public, far outweighed any consideration to a lesser sentence.

In that respect, in dismissing the application for special leave to appeal, Justice Mc Hugh stated:

Law and order is such a powerful, political tool these days because there is a public perception that courts are out of touch with what the public or what the community standards require…on any view in this case, supposing you gave this man 15 years. He is not insane; he could not even qualify for a defence of diminished responsibility. What would the community think of a sentence of 15 years to 18 years for six murders in those circumstances? It would be an outrage and that is what the Chief Justice, in this

369 *R v Malcolm George Baker* [1993] Unreported, Supreme Court of NSW, Newman J, 6 August 1993. It was interesting that almost two weeks after Baker was sentenced to penal servitude for life, Judge Newman, in the case of a 20-year-old rapist and murderer, only imposed a maximum of 24 years with a non-parole period of 20 years based solely on the young age of the offender. See *R v Malcolm James Hungerford* [1993] Unreported, Supreme Court of NSW, Newman J, 17 August 1993.

particular case, took the view that this was a proper case for a life sentence. [370]

From all reports, serving his life sentence was not easy, with Baker being medicated from time to time and transferred to different prisons, including both Long Bay and Silverwater Correctional Complex. In addition, given the nature of his crimes, he was frequently physically abused by other prisoners and also had his ribs fractured as a result of one assault. In 2006, his status was upgraded and he was transferred to the High Risk Management Unit at the Goulburn Correctional Centre in 2009. There were also many times when he was hospitalised under community treatment orders, due to his fluctuating mental health condition.

I don't think anyone would have much sympathy for this callous murderer who committed one of the worst massacres in the history of Australia. The community would certainly have untold empathy for the families of his victims, in particular, the mother of the two Gannan sisters. She, understandably, struggled after losing her much loved husband, daughters and unborn grandson, spending over three years both drug addicted and homeless.

At the time of his sentencing in 1993, Baker was given the privilege of sitting behind a screen in court, so he wouldn't have to look at any of the victims' family. This would have been very distressing but, to her credit, and thanks to counselling and the support of her two sons and grandchildren, this grieving mother was able to eventually remove herself from what was, understandably, a very dark place.

370 *Baker v The Queen* S139/1995[1996] HCA Trans 346(9 September 1996).

As for Baker, he also received the privilege of prison visits from some of his children and grandchildren but that ended when he passed away in prison palliative care on 22 June 2024.

35
THE TOMAHAWK BEAST

On Monday, 22 February 1993, Queensland resident, Evalyn Clow, received a telephone call from her brother. He advised Evalyn he had just heard over their local radio that a woman and her three children had been found murdered in Greenough, a country town about 400 kilometres from Perth, Western Australia. As the age of the murdered woman was the same as her sister, Karen McKenzie, who also lived in Greenough and was the mother of three children, Mrs Clow righty became concerned. She then tried calling Karen but the phone either rang out or would be engaged.

Back in those days, mobile phones and online up-to-date news was not yet available so she had to wait, fearing the worst. Her concerns were realised when, after watching a news bulletin that evening, which still had not revealed the names of the victims, there was a knock on her door. Local police had the unenviable task of confirming what she already knew in her mind. The victims were her sister and much-loved nephew and two nieces.

Greenough police had been advised earlier that day, by a friend of the family, of the body of 16-year-old Daniel McKenzie he found lying dead in the yard of the home. On attending, police would be confronted with an horrific scene, also finding the mother deceased on a mattress in the lounge. On moving upstairs, her two youngest children, Amara, who was seven and Katrina, being the youngest at five years old, had also been murdered.

It was obvious that the four victims had all been bludgeoned to death with some sort of axe. The two young girls had been sexually penetrated, with one found with an implement inserted in her vagina. It was also apparent their mother had also been sexually abused. Such was the horrendous scene that even very experienced homicide detectives vomited, with others later leaving the squad as the memories of what they had witnessed just became too much.

The crime scene would, however, eventually lead to the identity of the perpetrator, first with the discovery of a substance on an interior door, later identified as Sorbolene cream. Whilst that was of some interest, hidden behind it was a partial palm print. The door was subsequently removed for closer examination and investigators in the interim started to focus their enquiries on a number of persons known to the McKenzie family.

One, in particular, was 22-year-old William Patrick Mitchell, a local farmhand who was known for his drug abuse after experiencing an unhappy childhood. Mitchell was one of six brothers and sisters and was a recluse living in poverty, especially after his mother passed away when he was only 11. He had no friends and always went straight home after school. He mixed with local druggies but little did anyone know at the time, what sort of inhumane beast he would turn into.

Some five weeks later, on being questioned by police, he first denied any knowledge of the ghastly crime. After attempting to harm himself and finishing up in hospital, he finally admitted he was responsible for the four murders. The fact that his fingerprint matched the print from the interior door, left him with little choice. Mitchell detailed to detectives what had taken place, first on the afternoon of 21 February 1993, in which he consumed copious amounts of alcohol and drugs, including injecting himself with amphetamine.

According to his version of events, in the early hours of 22 February 1993 and totally under the weather, he drove out to the McKenzie household. He was happily met by the young lad, David, who knew him as an acquaintance of his mother. What David didn't know was Mitchell was carrying a tomahawk and he was fatally struck a number of times. Mitchell them moved into the home where, after sexually assaulting Karen, he then struck her several times, again molesting her as she lay dead.

Not satisfied with killing two innocent people, Mitchell then moved upstairs and located the two sleeping young girls in separate bedrooms. He caused terrible injuries to Amara, which was later described by the sentencing judge as to 'almost defy description.' After striking her with the axe, he then also murdered her younger sister, while she lay asleep in her bed.

On 8 September1993, Mitchell pleaded guilty to four counts of wilful murder,[371] three counts of indecently interfering with a dead body by sexual penetration and a further count of sexual penetration of a child under 13 years.[372]

---

371 *Criminal Code Compilation Act 1913* (WA) – section 282.

372 Mitchell also pleaded guilty to unrelated charges of stealing and armed robbery with threats of actual violence, which took place in early November 1991.

Supreme Court Justice Owen sentenced Mitchell to strict security life imprisonment on the wilful murder counts and varying concurrent prison terms on the remaining charges. His Honour determined that Mitchell went to the house with the sole intention of committing murder. Although under the influence of drugs, he carried out a totally meaningless, motiveless and mystifying set of horrendous crimes that had no boundaries.

His Honour was also mindful to comment that in respect of the murders of the victims, they were totally innocent and defenceless and had been subjected to 'sexual activity of the most depraved kind.' In his own words, Justice Owen then said, 'as far as I am concerned you will never be released…'[373]

On that basis, you would think the learned judge would make an order for Mitchell to spend the rest of his life in prison and not be eligible for parole.[374] However, Justice Owen declined to make such an order, given that Mitchell was under the influence of drugs and there was a possibility of his future rehabilitation. This would then become a rather drawn-out legal fight, all the way to the High Court of Australia.

In the first instance, the Crown appealed such a refusal, in that the sentencing judge erred on the penalty imposed which was, in effect, manifestly inadequate and in part:

> *… (2) failed to reflect community abhorrence of crimes of this type and proper public concerns as to the respondent (Mitchell)*

---

373 *The Queen v William Patrick Mitchell* [1993] unreported, Supreme Court of Western Australia, Justice Owen, 7 October 1993.

374 Such an order was available to be made courtesy of section 40D(2a) of the *Offenders Community Corrections Act 1963*(WA).

ultimately being released.'. (5) failed to reflect the need for general deterrence in cases of extreme severity...[375]

The Court of Criminal Appeal had no hesitation in allowing the appeal, albeit on a 2-1 judgment with one judge dissenting, that Mitchell not be eligible for parole. However, the High Court of Australia had other ideas and, in fact, found the Court of Criminal Appeal erred in displacing the initial decision of Justice Owen and allowed Mitchell the right to apply for parole, with an earliest possible release date in 2013.[376] This meant this murderer of four innocent victims could apply for parole after serving a measly 20 years.

It's fair to say the Australian public were absolutely horrified that, somehow, Mitchell may well be able to walk free, after serving only 20 years. This punished him, if he was granted parole, a measly five years for each of the four murders. Total dissent at such an appalling decision was made even more confronting in 2010.

It then became known he had been downgraded in his prison classification and was now deemed a medium security prisoner. The fact he had been transferred from Casuarina

---

375 *The Queen and William Patrick Mitchell*, Supreme Court of Western Australia, The Full Court -Court of Criminal Appeal, CCA No 191 of 1993- 29 April 1995- pages 5 & 6.

376 *Mitchell v R* [1996] HCA 45; (1996) 184 CLR 333; (1996) 134 ALR 449; (1996) 70 ALJR 313 (5 March 1996).

Prison to Bunbury Regional Prison beggars belief.[377] Thanks to an online petition, the parole application by Mitchell in 2013 failed[378] but he applied again in 2016.

This time, another online petition of over 18,000 signatures opposing any consideration for release, was brought to the attention of the State Parole Board and the WA Government. The letter penned by Karen's sister, Evalyn, was extremely sad and gut wrenching. In opposition to any consideration of release for Mitchell, she said to the Parole Board:

> *... I continually think of what sort of life my nieces would have had. They were very happy little girls who adored their mum and brother. They had beautiful smiles and had the innocence of life stolen from them in the most barbaric way. I cannot ever forget the way in which they died. Children are so defenceless and pure of heart, I do not understand how anyone with any sense of right or wrong could do what was done to them. My nephew, Danny, was a real rascal but he had a heart of gold. He would never have let his mum or sisters get hurt if he could help it... he would have fought with all his might to protect his family...Karen went through many difficult times and had to fight hard to achieve what she had in life until Mitchell cut her*

377 Casuarina Prison is the main WA male maximum security prison and has a special unit for intensive, high security supervision of offenders. On the other hand, Bunbury prisoners are allowed to assist with local community projects and one of its other main features is its market garden, which supplies the majority of fresh vegetables for consumption by prisoners throughout WA's prisons.

378 Mitchell appeared before the WA Prisoners Review Board which made a recommendation to the Attorney General that any consideration to parole should be rejected.

life short…She was the best sister, always looking out for me… it kills me to know that I wasn't there to protect her and her family when she needed me most…

Mitchell would be denied parole in 2016 and the three-year rule for further consideration for parole was amended to every six years in 2018. In November 2024, the WA Attorney-General again determined that Mitchell would be one of the three serial killers who would now not be considered for parole until 2030.[379]

If Evalyn has anything to do with it, Mitchell will never be released. It's best left to her to have the final say, after she visited this despicable killer in jail in 2010:

Mitchell knows what I think. I told him as long as I've got breath left in my body, I'm going to do everything I can to keep him inside.

379 WA Attorney-General John Quigley signed ministerial orders directing the Prisoners Review Board to further suspend parole consideration relating to Mitchell, Catherine Birnie and Peter Maloney, the latter being responsible for two murders in the late 1970s.

36
FRANKSTON SERIAL MURDERER

In the early hours of Saturday, 31 July 1993, I was working night shift when we were patrolling schools in the Frankston area, a seaside suburb about 40kms from Melbourne.[380] Apart from a vast number of police units also in the same location, the streets of Frankston and surrounding areas were unusually quiet after another spate of murders and attacks on women. Frankston had now become widely known as the suburb where a serial murderer lurked, looking for his next victim. Police had left no stone unturned trying to identify the culprit, all to no avail.

The first murder had occurred when the partially clothed body of 18-year-old Elizabeth Stevens was found in Lloyd Park situated in Langwarrin, not far from Frankston. Her throat had

380 In 1974, I was appointed as Head of School Security for the Victorian Education Department.

been slashed and a criss-cross pattern carved into her chest down to her abdomen. After leaving the library at Frankston TAFE on 11 June 1993, where she was a VCE student, Ms Stevens boarded a bus to take her to an intersection near Langwarrin, where she lived close by with relatives. She was last seen alighting from the bus and walking to her residence, with the family expecting her home by 8pm.

Two hours later, her concerned uncle notified local police after being unable to locate his niece. At about 5pm on 12 June 1993, a local resident discovered her body lying in a drain, partially covered by tree branches. Apart from the knife patterns on her chest, neck and face, a post-mortem also revealed she had been strangled to death by forced compression. At the time, the only clue they had was the finding of her school bags, books and a knife, which was possibly connected to the murder. Police suspected she was either a victim of a random killer or it was an attempted rape gone horribly wrong.

Around 5.50pm on 8 July 1993, a 41-year-old woman, after leaving Seaford Railway Station and walking along an adjacent road, was attacked. Carrying what appeared to be a homemade aluminium knife and a wooden imitation firearm, a male in his early 20s grabbed her and tried to drag her by the hair into a reserve toilet block. As she screamed and struggled, trying to escape from his clutches, she then bit him, so he let her go.

Producing a firearm, the assailant yelled words to the effect, 'I will blow your head off.' Somehow this brave woman escaped from him on two separate occasions, finally by hailing down a passing motorist. She was minus her shoes and wore torn clothing. Police now had a description of the male: he had a round face with large blue eyes and was about 180 cm in height.

Approximately one hour later the same evening, after leaving her vehicle unlocked, Deborah Fream attended at her local Seaford milk bar to purchase some milk. This 22–year-old mother left her 12-day old son at home with a friend who then called her boyfriend when she failed to return home. Police were notified around 8pm that evening and would subsequently locate her unlocked car on a nearby nature strip the following day. On finding blood inside the vehicle, which was later determined to be from the missing mother, witnesses also came forward to report the same car driving all over the place with the driver flashing its lights.

Four days later, on 12 July 1993, Deborah's body was located under tree branches in a bush track at nearby Carrum Downs. Similar injuries had caused her death from strangulation but this time by a cord and there were stab wounds to her neck, upper chest and abdomen. It was noted in the post-mortem that Ms Fream had obviously tried to fight off her attacker, with a number of defensive wounds found on her hands. What would later prove of some interest and then a connection to another murder, was a witness told police about a yellow Toyota Corona which had been observed near where her body was found.

At this point, police now had two unsolved murders and one attempted abduction to investigate and, despite extensive enquiries, were no closer to finding who was responsible. Under "Operation Reassurance", led by Detective Chief Inspector Peter O'Halloran, homicide detectives met on the early afternoon of 30 July 1993 to plan another extensive doorknock the following day.

At around the same time, 17-year-old Natalie Russell, a John Paul College schoolgirl, was quietly heading home after the day's lessons, along Skye Road, Frankston. Her usual way to get home more quickly was to walk along a bicycle track adjacent to the Peninsula and Long Island Golf Clubs.

Sadly, Natalie would not make it home that day. After being reported missing, police would find her body later that evening with horrendous injuries. These included, what appeared to be, stomp injuries on her back, with her head almost severed after her throat had been cut. Another knife wound started at the temple and continued down to the left side of her face. The crime scene examination also found three holes cut in the fence, which separated the two golf clubs.

Like the other two murders, the post-mortem confirmed this defenceless young girl had not been sexually assaulted by her assailant. This time, her killer had left behind damning evidence. On her body was a skin slither stuck by dried blood, which was not Natalie's. Police had no doubt it belonged to the killer who had most likely cut a finger in the vicious attack.

Police would now receive the breakthrough they were desperately looking for. About two hours before Natalie's school day finished, an alert postal worker observed a young male holding binoculars sitting in a yellow Toyota Corona, in close vicinity to the bicycle track near Skye Road. He appeared to slump down when he realised he'd been noticed. Her concerns were reported to local police, who later dispatched their afternoon patrol shift to check on the vehicle. When they arrived, the vehicle was empty but they logged its registration label details, as the vehicle had no number plates.

Unknown to them as they were leaving, the owner of the vehicle was walking back towards his car. On seeing the police divisional van, he put his bloodied hands inside his jumper and walked to his Seaford unit, which he shared with his girlfriend. It was only a short distance from Skye Road.

The following morning, a police vehicle registration plate number check revealed the owner of the suspicious vehicle was 21-year-old, Paul Charles Denyer. He was one of six children of English parents who migrated to Australia in 1965. When they eventually settled in Victoria in 1981, they started to experience problems with him when he was only 10 years old. He was their third child and attended Northvale Primary School in Mulgrave.

Denyer had put on weight and was finding it difficult to settle in at his new school. His attraction to knives became apparent when after practising on his sister's teddy bears, he slashed the throat of the family cat. This time, he used his brother's pocketknife. Denyer followed this up by killing a friend's cats by disembowelling them and then showing off his handiwork.

Three years later at the age of 13, he received a police caution for stealing a motor vehicle, followed by making a false report of wilful damage and theft. This was followed by again coming to the attention of police at the age of 15 years, when he forced a fellow student to masturbate in front of their classmates.

Denyer, now with the nickname of "John Candy", named after the Hollywood actor, thanks to his height and physical presence,[381] had moved into a flat with his then girlfriend in Frankston-Dandenong Road in 1992. He tried different jobs, all to no avail and by 1993, was unemployed. By this stage, his fascination with knives and daggers had increased, almost to the point of not only being totally obsessed with his collection but also the subject of macabre deaths.[382]

381 Candy was a well-known Hollywood actor who struggled with his weight and, at one stage, weighed in excess of 125 kg.

382 It was later found that Denyer had an obsession with watching horror movies such as The Stepfather, Fear and Halloween.

After confirming the owner of the yellow Toyota Corona, Homicide detectives were now ready to pay Denyer a visit. They became even more interested when their computer scan revealed that a similar-coloured Toyota vehicle was logged as being seen in the vicinity of where the remains of Debbie Fream were located. A knock on his unit door late on the afternoon of Saturday, 31 July 1993, found him not at home, so a card was left requesting he make contact with police. Later, being advised by his girlfriend that Denyer was at home, homicide detectives attended at the unit. He certainly was there, drying his runners on a bar heater.

Denyer was very cooperative and could even provide an exact timeline alibi of his movements regarding the enquiries being made. He even explained his vehicle had no number plates due to repairs and, in any event, he had a 28-day permit so he could still drive it. Detectives noticed Denyer had scratches on his hands in a number of places, so they pressed him for more details regarding his so-called alibi.

At this point, Denyer would elaborate further, confirming that, yes, he was in the vicinity of two of the murders. One explanation was, his vehicle had broken down in a location which happened to be in the vicinity of the Natalie Russell murder. As for Deborah Fream, once again, he was nearby but he used the excuse of waiting to pick up his girlfriend at the train station. With the hand scratches, that was supposedly thanks to an electric fan when he was carrying out repairs on his vehicle. Seasoned detectives, Mick Hughes and Charlie Bezzina, were in no doubt they had their man, so he was placed in the back of a police vehicle and driven to Frankston Police Station. Denyer, meanwhile, kept up his façade and was very courteous and certainly cooperative.

After being given his rights, police commenced a lengthy video record of interview. Denyer ultimately confessed but only when faced with the overwhelming evidence and when asked to provide a blood and hair sample for DNA matching with exhibits from each of the victims.

His short and blunt response was, 'Okay, I killed all three of them.'

Around 4am on the morning of 1 August 1993, Denyer provided extensive details of the three murders and the attempted abduction. Even hardened police officers were shocked with what he had done.

In the first murder, Elizabeth Stevens, Denyer said he saw her alight from the bus and instantly thought she would be his victim. He said he had a pocketknife which was tied to his right ankle by an elastic band. He was also armed with an imitation firearm, which was hidden in the front of his trousers. When this young, innocent girl turned into a street, he grabbed her from behind with his hand over her mouth. Denyer then placed the imitation gun against her head, saying if she screamed, she would be shot dead. After walking down the street, with his victim holding his hand, under the pretext they were a couple, he then viciously attacked her in a secluded bush area in a local park.

Denyer then said he literally throttled her and, when she fell to the ground, he stabbed her in the neck with enough force to snap the knife. He said, somewhat nonchalantly, that Elizabeth somehow regained her balance but he managed to hold her down and by placing his foot on her neck, she stopped breathing. Knowing she was dead, he slashed her chest and abdomen leaving a criss–cross pattern.

After Denyer dragged the body for about 30 metres, he

placed broken tree branches to conceal her remains, which he left in a drain. Denyer, in a joking manner, said on the one hand, he was not only angry with himself but also happy, which then turned to some sort of sadness. Denyer finally walked home, disposed of the broken knife and tucked into his evening meal with his girlfriend and her mother.

With his next victim on 8 July 1993, he again admitted he had gone to the area hoping to find someone he could attack. Denyer said he observed a woman walking away from the Seaford Railway Station. Armed with a homemade aluminium knife, a black cord and his favourite imitation firearm, he stealthily came up behind her and placed his left hand over her mouth. This victim courageously fought back on two occasions and, after seeing her flag down a passing motorist, Denyer said he took off into a nearby reserve. When questioned further by detectives, he admitted his intention was to drag her into the park and kill her.

After not satisfying his lust for murder, an hour later he saw Deborah Fream walking into her local milk bar. He noticed she had alighted from her vehicle and not locked it, so he climbed into the back seat and crouched down. The unsuspecting Deborah then returned to her vehicle and started to head home but Denyer had other ideas. On becoming aware of someone in the rear seat, after doing a U-turn, Denyer stated she must have panicked and the car crashed into a brick wall. He then told police he said to her 'Shut up or will blow your head off.'

Denyer then gave her explicit instructions of where to drive, repeating his threats not to try and alert anyone or he would 'decorate the car with your brains.' Unbeknown to Denyer though, the understandably panicked victim started flashing the car lights in desperation and even swerved at one stage onto the wrong side of the road. All this was to no avail. After driving to an area in Taylor's Road, Carrum Downs, which Denyer said to police he was familiar with, she was told to get out of the vehicle.

Denyer went into explicit detail of how he first walked behind Deborah with the imitation firearm pressed against her back. On reaching some scrub, he placed a black cord around her neck and continued to strangle her until she passed out. After falling onto the ground, Denyer took out the aluminium homemade knife and, by kneeling on top of her in order to pin her knees, then stabbed the defenceless woman a number of times in the neck and upper chest area. Denyer, in a somewhat casual manner, said his victim started breathing out of her neck, just like his first victim did.

He stated he was impressed with the way Deborah started to fight back, leaving several wounds on her hands, as she desperately tried to defend herself against the savage assault. He said to detectives, 'I could just hear bubbling noises' after stabbing her repeatedly.

On being asked what happened next, he said he still wasn't satisfied even after she was obviously dead. He then lifted the top she was wearing and, after ostensibly looking at her breasts, Denyer plunged the knife into her, in his words, "guts". Following his normal pattern, he dragged the body into a bushy tree area and tried to conceal the bloodied remains by placing tree branches over it.

Denyer admitted he became concerned he had left behind crucial evidence, in particular, the weapons of choice he had previously dropped after killing Deborah. He said he spent five minutes looking for them and when he found both the knife and imitation firearm, he drove her vehicle to Madden Street in Frankston and parked it on a nature strip. Not to be outdone, so he thought, he took off his jumper and used it to wipe down and remove any fingerprints he may have left on the steering wheel, handbrake and door handles.

After walking home, he said he washed the homemade knife to remove any blood, took off some insulation tape that was wrapped around the handle and hid it in various parts of his unit. As far as he was concerned, nothing had happened. He made a call to his girlfriend at work, then drove to Kananook Railway Station to pick her up.

He then detailed how, the following morning, he went back to Debbie Fream's motor vehicle and helped himself to the items she had purchased the night before at the milk bar. Now concerned that if they were found in his possession, it might connect him to the murder, he decided to dispose of them, other than a $20 note which he found in her purse. He burnt everything else, including her driver's licence and credit cards and buried what was left at a bike track at the nearby golf course. This location would be the subject of his third and final murder.

By this stage, he had been interrogated for over 12 hours and what he was about to detail in the murder of Natalie Russell, was even more confronting for the experienced detectives. Denyer said he knew the bicycle track which runs between the Peninsula and Long Island Gold Clubs extremely well. In particular, he was aware it was used as a way home by many schoolgirls living close by.

As far as he was concerned, it was a perfect scenario to carry out another vicious attack on any young woman who happened to be walking by. In the early morning of 30 July

1993, he cut three holes with a pair of pliers, each some distance apart in the cyclone fence between the golf clubs. According to Denyer, these holes would be big enough for him to climb through, as well as force any chosen victim.

Around 2.30pm, while waiting in his vehicle parked in Skye Road, he saw Natalie carrying her school bag. Knowing she would be his next murder victim, he climbed through one of the holes and hid in the bushes. After Natalie walked past, he followed her along the grass edge so she would not hear him. He then quickly ran up behind her, placed his hand over her mouth and pressed a knife against her throat. Denyer stated that he dragged her back through one of the holes he had cut and forcibly took her to a secluded area, near one of the golf courses.

Taunting her by running the knife up and down close to her eyes, he forced her to the ground. According to Denyer, the petrified young girl, obviously fearing for her life, offered him money and even to have sex with him. This deviate then said he was so disgusted by her last offer that he cut the side of her face. At the same time, he cut his own finger showing it to detectives who noted a piece of skin was missing on the thumb. With Natalie now screaming, he threatened to kill her unless she kept quiet. Using the leather strap from a pair of binoculars he was carrying, he placed it around her throat. After pushing her head back, Denyer proceeded to cut her throat.

Not satisfied with just the throat wound, he demonstrated to detectives how he did this but what he would then say was horrifying:

> Denyer: I cut a small cut at first and then she was bleeding. And then I stuck my fingers into her throat… grabbed her cords and I twisted them.

Detective O'Loughlin: Why'd you do that?
Denyer: My whole fingers…like, that much of my hand was inside her throat.
Detective O'Loughlin: Do you know why you did that?
Denyer: Stop her from breathing…and then she slowly stopped. She sort of started to faint and then, when she was weak, a bit weaker, I grabbed the opportunity of throwing her back and one large, big cut, sort of almost cut her head off…and then she slowly died.
Detective O'Loughlin: Why did you kill her?
Denyer: Just same reason as before, just everything came back through my mind again. I kicked her before I left.

Denyer stated, he walked back towards his vehicle with his hands covered in blood and concealed in his pockets but he saw two police officers looking over his car. He immediately turned back the other way and walked home. After washing all the blood off his clothes and throwing the murder weapon in the backyard rubbish bin, he resumed his normal life. After later collecting his vehicle and again washing his clothes, just to ensure there was definitely no blood on them, he went to dinner at his girlfriend's mother's home.

Prior to the conclusion of the record of interview, Denyer also confessed to breaking into a neighbour's unit in February 1993, where he cut the throats of two kittens. Denyer had also left a threatening note stating he would murder the female occupant by cutting her throat if he ever got the opportunity. It's fair to say, homicide detectives were really at a loss at his murderous rampage, other than he was a sociopath just waiting for the right opportunity. However, Detective O'Loughlin again put the motive question to him:

Detective O'Loughlin: Can you explain why we have women victims?
Denyer: I just hate them; I just hate them.
Detective O'Loughlin: Those particular girls, or women in general?
Denyer: General.

On 20 December 1993, Denyer appeared before His Honour Justice Vincent[383] after waiving a committal hearing, pleading guilty to three counts of murder and the attempted abduction. The only explanation of his behaviour was put by one expert witness, psychiatrist Ian Joblin. In his considered opinion, Denyer suffered from what was loosely described as a sadistic personality disorder. Joblin stated that Denyer was narcissistic and obtained immense satisfaction and gratification from not only humiliating his victims but by their mutilation leading to death.

There were submissions made by counsel for Denyer that he had been subjected to some sort of sexual abuse as a young lad by a family member. However, it was noted by Justice Vincent that Denyer had not shown any sort of remorse. If anything, the only regret Denyer had was that he was now before the court and about to face the consequences for his brutal crimes.

Denyer, at the young age of 21 years, was sentenced to three

383 Justice Frank Vincent was appointed as judge of the Supreme Court in April 1985. I had the pleasure of listening to him in 1994 when he was a guest lecturer at La Trobe University. As a soon-to-be lawyer, I was impressed with his laid-back manner and certainly his knowledge of the law. Judge Vincent then sat on the Court of Criminal Appeal from 2001 and was also a Chancellor of Victoria University. He retired in August 2009 and in 2012 was appointed as a commissioner with the Victorian Law Reform Commission.

terms of life imprisonment and for the attempted abduction, eight years. All sentences were to be served concurrently, which resulted in an effective sentence of life in prison as Justice Vincent then rightly considered that it was not appropriate to fix any sort of non-parole period. As to the gravity of the crimes committed by Denyer, the learned judge said:

> *...when looking at the seriousness of your conduct, is the fact that you took the lives of three young women about whom you knew nothing and for whose lives you cared nothing. They were selected simply by reason of their availability as suitable prey. Their lives did not possess any value in your eyes but they certainly do in the sight of a society before whose Bar of Justice you must now stand.*[384]

His Honour would also go on to say:

> *... it must not be forgotten that you harboured thoughts of killing since you were about 14 years of age. Rather than reject them, or seek assistance in relation to them, you nurtured them and fed them. Since the age of 17 years, you have been stalking women as, apparently, you waited for the time to arrive at which you felt strong enough to embark upon violent attacks.*[385]

You would like to think that Denyer would be taken from the court in handcuffs, never to be heard of again. Unfortunately, that was not the case. With no comfort to the families and

---

384 *The Queen v Paul Charles Denyer* [1993], Supreme Court of Victoria Criminal Jurisdiction. Transcript of Proceedings, Justice Vincent, 20 December 1993–page 90.

385 Ibid- page 95.

loved ones of his victims, he wanted to say something from the dock. He stated:

> *...look, I'm sorry truly for what I've done and my true feelings have not been expressed in this court. With, with God with me now, well, you know, I expect you to think that, but I'm truly sorry for what has happened, and I will do my sentence, and I will become a better person and I will not re-offend. That's my promise to God as well as to the people of Melbourne. Thank you.*[386]

Now with God obviously on his side, the next we would hear from Denyer was his appeal to the Full Court of the Supreme Court, against the severity of his sentence in not imposing a non-parole period. In essence, it was based on whether Judge Vincent erred in forming the view that the nature of the offending by Denyer and his past history, meant there was never any prospect of rehabilitation. Given that, he should then remain incarcerated for life without a minimum term.[387]

This appeal was successful with the Full Court, ordering a non-parole period of 30 years, much to the dismay of the community.[388] The Crown, quite rightly, appealed this decision to the High Court of Australia, but the appeal failed, meaning

386 Ibid- page 98-99.

387 Section 11 of the *Sentencing Act 1991*(Vic) provides that a court must fix a non-parole period unless it considers the nature of the offence, or the offender's past history, determines it inappropriate to set such a period.

388 *R v Denyer* [1995] 1 VR 186, 24 June 1994. This non-parole period was the equal highest ever imposed at the time in a Victorian Court, the other being in respect of Ashley Coulston.

Denyer could be considered eligible for parole in 2023. The Court accepted the submissions of his counsel, when, in part, he put forward that the Full Court in a majority were correct in that:

> *...there is nothing in the past history of the offender, he had no relevant prior convictions... and because he was of young age and because although the murders were heinous...that was recognised by all the judges...but what the majority decided, in exercising their discretion which they are entitled to...found the sentencing judge's discretion erred...they believed a non-parole period should be set.*[389]

Denyer would still stay in the public spotlight as he was considered a suspect in the 1990 disappearance of Sarah MacDiarmid, after blood stains were found beside her vehicle parked at the Kananook Railway Station at Seaford. He vehemently denied any involvement. Denyer was also eliminated in 2011 as a suspect in the murder of Michele Brown, who disappeared from near the Frankston Railway Station on her 25th birthday on 1 March 1992. Her body was found two weeks later in a shed at the back of a gun shop in Playne Street, Frankston.

In prison, Denyer, now wanting to be known as "Paula", began to dress as a woman with long hair. In April 2012, he was accused of four rapes involving inmates believed to have intellectual disabilities. While waiting to see if his transition would result in sex reassignment surgery, he was also known to have befriended fellow cell mate and murderer, Robert Arthur

389 *The Queen v Denyer* M77/1994 [1995] HCA Trans 83, (17 March 1995)-page 9.

Selby Lowe. It was rejected, so Denyer then eventually reverted to simply being known as Paul.

In May 2023, Victoria's Parole Board rejected his bid for release after he completed the 30-year sentence. In late 2023, a bill was passed by the Victorian State Government to amend legislation by imposing stringent conditions in which a parole board may only release Denyer. Such conditions included: an imminent danger of dying or seriously incapacitated and that he can demonstrate he does not pose any risk to the community.[390]

Hopefully, this low life will never be released.

390 *Corrections Amendment (Parole Reform) Act 2023*(Vic) No 36 of 2023. In order to succeed in any application, Denyer would have to demonstrate he was suffering a terminal illness, was bedridden and that death was imminent. Any decision is ultimately a recommendation to the governor by the Victorian Premier that it should be granted.

37
A GUN FANATIC

The question of gun control in Australia was starting to become an issue in the early 1990s and it would certainly rear its ugly head, following the Port Arthur massacre in April 1996.[391] Three years earlier in August 1993, John Paul Lascano, perhaps disillusioned with the laws surrounding the issuing of a pistol licence to him, took it upon himself to bring his obsession with guns to fruition.

In 1987, at the age of 18, Lascano and his family came to Australia from the Philippines. For all intents and purposes, he had a normal well-educated upbringing and, after completing year 10, he gained employment with a motor company in Port Melbourne, Victoria. By this time, he had two obsessions

391 On 28 and 29 April 1996, Martin John Bryant shot and killed 35 people and injured another 23 in what became known as the Port Arthur massacre in Tasmania. He is currently serving multiple life sentences without any possibility of parole. As a consequence, the Australian Government introduced firearms restrictions on all types of firearms- (see chapter 51).

which were guns and drugs. His initial large quantity drug use of Valium perhaps accelerated his absolute fascination with firearms, in particular, high-powered guns.

By 1992, due to his continued absence from his workplace, most likely due to his substance abuse, he lost his job. This heavy misuse of drugs and other substances, which now also included injecting himself with heroin and consuming large quantities of alcohol, would lead his medical practitioners to become concerned about his mental state. However, at the same time, he was still able to function with a relatively normal lifestyle, especially when trying to satisfy his obsession with guns.

Lascano would spend every available opportunity collecting and reading all types of material and any paraphernalia he could get his hands on, about different types of high-powered guns. He became somewhat of an expert about the characteristics of guns and ammunition and, at this point, he desperately wanted to obtain his own weapons, complete with applicable ammunition.

He obtained a shooter's permit, enabling him to purchase weapons collectively referred to as "long arms".[392] On obtaining the required permit, he attended a gun shop, known as Taylor's Firearms, in Springvale, Victoria and purchased a Winchester shotgun. He would become reasonably well known to its owner, Richard Taylor, visiting his outlet on several occasions.

Around the same time in late 1992, Lascano, in keeping with his passion, joined the Antique and Historical Arms Collectors Guild of Victoria. This guild was established in 1963, the main aim to provide private collectors the means to

392 This is generally a category of a weapon with a long barrel and designed to be held by two hands. Contrast that to a handgun (pistol), which can be fired using only one hand.

enjoy their passion of all types of antique guns. As a member, Lascano would be eligible, under certain conditions, to also secure a pistol collector's licence after the expiration of a six-month period. He would also become very well known to the guild's treasurer.

However, his level of frustration to meet his obsession with handguns, was not helped by a pre-requisite. In order to obtain such a collector's licence, you also had to have a pistol safe for the weapon. Given Lascano was unemployed, he simply couldn't afford one.

Lascano joined a pistol club with a view to obtaining a pistol licence, which differs from a collector's licence. This would allow the holder of such licence to use pistols, other than just possess them as a collector. Regarding pistol ammunition, for some reason it was not covered in any firearms legislation and it could be purchased unrestricted on the production of a shooter's licence.

On Wednesday, 18 August 1993, with Lascano becoming increasingly frustrated in his attempts to fulfill his pistol passion, he attended the Springvale Gun Shop to pay a deposit on a .22 rifle. He also had with him a shopping list, which included a Smith & Wesson 9 mm Parabellum semi-automatic pistol. On the morning of 21 August 1993, Lascano again attended Taylors with a loaded magazine for use in the same type of pistol, which he was able to previously purchase such magazine without any restrictions.

He would be observed by another customer examining the Smith & Wesson, which did not have a magazine and was unloaded after it had been handed to him by its owner, Richard Taylor. Little did he know, Lascano was equipped with an unloaded magazine which he was about to insert into the pistol undetected, once it was removed from its carboard box. It would later be revealed that Lascano had gone to the Springvale Gun Shop, following a substantial amount of planning and preparation, with the sole intention of stealing a quantity of handguns.

It was apparent that around midday on 21 August 1993, Lascano saw his opportunity and shot dead three people, which included Taylor, his 14-year-old daughter, together with a friend, Kevin Simpkins. He then chose several firearms and ammunition from a vast range on display to take with him. After loading the goods into his car, which was parked outside the gun shop, he returned and set fire to the premises to destroy any evidence, including a history of his transactions.

He returned to his flat around 2pm that afternoon where he lived with his girlfriend. The following evening, the triple murders were on the evening television news bulletin and, of all things, the extensive coverage included a sketch of a male seen leaving the gun shop. Remarkably, this drawing looked very similar to Lascano, which was observed by his girlfriend, who would later be a Crown witness.

Despite Lascano setting fire to the shop, the bodies were not burnt to a degree that prevented an autopsy from determining the cause of death. Each had been shot more than once. The bullets removed from each of the deceased were 9mm Parabellum from a Smith & Wesson 9mm semi-automatic pistol. These types of bullets were difficult to purchase, so homicide detectives quickly ascertained that a gun shop in in Elgin Street, Carlton, was one of a very select few dealers that sold this ammunition. On examining their shop records, lo and behold, Lascano had indeed visited the dealer on a few occasions in 1993, the last on 7 August, only two weeks before the murders. He was there to purchase the 9mm Parabellum fully jacketed fatal ammunition.

Thanks also to number of witnesses, they were able to place Lascano at, or very near, the Springvale gun shop on the day of the shootings and subsequent fire. Police knew who they were looking for and, three days later on 24 August 1993, he was taken into custody wearing two concealed, unloaded firearms. A subsequent search of the vehicle he was driving when arrested also contained a further 10 unloaded firearms belonging to the Taylor's Springvale Gun Shop. On the front passenger seat, they found the murder weapon, together with its Parabellum magazine. A further search of his East Kew flat and his parents' residence, would also reveal a number of other guns belonging to the same outlet.

On speaking with his girlfriend, who would later give the same evidence in court, she said on the morning of the murders, Lascano said he was going to the supermarket and other shops. When he returned some four hours later, he went straight to their bedroom and closed the door. The following night, on seeing a sketch on television of the suspect, she told him it looked remarkably like him. He agreed, then held his head in his hands.

With Lascano on remand for charges of murder, arson and theft, further enquiries would also ascertain that Lascano had visited a few other gun shops, with one in particular of some interest. On visiting a dealer in Surrey Hills a week before the murders, he loaded a 9mm Smith and Wesson pistol, which the dealer quickly took back from him. Lascano apologised and said all he was doing was testing to see if the 9mm bullet would fit. Their evidence and that of the guild treasurer, who also had an incident with Lascano when he tried to steal a 7.65 mm

Beretta pistol, would paint an overall picture, leaving no doubt in the minds of prosecutors, Lascano was guilty as charged.

In a subsequent jury trial in the Supreme Court of Victoria before Justice Frank Vincent, despite the overwhelming incriminating evidence, Lascano pleaded not guilty to the four main charges but guilty to theft. What Lascano didn't know was, during his period on remand, he shared a prison cell with a well-known crook who would later turn Crown witness. He told the jury Lascano had said when Paul Taylor was distracted, he slipped the loaded magazine from his pocket into the gun that had been placed in a bag. The friend of the owner then came out from the rear of the shop, so Lascano shot him dead with a bullet to his forehead.

Taylor was next, shot three times in the chest, followed by his daughter who, on hearing all the noise, came out to see what was going on. Tragically, she knew what was about to happen and, according to Lascano, she yelled out, 'I love you, Dad,' before she was shot in the chest.

Just for good measure, Lascano would shoot them all again, to make sure they were dead. Justice Vincent, after hearing the evidence from Lascano's cell mate, appropriately warned the jury about accepting such evidence but, at the same time, said Crown witness had no reason to lie.

After the Crown had finished their evidence before the jury from a number of witnesses, Lascano had his turn. I think it's fair to say his version of events defies imagination, even bordering on ludicrous. He agreed he had visited Taylor's Gun Shop on a few occasions, even examining the murder weapon days earlier on 18 August 1993. Furthermore, he did attend the gun shop on 21 August 1993 to allegedly pay $20 off a rifle lay-by and, as he was about to enter, he observed a person wearing jeans walking out and carrying what appeared to be a pistol case.

He stated, after finding the three dead bodies, he had some sort of "brain snap", which makes it even more pathetic. After checking for any pulse of Taylor, who was obviously dead, Lascano decided to take several guns with him, one which happened to be the murder weapon. Lascano said he was carrying a green bag and, on seeing a gun display open with the Smith & Wesson pistol lying on top, he put that gun in his pocket. After being disturbed by two males who had approached the shop, Lascano told them to leave. He admitted to then setting a fire but it was an accident as he only meant to burn his lay-by papers, in order to cover up the theft. As to his inconsistencies in the police record of interview, that was due to consuming too much Valium.

It was no surprise the jury rejected his "story telling", finding him guilty on all three counts. Lascano, now aged 25, appeared before Judge Vincent on 7 December 1994 for sentencing. His Honour accepted that Lascano, who had no prior convictions, had an increasing level of psychological agitation and mental disturbance, with a degree of low self-esteem. Substance abuse was also a mitigating factor. It was obvious he had a fascination with guns but, taking all factors into account, including his potential rehabilitation, this did not in any way alter the principles in which he must be sentenced.[393]

Regarding Lascano's offence, Justice Vincent stated:

> *The actions in which you engaged were...the product of a substantial measure of planning and preparation. I am satisfied that you anticipated the necessity, if you were to avoid detection,*

393 See sentencing guidelines–*Sentencing Act 1991* (Vic)–section 5.

of shooting, at least, the gun shop proprietor, who would have been in a position to identify you. I am also satisfied that the decision to kill other persons, if they were present or when you found them to be present, constituted no difficulty for you.[394]

The learned judge, after hearing a plea for leniency, sentenced Lascano to life imprisonment on each of the three murder charges, three years on the one count of arson and 12 months for theft. Although the total effective sentence was life imprisonment, a non-parole period of 27 years was fixed, taking into account a total of 473 days for pre-sentence detention. This meant, if Lascano behaved himself, he could be released on parole around late 2019 to early 2020.

In 1995, Lascano lodged a notice of application for leave to appeal against conviction and sentence. The appeal was based on Justice Vincent allowing certain evidence to be admitted, which included Lascano previously visiting gun shops and the purchase of the 9mm murder ammunition. The evidence from his cell mate was not a point of contention in the appeal. In order to be successful, Lascano would have to demonstrate, in all the circumstances, it was not open to Justice Vincent to allow the evidence and then impose the sentence he did.

However, the Supreme Court of Victoria Court of Appeal on 7 December 1995 dismissed the application and, in that regard, said further:

...We are of opinion that these crimes were so horrendous in their nature and execution that, notwithstanding the mitigating factors put forward by the applicant, it was open

394 *The Queen v John Paul Lascano* [1994] Supreme Court of Victoria, Justice Vincent-Transcript of Proceedings- page 5.

to the sentencing judge to impose life sentences. So far as the murder of Mr Taylor, at least, is concerned, there is the further exacerbating factor of premeditation. As to the non-parole period, upon any view a very lengthy term was called for and it was so conceded by the counsel for the applicant. We are not of the view that the period of 27 years lay beyond the permissible range.[395]

So, what has happened to Lascano? There has been nothing heard of him since and, for all we know, he may well be back in the community behaving himself.

We can only hope.

---

395 *The Queen v John Paul Lascano* [1994] No 308/1994, Supreme Court of Victoria, Court of Appeal-7 December 1995-page 16.

38
VALENTINE'S DAY MURDERS

Valentine's Day on 14 February of each year is a celebration, albeit somewhat a commercial one, about romance and love. Sadly, two women, Kerrie Pang and Fatma Ozanol, were unable to celebrate it as they would both be shot dead. For Kerrie, she would never be able to spend a romantic evening with, who she thought was, the love of her life, as the murder was, in fact, carried out on the instructions of her de facto partner, Mark Lewis.

It appeared to some they had a loving relationship of three to four years before her murder. They also had a 15-month-old son and lived together in a rented house in the NSW suburb of Cherrybrook. Kerrie also had four other sons from previous relationships but, as events would later reveal, Lewis was not a happy man. According to statements he subsequently made to police, including a record of interview the following morning after the double murder, Kerrie was working at her business premises in Gladesville, NSW at approximately 5.30pm on Valentine's Day, 1994.

Her business was renowned for being a well-known "relaxation centre", known as "Kerrie's Oasis". Unfortunately, her employee, Fatma, was also working but not expecting the day to be any different to her usual duties. Lewis said he was at his own business address in West Ryde, which also happened to be a massage parlour, a 10-minute drive away from Gladesville. Lewis telephoned her at approximately 6.15pm and said he was not feeling well, purportedly requesting that she pick him up and drive him home to their residence.

On Kerrie's arrival around 6.50pm, Lewis changed his story, telling Kerrie he had received a telephone threat from an unknown person, purportedly saying he was going to kill her. They reported the death threat to police and on the way back to Kerrie's Oasis, both driving separate vehicles, they stopped at a shop to purchase some bread and other items. On arrival at Kerrie's work at approximately 7.20pm, Lewis would tell police he walked Kerrie to the front door and, after she safely entered the premises, he left to drive back to West Ryde in his white Tarago van.

Lewis also mentioned a bag containing a .22 rifle which was taken from the boot of his car. Kerrie, according to his version of events, wanted to take the rifle inside to the premises but Lewis was against that idea and placed it back in the boot, before driving off around 8pm. Lewis then said he closed his business premises about 9pm and drove back to Kerrie's Oasis, purportedly to pick her up and go home. On arrival, he was shocked to find the building had been set on fire. He said he was told by police that Kerrie was dead and he had collapsed in shock, allegedly suffering a heart attack and had to be taken to hospital.

Regarding the events that had transpired prior, police were advised by a neighbour at about 7.15pm, she heard a single gunshot coming from Kerrie's Oasis. Smoke was then seen coming from the premises, with firefighters and police arriving at 7.42pm.

They would find the bodies of both Kerrie and Fatma and a subsequent post-mortem revealed Lewis' deceased partner she had been shot a number of times and also stabbed. Whilst the timing of events was firmly established from Kerrie's telephone and mobile phone communication, Lewis was not quite truthful, leaving out a lot of the facts of exactly what took place.

Lewis, for a start, omitted to tell police his relationship with Kerrie was not a happy one. Several Crown witnesses at his subsequent trial for murder, would give evidence that it was marred by jealousy and many arguments. One other witness also stated she had been told by Kerrie, just days prior to her murder, it was all over with Lewis and she wanted him to pay $500 a week for the care of their child. Lewis was also known to be dissatisfied with her line of work. However, another witness painted a different picture in that Kerrie loved Lewis, despite all his faults and he was not a violent man.

So, what really happened on 14 February 1994?

Lewis had, in fact, engaged the services of an acquaintance by the name of Lindsey Robert Rose, to kill Kerrie and would pay him the sum of $20,000. Rose was known to Kerrie, with even some suggestion, for reasons unknown, he disliked her immensely. Given that Kerrie knew Rose and would recognise him, he enlisted the services of Ronald Waters and was to pay him $500 to assist in gaining entry to Kerrie's massage parlour.

Rose had a rather interesting background, born on 2 May

1955, with the surname of Lehman and brought up initially in North Sydney. His mother would leave his father and remarry, so he changed his surname. After moving to the Western Suburbs of Sydney, he finished a fitter and turner apprenticeship before joining the NSW Ambulance Service in 1976 where he met his wife. During his short ambulance career as a paramedic, Rose was, in fact, one of the first responders at the Granville rail disaster in 1977.[396]

In 1979, he decided to become a private investigator but his life would spiral into a life of crime. At one point and with a young daughter, his wife divorced Rose, seeing him as a changed man, particularly after he savagely assaulted her. What would further take place beggars belief as, prior to Rose carrying out the contract murder for Lewis, he obviously had a passion for this type of crime.

It would take, however, many years before he was sentenced for his horrific crimes but his first foray into murder occurred in January 1984. On this occasion, he shot and killed a couple in their home in Sydney's Hoxton Park. As he would later admit to investigators, this was a revenge killing of the male victim, supposedly over him beating up a friend of his. The partner of the male, sadly, just happened to be a witness of what took place, so he also shot her dead.

Investigators at the time had absolutely no idea who carried out the killings and it was the same with a further murder in 1987. This time, Rose forcibly entered a house in West Ryde belonging to a wealthy businessman, with the

396 On 18 January 1977, a crowded commuter train derailed and crashed into an overhead bridge, which then collapsed onto two of the train's passenger carriages. It became the worst rail disaster in the history of Australia with a total of 84 victims dying and 213 injured.

intention of carrying out a burglary. On being observed by his partner, she was stabbed using a screwdriver and vegetable knife. He hogtied her to a chair and escaped but his victim would later die from her injuries.

For want of a better expression, his next "claim to fame", this time in company with Waters and one other person, notably Lewis, was the Kerrie's Oasis double Valetine's Day murders. It would be the evidence of Waters in November 1999 at the subsequent trial of Lewis, that would result in a conviction and life sentence. But before turning to the trial admissions of Waters, it's fair to say, in 1996, Lewis would have been rather worried he was about to be implicated in the murder of his de facto partner and her employee.

Rose, at this point, had not been identified as a suspect in any of the five murders. However, he told an acquaintance, who knew a corrupt police officer, about some of the murders, thanks to inducements. Rose only told him about the first two murders but that was enough for his so-called mate to inform his NSW police colleagues. Detectives interviewed Rose and, on making no admissions at this point he was released. However, on 4 July 1996 he was placed under covert police surveillance.

It was obvious he became a wanted man, so he relocated to Adelaide and used his birth surname of Lehman to find employment. It would, however, only be a matter of time and, after his mug shot was widely displayed on evening news bulletins, he was taken into custody by South Australian Police on 9 April 1997. Now, for reasons only known to Rose, he readily admitted to the five murders and it wouldn't be long before both Waters and Lewis were taken into custody, no doubt, thanks to Rose giving them up. The latter two were charged with the Valentine's Day double murders and remanded in custody.

Rose pleaded guilty on 18 June 1998 to not only those two murders but also the other three he had readily admitted to. On 3 September 1998 and represented by the famed Stuart Littlemore QC, Rose would be sentenced to five consecutive life terms of imprisonment, without the possibility of parole.[397]

The severity of his sentence would be a point of contention and subject of an appeal to the Court of Criminal Appeal. The issue was that Rose should have been given a discount on his sentence in view of his cooperation with police and a plea of guilty, notwithstanding the hideous murders were clearly in a worst-case category. This was, in fact, conceded by his counsel but, at the same time, they said Rose should be entitled to 'see the light at the end of the tunnel.'

The Court of Criminal Appeal were having none of that and on 11 October 1999, dismissed the appeal against sentence. Indeed, the learned justices referred to what His Honour stated when he had sentenced Rose to the five terms:

> *...when one totals up, as it were, the crimes, the criminality, the career of breaches against the criminal law to which the so-called confessions and admissions were made by this prisoner and weighs against their individual and overall utility, the objective and horrific seriousness of the five killings to which he has pleaded guilty, one cannot come to any other view than that to allow a reduction by reason of this so-called assistance to authorities and promises of co-operation, would produce*

397 Some three months later, in December 1998, Rose would be sentenced for other crimes he had confessed to, including conspiracy to pervert the course of justice, robbery, kidnapping, armed robbery and malicious wounding. The sentence was 39 years all up, not that it made any difference to his five consecutive life sentences.

a sentence unreasonably disproportionate to the nature and circumstances of the five murders with which this sentencing procedure is concerned.[398]

The Court of Criminal Appeal further acknowledged and accepted again the trial judge's reasoning, in which he said further, on sentencing:

The prisoner has indicated no contrition or remorse; he had admitted to the violent murder of five people, murders of revenge and gangland style and of opportunity...There is simply no warrant or leniency in this case even taking into account the burden of custody under protection and the "positive" advanced for him- assistance to authorities- if given the weight sought, would result in a sentence disproportionate to the criminality.[399]

The only one left to cooperate with authorities was Waters, as it was readily apparent there was nothing to be gained further from an uncooperative Rose, for a reduction in sentence. Waters was certainly going to turn Crown witness against Lewis as, after being charged with the two 1994 Valentines Day murders, they were withdrawn.

On 7 May 1999, Waters pleaded guilty to the lesser charge of two counts of being an accessory after the fact to the murders and was only sentenced to 18 months imprisonment, to be served concurrently.[400] His sentence was downgraded further, in view of his cooperation with police, so his custodial sentence

398 *R v Rose* [1999] NSWCCA 32–page 2.

399 Ibid- page 2-3.

400 The maximum penalty for committing such as offence is 25 years imprisonment. *Crimes Act 1900*(NSW)- section 349.

could be served periodically, normally between a Friday and Sunday evening.[401]

In early November 1999, Lewis appeared in the Supreme Court of NSW before a jury pleading not guilty to two counts of murder. The trial would last 14 days and the jury, no doubt, listened intensely to the evidence of Waters, as he described what transpired on that fateful day. He stated he was in attendance with Rose and the part he was to play was to knock on the door of the parlour, to gain entry. For this, he was to be paid a measly $500 and, as it turned out in any event, he never received payment.

Waters said, around 6.30pm he drove with Rose to the premises and, after knocking on the door, it was answered by a person he knew to be Fatma Ozanol. After he was let in, Rose stormed in, armed with a pistol. When told Kerrie was out with Lewis, ostensibly at a doctor's appointment, they waited inside, keeping a look out for them.

A man, in company with Kerrie, arrived shortly after and, as they were walking towards the building, Rose shot Fatma in the head. When Kerrie walked in, she saw Rose armed with a pistol. He told her she would be killed as well. A male came in, armed with a .22 rifle and was disarmed by Waters, with Rose saying, 'Leave him alone as he is paying for this.'

Kerrie, in a panic, fought with Rose over the pistol, which was fitted with a silencer. The male, supposedly unknown to Waters, yelled out, 'Hurry up and get it done,' or words to that effect.

The last thing Waters saw was Rose running after Kerrie

401 Periodic detention was introduced in NSW in 1971 but was replaced by non-custodial sentences in 2010, such as intensive corrections orders.

and when he came back, told them to get out as the building was on fire. Waters said they quickly ran outside and he was told to leave the door open so the premises would burn more quickly. He saw the other man place the rifle in a bag, with Rose telling him to drive home.

At no stage did Waters say in his evidence that the male person was, in fact, Lewis, as it appeared he had no idea who he was. At first glance, the only possible incriminating connection to Lewis, when examining the testimony of Waters, was the comment about the Tarago van and being told to pretend to police he had suffered a heart attack. Lewis did drive a Tarago van and he had collapsed in shock, allegedly suffering a heart attack, when told of Kerrie's death.

The forensic evidence presented in Lewis' trial to the jury also left a burning question of his involvement. This included blood stains on the rifle bag found in the Tarago vehicle that contained Kerrie's DNA, as did the clothes he was wearing. The Crown did not produce the murder weapon and the knife used in Kerrie's murder, with Lewis also choosing to remain mute and not provide any testimony. In the evidence of Waters, the judge gave appropriate instructions to the jury in that he had previously benefited from a lesser sentence for the same murders, in view of his cooperation with the Crown. The judge was also mindful to caution the jury that the evidence of Waters may be unreliable. However, if they were satisfied beyond reasonable doubt that his evidence was true, they may convict.

On 19 November 1999, the jury did exactly that, returning a verdict of guilty being satisfied beyond reasonable doubt. On 9 June 2000, Lewis was sentenced to life imprisonment for the murder of Kerrie and 18 years for the murder of Fatma. Lewis had no hesitation in contesting his conviction and sentence, which proceeded before the Court of Criminal Appeal in late 2001. Lewis appeared without counsel and the main focus of his appeal, apart from challenging the blood and subsequent DNA evidence, was the testimony given by Waters.

On 9 November 2011, the appeal against conviction and sentence was dismissed, with the Court of Appeal saying in respect of Waters:

> *If the jury could have been reasonably satisfied of this beyond reasonable doubt, there is...no possible doubt about the identification of the appellant as this third person, even though Waters was not able to identify the appellant...Mr Waters gave evidence of Ms Pang and the third person walking from two cars parked side by side outside Kerrie's Oasis minutes before the murders; the appellant had driven with Ms Pang in two cars to Kerrie's Oasis, arriving within about five minutes of the murders and then walked with her to the door...after the murders, Waters said the third person put a rifle bag in a white Tarago van, being one of two vehicles from [which they] had walked a few minutes earlier...it is inconceivable that a person, other than the appellant, could fit into this scenario.*[402]

The Court of Appeal, after accepting the DNA evidence of Kerrie's found on the rifle case and the clothing of Lewis, would say further:

> *Even without Waters' evidence, all those circumstances amounted to an extremely strong circumstantial case that the appellant went into Kerrie's Oasis with Ms Pang and, in so far as the*

402 *R v Lewis* [2001] NSWCCA 448- para 53.

jury's verdict involved satisfaction beyond reasonable doubt that the appellant went inside, was present during the murder of Ms Pang and left with Rose and Waters after the murder, the jury's finding to that effect could not be unreasonable.[403]

So, what has happened since to the three partners in crime? Nothing has been heard of Lewis since then but, no doubt, he's reflecting on one's life's mistakes as he bides his time in a lonely prison cell. Rose, on the other hand, spends his life prison sentence in Goulburn Gaol's High Risk Management Unit, even smuggling out letters of complaint over his harsh conditions. According to him, to make his plight even worse, Rose also became extremely unhappy with other inmates converting to Islam, as he alleged in 2005 and again in 2007. He obviously has nothing better to do with his time than complain.

In early 2016, Waters, no doubt trying to make amends for his involvement in the Valentine's Day murders, joined the Australian Anti-Paedophile Party hoping to be elected as a senator. Given his somewhat tarnished background, a number of constituents lodged complaints with the Australian Electoral Commission and the party was voluntarily deregistered in late 2016.

We can only trust we will never hear about Waters again.

403 Ibid- para 56.

39
A QUESTION OF INNOCENCE–PART ONE

A wrongful conviction of a person, later deemed innocent, can only be described as being totally let down by Australia's justice system. In other words, they are convicted of a crime they didn't commit, because of a variety of other factors. Convictions have sometimes resulted from jury trials or occasionally judge-only trials, based on circumstantial evidence, witness identification of the accused or forensic evidence later found to be totally flawed and unreliable. [404]

Compensation for a wrongful conviction, other than in the Australian Capital Territory,[405] does not automatically

404 Other factors may include incompetent police investigations and, on some occasions, thanks to corrupt and overzealous police.

405 A person has a right to be compensated under section 23 of the *Human Rights Act 2004*(ACT) following a conviction and sentence, which is reversed or in cases of a pardon, on grounds which may include new evidence which demonstrates that there has been a total miscarriage of justice.

follow, despite the terminology laid out by the International Covenant on Civil and Political Rights.[406] In that respect, any person affected by a wrongful conviction may make application for an ex-gratia payment as a form of restitution, to compensate them for what can often be traumatic outcomes.

After being wrongly convicted and then sent to prison, only then to be released when deemed innocent, can result in a personality change often diagnosed as a post-traumatic disorder. While some form of compensation may play a small part in addressing their suffering, ex-gratia payments are made only at the discretion of the applicable state or territory Attorney-General.

Australian statistics suggest that since 1922, there have been almost 100 cases of wrongful convictions, three which became high profile and etched as a miscarriage of justice. These included, on some occasions, an appeal, which initially failed to have the conviction and sentence overturned.

One prime example was New Zealand–born Australian woman, Lindy Chamberlain. Despite her saying words to the effect, 'a dingo ate my baby', she was imprisoned for three years after being wrongly convicted of murder. Lindy was adamant her nine-week-old daughter was taken by a dingo, when camping with her husband and children at Ayers Rock in the Northern Territory in 1980.[407] Thanks to a plethora of failed forensic evidence and sensational media reporting, this

406 Article 14(6). This key international treaty came into force on 23 March 1976.

407 In 1873, a European explorer named it Ayers Rock in recognition for unexplained reasons of the then South Australian Premier, Sir Henry Ayers. In October 1985, the Australian Government returned traditional ownership to the Anangu people and in 1995, it was officially renamed Uluru.

distraught mother was still jailed for murder in October 1982. What followed were failed appeals all the way to the High Court of Australia.[408]

In February 1986, the baby's matinee jacket was found partially buried near a dingo lair, not far from where they were camping. On 2 June 1987, a Royal Commission delivered findings that the trial verdicts were considered unsafe and unsound.[409] Both Chamberlains were then formally pardoned with their convictions quashed by the NT Supreme Court in 1988.[410] As a consequence of Lindy spending nearly four years in prison, she received an ex-gratia compensation payment of $1.3 million in 1992 from the NT Government.

Former public servant, David Harold Eastman, was another innocent who was wrongfully convicted of murder. On 10 January 1989, senior Australian Capital Territory police officer, Colin Winchester, was shot dead as he alighted from his vehicle near his home in Deakin Avenue, Canberra. Eastman had been charged with an unrelated assault matter and was upset after meeting Winchester in a failed bid to overturn the charges. He allegedly then made threats to kill Winchester and was subsequently convicted of his murder in late 1995. The Crown presented what was considered to be a strong circumstantial case, which also included over 200 witnesses,

---

408 *Chamberlain v The Queen (No 2)* [1984] HCA 7 (1984) 153 CLR 521.

409 Royal Commission of Inquiry into Chamberlain Convictions. Report, Commonwealth Parliamentary Papers (1987), volume 15, paper 192.

410 Reference under s.433A of the *Criminal Code Act 1983* by the Attorney-General for the Northern Territory of Australia of Convictions of Alice Lynne Chamberlain and Michael Leigh Chamberlain, 15 September 1988.

7,000 pages of transcripts and an abundance of exhibits. Eastman was subsequently convicted by a jury and sentenced to life imprisonment without parole.[411]

After a number of failed appeals, including to the High Court of Australia,[412] following a fresh inquiry in 2014,[413] the ACT Full Court quashed his conviction and ordered a new trial. This was on the basis that the interests of justice demanded such new trial on what appeared to be deeply flawed forensic evidence, leading to a miscarriage of justice.[414] As a consequence, Eastman was found not guilty by a jury in the ACT Supreme Court on 22 November 2018. This led to one of Eastman's former lawyers saying, 'The first trial was an absolute disgrace...a shambles...the forensic evidence was almost certainly fabricated in some respects.'

After spending 19 years in prison for his wrongful conviction, the question now remained, what amount of compensation Eastman would accept. He initially rejected an ex-gratia compensation offer of $3 million and his civil claim was ultimately successful. On 14 October 2019, the Supreme Court, in accordance with the Human Rights Act, awarded him $7.2 million, together with an order for his legal costs of the proceeding to be paid by the ACT Government.[415]

---

411 *R v Eastman* [1995] Unreported ACTSC, Carruthers AJ, 10 November1995.

412 *Eastman v The Queen* [2000] HCA 29;(2000) 203 CLR 1.

413 Report of the Board of Inquiry. Inquiry into the Conviction of David Harold Eastman for the Murder of Colin Stanley Winchester, 29 May 2014.

414 *Eastman v Director of Public Prosecutions (No 2)* [2014] ACTSCFC 2.

415 *Eastman v The Australian Capital Territory* [2019] ACTSC 280

In early May 2013, the South Australian Government introduced into legislation, a statutory right for a further and subsequent appeal, for any conviction on the basis of 'fresh and compelling evidence that should, in the interests of justice, be considered on appeal.'[416] Prior to such legislative amendment, the concept often defined as the "finality principle" stood, which effectively meant once convicted there only existed one statutory right of appeal.

This was also applicable at the time in other state and territory jurisdictions, which allowed such appeal, usually based on a question of law or with leave of the court on other grounds, such as manifestly excessive sentence. In other words, Australian courts would not consider any appeal against a criminal conviction, other than the one statutory right of appeal. This was also supported by the High Court of Australia, so once you exhausted that appeal process, what remained was only a prerogative power of mercy vested in the applicable jurisdiction's Attorney–General.

It's fair to say that if it wasn't for the fresh and compelling evidence appeal, as allowed following the amended by the SA Government in 2013, Henry Vincent Keogh may still be behind bars. He grew up in Adelaide, was well educated and had met the love of his life, Anna–Jane Cheney in the early 1990s. She worked in a senior position with the Law Society of Australia but, at the age of 29 years, three days after her birthday, she was found dead in a bathtub. Keogh said he returned home on the night of 18 March 1994 to find his fiancée deceased and it appeared, at first glance, she had drowned.

However, an autopsy carried out by Dr Collin Manock determined, in his opinion, that the deceased was conscious when

416 Section 353A of the *Criminal Law Consolidation Act 1935*(SA).

her head was submerged in the bath. Manock, after carrying out a further examination, also found what he considered to be evidence of bruises to her lower left leg, which appeared to be consistent with the use of a hand type grip, which then forced her body under the bath water. He also considered the bruises to her head and back of the neck were as a result of her head forcibly hitting a hard part of the bath. What also raised the attention of police, now that they were dealing with a murder, such bruising occurred within four hours prior to her death.

Keogh was immediately considered to be more than just a person of interest, when investigators uncovered that he would benefit from over a million dollars in life insurance policies. He had recently instigated the policies in her name and it appeared he had forged her signature. Keogh was subsequently charged with murder and after his first trial in February 1995 resulted in a hung jury, he was again presented before a jury in August 1995.

The Crown presented what was largely a circumstantial case, including the expert forensic evidence of Dr Manock, together with the insurance claim motive. Keogh maintained his innocence saying, when he arrived back at the residence, he found his fiancée lying on her side, with her face under the water. He stated that on removing her from the bathtub, he attempted resuscitation without success. As to the insurance policies, they were taken out to prevent them relapsing, with the Crown conceding that Cheney was aware of at least two of the policies being signed by Keogh. Nonetheless, on 23 August 1995 the jury found him guilty of murder and 41-year-old Keogh was sentenced to life imprisonment, with a non-parole period of 25 years.

Over a number of years, Keogh effectively exhausted all

his formal rights of appeal. His first appeal to the Court of Criminal Appeal in December 1995 was dismissed,[417] followed by further unsuccessful appeals all the way to the High Court of Australia in 2007.[418] In 2013, Keogh had spent nearly 20 years in custody, which included his pre-sentence detention, however, his life in due course was about to change for the better.

On learning of the amendment by the SA Government to allow a further appeal on the basis of fresh and compelling evidence, a further application was filed. His legal team had maintained, for some time, that the so-called expert forensic evidence of Dr Manock was flawed. Indeed, around this time, the good doctor had also recanted his earlier evidence and no longer maintained that Cheney had been forcibly held under water until she drowned. This was, no doubt, due to the learned opinion of a Professor of Anatomy at the University of Adelaide, which was corroborated by other senior pathologists.

In their considered view, it was not possible to drown Cheney by simply grabbing her calf muscle then pushing her head under water. This was on the basis that her leg would have exerted greater power over the fingertip grip of Keogh. Furthermore, after measuring the physical location of the bathtub against the wall, it meant, if she was forcibly drowned, Keogh would have had to position himself where the wall was located, which was virtually impossible.

They also raised the possibility that Cheney had fallen, which had caused the head injury rendering her unconscious, then landing accidentally into the bath. Notably, this was

417 *R v Keogh* [1995] Unreported, Court of Criminal Appeal South Australia, Matheson, Millhouse and Mullighan, 22 December 1995.

418 *Keogh v The Queen* [2007] HCA Trans 693 16 November 2007.

never considered as a possibility or ever raised at trial. As to the bruises on her body, they would have been sustained in a shorter time frame than within the four hours of death, giving further support to the fall scenario.

The application for leave to appeal and against conviction was upheld in a unanimous judgment of the Court of Criminal Appeal in December 2014. The court came to the only sensible conclusion in respect of the "fresh and compelling evidence", that the original trial of Cheney was indeed "fundamentally flawed", leading to a miscarriage of justice. As for the now recanted forensic evidence of Dr Manock, it was highlighted that he had misled, not only the jury but the trial judge, the Crown and opposing defence counsel for Keogh. On that basis, the conviction and sentence of Keogh was quashed and a new trial ordered.[419]

The retrial didn't happen as, following the release of 59-year-old Keogh on bail on 22 December 2014, the Director of Public Prosecutions determined it would no longer proceed to a fresh trial, which had been listed for early 2016. On 1 July 2018, it was announced by the SA Government that an ex-gratia payment of $2.5 million would be made to Keogh, as compensation for his wrongful conviction.

This meant he would receive just over $100,000 for each year in prison. I will let you be the judge as to whether this was fair and just compensation for the loss of 20 years of a meaningful life.

419 *R v Keogh No 2* [2014] SASCFC 136.

40
A QUESTION OF INNOCENCE–PART TWO

'I am an innocent man…you have not heard the last of this'.

Truer words could not have been spoken as 33-year-old Andrew Mark Mallard was led away in handcuffs from the dock of the Supreme Court of Western Australia on 15 November 1994. He had just been convicted of the murder of Pamela Suzanne Lawrence, for which Mallard was sentenced to life imprisonment by Justice Murray, with a minimum of 20 years. It would take a prolonged legal battle over 12 years, when the case against him was ultimately dropped by prosecutors in February 2006. This was after the High Court of Australia quashed his conviction and sentence, declaring a miscarriage of justice.

The case against Mallard centred around the severe bashing and death of Pamela, who was found lying face down on the floor of her jewellery shop in Glyde Street, Mosman

Park, a 15-minute drive from Perth. On 23 May 1994, this unfortunate shop keeper suffered severe head injuries due to her skull being fractured in three different places. There were also several injuries to the right side of the front of her skull and it was apparent she had been struck with a blunt instrument. She was found by her husband around 7pm but passed away in the back of an ambulance before reaching the hospital. A subsequent postmortem would find a total of 12 lacerations to her head, together with evidence of some shavings of what appeared to be blue paint.

Police didn't have much to go on, apart from a witness who said she had seen a male in the shop standing near the counter, late that afternoon as she had walked by. He was described as 30-35 years old with a ginger beard, just under six feet tall and wearing a gypsy type bandana. When the male saw her, he bobbed down, as though he didn't want to be seen.

Another two witnesses advised police they saw a man wearing a similar bandana on his head. He was behaving erratically approximately three kilometres from the murder scene, several hours before it occurred. However, there were issues with these three statements as Mallard was a lot taller, being around six foot seven, and he was, in fact, locked up at the time at the East Perth Police Station, before being transferred to a mental facility. Police, in any event, released an identikit description of the male they were looking for.

A crime scene examination with photographs, later tendered at the trial of Mallard, would show a large amount of blood on the floor of the jewellery shop. The lead chemist, attached to the police forensic science laboratory, would examine foreign matter in the specimens obtained from the head wounds of the deceased. On further testing, those specimens showed minute amounts of dark blue smears containing iron or iron oxide particles, suggesting the murder weapon was a type of iron or steel implement, but certainly not a wrench.

Along with over one hundred other suspects, it was obvious that Mallard quickly became a person of interest in the Lawrence murder. He was known to live on the streets around Mosman Park, occasionally squatting at a friend's place nearby. He had only been in Australia since 1967, when his parents migrated to reside in Perth. Mallard had trouble settling in and, after leaving school at the young age of 16, his life was mainly spent unemployed, dabbling in smoking marijuana and dancing in nightclubs. He tried to join the army without success, moved to his birthplace in England for a brief time before returning to Perth. By 1994, this six foot seven young man was basically homeless and sadly lacking in confidence.

On 24 May 1994, after suffering a nervous breakdown and being admitted to Graylands Psychiatric Hospital, he was charged by police for an unrelated matter. This allegedly involved him carrying out a burglary and impersonating a police officer, supposedly saying he was an undercover drug agent. This would be the first time he came to the attention of police and he certainly had no history of violence. While in hospital, he was also interviewed by police about his movements on the day of the murder but was not offered access to any legal representation, let alone even a mental health nurse.

When released on bail on 10 June 1994, he was again interviewed in which he denied any involvement in the jewellery shop murder. He did, however, originally admit, during this unrecorded interview, which he later denied, that he had entered the shop on the day of the murder. Mallard would then speculate during this interview that he committed the murder but then again denied such act, saying it 'must be lies…it's all lies.' He kept speaking in the third person when referring to the murderer, saying whoever did it was an 'evil person' and 'its murder and that's not me. I'm innocent.'

For the next seven days, with police believing he was the culprit, Mallard was befriended by a male, who introduced himself as Gary. In Mallard's confused and dazed state, Gary took him around Fremantle splurging on hotel rooms and copious amounts of alcohol and drugs. Little did Mallard know but our man Gary, was in fact an undercover police officer trying to elicit some sort of confession from him.

A further police interview then took place on 17 June 1994, in which Mallard again made further speculative admissions. He first admitted he had struck the victim up to 12 times and even drew a sketch of the weapon he said he used. He said it was a rusty Sidchrome pipe wrench, which he found in the backyard shed at the rear of the shop near some gas bottles. Mallard said she was wearing dark slacks and a jumper but changed that to some sort of skirt.

Again, as in his previous interview, he repeated that it was all lies and he was simply making it up in what could be classified as a very unusual interview. This somewhat all-over-the-place interview, after he said, 'I want it to be videotaped so that I can be cleared,' was further evidenced by the following lines:[420]

Officer: We brought you in this morning and we had

420 The extracts, in respect of the line of questioning in the police interview of 17 June 1994, are not in exact sequence, as it was transcribed from both the High Court Appeal and the ABC Australian Story of May 2019.

a conversation in relation to the murder of Pamela Lawrence at Mosman Park. Do you agree with that?

Mallard: I do…I had, over the course of my life, suffered from a behavioural situation where I was… I would always acquiesce. I would try to please people. I was a people pleaser.

Officer: You said that you approached her from the rear of the shop and she asked you, 'what are you doing here?'

Mallard: Yeah.

Officer: Is that right?

Mallard: That's right.

Officer: Okay. And that you said to her that you were going to rob her. This is what you told us. Okay?

Mallard: This is what I imagine this person would say.

Officer: … Now you also said that she gave you a purse?

Mallard: A purse.

Officer: All right.

Mallard: I would say it would have to be a matching purse. Being a woman of taste, she would have a matching handbag and matching purse. At a last resort, I would have gone for a Glomesh bag.

Officer: Okay. All right. You told us that she was dressed in what?

Mallard: A skirt of some sort. Again, being a woman of taste and sophistication, she would have had to be…. worn a nice skirt like this, but one that joins up.

Officer: Right, and I think you said that you virtually ran there (the Stirling Bridge) from the scene?

Mallard: Would have had to.

Officer: Yeah.

Mallard: Or caught a train much…probably at North

Fremantle but I don't think so because the tapes…there's no videotapes of that day.
Officer: No problems.
Mallard: So, he was either very fit or he had a push bike.
This police interview also included at one point with the following exchange:
Mallard: …May I say something else?
Officer: Okay, yeah. Go on.
Mallard: If Pamela Lawrence was locking the store up, maybe she came in through the back way and the front door was already locked and she left the key in the back door and that's why he had easy access and that's why she didn't hear him…
Officer: We'll go on with what you told us earlier okay, before we go into anything else… the fact is that you told us all these things and you now say that that was a complete pack of lies, that is the things you told us was.

It was somewhat perplexing that police had not recorded the earlier interview of 10 June 1994. The majority of the second interview seven days later was also not videotaped, apart from a short recording near the end. Mallard said he had never been anywhere near the shed and probably obtained the wrench from somewhere else. He also mentioned he had been under the influence of drugs after being released by police but, given he had no money at the time, it questioned whether he could have been drug affected. His final words at the end of the interview, were to the effect:

Mallard: My version, my conjecture, of the scene of the crime… its murder and that's not me.

Officer: Okay, no worries. We'll leave it at that. End of story. Thanks very much.'

It was also clear Mallard was merely speculating about the conduct of the victim and not just what he had allegedly observed. In addition, to a lot of what he said, it would later be suggested, it was from details fed to him by his newfound friend, Gary, the undercover police officer. Other issues, in any event, would be raised in the subsequent appeal to the High Court.

On 19 July 1994, Mallard was charged with the wilful murder of Pamela Suzanne Lawrence and remanded in custody. On 2 November 1994, Mallard pleaded not guilty at his jury trial before Justice Murray in the Supreme Court of Western Australia. The Crown contended that Mallard was guilty of murder beyond reasonable doubt, repeatedly submitting that the victim had been killed using a wrench. They said the wrench had been obtained by Mallard from the back of the shop, emphasising to the jury that the accused even drew the wrench, during an interview with police. The prosecution tendered the sketch as an exhibit, noting the murder weapon had not been located.

Mallard, in his sworn evidence before the jury, emphatically denied he had admitted to police he killed Mrs Lawrence with a wrench. In that respect he stated:

'A sketch of a supposed weapon that we were talking about in our theory which I said was a gas wrench to be used on acetylene equipment. I have no idea what a gas wrench looks like. That is what I assumed it would look like in my theory…'

What was also in Mallard's favour on a question of innocence was the fact that, despite a number of crime scene photographs of a large pool of blood, they were not tendered before the jury. Given the horrendous nature of the attack, it would, in all likelihood, have left the deceased's blood on the perpetrator and particularly the clothing being worn at the time. None in fact was found on Mallard which would have linked him to the crime, for which he had been charged.[421]

The Crown, of course, has a duty of disclosure and such ongoing obligation in any criminal trial to provide full disclosure to the defence, of all relevant evidence in its possession. Now, this is where it gets really perplexing and indeed outrageous in the first instance of what was withheld by the prosecution. The lead prosecutor in that respect breached his obligations on disclosure, in that the victim's injuries did not in any way match the type of wrench referred to in the sketch.

The Crown had, in fact, a report from forensic pathologist, Dr Cooke, that clearly stated a wrench could not have resulted in the injuries to the victim's head. His expert opinion was set out in a comprehensive report saying, the wrench, as drawn by Mallard, did not match the injuries sustained by the victim. This view was formed by conducting an experiment using a pig's head, which did not replicate any of the deceased's injuries. In addition, there was a separate chemical report which determined the murder weapon was, in fact, a blunt iron or steel implement, either painted blue or had blue type paint marks. This was obtained from foreign matter obtained from fragments in the head wounds of Mrs Lawrence.

To make matter more compelling on the innocence of Mallard, the Crown prosecutor not only failed to tender this exculpatory forensic evidence but also omitted to properly

421 A small spot of blood was found on the only shoes he owned but it was, in fact, his own blood and certainly not from the deceased.

question key witnesses. In that respect, the forensic pathologist was not asked whether the wrench, as drawn by Mallard, was the murder weapon. In addition, the expert who prepared the chemical report was also not questioned whether the wrench sketch was or could have been, the murder weapon.

Despite withholding forensic evidence and the legal argument over whether the police interviews with Mallard were admissible, given his psychosis, on 15 November 1994 Mallard was found guilty. It was clear the jury was satisfied beyond reasonable doubt, in respect of the bumbling so-called unsigned confessions of Mallard but only supported by the last 20 minutes of the video-recorded police interview. Mallard was sentenced to life imprisonment, with a minimum of 20 years.[422]

Not only did Mallard profess his innocence but his family, outside court on the day of his sentencing, also vowed they would not rest until he was exonerated. His brother said to the waiting media:

'Andrew was convicted on unsigned and unseen statements written by police…there are so many holes in this case it's not funny…'

But it would take over a decade to right the wrong and for 'justice must not only be done but must also be seen to be done.'

Within five days of being convicted and sentenced, Mallard lodged an appeal in his own right against conviction. This was on the basis that the learned trial judge erred in allowing and admitting into evidence some of the oral conversations applicable to the police interviews of 10 and 17 June 1994. He was then represented by counsel asserting there was new and fresh evidence, which would be filed prior to any hearing of

422 *The Queen v Mallard* [1995] Unreported, Supreme Court of Western Australia, Justice Murray, 15 November 1995.

the appeal. However, those further and better particulars were never filed and the appeal was dismissed on 11 September 1996 by the Court of Criminal Appeal.

Although fast losing patience and confidence in the justice system, his family had not given up by this stage. They enlisted the assistance of the then Labor Member of Parliament, John Quigley, and lawyer, Malcolm McCusker.[423] On 8 July 2002, along with well-respected journalist, Colleen Egan,[424] they served a petition for clemency on the WA Attorney General on the basis of, amongst other grounds, the forensic evidence which had not been disclosed at Mallard's original trial. This was regarding the wounds suffered by Mrs Lawrence, which could not have been inflicted by the alleged murder weapon, namely the wrench.

In accordance with legislation applying to the clemency petition,[425] it was then brought for hearing before the Court of Criminal Appeal in 2003. It was therefore of no surprise as a ground of appeal, arguing a miscarriage of justice for the non-disclosure of the fresh evidence concerning the deemed murder weapon. The alleged statements made by Mallard that were, in

---

423 John Quigley was also a lawyer and represented the Western Australian Police Union for 25 years. In 2007, his life membership of the Union was withdrawn after he threatened to reveal the identity of an undercover police officer involved in the Mallard case, for which he was fined $3,000 by the State Administrative Tribunal. From April 2009 to March 2017, he was the Shadow Attorney-General and then became Attorney General. Malcolm McCusker would subsequently be appointed as the 31st Governor of WA holding office from 2011 to 2014.

424 She went on to become Chief of Staff for Attorney-General John Quigley and in 2025 was elected to Parliament as the member for Thornlie.

425 *Sentencing Act 1995*(WA)- section 140(1)(a).

fact, not confessions but third party or theorising statements, were also a further ground of appeal.

On 3 December 2003, the Court of Appeal, in an 83-page judgment, dismissed the appeal.[426] This was despite describing the so called "confessions" of Mallard as not only "peculiar' but, at times, several things he said were "odd". In that respect and to the contrary, it was submitted by the Crown that a total of 15 facts could be identified in his confessions, which only the person who committed the murder would know. In response, counsel for Mallard submitted that these were said in truth but were inconsistent with the known or established facts. For some reason, the Court of Appeal, which would later be found to be in error, did not consider this submission.

As to the drawing of the wrench by the appeal petitioner Mallard, the Court of Appeal stated:

> *Looking at that material in light of the petitioner's description and drawing, the evidence would appear to support two propositions; first, that the petitioner had not drawn the murder weapon with precision; second, that an implement with some similarities to that drawn by the petitioner might have been capable of being the murder weapon. The evidence before us of Mr Hogan, the petitioner's counsel at trial, was that he understood (in our view accurately) that the Crown asserted the weapon to be "similar" to that drawn by the petitioner, and that he always took the view that the jury could have found that the weapon was not a wrench.*[427]

---

426 *Mallard v The Queen* [2003] WASCA 296.

427 Ibid-para 104.

In respect to the non-disclosure of the finding of Dr Cooke about the murder weapon, the Court of Appeal said:

> *In our view, nothing in the evidence before us, relating to the likely murder weapon, alters the position at it was seen to be at trial. The more detailed material which is before us as to the experiments of Dr Cooke, both before and after the trial, with different implements and the material concerning the efforts to find an appropriate implement, go no further than establishing that no wrench, which can clearly be said to be capable of inflicting injuries of the type seen on the deceased, has been found. Indeed, no implement capable of inflicting those injuries has been found.*[428]

To their credit, the supporters of Mallard and notably his legal team, did not give up. In October 2004, special leave to appeal to the High Court of Australia was granted with Mallard again being represented by Malcolm McCusker QC. The main thrust of the appeal seeking a retrial, was again that there had been a miscarriage of justice, in that the evidence before the jury could not be supported. On that basis, it followed that the Court of Appeal erred in refusing to consider the whole case and the evidence adduced at trial.

On 15 November 2005, in a unanimous decision by the five High Court Justices after hearing submissions over two days, the conviction of Mallard was quashed and a new trial ordered.[429] It was very clear that the High Court supported the contention that had the jury known a wrench could not possibly have been

428 Ibid- para 105.

429 *Mallard v R* [2005] HCA 68;(2005) 224 CLR 125(2005)222 ALR 236(2005) 80 ALR 160.

the murder weapon, which was not disclosed at trial, doubt would then have been cast over the "confessions" by Mallard.

In that regard, the High Court said:

> *...his assessment of the number of blows struck was, for example, approximate and varied from time to time. There was, in fact, no necessary correspondence between the appellant's description of Mrs Lawrence's clothing and what, in fact, she was wearing when she was attacked. Similarly, there were discrepancies between the appellant's description of the premises and its actual configuration. The appellant denied that he had said much of what was attributed to him in the interviews by the police officers. The absence of any recording of most of the interviews in these circumstances is most unfortunate.*[430]

The High Court then came to the following conclusion in respect of the material non-disclosures stating:

> *A review of the...evidence which was not disclosed to the appellant's counsel at trial, but which was in possession of police and, at the least, available to the prosecution, suggests strongly that material evidence was not disclosed that bore upon the guilt of the appellant of the crime charged in the indictment. Whilst the non-disclosure of one or two of these items...taken alone or perhaps together, might not have been sufficient to produce an unreasonable or unsupported verdict, with a miscarriage of justice in the trial, a consideration of the totality of the unrevealed evidence raises a stark question as to the safety of the appellant's conviction.*[431]

430 Ibid- page 11.

431 Ibid-page 16.

The Director of Public Prosecutions was not happy with the High Court ruling that the errors which took place in the trial were indeed substantial. Initially, after Mallard was released on 20 February 2006, after serving almost 12 years behind bars, the DPP, after announcing a re-trial would not proceed, still took the view that he remained a prime suspect for this murder. John Quigley summed it all perfectly though in his speech to Parliament when he said:

'Here's a man that's been in jail now for 11 years and the High Court has said it's because the police and prosecution suppressed evidence…Anything in the brief that didn't fit with their theory that Mallard was a murderer, they simply went back to a witness and got them to change the statement.'

Following this decision not to proceed, a police cold case review of the murder of Mrs Lawrence then took place and what was found completely exonerated Mallard. What cold case detectives located on file, allegedly due to advanced digital technology, was a palm print found at the Lawrence's store which was that of convicted murderer, Simon Rochford. After he confessed to the murder of his girlfriend on 15 July 1994, which was only seven weeks after the Lawrence murder, he was given a minimum 15-year prison sentence and to be deported upon release.[432]

In addition, it was also confirmed that the weapon, which was located in his backpack, had been used in both murders, inflicting similar injuries and was a wooden stick with a blue weight attached. This "rediscovery" would lead to Shadow Attorney-General John Quigley, being somewhat perplexed

432 While in jail, Rochford was also questioned by British police over the murder of a German tourist in 1993.

and even infuriated it took so long for it to magically be brought to light.[433]

The resultant repercussions for both murders, saw Rochford commit suicide in prison in May 2006 after he was interviewed as a significant person of interest in the Lawrence murder.[434] There were also repercussions for the investigating police officers and even the Crown Prosecutor in the Mallard prosecution. The WA Crime and Corruption Commission in 2008 found that two police officers, who were both now assistant commissioners, were guilty of misconduct, including the altering of witness statements in the prosecution brief. Regarding the Mallard trial prosecutor, he was reprimanded and ordered to pay a total of $13,000, being a fine together with costs.[435]

After receiving $3.25 million in compensation in 2009 from the Western Australian Government, an innocent Andrew Mallard even graduated with a fine arts university degree. At the age of 56 and about to marry, he died when fatally struck by a motor vehicle while crossing a road in Hollywood, USA.

Prior to his death in 2019, he appeared in an ABC Australian Story episode in which he stated he had no choice but to leave Perth and reside overseas. This was due to how he

---

433 John Quigley was fined $3,000 by the State Administrative Tribunal in late 2011 for threatening to reveal the identity of the undercover police officer, 'Gary'.

434 See statement by Minister for Corrective Services-Death in Custody-Simon Rochford. Extract from Hansard -Assembly 30 May 2006.

435 The two police officers were reported in the media as having resigned before they faced any disciplinary hearing. In respect of the Crown Prosecutor, see Legal Profession Complaints Committee and Bates [2012] WASAT 150.

was treated by disgruntled members of the Perth community who still treated him as a murderer and, in his words, 'some sort of psycho.'

This was all despite being, 'Not Guilty Your Honour.'

41
POLITICAL RIVALRY

To be one's rival usually means you are trying to defeat another person for benefit or gain some sort of advantage over them. Political rivalry usually occurs more frequently and intensely when, as candidates, they are running for the same seat in order to be elected to Parliament. You will often read several quotes in the media like 'as a political rival, he was as tough as they come' or 'political rival humiliated but at what cost'.

There is also an often-quoted maxim, 'one political rival described him as "feared" and known to always get what he wants.' It could not have been a truer word spoken regarding budding and hopeful politician, Phuong Canh Ngo. The only problem was, eventually he would be jailed for murder and sentenced to life imprisonment. So, what went wrong?

Born in 1958 to wealthy parents who operated a chicken farm in South Vietnam, Ngo witnessed the horrors of war. Following the fall of Saigon in 1975, he and his brother arrived in Australia in 1982 to begin a new life. He initially worked for a flyscreen company in Punchbowl, NSW and quickly became quite successful as the founding member and then inaugural Honorary President of the Mekong Club following its inception in Cabramatta in 1990, with it officially opening in 1993. Ngo was also instrumental in assisting Asian people, in particular local Vietnamese, with the club providing much needed ethnic support to its members. Thanks to his soon-to-be initiative, one of its employees, Quang Dao, would later gain infamy and not just in his role as a club social worker.

Ngo also entered into the foray of local politics and was the first Vietnamese-born Australian to gain a seat in local government. In September 1987, he was elected to the Cabramatta Ward for the Fairfield City Council. In partnership with the well-known Rodney Adler,[436] they set up a Vietnamese language newspaper and in 1990, Ngo was elected Deputy Mayor of the Fairfield City Council.[437] In May 1991, believing his chances of being elected to the NSW Parliament were favourable, he stood for the seat of Cabramatta. However, he was not elected, with the electorate again favouring the sitting Labor member, John Newman.[438] Little did anyone know at the time they would become more than just political rivals.

Of Austrian background and under his birthname of Johann Grauenig, Newman came to Australia in 1950 at the age

436 Adler was also a director of HIH Insurance, which went into liquidation in early 2001. He was jailed in 2005 for dishonesty offences, being released two years later on parole.

437 Ngo was also a Commissioner with the NSW Ethnic Affairs Commission.

438 Just prior to the election, there was a report that Newman had raised issues as to the refugee status of Ngo and that he had an alleged connection with local Cabramatta gangs.

of four. His name was changed by deed poll when his mother remarried and, as a member of the now Newman family, he was able to attend local schools, including the Cabramatta Public School. After graduating from high school, his attraction to the Australian Labor Party became apparent, as he worked for many years as a union delegate for the Federated Clerks Union.

Like his soon-to-be rival, he was also a Fairfield City Councillor from 1977, reaching the status of deputy mayor in 1985. His life, at that point, had been marred by tragedy, losing his pregnant wife and infant son in a motor vehicle accident in 1979.

Obviously well respected by the ALP, he was elected to the Legislative Assembly of the NSW Parliament, a position he held in the lower house as the sitting member for Cabramatta from 1986. Newman represented his constituents with some passion, particularly in his efforts in the fight against Asian organised crime.[439] They obviously took exception, as he received several death threats and his home was vandalised. He also undertook several leadership roles for sporting organisations and as fifth–dan karate master, he was President of the Federation of Australian Karate-do Organisations, serving from 1978 to 1987. As a strong advocate for road safety, he diligently served on its joint standing committee from May 1989.

In March 1994, he successfully retained preselection for the same seat for the pending 1995 State election. It was obvious though that Ngo had other ideas.

By this stage and on an invitation, Ngo had joined the ALP. Still wanting to become a member of the NSW

439 Newman was instrumental in the formation of NSW Police Task Force Oak targeting Asian-influenced crime in particular drugs and prostitution.

Parliament, this put him in direct opposition to Newman. Given the popularity of his opponent,[440] the chances of him being pre-selected were effectively non-existent. Regardless, Ngo was seen as the favoured son by the ALP, even having his photo taken with a big smile on his face, alongside the then Australian Prime Minister, Bob Hawke. Given the position Ngo held as Honorary President of the Mekong Club, he also had the pleasure of Bill Hayden, a former ALP stalwart but now Governor General of Australia,[441] officially open the club, which Ngo was using to conduct branch meetings. This was all pending a fast track to Parliament in the forthcoming election. Would all this be enough though to be preselected and then win the much-anticipated seat, currently held by Newman?

Around 9.30pm on 5 September 1994, following a party meeting, John Newman returned to his home in Cabramatta. After alighting from his vehicle, he was standing in the driveway talking to his fiancée, Lucy Wang, when a dark green or white motor vehicle drove up. Wang later told police she saw and heard a hooded gunman firing shots in Newman's direction, then return to what she thought was a green-coloured vehicle which was quickly driven away.

Local neighbours also confirmed seeing a similar vehicle but one witness told police there were two vehicles, one green and one white, leaving from what was now a murder crime scene. Newman had been mortally wounded, after being shot

440 When he first stood against Newman in the 1991 election, he only received a total of around 11% of the vote.

441 Bill Hayden was leader of the ALP from 1977 to 1983 and was the 21st Governor General of Australia from 1989 to 1996. Bob Hawke was first President of the Australian Council of Trade Unions and then ALP Leader and was the 23rd Prime Minister of Australia from 1983 to 1991.

twice in the chest and was later honoured with a state funeral, attended by various dignitaries, including the then Prime Minister, Paul Keating.[442]

The initial suspect in the murder was Cabramatta gang leader, Tri Minh Tran,[443] a much-feared criminal identity with whom Ngo was known to associate. One of Tran's relatives reportedly told police Ngo had approached Tran offering him $10,000 to kill Newman. It was alleged further that Tran rejected the offer, supposedly on the grounds the murder of a politician would create too much publicity and, no doubt, police attention.

Ngo was interviewed by police on two occasions, the first being a few days after the murder and later in December 1994, because he still remained a person of interest. As for 20-year-old Tran, he would be shot dead by members of his own gang in August 1995, apparently because he broke the legs of one of his second-in-charge. What was of further interest to homicide detectives was Ngo attended the funeral.

Despite an exhaustive investigation, it was not until 13 March 1998 when Ngo was taken into custody and charged with murder. The police were confident Ngo was responsible

442 Media reports suggested this was Australia's first political assassination, but that 'title' may well be held by another member of the NSW Legislative Assembly, being Thomas Ley. One of his opponents being state legislator Hyman Goldstein also a much vocal critic of him, apparently 'fell' to his death from Suicide Point in Coogee, NSW in 1928. Arthur Calwell who led the ALP from 1960 to 1967 was lucky to survive an attempt on his life when in June 1966 he was shot at point blank range at an anti-conscription rally, only suffering minor facial injuries.

443 Tran was the leader of the Vietnamese 5T crime gang and by the age of 13 was believed to be involved in a number of murders, although he was never charged.

for the murder of Newman, thanks to admissions made by two accomplices. They had nominated, not only Ngo, but two employees from the Mekong Club: Quang Dao and David Dinh.

After the first jury trial, which ran from June to August 1999, it was aborted for legal reasons, noting one of the two accomplices had also been indicted for murder. With both Ngo and Dao now facing the same murder charge, the second trial from February to May 2000 resulted in a hung jury, unable to agree on a verdict.

The Crown was not perturbed and a third trial before Justice Dunford commenced on 7 March 2001. This time they added Dinh to the indictment for murder, so the now three joint accused would face a jury of their peers. To a large degree, the Crown case would depend on the testimony of one accomplice in particular, who was also an employee of the Mekong Club. On the basis of his evidence, he had been granted immunity from prosecution. To protect his identity, he was referred to as "W2" during the trial.

His evidence was to the effect that in early March 1994, Ngo approached W2 and another employee, requesting they purchase firearms for him. On obtaining the weapons, which included a .32 Beretta pistol, a plan was then hatched to murder his political foe. After several failed attempts to carry out the murder and, given that Ngo couldn't find anyone to complete the task, he was left with no choice but to put his own plan into action.

On the night of 5 September 1994, at the instigation of Ngo, W2, in company with Dao and Dinh, drove to Newman's house in a Ford vehicle, followed by Ngo in a white Toyota Camry. W2 stated he had been lured into the vehicle on some other pretext and had no idea of what was to take place. When the unsuspecting victim arrived home from his ALP meeting around 9.30pm, W2 said Dinh, armed with the pistol, shot him dead. They immediately drove off with witnesses reporting seeing two cars, one being a Ford and the other a white vehicle. Dao and Dinh then met Ngo at a nearby service station, with Dinh handing the pistol to him, together with a jacket and gloves.

The jury was not prepared to accept all the evidence given by W2, acquitting both the alleged shooter Dinh, and Dao. They were not satisfied beyond reasonable doubt but the same could not be said for Ngo. The evidence that he was the instigator of Newman's murder was overwhelming, particularly in respect of his movements that night. The police investigation had uncovered evidence of telephone calls made from the Toyota Camry car phone, driven by Ngo, in close location and also seen near the Newman home.

These calls were not just within minutes following the murder but also, obtained from Telstra records, around 9.36pm the evening before, when his house was being looked at in preparation. In addition, there was evidence of other calls made by Ngo from the Toyota Camry to the Mekong Club. On listening to some of the calls, one Crown witness stated it was definitely Ngo's voice, with one other call where he actually identified himself.

Police were also able to trace the movements of Ngo after he had been handed the pistol and clothing. The Telstra mobile phone records showed the Toyota Camry, driven by Ngo, went first to his home and then briefly to Voyager Point, about 10 kilometres from the murder scene. It was noted that around 10.30pm, Ngo arrived back at the Mekong Club in the white Toyota Camry. This even gave him time to watch the television news reporting the death of Newman.

A coronial inquest into the death had previously been held and the importance of the Telstra records, regarding Ngo's movements, quickly became apparent. After the inquest, it was brought to the attention of police that they should search the Georges River at Voyager Point. Four years after the murder, a pistol was located in the river. In all likelihood, it was probably the murder weapon but, due to the time it had been submerged, it was not in a condition to confirm if it was indeed the missing pistol.

Ngo declined to give any evidence at trial which, of course, was his right but his defence team attacked the credibility of the Crown's witnesses. Particular focus was directed at W2 and perceived discrepancies in his evidence in that it was all his doing, including the purchase of weapons and approaching others to carry out the murder. In addition, testimony was given about the alleged disharmony between Newman and his fiancée, with one neighbour stating hearing disagreements between them. Furthermore, in trying to point the finger at other individuals as the perpetrators, evidence was led that Newman was not a popular man with his staff and other ALP colleagues.

The jury, however, was not satisfied with the innocence of Ngo, finding him guilty in instigating and organising the murder. On 14 November 2001, 43-year-old Ngo appeared before Justice Dunford for sentencing with the judge agreeing that while he was not the actual shooter, he was indeed the principal offender. As to motive, His Honour said:

I am satisfied to the criminal standard that Phuong Ngo's motive for the killing of John Newman was naked political ambition and impatience. He wanted to be the Legislative

Assembly member for Cabramatta... he could not wait until the next general election...so he needed to remove John Newham as the sitting member in order that he could run in the pre-election ballot which, on the numbers, he had a very good chance of winning. The method he chose was to have John Newman killed.[444]

Justice Dunford clearly saw the political murder in the worst type of category and stated further:

In my opinion, the killing of a member of parliament for political purposes, involving, as it does, an attack on our constitutional system of parliament democracy and particularly committed for personal political gain, gives rise to such culpability that the 'community interest in retribution, punishment, community protection and deterrence' can only be met by the imposition of a life sentence.[445]

Penal servitude for the term of his natural life it was but an appeal against conviction on 12 grounds in 2003 was filed. Of these, two were deemed to be possibly relevant, namely that Justice Dunford failed to give adequate directions to the jury, particularly in respect to W2. Furthermore, the judge also failed to give appropriate directions to the jury as to the significance of the acquittal of Dinh and also Dao. The Court of Criminal

444 *R v Ngo* [2001] NSWSC 1021-para15. Under section 61 of the *Crimes (Sentencing Procedure) Act 1999* (NSW) a court must impose a life sentence when the level of culpability is extreme in order to meet community expectations.

445 Ibid-para 32.

Appeal, however, dismissed the appeal on 3 April 2003,[446] as well as the application for special leave to appeal by Ngo to the High Court of Australia, which was refused in May 2004.[447]

This was followed by a Judicial Inquiry in 2009, following an ABC *Four Corners* report, suggesting there was some impropriety in the case put forward by the Crown. Nothing could be further from the truth and the general conclusion reached by the inquiry was, the Crown had no choice but to call witnesses who had also engaged in the criminal activity. It also concluded that the cross examination of them on behalf of Ngo was vigorous. In addition, the jury was properly instructed by the judge of any inconsistences and discrepancies in what was clearly a strong Crown case. In fact, the Judicial Inquiry reached an unbiased conclusion in that, '…material put before the Inquiry increased rather than diminished the strength of the Crown's case at trial.'[448]

Despite calls to pardon Ngo, he remains behind bars today, even now being touted at 66 years of age as a model prisoner and still claiming his innocence. John Newman has been rightly remembered by having a swimming pool in the suburb of Prairiewood named after him in 2002.

It remains to be seen whether any mercy will ever be granted to Ngo but as his papers have been marked 'never to be released', he will most likely die in prison.

---

446 *R v Ngo* [2003] NSWCCA 82.

447 In refusing the appeal, Chief Justice Gleeson said at the time, 'We are of the view that in this matter there are insufficient prospects of success of an appeal to warrant a grant of special leave and the application is dismissed.'

448 Report to the Chief Justice of NSW of the Inquiry into the Conviction of Phuong Canh Ngo for the Murder of John Newman, 14 April 2009-para 500.

42
IT WAS NO ACCIDENT

Around 7am on the morning of 4 October 1995, neighbours who lived next door to the Smith family heard a smoke detector alarm. On looking outside, they saw that the Hoppers Crossing house in south-western Melbourne, Victoria, occupied by Nicole Smith, her husband Mark and their two-month-old son Adrian, was on fire. They immediately called the fire brigade and, on rushing into the backyard, saw Nicole lying in the doorway of her home near the patio. In excruciating pain from burns, particularly over one arm, she told them her baby was still inside.

Rushing into the burning building with Nicole, they forced open the door to the bedroom which was consumed with heat and smoke. On seeing a flame near the left side of the main bed, it was apparent the baby was on fire and there was little they could do. Nicole and her neighbours waited outside until emergency services arrived. Sadly, they later confirmed the baby had died from being badly burnt. Nicole was rushed to Werribee

Hospital and, in view of the extensive burn injuries to her right arm, which was now distorted and contracted, she was transferred by helicopter to the burns unit at the Alfred Hospital.

After being advised of what had transpired, her husband, Mark, immediately drove to the hospital from the Royal Australian Air Force base at Laverton, where he worked in electronic engineering. Nicole would later reveal, when telling Mark she remembered being held down, he told her it 'didn't happen like that.'

To those who knew him well, Mark appeared to be devastated about the loss of his child and Nicole's serious injuries. However, one soon-to-be former workmate, who was his Squadron Leader, noted Mark seemed quite calm and sociable at baby Adrian's funeral a week later.

Police obtained a written statement from Mark on 11 October 1995 about his recollection of that fateful morning. He stated he had prepared to leave for work around 6.30am but took the baby into the bedroom and placed him at the foot of the bed where Nicole was sleeping. He noticed she was still breathing very heavily from a cold so, as was his usual method, placed some Vicks VapoRub on a tissue and put it over her face. According to Mark, Nicole woke up with a fright and, after grabbing him, tried, without success, to pull him down onto the bed. After placing Adrian alongside her, he took the aromatherapy oil burner from the lounge room which had been purchased some days earlier and, after lighting it, placed it on a bedside table.

He assured police in his statement, he made sure the lit burner was not too close to the bed or the tissue box. After kissing Nicole goodbye with her response being a mumble and, satisfied everything looked safe, Mark left for work around

7am. At this point, police came to the view the fire and death of their baby was an accident, caused by the lit aromatherapy device which somehow spread to the bed.

Nicole remained in hospital for nearly two months and was initially supported by Mark. Her horrific injuries were full thickness burns to her ears and the whole of her right arm, plus partial burns to her other arm, face and scalp. Her treating doctors were perplexed as to why there was so much severe burning to the right arm, whilst other parts of her body were not so badly affected.

Based on their experience with burn victims, there should have been a greater degree of burning injuries to other parts of her body. In addition, Nicole had initially slept through being burnt from the fire, which was highly unusual as the pain would have been excruciating.

Usually, to sleep through such horrific injuries is confined to sleeping victims under the influence of alcohol or drugs. They would suffer extreme burns and not just to one confined area. It just didn't make sense.

As part of her early treatment, Nicole's little finger on her right hand had to be removed. Also, her right arm would have to be amputated below the elbow at a later date. Meanwhile, some weeks later, following the tragic loss of her infant child, Nicole's sad life would take another turn for the worse.

As far as she was aware, her relationship with Mark was stable after marrying him in July 1991. A sergeant in the RAAF, he was originally stationed at the Amberley Air Base in Queensland, then posted to working on F1-11 aircraft in the United States of America. During his deployment, they did have a difficult time in their relationship when trying to conceive their first child.

Nicole discovered Mark had become very friendly with an attractive woman named Donna Wilkinson. She was employed by an American company who were also involved in the same type of work on aircraft as Mark was. On finding out he had accompanied Wilkinson to a pregnancy ultrasound test, Nicole became quite angry. They argued over why he went with her but, with Nicole now pregnant, decided they needed to forget about it and get on with their lives.

In December 1994, the Smiths returned to Australia and, in January 1995, Mark was posted to the Williams Air Base in Laverton. Although Nicole knew he had been talking to Wilkinson by phone, she was unaware she had also temporarily relocated under a visa to Australia and was pregnant to another RAAF member. Wilkinson remained in Australia until late September 1995 then returned to the States with her own baby, who was born some months earlier in May 1995.

Nicole thought her marriage to Mark at that point in time was now stable and he was looking forward to the birth of their son. What Nicole didn't know though was Mark had already applied for a discharge from the RAAF and he was planning to return to the USA, not only to work but to reside with Wilkinson. Now, facing a life without their precious baby and the difficulties of adjusting to managing her burn injuries, their four-year marriage was on the rocks.

Around this time, Mark was telling people he had problems in his marriage and that Nicole would blame him for the loss of their baby son. He also made the comment that there was no way he could live with Nicole who, when looking at her amputated arm, would continue to blame him for the fire and that everything was his fault. On Monday, 25 November 1995, Mark visited Nicole in hospital and, after helping her get ready for breakfast and as he headed out the door, turned around and said he had made two decisions. The first was he wanted a separation, followed by that he was leaving the RAAF. Nicole, obviously devastated, was given no reason why, as she watched him walk away.

After being discharged from hospital and, no doubt, still in shock at what had transpired, Nicole went to live with her parents in Queensland. She had to have multiple skin grafts which would continue for at least 18 months. In late January 1996, they had reached a partial separation settlement, with Nicole retaining the family motor vehicle and a small division from their joint bank account.

Nicole received two letters from Mark who told her he was visiting friends in America, before travelling to London. This was another lie as he had been with Wilkinson and her child. He made the mistake of returning to Australia with her in March 1996, for what was meant to be only a short visit.

Nicole was now aware Mark had kept all his superannuation funds, which had been transferred to the United States. He was also not providing any financial support for Nicole and, after obtaining legal advice, she commenced proceedings in the Family Court of Australia by way of an ex-parte order for an injunction.[449] Mark tried to return to America with Wilkinson in April 1996 but his passport was seized and he was prevented from leaving, thanks to the injunction obtained by Nicole. Wilkinson was left with no choice but to take her child back to the States. Despite some dubious attempts, on 1 February

449 Such order is made by a judge without the presence or notification of the other party involved. It is usually granted in urgent matters in family law disputes.

1997, to obtain a passport under false pretences, Mark was forced to remain in Australia.

The sequence of events which transpired next and why police became suspicious, is somewhat cloudy. It could have been a further statement obtained from Nicole which conflicted with Mark's version of events or compelling fresh forensic evidence that came to light. The question was whether Mark, wanting to be with Wilkinson, had decided to eliminate both Nicole and the baby under the guise of a fatal accident, rather than leave them unscathed but having to pay on-going financial support.

Let's start with Nicole and whether she shed some light on exactly what transpired. The fact she survived was remarkable, let alone remembering enough of what took place. Nicole told police that in the weeks prior to 4 October 1995, she became a tad uneasy regarding certain events involving her now ex-husband. She said that after he came back from a conference in Canberra in early September 1995, she smelt gas on waking up from a deep sleep. She roused Mark but unable to locate the problem, opened all the windows for fresh air before returning to bed. Their premises were checked the following day by a plumber, who was unable to find any evidence of a gas leak.

On 26 September 1995, Nicole was again woken up by smoke alarms going off. Upon investigating, she saw Mark holding a fire extinguisher, trying to put out a fire in their kitchen garbage bin. Once the flames, which had soared as high as the ceiling, were extinguished, Nicole saw Mark take the bin outside. Somehow, it rekindled, so he used the extinguisher again to douse the flames. She told police it was after these two incidents that she had purchased an aromatherapy burner, placing it on the bedside table next to a box of tissues.

This was with the forlorn hope it would calm her because she was particularly stressed by this stage. Nicole also said Mark had a glass jar beside the computer he used when working from home. Looking like something out of a science laboratory, the jar, with its glass stopper, contained what appeared to be clear liquid. On asking Mark what it was, he said he used it to clean his computer parts.

Regarding the events that led to the fateful fire, Nicole stated that on the night of 3 October 1995, she stayed up later than Mark, which she usually did, to feed the baby. Adrian always slept in a bassinet in the lounge room opposite the main bedroom. In keeping with her normal practice, the baby was fed again at 5.30am and, after he finished, she placed him in his normal sleeping place. Nicole agreed she had a cold at the time but, nonetheless, this did not prevent her from waking up regularly and when the baby cried.

Her next recollection was waking up and struggling for breath, whilst also thinking she was being held down. Nicole stated that something with a strong smell, like being in a dentist's chair, was placed over her face. She remembered kicking out and trying to push away whatever it was from her face, so she could breathe. At this point, she was down on her hands and knees on the bed facing the front and screaming, 'No! No!'

Nicole said she distinctly remembered seeing the outline of a body alongside her in the bed. It was later found to be her baby son. Nicole, however, said that she had no recollection of Adrian ever being placed alongside her in the bed. Her next memory was when she was outside on the patio and being helped by neighbours. When asked by police what woke her, Nicole was unable to say whether it was the pain or simply not being able to breathe.

At this point, it was apparent to police the candle theory causing the fire was indeed questionable. In particular, Nicole's statement effectively meant that some type of strong chemical smell had emanated from whatever was placed over her mouth. Police now needed to obtain further forensic and medical analysis to determine if the candle theory still carried any weight or was it something other than just an accidental fire?

After inspecting the scene, a forensic scientist was suspicious it was not simply an accidental fire. He noted that most of the burning was in the southwestern area of the top half of the bed. The damage extended almost down to the floor level and its ignition point was beside the bed next to a chest of drawers. Given that the watch beside the bed had stopped at 7.15am meant, at this point, it was progressing at a reasonable pace. The electric lamp was excluded as a possible source of ignition, which would later be confirmed following a further laboratory examination.

The aromatherapy candle was removed for further testing which found only one third of it had been destroyed. Its aluminium base had not melted and the accompanying bottles of oil were found to be normal. Further burn testing was conducted by the Metropolitan Fire Brigade who emulated the fire scene as closely as possible, including the box of tissues. Such testing showed if the candle was the cause, there would have to be a lot more burning to the base of the bedhead and the top of the bedside drawers. On that basis, the candle was effectively eliminated as the cause of the fire.

Whilst there was no direct smell of any accelerant, further forensic analysis of the fire scene came to the view that it was most likely started by a volatile solvent. This could have been acetone, ether or chloroform, all having the ability to leave no trace. Given the fire had progressed at a rapid rate, this now led to the inevitable conclusion. It was deliberately lit.

The initial concerns raised by the medical team at the burns unit, of Nicole somehow sleeping through a substantial part of her injuries, was also now looked at. A report was obtained from a specialist anaesthetist who confirmed that after looking at photos of Nicole's burn injuries, it would have been difficult for her to sleep though such a painful infliction, unless she had been administered an anaesthetic substance.

The only alternate explanation, in that event, was Nicole had been deprived of oxygen or had been affected by carbon monoxide poisoning, thereby losing consciousness, which wasn't the case. The logical conclusion was ether was used to temporarily render her being unaware of any pain, for a short period of time. It was noted that such a powerful solvent such as ether is a colourless clear liquid, which may have been contained in the glass jar beside Mark's computer.

On 26 February 1997, Smith was interviewed again by police and effectively stuck to the same story he had provided in his first interview. He agreed he had placed the baby in the bed alongside Nicole which, according to him, occurred on a daily basis. As to the Vicks VapoRub, he and the family used it from time to time when suffering from colds. When he placed it over Nicole, he said he now recalled she went crazy and pushed him, where he landed on the other side of the bed. He agreed he did have a cleaning fluid in a beaker in a glass jar, which he kept at home alongside his computer, but denied it was ether.

Smith also denied the sequence in respect of the rubbish bin fire, to the point where he said he was woken up by Nicole who told him to put it out. As to how it started, he had no idea. Smith agreed he had met Wilkinson in America, describing her as very attractive and that she brightened up the office. The relationship with Nicole did end and his words were they, 'had been unhappy for some time.' He agreed he had applied for a discharge from the RAAF around two months prior to the fire and stated during this interview, it was just as a 'means to an end.'

The end for Smith was approaching but it took until August 1999 before he was finally arrested. Now armed with incriminating forensic and medical analysis, police still needed to gather more evidence. This included looking at his conduct, not only before but after the fire, to add further weight to satisfy a jury beyond reasonable doubt. The fact he applied for the RAAF discharge two months prior to the fire, as well as other matters, would show he was indeed a callous murderer.

As part of the ongoing investigation, Victoria police, together with assistance from the Australian Federal Police and their counterparts in the United States, uncovered various financial transactions put in place by Smith. This also included a search of the flat now occupied by Smith and Wilkinson, carried out by Federal Bureau of Investigation agents and local police. With one cheque payment made out to Wilkinson on 12 October 1995, they located a letter in which Smith told her he didn't love Nicole anymore:

...I'm not cold and heartless either. I'm looking forward to so many things when we get started in the US...any amount of money I send over can be used for whatever purpose you see fit...Talk to you soon. Love Mark.

What was of further interest, adding to the totality of the evidence gradually being amassed against Smith, was that this letter and cheque were sent only eight days after the fateful fire. On 14 January 1996, Smith had spent $5,000 on an engagement ring for his new partner and some months later in April 1996, a further handwritten document was uncovered. This was giving Wilkinson permission to operate his bank accounts as she saw fit, together with two cheques totalling $70,200, all payable to her.

Police were now satisfied that Smith had a motive to burn both his then wife and baby to death, allowing him to continue a full-time relationship with Wilkinson. They also had no doubt there had been a pre-existing covert relationship in place. Smith clearly didn't want to be faced with any ongoing financial burden should he separate from Nicole and then have to pay ongoing maintenance and child support.

On 5 August 1999, police attended the Northen Territory home of his parents, where he was living and working in the computer industry. He was taken into custody and was subsequently extradited back to Victoria. After being charged with one count of murder and one of attempted murder, he was refused bail to face a jury trial commencing in the Supreme Court of Victoria in October 2000 before Justice Frank Vincent.

Supported by expert evidence and testimony from Nicole, the Crown's case was largely based on several arguments, namely that Smith first used ether to anaesthetise Nicole. He then took the baby into the bedroom and placed him alongside his mother, for the sole purpose of setting them both on fire so they would burn to death. This occurred when Smith used an accelerant, most likely ether, to set fire to the bed.[450] As to motive, the Crown was under no obligation to prove what

450 Ether is extremely flammable by evaporating quickly and forming vapours that can easily ignite.

was behind the callous act but would also rely on the overall conduct of Smith in the relationship with Wilkinson.

Counsel for Smith determined not to call him to give evidence, so he remained mute. As to how the fire started, the aromatherapy device was the culprit and not the accused. Great reliance was placed by the defence on the evidence of the specialist anaesthetist who, under cross examination, had conceded to a point that it was possible Nicole had not been anaesthetised. On that basis, her burns may have been as a result of only short exposure to intense flames.

The Crown though, in summing up to the jury, stated Nicole's accounts of events was consistent with not only the administration of an agent such as ether but her coming out of an ether-type anaesthetic. As to her injuries, they were so severe that any person in a normal type of sleep would have immediately woken up but she didn't as she had been temporarily rendered unconscious.

On question of motive, as mentioned above, the judge's direction to the jury pointed out it was not a necessary element for the Crown to prove. In other words, they did not have to show Smith acted the way he did because of some powerful factor, leading to him committing murder. However, the jury was instructed to derive some assistance out of the presence or absence of motive. Nonetheless, it was not required to have any bearing on their overall judgment for reaching a verdict and be satisfied of guilt beyond reasonable doubt. Indeed, the jury did reach such a unanimous verdict beyond reasonable doubt, finding Smith guilty on both counts as charged.

On 6 December 2000, he appeared before Justice Vincent for sentencing. His Honour accepted that Smith had no prior convictions and had good prospects of eventual successful reintegration into the community. However, as to what took place on that tragic morning, the learned judge didn't hold back saying:

> *...at about 7 o'clock, you placed a cloth impregnated with a volatile anaesthetic, possibly ether, over the face of your sleeping wife. She awoke and struggled as she inhaled acrid fumes but you held her down until she lost consciousness... using an aromatherapy burner that had been purchased only a few days earlier, you staged a setting designed to indicate that an accidental fire had occurred and set fire to the bed. You left the house and went to work as if nothing abnormal had happened.*[451]

It was certainly no accident and in that regard His Honour said:

> *You are, I consider, a calculating individual, who, having decided what he wanted, was prepared to let nothing stand in the way of achievement of his desires, not the life of his child and certainly not that of a wife of whom he had grown tired*[452]*...You almost succeeded in your design but, fortunately, Nicole Taylor survived and was able to recall enough of what had happened so that an extensive investigation involving the police services of both countries was conducted and you were brought to this court and a jury of your peers.*[453]

Smith was sentenced on both counts to an effective term

451 *R v Smith* [2000] VSC 561-para 22.

452 Ibid-para 51.

453 Ibid-para 52.

of imprisonment of 26 years with a non–parole period fixed at 22 years. A subsequent application for leave to appeal was dismissed in the Court of Appeal on 20 December 2002.[454] Following his rather lenient sentence of a non-parole period of 22 years, with time already served in pre-sentence detention of 490 days, this meant Smith, at 58 years of age, would have been eligible for parole around August 2021.

For all we know, he is now enjoying what life has to offer as a free man. It is a pity that this low life of a human being didn't allow Nicole the same privilege. Sadly, she must live her days suffering from horrendous injuries and the loss of her adored infant child.

---

454 *R v Smith* [2002] VSCA 219-The failed appeal was on the grounds of whether there was a motive link, were the directions sufficient as to lies and admissions and the directions given in respect of expert evidence. The Court of Appeal went into some detail in their 128-paragraph judgment in dismissing the appeal.

43
ONE DISTURBED MIND

A question of motive can assist a criminal jury to reach a conclusion why the accused committed the crime and also what the intention was. However, as we know, motive is not an essential element in order to prove guilt and, providing the Crown has a strong circumstantial case, the criminal trial may simply proceed on the basis of no evidence of motive.

It certainly became a question of "why" in the horrific murder of a mother and two of her children. Around 9.30am on Wednesday, 12 March 1996, their three bodies were found in the family home in Albion Park Rail, a 15-minute drive from Wollongong in NSW. In a visibly upset state, Matthew De Gruchy had yelled out to a neighbour, 'There is something wrong with Mum and Sarah.'

On finding their mother, Jennifer Anne De Gruchy, deceased in bed with a towel covering her head, the neighbour quickly contacted emergency services. Police and ambulance officers found the 18-year-old De Gruchy lying by the side of the road in a very distressed state, requiring transfer to a local hospital.

When entering the house, police located another two dead victims and were faced with a massacre that was truly horrific. De Gruchy's 15-year-old sister, Sarah, was found in her bedroom with a cushion over her head and his brother Adrian in the garage, both suffering massive head wounds. Adrian also had extensive injuries to the lower part of his body, with his arms blistered and his clothes soaked in petrol. Crime scene detectives found a jerry can containing petrol near Adrian's body, with large tufts of carpet cut and removed from different areas of the main bedroom.

While most of the household valuables had been left untouched, De Gruchy's father noticed several items, including a video recorder, were missing, so it was highly probable a robbery had taken place. Crime scene detectives also found a wall unit and wardrobe drawers open, with numerous blood smears in various parts of the home, later providing detectives with valuable DNA evidence.

Postmortem examination of each of the victims revealed the terrible extent of the children's injuries, describing them similar to plane crash victims. The opinion of the time of death of each deceased was late on the evening of 12 March 1996, or even up to as late as 3am the next morning. In respect of Mrs De Gruchy, she suffered not only a depressed fracture between her eyes but extensive underlying brain trauma, most likely inflicted by either a wheel brace or sledgehammer while she was asleep. Her brain had almost been severed from her head, with blood in her airways suggesting she was still alive for a short time after the attack. Her face was so disfigured, her identity could only be confirmed from a DNA match.

Adrian had suffered a total of 21 injuries, which included fractures and lacerations to his neck and head. There were also injuries to his trunk and bruises on his chest, leading to a conclusion that a similar weapon had been used. Peeling on his skin was noted and consistent with petrol being poured over him, most likely in preparation to set him alight. Defence injuries were found on the right arm of Sarah De Gruchy, with similar skull fractures. In her case though, a tyre lever was suspected as the murder weapon.

De Gruchy was interviewed by police the day after the terrible events and again, four days later. He stated he last saw his family alive on the night of 12 March 1996, before he left to spend the night at his girlfriend's place. His father, when questioned of his whereabouts, said he had spent the night at his parents' house, which he often did due to work travelling commitments. This was confirmed by his parents, who said he had indeed slept at their home overnight. De Gruchy's girlfriend confirmed he had spent the night at her place, after arriving around 11 to 11.30pm and did not appear to be stressed in any way. She also said there was no evidence of any blood on him or his clothes.

However, she mentioned he had informed her of receiving threatening phone calls earlier in the evening, which delayed his arrival at her residence. Prior to leaving the next morning, around 8am, he also said the telephone threats were to his mother, which included a statement that 'three people in your family would be deceased.' Matthew, however, made no mention of these alleged telephone calls, when he was interviewed by police on 13 and 17 March, 1996.

Homicide detectives were building a strong circumstantial case against the young lad, suspecting he was the perpetrator.

In the Toyota Corolla he drove that evening, they found a small piece of carpet matching his mother's bedroom and expert evidence would confirm it was most probably from the same carpet. The carpet also contained a small red blood stain which did not match either his mother or father. However, it matched De Gruchy with also a smear of his fingerprint on the blood of a doorknob from a vanity unit in the main bathroom. Other blood spots throughout the house were also found to match their now main suspect, De Gruchy. In addition, a petrol container found near his brother's body also bore his fingerprints.

Two months after the murders, some of the family's missing items were found near a dam behind the old Woonona brickworks. This dam was only two kilometres from his girlfriend's place and around 31 kilometres from the De Gruchy family home. A red and white bag found by children contained a sheet, a piece of similar carpet and a small sledgehammer with a towel wrapped around it. A further search by police then uncovered a black backpack and a quantity of loose items, together with pieces of carpet. The items now recovered, amongst other household items, also included a video recorder, credit cards and a driver's licence in the name of Mrs De Gruchy.

One of the bags contained torn pieces of paper sealed in a plastic zip-lock bag, which later became significant evidence in the case against De Gruchy. The police determined that the note was written in his handwriting. It contained a list of instructions in what could loosely be described as a "how to do it" checklist, including the names of the three deceased victims written in blue. The checklist stated such things as "have a shower", presumably suggesting it was to be done after the murders. Other words included "hit arm with pole…hit leg with pole…cut somewhere with knife" and also "throw hi-fi down back…throw things down wall in roof…."

De Gruchy was placed under covert surveillance by investigators as he was clearly more than just a person of interest. In the absence of any further incriminating evidence, a decision was made to take him into custody on 22 June 1996. He exercised his right to silence, which was most likely on legal advice. Detectives then conducted a further search of the De Gruchy home, particularly his bedroom. Their initial search, based on the handwritten note, proved unsuccessful, as nothing was found in the roof cavity or thrown down any wall space. However, this time, police located a single sheet of note paper similar to the one previously reconstructed and an expert opinion confirmed it was in De Gruchy's handwriting.

At his contested 1998 Supreme Court trial on three counts of murder, the Crown contended that the accused murdered his mother and two siblings, sometime after 8pm on the night of 12 March 1996. After driving to the old Woonona brickworks in the Toyota Corolla, to dispose of the various household items in the dam, he then went to his girlfriend's house. The following morning, De Gruchy feigned surprise and anguish at the discovery of the grisly scene.

The Crown, from the outset, accepted their case was based solely on circumstantial evidence, conceding there was no identified motive for the murders. However, such evidence also included DNA and fingerprints linking De Gruchy to the crime scene, the comparable handwritten note found in the dam and his bedroom and inconsistencies in his two earlier police interviews.

De Gruchy gave evidence at his trial where he steadfastly maintained his innocence, stated he loved his mother very much and that he'd last seen her and his two siblings alive at around 10pm on 12 March 1996. His reason for omitting to tell police about the threatening phone calls was because of the medication he was taking after being hospitalised. In his opinion, the murders had been carried out by someone else and he even suggested, at one point, that his father was the culprit.

The defence also submitted that the alleged telephone threats, forecasting the demise of the three family members, were significant. Additionally, they contended a note dated 19 March 1996, left by a male who had committed suicide fearing he would be held responsible for the murders, was considered relevant. Counsel at the trial tried but failed to subpoena police records of the two murders that happened in the same area after the De Gruchy killings.[455]

As to the incriminating DNA and fingerprint evidence, De Gruchy admitted he had left blood in the house at some point, all innocent though. Regarding the carpet offcuts, they were regularly placed in the car, to assist when transporting heavy objects. The petrol container was often used by him so that explained the fingerprints. He acknowledged the handwritten notes were his but, aside from activities related to his 18th birthday, he did not recall writing them.

What was surprising was the Crown Prosecutor, in his closing address to the jury, suggested the person who committed the murders, 'must have had a disturbed mind.' Rightly, counsel for the accused objected to the Crown proffering an explanation in the absence of any motive. Given there was absolutely no evidence to prove such disturbed mind, it was submitted such

455 In June 1998, two violent murders, with one victim living within 1.7 kilometers of the De Gruchy home, occurred leading to the arrest of Mark Mala Valera (see chapter 45).

a comment must be withdrawn. Although the trial judge correctly dealt with this comment in his directions to the jury, it would later become a point of contention in an appeal all the way to the High Court of Australia.

Although his defence team had relied heavily on the absence of any proven motive and he was of excellent character, which was supported by his father and girlfriend, it was all to no avail. On 14 October 1998, a jury convicted De Gruchy on three counts of murder and he was sentenced to concurrent minimum terms of 21 years, in addition to further terms of seven years. This meant, at the time of sentencing, taking into account his time in custody on remand, he would not be eligible for parole until at least June 2017.

With absolutely no disrespect to the sentencing judge, such a term of imprisonment seems rather lenient, given the murder of three innocent family victims. In effect, if De Gruchy was to see out his full term behind bars, arguably, it could be looked at as a little over nine years for each of the victims. This may not have provided any solace to the family, especially his father, who experienced the profound loss of his beloved wife and children. Credit is due to his father for supporting his son during the trial, as he believed in his innocence.[456]

Clearly, his defence team also thought he was not guilty, as an appeal against conviction and sentence was subsequently filed with the Court of Criminal Appeal.[457] This was on the basis of (1) the unreasonable verdict could not be supported by the circumstantial evidence; (2) exclusion of evidence of other

456 Some years later it was reported in the media that Mr De Gruchy had again approached NSW Police requesting access to all the evidence that convicted his son.

457 *R v De Gruchy* [2000] NSWCCA 51.

violent murders and (3) directions given to the jury by the trial judge about the "disturbed mind".[458]

Despite the circumstantial nature of the Crown's case and the reliance on incriminating evidence, ground one was deemed of no relevance. The court highlighted the substantial evidence that unequivocally established De Gruchy's guilt beyond reasonable doubt. Indeed, it was summed up succinctly by Chief Justice Wood when he said:

> *When all the factors, identified by the Crown, are taken into consideration, in combination, I am not persuaded that the case is one in which the jury ought to have obtained a reasonable doubt. In particular, the combination of the note, the presence of the appellant's fingerprint on the cabinet door knob, the DNA recovered from the carpet tuft and from the spots of blood in the hallway and bedroom…the appellant's unconvincing evidence concerning the note, the absence of any mention to police of the prophesy as to the death of three members of the family, the appearance of a staged robbery and the finding of items in a dam with which he was familiar, constituted a powerful circumstantial case. It may also be assumed from the verdict that, having seen and heard the appellant give evidence, the jury were not impressed with his credibility-a conclusion well open to them by reference to the matters I have mentioned.*[459]

Regarding the other murders in the same approximate location, the Court of Appeal considered this as pure conjecture

458 An additional ground was on the basis of an unbalanced jury summing up by the trial judge which was also dismissed outright by the Court of Criminal Appeal. See Ibid- paras 86-92.

459 Ibid-paras 93-113.

for the existence of an alternative hypothesis. The Court of Appeal did, however, express some criticism at the remarks made by the Crown Prosecutor, in his closing address to the jury regarding the appellant's 'disturbed mind'. In that regard, Chief Justice Wood stated:

> *The approach taken by the Crown Prosecutor in this regard was both ill-advised, and curious since the comment did not necessarily advance the prosecution case. It also involved a degree of circularity. In the absence of any evidence that the appellant had a disturbed mind, the comment was capable of being understood as pointing to some other person other than the appellant as the culprit. To that extent, it favoured the defence case. However, the complaint of the appellant lay in the submissions that it offered a possible explanation for the appellant acting in a most disturbing and violent way, which was apparently out of character for him.*[460]

However, with the other two justices agreeing to also dismiss this ground, Chief Justice Wood said:

> *I am satisfied that the jury would have understood the remarks of His Honour to have been directed to that matter and, in that respect, to have neutralised the somewhat ill-advised and circular observation of the Crown Prosecutor. Once these directions were given, there is no reason for supposing that the jury were left with the apprehension that there might have been some uncalled evidence available to this effect or that they*

460 Ibid- para 72.

might properly speculate that the accused had been suffering from a disturbed state of mind. [461]

Following the dismissal by the Court of Appeal on 2 March 2000 for conviction and refusing leave to appeal against sentence, a further appeal was heard in the High Court of Australia. Again, such grounds revolved around the directions given to the jury by the trial judge that were either wrong or inadequate, particularly on the issue of "disturbed mind". In addition, it was submitted by counsel for De Gruchy, whether the jury's verdicts were unreasonable, based on purely circumstantial evidence in the absence of motive.

On 8 August 2002, the High Court was unanimous in its 25-page judgment dismissing the appeal and finding the jury's verdict was not unreasonable. Regarding the trial judge's directions with absence of motive and the disturbed mind issue, the learned justices stated:

It clearly appears from the trial judge's directions that much emphasis was placed on the absence of motive in defence counsel's final address. Apart from instructing the jury correctly that the prosecution did not have to prove motive, nothing was said by the trial judge to detract from the force of the defence counsel's submissions in that regard. Moreover, given the trial judge's repeated directions that the question of "disturbed mind" was irrelevant[462]*...neither prosecuting counsel's references to a disturbed mind, nor anything else in the case, required any specific direction with respect to motive other than that motive*

461 Ibid-para 84.

462 *De Gruchy v The Queen* [2002] HCA 33-para 31.

was not an essential element of the crime charged and, thus, did not have to be established by the prosecution…[463]

You'd like to think that De Gruchy would disappear from the face of the earth and quietly serve his sentence, given that eventually he could be released on parole. However, it wasn't to be. In February 2007 and in company with several other notorious inmates,[464] they allegedly bashed two members of the infamous "K" brothers, with one almost dying from his injuries. This duo, along with two other siblings, were sentenced to a total of 70 years in prison for committing multiple gang rapes in Ashfield, NSW, during 2002.

I use the word "allegedly" because the outcome of the charges, which included two for maliciously inflicting grievous bodily harm, did not appear to be reported in full in the media.[465] Regardless, even if De Gruchy and others were found guilty, most likely, any sentence imposed would be served concurrently with their existing prison time.

In April 2017, after earlier being transferred from maximum security at Goulburn Prion to Junee Correctional Centre, it appeared De Gruchy may have mended his ways. Not only was it reported he was now a model prisoner but he had also been given the right to leave prison on day leave. This was for approved reasons, such as education and work. In respect of the latter, this triple murderer was also working

463 Ibid-para 32.

464 One of his alleged cohorts was Craig Andrew Merritt, who was serving at least 27 years for the 2001 murder of his three young children. See further *R v Merritt* [2004] NSWCCA 19.

465 The only media report appears to be in March 2009 in respect of a mention hearing at Goulburn Local Court.

in a Junee abattoir, pending his application to be released on parole. Regarding his duties at the abattoir, Corrective Services assured the public De Gruchy was only carrying out work in the chill room and did not have access to any knives.

It was obvious that, pending his first application for parole in May 2017 when he was 38 years old, he was reasonably confident he would soon be released. So confident was he that he sent a card to a family member sending his love and making a reference that 'things were about to change for the family.' This could be taken two ways, namely, he would soon be free or their peaceful lives would change drastically when that happened. One family member, who asked not to be identified, told media at the time:

'Every now and then, I do get flash backs and remember [the state of their bodies] …Matthew is the stuff nightmares are made of. But we just want to get on with life… They can't be rehabilitated…'

Their prayers were initially answered in late May 2017, when his first application for parole was rejected. The NSW Parole Authority refused his bid for release pending a further psychiatric report as he was still considered an unacceptable risk. In addition, De Gruchy had not participated in their required external leave programs and arrangements for post-release accommodation were still to be finalised.

It was another two years before he was released. After serving 23 years of his maximum sentence, in August 2019 41-year-old De Gruchy walked out of Long Bay Correctional Complex a free man. It was under strict parole conditions which would expire in June 2024, including making no contact in any form with members of his family, other than his father and an aunt who still supported him. In addition, under no circumstances was he allowed to visit the Illawarra or Shoalhaven local government areas.

According to the Parole Authority, De Gruchy's conduct behind bars had been exemplary, apart from the 2007 incident and one other matter. He had also obtained trade qualifications and had found suitable accommodation. His release was approved, despite the NSW Government expressing strong opposition due to the seriousness of his offences.

The final say should be left to De Gruchy's uncle and another advocate, who commented on his release:

'The family feel three lives were taken and De Gruchy should have been sentenced to three life terms and should never be released…no matter what sentence you give to the offender, we are the ones who get the life sentence.'

Truer words have never been spoken.

44
A BRUTAL ACT

In some jurisdictions, being sentenced for murder means you will be imprisoned for the term of your natural life, never to be released. In a number of states in the USA, the death penalty for first degree murder is handed down, particularly in the state of Texas.[466] In our sun-blessed country down under, life imprisonment is the most severe penalty that can be imposed for the most heinous of crimes, including murder.

However, a life sentence for murder in Australia does not necessarily mean life. Even in respect of a triple murder,

---

466 Since 1976, over 30 per cent of the total number of executions in the US were carried out in the state of Texas. Each of the states in order to impose a death sentence requires the finding of aggravated circumstances or factors such as the murder of a law enforcement officer, a killing by a hired assassin or to prevent lawful arrest, or the murder of a witness. It can also include that the murder was particularly heinous, atrocious or cruel.

a minimum non-parole period may still be imposed.[467] The final say for time to be served is left with the sentencing judge, subject later to any appeal and is determined by the severity of the crime, prior criminal history and factors in mitigation, such as mental health issues, even remorse and an early plea of guilty. After completing the minimum period, the offender may then apply for parole but that does not mean it will be automatically granted.

Unfortunately, we have seen many examples where both the head sentence and non-parole period involving a murder have been manifestly inadequate. Case in point, was the January 1997 murder carried out by 19-year-old Mark Thomas England in West Geelong in Victoria. I must warn you, if you think what you have read in the preceding chapters has been confronting or distressing, I suggest you give the following a complete miss.

The port city of Geelong is approximately 75 kilometres from the Melbourne CBD, with a population of around 285,000. Apart from its well-known AFL football club, the Cats, being the second oldest competitor in the code's history,

---

467 Prior to 1999, life sentences in Australia did not impose a maximum time duration. Since then, all states, for example, have put in place legislation setting a maximum period and once completed must then be reviewed by a parole board or judge. A period of 25 years applies in Western Australia, South Australia, Victoria and New South Wales. A lesser period of 15 years applies in Queensland and in Tasmania it is 20 years. The usual range is anywhere between 10 years to 25 years, other than the most vicious of murders. However, in respect of the murder of a police officer, a conviction means mandatory life without parole.

it also provides a valuable transport corridor.[468] Unfortunately, it has also been the subject of a number of high-profile murders, including some which still remain cold cases.[469]

One that will remain forever etched in the history of Geelong, was the murder of a 75-year-old woman who was only ever referred to as Mrs Findlay, or Mrs F, in subsequent court proceedings. In the early hours of Sunday, 12 January 1997, a fire burning ferociously in a house in West Geelong was reported. After quelling the blaze, emergency responders found the badly burnt body of the owner who resided there alone since the death of her husband in 1969.

Following a victim identification by loved ones, which understandably caused great distress, a post-mortem determined that Mrs F had in fact been murdered. She had suffered extensive blows to her head, possibly from a heavy, blunt instrument. What was not known at the time though was the full extent of what had taken place, particularly after she had died and before the fire was set.

After homicide detectives conducted a thorough investigation, they quickly identified England as a person of interest. He had been a previous tenant of a flat owned by Mrs F, until the tenancy ended abruptly over unpaid rent. To try

468 It is also known as a 'Gateway or Second City' playing an important role in Australia's national economic and social prosperity.

469 The January 1973 murder of Geelong pinball operator, Bert Driscoll, remains unsolved as does the bashing and strangling to death in December 1992 of 13-year-old, Clare Morrison. Another cold case that would take 23 years to bring to justice was the stabbing murder of Ricky Balcombe in May 1995. In June 2018, his killer, 44-year-old Karl Michael Hague, was sentenced to 26 years imprisonment, with a minimum non-parole period of 20 years. (*The Queen v Hague* [2018] VSC 323).

and recover the arrears, Mrs F withheld some of his furniture and clothing. Police then spoke with a woman who had also boarded with England in the same flat. She told police of threats England had made at the time of the dispute. After both being told by Mrs F to move out, England said, in no uncertain terms, that he would get her back and that:

'She's going to die. I'm going to kill her for this…she's going to get hers one day. I'll make sure of that.'

Investigators recovered a watch, which was identified as being from the home of Mrs F. After learning that England had given this watch to his former girlfriend not long after the murder, police pounced, taking him into custody on 4 February 1997. Initially, England denied having anything to do with her death and provided a questionable account of how the watch came into his possession, saying it was given to him by an innocent third party. The police interview, comprising 1200 questions and answers over long protracted stages, finally saw England admit to forcibly entering her house to steal money and other items. His detail of what actually took place, even astonished hardened homicide detectives.

England said, initially his sole intention was to steal money from Mrs F, as he had knowledge of her regular habits from when he was a tenant. He was very aware of money kept in her house, after she collected the rent from her flat tenants. England stated that he forcibly entered the home in the early morning of 12 January 1997, arming himself with a long crowbar he found in the kitchen. He proceeded along the hallway to the main bedroom where he found Mrs F asleep. She woke up screaming at him and saying, 'You beast!' when he demanded money from her.

When told she had no money because it was with her

relatives, he started hitting her with the crowbar. England said the blows to her skull did not knock her out, as it seemed like she was wearing some sort of steel plate in her head. Unperturbed, he tried using the claw-like end of the crowbar, inflicting further injuries to her hands and forearms as she was trying to defend herself.

After she fell on the floor, England stomped on her and placed one foot on her throat but it didn't kill her. He then grabbed a belt hanging off the bedroom door and strangled her until she finally stopped breathing. Following this, he dragged the now deceased Mrs F across the bedroom floor, removed her nightie and had sexual intercourse with her dead body, even stating to police he ejaculated.

England then located her handbag, which contained about $1,000 and, after removing the watch from the bedroom, he went into the garage where he found a can of petrol. The contents were poured over her dead body, the hallway and throughout the house and lit before he left via the back door. On arriving home, he washed all his clothes and gave the stolen watch to his former girlfriend sometime later. As to the money, he told detectives he used it to buy drugs and a Walkman device.

In October 1997, a contested committal hearing took place in the Melbourne Magistrates Court for a charge of murder.[470] Counsel for England cross-examined at least 20

470 Witnesses called by the prosecution at a committal hearing are subject to cross-examination by the defence, who may also call witnesses. At the conclusion, defence counsel may make submissions on the strength of the evidence. A magistrate will then determine, at such hearing, whether there is sufficient evidence to support a jury conviction and, in that event, the accused will be committed to stand trial on the charge of murder in the Supreme Court.

Crown witnesses, with the suggestion that there were issues with "continuity" of forensic samples. It also proposed that England might consider an insanity defence.[471] In August 1998, after some suggestion that he would change his plea to not guilty, England pleaded guilty. He appeared before Justice Coldrey[472] for sentencing in the Supreme Court of Victoria on 23 October 1998.[473]

Any suggestion of a defence of insanity was put to rest, following expert reports tendered before His Honour. One psychiatric report concluded, apart from his extensive use of cannabis, which was not connected to the murder offence, England had no mental impairment. There was no diagnosable mental disorder but he did have a low IQ, despite being of normal intelligence. Counsel for England went to some length in submitting. whilst post-mortem acts could be seen as an aggravating factor, it did not apply in this matter. This was on the basis of a loss of control, exacerbated by his dull intellect.

England's background included setting fire to a school he attended then leaving home at the age of 15 and being sentenced in 1996 to detention in a youth training centre. This

---

471 Mental impairment is a device available under section 20 of the *Crimes (Mental Impairment and Fitness to be Tried) Act 1997*(Vic).

472 Justice Coldrey earned a reputation as a notable Supreme Court judge from 1991 to 2008. He then served on the Adult Parole Board, followed by being appointed chair of the Victorian Institute of Forensic Medicine Council. He would often be brought to tears when reading victim impact statements and, in one trial, gave a suspended sentence for manslaughter, which has since been removed as an opinion available to judges. My perceived criticism of him in this matter in no way reflects on his extraordinary career.

473 *DPP v England* [1998]-Unreported VSC, Justice Coldrey, 23 October 1998.

was followed by further prison time in 1996 after an escape from custody and theft of a motor vehicle. He also had a few relationships, including fathering a child when he was 17 years old.

England was sentenced to a paltry 18-year imprisonment with a non-parole period of 14 years. It seems Justice Coldrey accepted and sentenced him on the basis that the act of sexual intercourse and setting fire to the body of Mrs F was in no way to be considered an aggravating factor. This, understandably, became a point of contention in a subsequent appeal filed by the Crown.

As to his reasons for sentence, the learned judge stated:

> *The crime of murder was, of course, complete at the death of Mrs Findlay and the shocking events which followed cannot, as a matter of law, be seen as aggravating the circumstances of that criminal act. However, having murdered Mrs Findlay in the course of the burglary, you did not recoil in horror at your brutal act. You certainly did not show any instantaneous remorse or regret for what you had done. Rather, you proceeded to defile the body of Mrs Findlay by sexual penetration of her corpse.*[474]

It was of no surprise that the question of the sentence being manifestly inadequate proceeded to the Supreme Court of Criminal Appeal. The DPP appealed on the basis that the post-mortem sexual intercourse and incineration of the body was certainly an aggravating circumstance, requiring a more appropriate sentence. The appeal grounds were heard in May 1999 with counsel for England maintaining the proposition that the crime of murder was in fact complete after death.

474 Ibid.

If that was to be accepted and it wasn't, this meant anything done after such a despicable act didn't matter and could not be viewed in any way as an aggravating factor. His counsel further argued that it would be inappropriate or even redundant, to consider the act of intercourse and the burning of the body as a significant factor, possibly interpreting it as a form of negative remorse.

The Court of Appeal accepted, as submitted by the Crown Prosecutor in the original trial, that the interfering with a corpse, including the burning of the body, clearly demonstrated an entire absence of remorse. In that respect, it must therefore be considered as a serious mitigating factor in the commission of the murder. On 25 June 1999, the appeal was upheld but only with a substituted sentence of 23 years imprisonment imposed, with a non-parole period of 17 years.[475]

In that regard Justice Batt said:

> *...On the main point, I would say in two sentences that I cannot accept that it would be improper to impose the same sentence for murder where there was post-death defilement, mutilation or burning of the corpse as, where they were absent, if the circumstances of the offence and of the offender were otherwise the same. To do so seems to me...to be contrary to commonsense...*[476]

It could be argued that commonsense would see a sentence of life imprisonment without parole for England. Alas, it was not to be. Given that his pre-sentence detention in June 1999 was around two years and six months, in all likelihood, the now

475 *DPP v England* [1999] VSCA 95.

476 Ibid-para 41.

35-year-old may have been released on parole sometime in late 2013.

Our community may never know if he was released and enjoying life again. Sadly, his victim will never have that chance. It is not uncommon for the media to publicise details regarding the conviction and sentencing and the parole of certain individuals, however, this has not occurred in England's case. After reading the horrendous facts, as set out in the Victorian case law unreported judgment followed by his appeal, the lack of media reporting is understandable.

Perhaps it might be in this low life's better interests that the general public are kept guessing when England was released on parole.[477]

---

477 The Adult Parole Board provides details on parole of prisoners to a Victims Register. A person who has been impacted by a crime may be eligible to join such register. Once accepted as a registered victim, information is available, including whether the Board has granted parole.

45
LIKE BROTHER LIKE SISTER

Two horrific murders which almost defy description, took place in June 1998 in the NSW towns of Albion Park and Wollongong. The initial murder was that of local shopkeeper, 59-year-old David O'Hearn, who was found mutilated on the floor of his townhouse on the morning of Saturday, 13 June 1998. He had been decapitated with his head found lying in the kitchen sink. His left hand had also been severed and was located on the couch in his lounge room.

The murder scene was so grisly even seasoned police officer, Detective Inspector Woods, was utterly horrified when he said:

'… It was a scene I'd never encountered in all my years in the police…'

A postmortem determined extensive wounds intersecting and parallel from O'Hearn's chest down to his stomach. His skull had been fractured and the left eyeball punctured by a sharp object. Given there were also extensive lacerations to his brain, it was determined that the numerous head wounds would have been caused by at least 10 blows of severe force. The mutilation of the body was considered as carried out after the victim had died.

What the crime scene also revealed was a hammer had been inserted into his anus and his penis mutilated. A piece of bowel was found on a silver-coloured tray, with parts of his intestine on the breakfast bar in the kitchen. Exhibits bagged by police included knives, a small metal saw, a razor blade and other implements used in the mutilation of the victim. The word "Satan" had been scribbled in blood on a table mirror and again in the lounge room near the severed hand. On the wall close to the television set, an inverted cross was visible as was a pentagram, again drawn using blood.[478]

Two weeks later on 27 June 1998, another savage attack resulted in the death of 68-year-old Francis Arkell.[479] His mutilated remains were found in his weatherboard home in Wollongong, with his body left lying in his converted garage granny flat. His face was covered in blood, as was the tiled floor in the bathroom leading to the doorway. It was apparent he

478 A pentagram is a five-pointed star and has been used over time as some sort of magic or occult symbol.

479 He was a NSW politician as the member for Wollongong from 1984-1991. Arkell also served as Lord Mayor of Wollongong and his reputation would be brought into disrepute following his murder. This was in respect of allegations that he was known as a paedophile which he vehemently denied. Arkell was also believed to have been investigated as part of the 1995-1997 Wood Royal Commission that investigated police corruption and paedophilia but was cleared of any wrongdoing on his part.

had been strangled by a leather belt found around his neck and an electrical cord was also used. Police located a pair of boots and tracksuit pants with bloodstains. Since the deceased was found wearing pants and a white singlet, these items were also of some evidential relevance to the investigators.

Postmortem results determined he had also been mutilated after death: three tie pins were embedded in his face and a splinter of timber was found in his neck. A total of over 30 injuries had been inflicted on Arkell's head by a blunt instrument, confirmed to be the broken timber lampstand found by police. The victim's right ear was crushed, cartilage and muscle were exposed, the left jugular vein had been punctured and there was confirmation he had been strangled. His teeth had been fractured and there were similar injuries to his rib cage.

Following media coverage that included photographs of both the boots and tracksuit pants discovered at the Arkell crime scene, 19-year-old Mark Mala Valera walked into Wollongong Police Station on the night of September 30, 1998. Confessing to both murders, he initially said to stunned detectives it 'seemed like the right thing to do and to get shit off my chest'.

Before attending the police station, he had confessed to his girlfriend and his martial arts instructor that he had done, 'some really bad things.' Even if Valera had not presented himself to police, it would have only been a matter of time, in any event, before he would have been arrested. Police already had information that the bloodstained clothes belonged to Valera and had matching fingerprints from the O'Hearn crime scene.

Valera grew up with his younger sister, Belinda. They were

the children of Jack van Krevel. His mother played no role in their upbringing and Valera found irregular employment after leaving school at the age of 15. He had experienced some learning difficulties, coupled with a slight speech impediment. Valera practiced tae-kwon-do and had no known interactions with law enforcement.

At some point in his teenage years, he had abandoned the birth surname of van Krevel and then resided in different places locally but also lived within walking distance of the O'Hearn house. It was known to his friends that he involved himself in Satanism and would play music that depicted mutilation. One of Valera's longstanding good mates, Keith Andrew Schreiber, who had known him since childhood, would spend many hours with him discussing how to dissect a body. Little did anyone know at the time though, that they would both separately bring their morbid fascination into reality.

Later, it would be revealed that Valera's father subjected him to physical and emotional abuse from the early age of five. The abuse included regular beatings with either a fist or open hand, kicking him and, on one occasion, a gun was held to his head. Valera has also been admitted to the hospital, following a severe beating by his father. There were allegations of sexual abuse but that was later strenuously denied by his father and also rejected by the Supreme Court in the subsequent trial of Valera.

On 1 October 1998, police, over seven hours, obtained a detailed confession from Valera in an electronically recorded interview.[480] At his subsequent trial, the court deemed the

480 Any admissions made in an electronically recorded interview with a suspected person (ERISP), then forms an essential element of the case put forward by the Crown.

ERISP to be fundamentally reliable. In addition, Valera accompanied police to each crime scene, walking around pointing out what had occurred. At one point, he even showed the officers a spot on the kitchen bench stating, 'There was a piece of intestine about a metre long there.'

In O'Hearn's murder, he readily admitted he did not know him and just picked his house out and, in his words, 'at random', so '1 could kill someone.' He stated that after he'd knocked on the townhouse door, he was able to enter on the pretext he was looking for rental accommodation. Valera was invited inside and, without warning, he struck the victim 10 times with a decanter. He said he knew how many blows there were because he counted each one. On checking O'Hearn had no pulse, he found items upstairs with which to mutilate the body. He also confirmed the severed hand was used to draw the inverted cross and the pentagram.

Valera acknowledged knowing about Arkell and was aware of the community's reported dislike for him. Pretending to be gay and with the sole intention of killing Arkell, he telephoned the unsuspecting victim stating his desire to call around to see him. After arriving at the house and talking for a few minutes, Valera said he picked up a lamp and smashed Arkell's head approximately 40 times. As the victim tried to defect the blows and crawl away, Valera grabbed and strangled him with a lamp cord.

Then, in a nonchalant manner, Valera stated in the ERISP after seeing his victim was dead, he still kicked him a few times just to make sure. Valera confirmed he stuck the two tie pins into Arkell's cheek and his eye, as he wasn't satisfied with what he had achieved. He also tried to insert a fork into the neck of his victim but the wooden handle broke.

As to a motive for the horrendous killing, Valera confirmed to police he didn't like Arkell and had read 'all the nasty things he had done to kids…heard about him in the papers and the media.' He said he left the house wearing a pair of the deceased's pants, leaving behind his boots and tracksuit pants because they were covered in blood.

Given the admissions Valera had made in the ERISP confirmed what police knew, particularly in respect of the mutilations, the crimes carried out were clearly a case of horrendous murder. However, when presented before the Supreme Court of NSW on 12 July 2000 on two counts of murder, Valera pleaded not guilty, but guilty to manslaughter, on the basis of provocation and by reason of abnormality of his mind.[481] It was of no surprise that such pleas were not accepted by the Crown and the trial proceeded before a jury.

Over the next 20 days and concluding around 8 August 2000, the jury heard a plethora of incriminating evidence submitted by the Crown. Testimonies were also heard from Valera, his father and his sister.

Valera then changed his story, telling the jury he had lost self-control and was provoked, when each of his victims wanted to have anal sex with him. He stated he had been sexually abused by his father from a young age and when encouraged by his soon-to-be victims into having sex, he lost control after

481 The defence of extreme provocation is set out in section 23 of the *Crimes Act 1900*(NSW) which provides that if the act or omission that constituted murder was in response to extreme provocation by the deceased, the accused must be found guilty of manslaughter. Section 23A provides a partial defence to murder based on mental health or cognitive impairment. Provocation as a defence in Victoria was abolished in 2005 but still has relevance in respect of when sentencing for murder.

having flashbacks. The suggested sexual abuse by his father, Jack van Krevel, was supported in evidence from his sister, Belinda. His father steadfastly denied any such conduct, although freely admitting to other physical abuse.

As to the defence of substantial impairment, expert evidence concluded that, in effect, it didn't exist as Valera knew exactly what he was doing, knew it was wrong and had sufficient presence of mind to control himself. Evidence of his state of mind and the pleasure he got from his murderous rampage, was further demonstrated by entries he had made in a book he had read titled, "The A to Z of Serial Killers".

Not only did the book include the names of his two victims but under "my list" he had pencilled in, 'Who will be my No 3?' followed by, 'Not anyone in particular.' Several inconsistencies were also identified in Valera's testimony, particularly regarding his credibility and statements previously admitted during the ERISP, which were corroborated by both crime scene and postmortem evidence.

The jury found the defendant guilty of murder on each count, concluding there was no provocation or abnormality of mind. On 21 December 2000, after the learned judge had previously heard final submissions from both the Crown and defence counsel, Valera appeared before His Honour for sentencing.

In finding both crimes in the worst category of heinousness, Justice Studdert said:

> *...David O'Hearn was subjected to a most savage attack and I am satisfied beyond reasonable doubt that the prisoner acted in such attack with intent to kill and that it was a random and utterly senseless killing. The way in which the prisoner mutilated the body of this victim showed utter contempt for*

his victim and so too did his use of the severed hand and his writing on the wall and the mirror. Indeed, this first crime scene exuded evil of the prisoner's making. Francis Arkell was likewise subject to the most brutal attack...with intent to kill. The prisoner sought to explain and, indeed, to justify his attack upon an adverse judgment he had formed of his second victim... utter contempt for his victim after inflicting the savage injuries which inevitably would have led to his death by inserting into the head of the body the three tie pins...also endeavoured to force into the victim's neck the timber peg. I find a complete absence of any facts such as might mitigate the seriousness of either crime.[482]

Although His Honour expressed a degree of sympathy for Valera, the only mitigating factors identified were his lack of prior convictions and his youthful age at the time the two murders were committed. However, it was clear Valera was a long-term risk and the potential for him to be rehabilitated in order to be readmitted into society was, likely, non-existent. Regardless, the court did not have the power, under existing legislation, to impose a non-parole period for a service of life imprisonment for murder.

On that basis and in line with the current sentencing legislation that came into effect on 3 April 2000,[483] Justice

482 *R v Valera* [2000] NSWSC 1220- para 102.

483 Section 61 of the *Crimes (Sentencing Procedure) Act 1999*(NSW) stipulates : A court is to impose a sentence of imprisonment for life on a person who is convicted of murder if the court is satisfied that the level of culpability in the commission of the offence is so extreme that the community interests in retribution, punishment, community protection and deterrence can only be met through the imposition of that sentence.

Studdert sentenced Valera to life imprisonment on both counts of murder, without a non-parole period saying:

> *...The level of heinousness involved in these two killings does not allow for the imposition of anything less than imprisonment for life.*[484]

The history of the van Krevel family had become increasingly complex, particularly with one member now serving a life sentence in prison, after having chosen to renounce the family surname. Although the court in the trial of Valera rejected the allegations made against the father, Jack van Krevel, on the balance of probabilities, it would turn out his days were numbered. It soon became evident that a propensity for violence was present within the family, with similar tendencies further observed between its two siblings.

Following Valera's conviction and sentence, his sister, Belinda van Krevel, publicly expressed strong negative feelings toward her father, stating she harboured deep resentment against him and wanted him dead. As far as she was concerned, it was his fault that her brother would now spend the rest of his life in prison. To make matters worse, her five-year-old daughter, who was born when Belinda was only 17 years old, had told her mother she had been allegedly sexually abused by "Poppy".

Valera's best mate Schreiber was now currently in a relationship with Belinda, and he also had an immense dislike of Jack van Krevel. Schreiber was aware of the alleged physical

484 *R v Valera* [2000] NSWSC 1220- para 122. His Honour did say at para 124 that if he had been empowered to provide the possibility of parole, he would have done so.

abuse Valera had suffered at the hands of his father and also believed the allegations, made by Belinda's young daughter, had some substance. Another purported motive to get rid of van Krevel was that both Belinda and her brother were designated as the sole beneficiaries of their father's considerable estate.

According to Belinda's initial version of events, in the early hours on 18 August 2000, she and her daughter were woken by blood-curdling noises coming from the bedroom where her father slept. Although knowing what was happening, Belinda hid under her bed covers and later told police she heard strange noises that sounded like someone being killed. Once there was silence, Belinda, with her daughter, left the house and drove to Wollongong Police Station. She informed the police of her observations, including hearing certain sounds and noticing traces of blood. She also told investigators that her daughter had asked, "What's happening to Poppy?"

A crime scene was established after police found the mutilated body of van Krevel, who had been repeatedly struck with an axe and knife. A fire poker had also been used with evidence of post-mortem mutilation; his head was almost severed and there was blood splattered over the walls and ceiling. Belinda, who was present with the police during their initial visit to the house, reportedly said words to the effect of, 'He's dead, isn't he? Something bad has happened, hasn't it?'

After being informed of her father's death, she maintained a theatrical appearance of innocence and asked, 'Was he shot? How did he die?'

In the course of a homicide investigation, detectives typically begin by closely examining individuals who were closest to the victim. This includes immediate family members and acquaintances, who may possess relevant information regarding the circumstances of the case. Belinda was already known to have made allegations about her now late father, with her boyfriend, Schreiber, also believed to practice in Satanic rituals and other bizarre practices. Schreiber was also known to police, following a conviction in 1999 for armed robbery. In addition, a week before the murder, he had raised concerns about the alleged sexual assault by van Krevel on Belinda's daughter.

That evening, following the horrific murder, Port Kembla police brought Schreiber in for questioning. He initially professed to have no knowledge of what had transpired. It wasn't long though before he did a complete turnaround, in which he confessed to the murder. It was carried out, according to him, because of the painful and sadistic assaults van Krevel had committed on his family, notably Valera, Belinda and her daughter.

He initially stated, at some point during Valera's trial, Belinda asked him if he would murder her father but he didn't take her seriously. He was emphatic though that Belinda had played no part in the murder but his interview had inconsistencies, which led detectives to believe that Belinda was also definitely involved.

As to what took place in the early hours of that fateful morning, Schreiber said he gained entry though an open window and, although he was unarmed, he came with the sole intention of murdering van Krevel. On finding an axe near the garage door, he stood over his victim and said words to the effect, 'You fucking paedophile bastard. You'll never molest another kid again.'

After striking him a number of times with the axe, he turned on the bedroom light enabling van Krevel to recognise his attacker. The victim screamed for mercy but to no avail. Schreiber, now also armed with a fire poker, made sure it was his victim's last breath. Schreiber then said he found a knife to carve up the body, before drinking a glass of water and quietly walking away.

Police were still not convinced of Belinda's innocence and the following questions and answers, in a rambling record of her boyfriend's interview, would effectively seal her fate:

> Q151. How long ago did you start thinking about killing him?
> A. I'm not sure. Don't know. For a little while but Belinda's told me he, they got into an argument and Jack said to her, 'I hope that pissy little ant and poofter Keith fucking come here and kills me, tries to kill me.' That's what Belinda told me, so, I can, he only got what he asked for anyway.
> Q152. So, did that, that sort of thing spur you on a bit?
> A. Yeah, a bit.
> Q153. Was it then that you decided you were going to do something about it, or you-?
> A. Yeah, sort of.
> Q154. Had you discussed with Belinda what you were going to do?
> A. No.
> Q155. Did she ask you to do it?
> A. Yeah, I knew she wanted, she wanted him done.
> Q156. She wanted him done?
> A. Mm.
> Q157. When did she tell you that?
> A. A while ago, when, when Mark's trial started.

Q158. Did she ask you to do it?
A. No. I think so, she, 'Would you do it?' Yeah. I said, 'No, I don't know, not really'.
Q159. You declined her offer?
A. I don't know if she was serous or not. Don't think so. She might have been.

Schreiber was charged with the murder of van Krevel and, in the interim, detectives continued their enquiries into Belinda's involvement. A statement was obtained from van Krevel's ex-wife who had, by this time, partially reconciled her relationship with her estranged daughter, Belinda, especially following her son's life sentence.

According to her version of events, Belinda had offered Schreiber a payment of $2,000 together with her car, if he killed her no-good father. Belinda even told her mother that the plan was to hack him into small pieces and throw the remains into a local blowhole. Belinda was subsequently arrested on 1 June 2001, charged with murder and remanded in custody.

As for Schreiber, he appeared before Supreme Court Justice Hidden on 19 December 2001, following his plea of guilty for the murder of van Krevel. In a somewhat lenient sentence, he only received a maximum of 16 years imprisonment with a non-parole period of 12 years, meaning with presentence detention he would be eligible for parole in August 2012.

His Honour not only took into account the plea of guilty at the first available opportunity but also said, in support of the lenient sentence:

...the offender's crime is explicable by his relationship with Mark Valera and Belinda van Krevel...I am not persuaded that he is

a continuing danger to society. Indeed, if he has the benefit of the psychotherapy recommended…I have some confidence that he will not re-offend in a violent way. His expression of remorse…while not complete as one might wish, demonstrates an insight into the enormity of his crime. I think that he has reasonable prospects of rehabilitation, particularly as he will enjoy the continuing support of members of his extended family.[485]

On 12 April 2002, Belinda Jean van Krevel was formally committed to stand trial and entered a plea of not guilty. It was with some interest that on the same day, a decision was also handed down in the Court of Appeal for her brother. Valera had appealed against the severity of his life sentence, largely on the grounds it was manifestly excessive.

In a short three-page judgment, the court dismissed the appeal and agreed with Justice Studdert that the proper sentence was life. As to the subjective features of the case and whether any discount should apply to modify the life sentence by way of parole, Justice Meagher said:

… *Mr Valera was very young, less than 20 years, in fact; that he had had a miserable early life, his father bashing him regularly and with great brutality; that, instead of waiting to be arrested, he gave himself up and thereafter co-operated with police and that he had no prior convictions. Contrition, however, was expressly negatived by His Honour. There was no provocation; nor was there any element of mental impairment. On balance, his Honour came to the conclusion that none of these factors required the sentence to be less than life imprisonment.*[486]

485 *R v Schreiber* [2001] 1184-para 22.

486 *R. v Valera* [2002] NSWCCA 50- para 6.

However, there was a statement made by the Court of Appeal that I believe would have been universally acknowledged at the time and supported within the local community. In rejecting the lesser sentence arguments of counsel for Valera, it was summed up perfectly:

> *...one might be tempted to suggest that the circumstances of the present case call for punishment a good deal more severe than mere life imprisonment.*[487]

Prior to Belinda's trial, her lawyers offered a plea of guilty to an alternative charge of soliciting Schreiber to murder her father.[488] It was of no surprise that this plea to the lesser charge would be rejected by the Crown. In a long-drawn-out process, two trials took place in July 2002 and again in February 2003 with the jury being discharged on both occasions. The Crown agreed to amend the indictment from murder to the soliciting to murder her father, Jack van Krevel, for which she would plead guilty.

On 4 April 2003, Belinda appeared before Judge Barr for sentencing. The judge acknowledged that her request to Schreiber to kill her father stemmed from her intense animosity toward him. Her animosity was, understandably, based on her perception of the facts regarding his behaviour and the alleged sexual misconduct. The judge also considered her guilty plea and evidence of post-traumatic stress, related to her childhood experiences, while also noting concerns about her conduct in prison during remand. After being taken into custody, she

487 Ibid-para 9.

488 See section 26 – *Crimes Act 1900*(NSW) which carries a maximum penalty of 25 years imprisonment.

tried to escape and was placed in segregation, followed by a further 16 breaches which included intimidation, damaging or destroying property and using threatening language.

His Honour further acknowledged Belinda's need for intensive psychological treatment, expressing some hope she would participate in rehabilitation programs after sentencing. Taking all these factors into account, a sentence of imprisonment of six years was imposed with a non-parole period of four years.

In summing up her offending, Justice Barr stated:

> *... the offender's importunity was hot-blooded, borne of her belief, reinvigorated by the trial about the deceased's responsibility for the predicament that Valera, she and her daughter found themselves in. I take into account that as the offender well knew, her solicitation was likely to produce the result she desired.*[489]

On 1 June 2007, Belinda was released on parole. It was expected that this would conclude her involvement with the justice system. It didn't happen though-like brother like sister. On 26 June 2013, Belinda took a knife to her then romantic partner in a state of frenzy, stabbing him at least five times and nearly killing him. For that indiscretion, she was sentenced to three years with her parole being revoked on two separate occasions. In November 2017, she spent another 18 months in prison for stealing an elderly woman's handbag.

Unfortunately, on 6 March 2023 she was at it again only, this time, taking a knife to her neighbour with whom she had formed a relationship. Despite suffering stab wounds to his

---

489 *R v van Krevel* [2003] NSWSC 227- para 35.

chest and left shoulder, he survived. Belinda received a further six years in prison, with a non-parole period of four years.[490]

District Court Judge Haesler, to a point, had some sympathy for her when he said:

> *An offender who has a start in life that van Krevel had does not bear equal moral responsibility as someone who had what might be termed a "normal" or "advantaged" upbringing. Her background has left her marked; it has damaged her.*[491]*…She will remain a risk when released to the community. A gaol sentence can only remove her from the community for so long… Her release to parole will be conditional upon the State Parole Authority being satisfied that community safety concerns can be met.*[492]

It seems we won't hear any more from Mark Valera, as he serves his life sentence at the Goulbourn Correctional Centre. As for Belinda van Krevel, her earliest parole date is 5 March 2027 and we all wait with some trepidation though, once she is released.

---

490 *R v van Krevel* [2024] NSWDC 146.

491 Ibid-para 50.

492 Ibid-para 51.

46
THE BROTHERLY FERNANDO COUSINS

The country town of Walgett is situated in northern NSW, not far from the Barwon and Namoi Rivers. A 2021 census taken from the population of just over 1,300, determined that nearly 24 per cent were of Aboriginal and Torres Strait Islanders descent and, in some way, deemed to be a socially disadvantaged community. Like many remote country towns and not just those with an indigenous population, the abuse of alcohol and drugs would result in on-going crime, even leading shop owners to protect their livelihoods with after-hours metal shutters on their premises.

Walgett was no exception and, once again, it would be brought into the national murder spotlight, following the abduction, sexual assault and murder of local nurse, Sandra Hoare. She had recently graduated and, at the age of 21, was expecting to live a fulfilling and happy life. Around 10.40pm on

8 December 1994, Sandra left her home which she shared with her loving partner, to commence a night shift in the geriatric ward at the Walgett District Hospital.

Approximately 12.30am the following morning, she had a telephone conversation with another nurse. Two hours later, night shift staff became concerned because a geriatric patient had been assaulted, suffering severe lacerations to the top of his head, with Sandra nowhere to be seen. Additionally, there was evidence of muddy footprints leading from the front hospital gate to a nearby motor vehicle owned by another nurse, which had been broken into.

A search was immediately carried out and around 4pm on Friday, 9 December 1994, Sandra's naked body was located in a paddock, approximately 400 metres from the hospital and not far from a sports oval. She had been viciously attacked with evidence of, not only multiple bruising but her head had almost been severed. A piece of blood stained blouse was loosely tied around her neck.

A postmortem would establish that the gaping incision from the left side of her neck extended right around to its base. A number of cut mark wounds, typical of a sawing motion using a machete type instrument, had been inflicted to numerous layers of muscle and the internal jugular vein. There were also similar scratch marks to the jaw and on the right side of her neck. The postmortem examination concluded that Sandra had been almost decapitated and had obviously suffered a very painful death.

A crime scene was quickly established, both at the location where the body had been found and also at and from the hospital. Thanks to earlier heavy rain, police were able to quickly determine that the muddy footprints first led from the hospital to the motor vehicle, which had a broken window and interior damage. The owner confirmed that property, including audio musical tapes in the glovebox, sunglasses and a family photograph, had been stolen from inside the car.

There appeared to be three sets of footprints which proceeded to a treed area, within walking distance of the hospital front gate. In an area of disturbed ground, crime scene detectives found a black-coloured hair elastic, some lens cleaning cloths and a pair of scissors which bore the name "Sandra". They also located a small metal button, later found to be identical in appearance to those on the blouse Sandra was wearing.

The three visible footprints led from that area to where Sandra's body had been located. At this point, police saw two sets of footprints which they measured to be about one metre apart, leading to a levee bank. More incriminating evidence was also located: a part of a Bon Jovi cassette cover and a screwdriver. A single set of footprints were determined to have crossed the levee bank and, after looping back, joined with the other set and disappeared into a street.

Investigators, at this point, were reasonably confident that two perpetrators were involved in Sandra's murder. They had very carefully taken cast impressions of each of the three sets of footprints and one set was confirmed as matching those of the victim. The following day, on 10 December 1994, during a search of a dam close to the paddock where Sandra's body had been located, police divers found two machetes and a screwdriver.

A subsequent forensic examination of these items determined it was highly probable at least one of the machetes caused, not only the fatal injuries but the head wounds of the elderly patient who had also been attacked. As for the screwdriver, it was most likely used in the forced entry into the nurse's vehicle parked near the hospital.

Various witnesses came forward with information relating to two indigenous men, who were seen in the early hours of 9 December 1994, in the possession of both a knife and a machete. One woman named both Brendan Fernando and his cousin, Vester Fernando, saying she saw Brendan throw a knife into some bushes after they observed a police vehicle approaching. After it drove past, Brendan retrieved the knife and gave it to his cousin who stuck it into his shorts.

Her brother confirmed what they both witnessed but stated Vester was also armed with a machete. In company with a third male, known as Michael Jackson, the cousins had walked off in the direction of the Walgett Hospital. The witness thought it was around 1.00am or possibly 2am. Another person also told police of an altercation he had seen around midnight involving Vester in a scuffle, noticing he was armed with a machete.

The two cousins, who were said to be like brothers, were well known to police. By the age of 24, Vester had significant convictions dating back to 1986, which included an offence of robbery with wounding in 1989. This was followed four years later in 1993, with further imprisonment for an assault in company with the intention to carry out a robbery. Vester was now on parole for that offending and, in December 1994, he took up residence at a drug and rehabilitation centre, being a one hour and 30-minute drive from Walgett.

Brendan, who was 18 months younger than his cousin, wasn't much better, having convictions for similar offending from around 1987. His last record of committing a crime was in 1991 for robbery and he was believed to now be residing with a girlfriend on the outskirts of Walgett.

The cousins were clearly persons of interest so on 10 December 1994, investigators visited the home of Vester's sister with a search warrant. What they found was enough incriminating evidence enabling them to take both cousins into custody. Vester's sister told police she last saw him at a local hotel around 10pm on the night of 8 December 1994 and then at her home the following morning.

Police conducted a thorough search of her home where they found an open clear plastic audio cassette cover, together with a portion of a Bon Jovi audio cassette. This matched what was found at the base of a tree near the levee bank. A search of the vehicle Vester was believed to be driving on the night of 8 December 1994, revealed a bag identified as belonging to him containing several items stolen from the nurse's vehicle. This included the name and address of the nurse's former husband, her children's sunglasses and a torn photograph of them.

After taking Vester Fernando into custody, he empathically denied being anywhere in the vicinity of the hospital around the early hours of 9 December 1994. He did admit to the confrontation around midnight but said he was only in possession of a small iron bar. He also agreed he met up with Michael Jackson and, together with his cousin, Brendan, they went back to his sister's place where they stayed after enjoying a smoke.

Vester had a few hurdles to overcome and not only because of what was found in the bag located in his motor vehicle's boot. The first problem was a record of interview police had with Michael Jackson on 11 December 1994. Jackson told investigators that on meeting the Fernando cousins in the street in the early hours of that fateful morning, Vester invited him to help them steal a car. He was also told by Vester not to worry about getting caught by anyone, as he was armed with a machete. On seeing the weapon and being told to use it if he needed to kill anyone, Jackson said he decided to leave. He also heard Vester say he was going back to his sister's place to get a screwdriver to use in the car break-in.

At this point, police had no doubt Vester and Brendan were involved in, not only the car's forced entry outside the hospital but the patient's assault and then the murder. However, they only had circumstantial evidence, albeit somewhat convincing and, therefore, needed more proof in order to connect the cousins to the murder.

They took an impression of the shoes Vester claimed he was wearing on the nights of 8 and 9 December 1994, confirmed by his sister. The shoe impression was then compared to the casts taken of the muddy footprints from both inside and outside the hospital leading to the murder location and then the two sets of prints leaving from there. They found the size of Vester's shoe impression was indeed similar in length to one set of casts taken from the crime scenes.

The other problem for Vester was his cousin, Brendan, who had also been taken into custody at the same time. On the way back to the police station, Detective Sergeant Pollock asked Brendan whether he was willing to participate in an electronic interview (ERISP), regarding the murder of the nurse at the hospital.

Brendan declined and was advised that such refusal would have to be recorded in any event. Prior to that procedure, Detective Sergeant Pollock asked him a number of questions, which he meticulously recorded together with the answers in his police notebook. On asking Brendan about the machete that Vester was seen carrying, by two separate witnesses, Sgt Pollock then questioned him, in part, as follows:

Q. Where is the machete now?
A. Vester threw it over the levee bank.
Q. Are you prepared to show us where…?
A. Yeah.
Q. Are you prepared to go with us to show us what happened with the woman and we will have a video made of what you show us?
A. I don't want to go too close to where it happened.
Q. Are you prepared to go with us to that area?
A. Yeah, but not too close.

In what would be later described as a "runaround"-type interview in an unsuccessful appeal against the guilty verdict by the Court of Criminal Appeal, Brendan agreed that the handwritten questions and answers taken by Sergeant Pollock were correct. Despite such initial evasive interview and, after showing police where the machete had been thrown, he then took part in a further detailed conversation after being read his rights.[493] This was recorded on a tape recorder with their actual crime scene visit also taken on video.

Regarding the murder of Sandra Hoare, the following extract of selected questions and answers, would, overall, also

---

493 In that regard, Sgt Pollock said, 'Now I want you to understand that you don't have to answer any of those questions or say anything unless you wish but whatever you say will be recorded and later given in evidence. Do you understand that?'

form part of a strong circumstantial case against the Fernando cousins:

> Q.70. Will you just tell me again where Vester took the girl's pants off? Underpants?
> A. Under a tree near…oval.
> Q.72. Did she walk with him to the tree…?
> A. He had a blade pressed to her throat and he had her by the head and his hand over…her mouth.
> Q.77. …then after he took the bra and pants off, what did he do then?
> A. He told her to lay down. She laid down.
> Q.85. You held her legs. Did he have sexual intercourse with her.
> A. Yeah.
> Q.88. And where did you have the knife when he was doing that?
> A. He had it up against her throat.'

Brendan denied he had sexually interfered with their victim but when asked, he did say in a somewhat confusing reply, that he'd already had sex. He also stated he walked away after hearing her screaming when Vester hit her with the machete. Brendan emphatically rejected participating in the vicious murder, including the earlier assault by Vester of the hospital patient. After attempting to cover her head with dirt, they both left and started to walk back to their relative's home.

They were carrying some of her clothing which was never located, together with the property stolen earlier that fateful morning. Vester was still armed with the machete he used to murder Sandra, which had been confirmed by Brendan as thrown in the dam, along with the other machete and screwdriver. The two sets of footprints leading away from the body left no doubt who they belonged to, indicating joint involvement of both the Fernando cousins.

On 6 May 1997, the Fernando cousins appeared before a jury in the Supreme Court of NSW. They were jointly indicted with the murder of Sandra Hoare, with a second charge of alleging aggravated sexual intercourse with their victim.[494]

The Crown essentially relied on strong circumstantial evidence against both the accused. The jury heard incriminating evidence, not only from witnesses observing Vester in possession of the machetes on the evening before the murder but also the stolen items recovered, matching those found at one of the crime scenes and at his sister's home. The compelling footprint evidence would also be relied on by the Crown with a probable matching impression to one set of shoes.

There was, of course, the recorded admissions made by Brendan. However, both defendants pleaded not guilty as charged, with Brendan, as was his right, choosing not to give any evidence or be subjected to cross-examination. As for Vester, he chose to give evidence and mostly kept to the same concocted story he originally told police.

Following a lengthy trial, the jury had no doubt finding them both guilty of murder as charged. As to the aggravated sexual assault, Brendan was deemed guilty but the jury found his cousin Vester not guilty. In that regard, His Honour Justice Abadee had previously directed the jury to find him not guilty on that count. The jury determined Vester guilty of assault

494 *Crimes Act 1900*(NSW) -section 61J which carries a maximum penalty of 20 years imprisonment.

with the intent to have sexual intercourse, without consent in circumstances of aggravation.[495]

On 21 August 1997, the Fernando cousins appeared before the court for sentencing. It was not surprising that on the count of murder, they were both sentenced to penal servitude for the term of their natural life, meaning they would never be released.

As to the role they both played, Judge Abadee stated:

> *Whilst I am satisfied that the actual wound(s) responsible for the death of the victim were actually, physically inflicted by Vester, I am also satisfied that, at the time of such infliction, Brendan was physically involved in holding the deceased. His attempt in the record of interview to distance himself from actual immediate physical presence, participation and involvement, and upon the basis that he was walking away at the time when the lethal injuries were actually inflicted, should be firmly rejected...*[496]

In respect of the assault with intent to have sexual intercourse, Vester received a concurrent term of 10 years, as did Brendan for the aggravated sexual assault. As expected, an appeal was lodged on behalf of both men against conviction and sentence. Such appeal was based on the confessions and admissions, including amongst a number of other questionable grounds, the right of Vester to have a separate trial.

In that regard, the Court of Appeal, in a lengthy judgment,

---

495 Ibid-section 61k which also carries a maximum penalty of 20 years imprisonment.

496 *Regina v Brendan Fernando: Regina v Vester Allan Fernando* Matter No 70071/95[1997] NSWSC 323- page 7.

found there was no undue prejudice and including the other grounds, dismissed both appeals.[497]

Despite the fact the Fernando cousins loved and treated each other like brothers, prison officials thought otherwise. In view of the confessional statement made by Brendan, in which he clearly implicated his older cousin, it was initially considered there might be some sort of payback. On that basis, they were locked up in separate prisons: Vester at the Goulburn Correctional Centre and with Brendan many kilometres away at Lithgow Prison. The alert to keep them segregated with no physical contact remained on the prison file until around May 1999.

Both prisoners approached their respective gaol governors requesting they be allowed once again to associate with each other, albeit behind bars. On 4 July 1999, Vester, obviously very keen to see his cousin, agreed to sign an acknowledgement which contained a few conditions, one of which stated as follows:

> *That I will not cause, attempt to cause, or have caused, any injury to any other inmate. That I have no problems or grievance with any other inmate at Lithgow Correctional Centre.*

It was not the only thing Vester would execute and on reflection such acknowledgment 'not to cause any injury' should have included '…except to my cousin Brendan.' On 22 September 1999, after being transferred from segregation to Lithgow Prison, Vester didn't waste any time and repeatedly stabbed Brendan during a music lesson in Lithgow's education block auditorium. His weapon was later described as a "shiv", namely one side of a pair of scissors with a plastic handle. An

497 *R v Fernando & Anor* [1999] NSWCCA 66.

autopsy would find the cause of death was a stab wound to his chest but there were also several similar wounds to other parts of the body.

Two days later, police attempted to interview Vester but he declined to make any comment. After being indicted on a charge of murder, he pleaded guilty. On 20 April 2001, Judge Howe sentenced Vester to a term of imprisonment of 30 years, with a non-parole period of 22 years. In effect, the concurrent sentence imposed really had no impact on him as he would never be released, in any event, in view of the life term without the possibility of parole for the murder of Sandra Hoare.

Arguably it begs the question, what was the motive behind the murder of his so-called brotherly cousin? His Honour, based on the facts before him, knew nothing about the motive that led to Vester attacking his cousin but it did have some unusual features. The fact the killing was premeditated with Vester first arming himself, clearly demonstrated he had every intention to kill Brendan.

What made it more questionable though, as to motive was, on the day of the stabbing murder, an application was pending to the High Court seeking special leave to appeal, which was subsequently refused. In that regard, Brendan had signed an affidavit, this time saying that his cousin was not involved in the Sandra Hoare murder, such "revelation" being known to Vester. On that basis, was it possible he did not kill Brendan because he initially held him responsible for giving false information to police, which resulted in his life conviction?

Taking all these matters into account, His Honour concluded, regarding the stabbing death of cousin Brendan:

Although it may be the case that the prisoner's conduct was spurred on by anger and resentment triggered off by the "revelation", the fact remains that the prisoner determined to kill his cousin because he blamed him for his conviction for murder and hence the life sentence imposed upon him. Even if there had been some reuseable foundation for this belief, it would have provided little or no mitigation for his conduct. In effect, it was an act of retribution for what the prisoner perceived were false accusations made by the deceased in his own defence.[498]

You'd like to think this would be the last time we would hear about Vester Fernando but not so. It appears there was not only an absence of brotherly love towards his now late cousin Brendan but also, he had no sympathy for another cellmate. In early April 2020, after he was transferred from Goulburn's Supermax Prison to the North Coast Correctional Centre near Kempsey, Vester carried out another frenzied stabbing attack.

It was noted on CCTV footage that while he repeatedly plunged the knife into the man's body, other inmates did nothing except sit back and watch, most likely laughing and enjoying the spectacle. Once again, Vester pleaded guilty and for this attempted murder he was sentenced in November 2021 to another 17 years and one month, with a minimum of 11 years and one month. All this sentencing was, of course, totally academic, as he will never be released.

Will this be the last we will ever hear about the exploits of the remaining Fernando cousin though? It remains to be seen.

---

498 *R v Fernando* [2001] NSWSC 294-para 24.

47
ONE OPEN AND SHUT CASE

The defence of provocation in cases such as murder first appeared in the English justice system during the 16th and 17th centuries. The usual plea was that the accused reacted after being provoked, particularly in domestic situations of rejection or infidelity by their partner.[499] Such a defence, if successful, would then hopefully reduce any pending conviction of murder to one of manslaughter, meaning a much lesser period of imprisonment.

Provocation as partial defence to murder was available

499 By way of further example, a Victorian Law Reform Commission study of 143 homicides that took place in Victoria during the period 1 July 1997 to 30 June 2001 found of those prosecuted, 31.5 per cent were homicides carried out in circumstances of 'sexual intimacy'.

in Victoria prior to 2005.[500] Robert Clive Parsons tried to rely on such a defence regarding the murder of his partner, Angela Elizabeth Parsons, carried out in December 1997. However, after final submissions at his subsequent trial, the learned judge ruled that provocation should not be left to the jury in its deliberations. During a failed Court of Appeal application, one justice immediately called it an open-and-shut murder case—and it was. But let's first look at what took place.

The Parsons began living together in 1983 and Angela, who was obviously very happy with the relationship, then changed her surname by deed poll to Parsons. After having a daughter in 1984, followed by a son in 1988, the relationship quickly soured. Parsons had a violent nature and, for reasons only known to him, he assaulted Angela so badly in 1990 that she took photographs of her facial injuries. They separated two years later and, despite having regular access to his two young children, Parsons decided to stop paying regular child support maintenance. Understandably, Angela couldn't afford the financial burden of raising two children on her own, so she commenced child support maintenance proceedings in early February 1997.

After Parsons made threats to kill her, Angela applied for an intervention order. Now, understandably, very concerned for her safety and that of the children, she continued with legal action in the Family Court of Australia at its Dandenong Registry. She was seeking orders pertaining to maintenance and custody of the children, including access and contact with

500 Any provocative conduct by a victim along with any other relevant circumstances is now taken into account in determining the appropriate sentence to be imposed for a crime of murder and also for non- fatal assaults. See section 5- *Sentencing Guidelines-Sentencing Act 1991*(Vic).

them by Parsons. Her application for an intervention order was dismissed in March 1997 but interim proceedings, in respect of their financial impasse, were listed in the Family Court for 8 December 1997.

Parsons walked in carrying a file under his arm. It was later noted he called it the "slag file". The outcome was not looking good for him as the interim order he was now facing for outstanding child support payments, was in the order of $47,000. During the hearing, he testified that he possessed only $300 in cash, however, subsequent findings revealed this amount was significantly understated.

Now, with the possibility of a discovery order that could reveal clear evidence contradicting Parsons's statements, the dispute escalated into a chilling confrontation. On Wednesday, 10 December 1997 around 2pm, when Angela was walking back to the court a short distance away along Robinson Street, Dandenong, Parsons was waiting for her. Armed with a long-bladed knife housed in a sheath, he attacked her as she was about to walk up the court steps.

Seizing Angela, Parsons stabbed her about 48 times, with numerous wounds to the neck and upper body. A postmortem later revealed that she suffered eight stab wounds into her heart, including her lungs and other vital organs. One stab wound went right through her neck coming out the other side. To make it even worse for the bystanders who witnessed this ferocious attack, Parsons then stabbed her twice in the legs, just to make sure she would not survive. Witnesses would later give evidence at his trial for murder that after he attacked Angela, he yelled out:

There, I've done it, you bitch... it's over now, bitch. It's over now...that's the fucking Family Court...you can blame the Family Court for this...

Parsons was quickly arrested by police and when asked why he carried out such a murderous act, he replied:

...she stole my kids...My name is Parsons. That is my wife... I've been dead for six years... I just saw red. I was in my car and she smiled at me. I just lost it. Sorry, I won't talk about it...

It came as no surprise that Parsons was charged with murder. After contesting the committal hearing and still maintaining a plea of not guilty, his trial commenced in the Supreme Court of Victoria on 7 May 1999. Parsons tried to put the blame back on Angela, telling the jury that she provoked him when he was walking up to the Family Court steps by saying, 'We've got you now, you bastard,' then supposedly throwing her head back and laughing.

Not only was that a lie but so was Parsons' claim that he couldn't afford child support. A search of his home uncovered $400,000 in cash buried in the backyard, with his total assets estimated in the order of $1 million. On 18 May 1999, the jury had no hesitation in finding him guilty of murder and not manslaughter, particularly after Justice Cummins gave them a direction that provocation was not to be a consideration in their deliberations.

On 24 May 1999, His Honour imposed a life sentence with a non-parole period of 25 years. The judge took into account that Parsons, now 55 years old, had no prior convictions and was the father of another daughter from a previous relationship. Parsons had, understandably, lost the support of his children and, no doubt, according to His Honour, prison would be a very difficult environment for him, given that his fellow cell mates don't take kindly to domestic violence-related murders.

However, in finding Parsons simply displayed a cold anger reflecting that he should not be crossed or suffer the consequences, Justice Cummins said further:

> *You have utterly no remorse for your crime. You do not even have any understanding of the total unacceptability of your actions. Indeed, the final question in re-examination of you at the conclusion of your evidence was this: 'You were asked a number of questions putting to you that what you did was that you killed your wife because of money?' You answered: 'No, that is not true. I killed her because she provoked me'. The law and our society, Mr Parsons, turns its face against such self-justification. We live in a civilised society ruled by law.*[501]

The Court of Appeal certainly had no sympathy for Parsons in his application for leave to appeal both conviction and sentence. Such appeal was largely based around the question of whether the jury should have been directed to consider provocation. In dismissing the appeal outright, apart from saying it was an open and shut case of murder, Chief Justice Philips stated:

> *... I desire to add that the offence of the applicant, characterised as it was by pitiless violence inflicted on an innocent and defenceless litigant, ranks as the most heinous single murders I have encountered during my involvement with the criminal law.*[502]

---

501 *DPP v Parsons* [1999] VSC 192-para 21.

502 *R v Parsons* [2000] VSCA 15-para 1.

Regarding the withdrawal of the defence of provocation by Judge Cummins in the jury instructions, Justice Brooking provided further clarification:

> *... No reasonable jury could have failed to be satisfied beyond reasonable doubt that the applicant's reaction to the victim's conduct fell below indeed, fell a long, long way below the minimum limits of the range of powers of self-control that must be attributed to the ordinary person. To hold that provocation arose in this case would be to encourage savagery at the expense of civilised behaviour. Many litigants, especially in the Family Court, are anxious, angry and disappointed. There is nothing out of the ordinary about the present case except the applicant's reaction.*[503]

Parsons would have been around 80 years old if and when he was released on parole, after serving the minimum period of imprisonment. For all we know, he may now be back living in society. If he is, I don't think anyone will have any sympathy for him.

503 Ibid-para15.

48
THE WAGGA WAGGA STRANGLER

Situated in the Riverina area of New South Wales, along the Murrumbidgee River, is the urban regional city of Wagga Wagga. It is well known as an important agricultural and transport hub of Australia, with a current population of around 57,000. It is also credited as the ninth largest inland city within Australia, with a travelling distance to Sydney of nearly 490 kilometres. Melbourne, Victoria is a tad closer, as it is only 370 kilometres from its central hub. Like many other towns down under, it would also become known for horrific crimes, this time for three separate strangulation murders in October and November 1998.

On or about 4 October 1998, the father of a next-door neighbour noticed the front door was open to the unit where 62-year-old Peter Wennerbom lived, with the television set blaring from inside. He knew this man suffered health issues following a stroke, so he went inside to check on him. On entering the flat, he found Wennerbom lying dead on the floor. Police and ambulance officers attended and, on inspecting the body, found a bruise on the right side of his throat. A crime scene was set up and a postmortem examination, carried out some days later, confirmed the victim, last seen alive on 1 October 1998, had been strangled to death.

Another murder was soon to follow when, on 18 October 1998, a 33-year-old woman, suffering from an intellectual disability, was also killed in a similar manner. Yvonne Ford, who lived on her own, had a part-time job as a dog walker for a local boarding kennel. The owner, on attending at the house to pick Yvonne up for the day's work, became concerned when she did not answer the door.

On hearing Yvonne's dog barking from inside and still with no response, a call was made to local police to report her concerns. Attending police found Yvonne lying naked and deceased in her bath. A postmortem was conducted but as the cause of her death was ruled inconclusive, there was nothing to suggest at this point in time she had met with foul play.[504]

On 4 November 1998, the father of Ronald Galvin was to catch up with his son but he failed to meet him as planned. He waited a couple of weeks and, again, after not hearing from Ronald, ascertained that his son's pension had not been withdrawn from a local credit agency. As this was unusual, he reported his son as a missing person. On 24 November 1998, as a part of their enquiries about the sudden disappearance of Galvin, police spoke with Matthew James Harris who lived

504 In January 1999 following a further review of the case, a pathologist would determine that the direct cause of death was consistent with manual strangulation.

next door to him in the same block of units. A rather laid-back Harris stated he last saw Galvin on Melbourne Cup eve, sitting with a chap he had never seen before.

As the detectives were leaving his flat, they noticed a collection of books with titles about non-fiction murders. No concerns were initially raised but a routine check of the database revealed Harris' prior convictions. Not only was he a known drug user but in May 1991 he served a minimum of two and a half years in prison for armed robbery.

Police also ascertained, although Harris was not engaged in paid employment, he did carry out driver duties for an organisation which provided transport for elderly and disabled persons. Again, another point of possible interest was that Yvonne Ford had used such service from time to time. On 30 November 1998, Harris became more than just a person of interest.

While he was serving his time in prison in 1991 for the armed robbery conviction, Harris became very friendly with Elaine De Jong, who had helped him track his birth parents as they had given him up for adoption. Mrs De Jong was involved with the Adoption Triangle Organisation and, after his release from prison, he lived in her family home for some months before moving into his own unit in Wagga Wagga. They clearly had a close friendship and police would later discover how Harris had met his first murder victim, Peter Wennerbom. He just happened to be Mrs De Jong's brother.

On 30 November 1998 around 3am, Harris telephoned his close friend, Mrs De Jong, on two separate occasions. She later made a statement to police that he said words to the effect:

'I need to talk to you. Will you stand by me no matter what? I'm going to be away for a long time, about 16 years.

Will you visit me? Will you promise not to die before I get out? I killed that bloke that's missing from next door...don't tell anybody yet. I want to do this in my own time. I love you.'

Mrs De Jong had no hesitation in immediately advising local police at 4am that same morning but at this point she had no idea that Harris had also killed her brother. She received another telephone call from Harris five hours later at 9.30am. Once again, Mrs De Jong made a police statement and later gave evidence of what transpired:

> Harris: I killed a lady in Phillip Avenue as well on Caulfield Cup Day.
> Mrs De Jong: How?
> Harris: In the bath. But I don't think anybody found her because I don't think there was anything in the newspapers about it.
> Mrs De Jong: Matthew, don't come back here thinking that you can talk me into being quiet. You know how I am.
> Harris: I don't know if I can do it.

After trying to commit suicide by taking an overdose of heroin, he was admitted to Sydney's St Vincent's Hospital. Upon his discharge, Harris was placed under arrest. On 1 December 1998, while being interviewed by police, the body of Robert Galvin was located near the town of Uranquinty, a 15-minute drive from Wagga Wagga. An autopsy conducted some days later confirmed he had also been strangled to death. Harris was advised of his rights in electronically recorded interviews over several days and he would later accompany police to the crime scenes.

In respect of Ronald Galvin and Yvonne Ford's deaths, Harris was told of the admissions made by him in telephone conversations with Mrs De Jong. After saying he could not recall ever saying anything to her, he readily confessed to both murders. He admitted he had strangled Ms Ford while she was having a bath, saying:

> *I just wanted to get into the bath so that I could strangle her…I live nearby, but then these thoughts started entering my head that I wanted to kill her…It could've been anybody. She was just unlucky…I just thought she would be easy to target, she wouldn't put up a fight…she would be relatively easy to kill…*

Regarding Galvin's murder, Harris admitted strangling him and then disposing of his body at Uranquinty. He said Galvin was:

> *…only a little bloke…I think it was just a lot of anger I was getting rid of and it was being projected on him…got away with [the earlier murders] thought well, why not go again…?*

In his police interviews, Harris originally stated he had no knowledge of the earlier death of Peter Wennerbom but, after expressing concern for Mrs De Jong, he admitted he did, in fact, strangle him. Harris said:

> *… I, at the time wasn't interested in robbing him, the only thing I wanted to do was to kill, that was my sole purpose… was an old man, there was no resistance at all. I had total, you know, control over the situation. He, he couldn't do anything…*

Understandably, this was very upsetting for Mrs De Jong and her family who later recalled that Harris, following her brother's death, had helped clear out his unit. He attended the funeral but did not enter the church and seemed withdrawn, which was now explained as he knew he was, in fact, responsible for the death of their family member.

On 3 December 1999, 31-year-old Harris was arraigned on an indictment, charging him with three counts of murder. On pleading guilty to each count, he appeared for a sentencing hearing before Justice Bell in the NSW Supreme Court on 24 March 2000. Her Honour heard evidence that Harris had been having murderous thoughts from when he was about 13 years-old, including killing his own family members. The Crown submitted that the murders of Ford and Galvin, in particular, called for nothing less than the maximum penalty for the term of his natural life.

A further psychiatric assessment determined that Harris had a personality disorder, together with being overwhelmed with on-going bouts of depression. Although he had killed three innocent victims, the learned judge still determined with appropriate psychological counselling over a lengthy period, he may in due course not pose a danger to the community. Given that the judge had a discretion to impose a lesser sentence than one of life imprisonment,[505] Harris was treated rather leniently.

On each of the three counts of murder, he was sentenced to imprisonment for a term of 40 years, to commence from the day of his arrest being 1 December 1998, but with a non-parole

505 Section 19A (3) of the *Crimes Act 1900*(NSW) provides for the passing of a lesser sentence than one imposed for imprisonment for life without parole.

period for each murder of 25 years.[506] This meant the earliest date for his release would have been 30 November 2023 when aged 54, allowing him to still enjoy life on the outside.

It was of no surprise that an appeal was lodged but certainly not by Harris, in respect of the sentence being manifestly inadequate. The Crown contended that Justice Bell had erred by not considering that the criminality of Harris fell into a worst category type of case, requiring the maximum sentence of life imprisonment without parole.[507]

The Court of Appeal on 20 December 2000 deemed there was an error in law, where the learned judge failed to give due recognition to the severity of the taking of three human lives. In that regard, with all three appeal judges concurring it fitted into a worst type of category, the court said:

> *It was the fact that : (a) the victims were aged, disadvantaged or physically slight and an easy prey…(b) the killing of Ms Ford involved a betrayal of trust; (c) Mr Wennerbom was the brother of the one person for whom the respondent[Harris] "had any degree" of emotional attachment; (d) the second and third killings were carried out for the satisfaction of the respondent,*

506 *R v Matthew James Harris* [2000] NSWSC 285. He was also sentenced to a concurrent term of three years imprisonment for an armed robbery he had committed on 20 June 1998.

507 Section 61(1) of the *Crimes (Sentencing Procedure Act 1999*(NSW) provides for life imprisonment for murder if the court is satisfied that the level of culpability is so extreme that community protection and deterrence can only be met by the imposition of such a sentence. It was also submitted that Justice Bell should have considered the operation of common law principles of worst-case category of cases and imposing a non-parole period under section 19A of the *Crimes Act* was incorrect.

as an exercise of power and to exact revenge on society… they were linked in a way aggravating each other; the three killings occurred within the space of only one month;(f) each killing involved considerable callousness and was such that the respondent could not have attached any value to the lives of those he killed.[508]

The sentences, in respect of the murders of Ford and Galvin, were quashed and Harris was sentenced to imprisonment for life with no parole period fixed. As for the original sentence imposed for the murder of Wennerbom, the Crown did not seek a similar life sentence without parole, so the Court of Criminal Appeal did not intervene.

Regardless though, this dangerous individual will never be released, spending the rest of his days in prison where he belongs.

---

508 *R v Harris* [2000] NSWCCA 469 -para 97.

49
THE TWO CASES OF COLIN EARL GRAHAM

From the time he was born in May 1955, Colin Earl Graham lived his life with a degree of respectability, or so it seemed. Graham, the oldest of six children with five younger sisters, left school at the end of Form 3. He was largely raised by his mother and grandmother after his parents separated when he was seven. His early foray into employment mainly centred around specialist technical roles and his hobbies included ten pin bowling, both as a player, coach and official.

In 1980, at the age of 25, he was married and working as a hospital orderly. They were not blessed with any children and after a few years, it appeared their marriage was just one of convenience and nothing else. In March 1986, Graham and his wife were living in a modest four-bedroom Ringwood home east of Melbourne, which they had recently purchased for $35,000.

Whilst working his shift at the Box Hospital, Graham formed a close relationship with a 25-year-old nurse by the name of Ina-Doris Warrick. The young lady, who lived about four kilometres away from Graham, was also a champion gymnast. She had recently lost her husband to cancer and, in her grief, had confessed to her friends that she was lonely, trying to live life as a single woman.

On the evening of 21 March 1986, Graham invited her out for a pizza. After, no doubt, enjoying their meal, he would later tell police of his own accord that he dropped Ina off at her home. He stated, he even walked her to the front door to make sure she was safe but never went inside. Ina didn't report for work to start the late shift that evening and it was not until four days later that her neighbours found her dead.

Becoming concerned that something was wrong, as her mailbox was overflowing with mail, they looked inside the house. Sadly, they saw the nurse lying dead on a bed. Police were immediately notified and a crime scene was set up, finding that Ina had been stabbed twice in the back. A postmortem would reveal that one of the stab wounds had punctured her lung. Police would also later ascertain the clothes in which she was found, fawn-coloured slacks and a blouse, together with high heels, was what she was wearing on the evening of the pizza dinner.

After making extensive enquiries, police narrowed the murder down to two possible suspects. One was her dinner mate, Graham, and the other was an anaesthetist she had met at the hospital, with whom she was having a relationship. He was interviewed on 2 April 1986 and agreed that he had spent the evening of 21 March 1986 with Warrick. He then stated he had only learnt of his lover's death from seeing it on the television's evening news, after returning home to be with his wife. He was still a firm suspect, with police accepting what Graham had told them, about only having a meal of pizza with Warrick and nothing else.

The version of events proffered by their now main suspect, the anaesthetist, also didn't stack up when they discovered he had returned to her house the following day. On being questioned again, he admitted he had gone to her home to leave her a loving handwritten note. He then said he went back on Sunday, 23 March 1986, but this time went inside to find Ina dead. According to his version of events, he panicked and, after retrieving the love note, quickly left in his white BMW vehicle. What was interesting to police was, he had failed to tell anyone about finding Ina dead. The problem faced was that police didn't have sufficient evidence to charge her married anaesthetist lover.

Still a person of interest in the Warrick murder, Graham would, once again, come to the attention of police, albeit some 13 years later. The body of 21-year-old hospital and university security guard, Hilary Stevens, was found lying dead on the front porch of her Wheelers Hill home, a suburb of Melbourne, in the early hours of the morning of 1 October 1999. Neighbours had earlier reported to police hearing muffled screams, followed by a car speeding off. Stevens had suffered several knife wounds to her arms and hands, before she was fatally stabbed four times in the back.

Detectives ascertained she was in a close relationship with Graham, having originally met him in early 1999, while he was still working as a hospital orderly. By this stage, Graham, who was now 43 years old, was still married but obviously enjoying discreet relationships. Friends and family members of Hilary told police she had developed a close relationship with Graham but, by September 1999, it was starting to cool off.

Detectives spoke with Graham not long after the murder and his initial statement to them would later be described by the sentencing judge as a mixture of trust and lies. In addition, Graham, in trying to deflect their investigations away from him, gave police false information about his movements on the night of 30 September 1999. In January 2000, police spoke with Graham again as he was still considered a person of interest. His story went round in circles on this occasion as Graham gave them a completely different version of events. It was all over for Graham in early February 2000 when he decided to cooperate with police, to a degree.

He admitted that after having dinner with Hilary at the local hotel, he took her home and left, already knowing what he was about to do. In the driver's side pocket of his car, Graham had a rather large knife. After leaving his car opposite the house where she lived, he entered her home and stabbed her to death. He gave no explanation to police why he carried out such an act, other than to say it was done on the spur of the moment. He did state she tried to ward off the blows, which was certainly evidenced by the wounds to her arms and hands. After plunging the knife a few times into her back, he quickly left and drove away.

Graham was charged with the murder of Hilary Stevens and remanded in custody, where he would spend a further 16 months before his trial. At his Supreme Court jury trial in May 2001, he pleaded not guilty to murder, obviously hoping for a verdict of manslaughter. Although the motive was unclear or perhaps it was because Graham knew the relationship with Hilary was at an end, the jury had no doubt in finding him guilty of murder.

On 18 June 2001, Graham appeared before Justice Bernard Teague[509] for sentencing, who said:

> *...I am not prepared to accept that you acted on the spur of the moment. It is not clear why you chose to act as you did. What is very clear is that this was a very serious case of a very serious crime. Just how serious is the more difficult to gauge because you are not a credible person. At times you merely twist the truth; at other times you are a brazen liar....it is impossible to be satisfied where the truth lies. I infer that the jury felt similarly... Their verdict was returned in what was these days an extremely short time; that was scarcely surprising given the number and character of the stab wounds and your lack of credibility.*[510]

After accepting that, at times, Graham showed some signs of remorse and the fact he had undertaken several programs while incarcerated, the judge determined he had good prospects for rehabilitation. In addition, Graham was suffering from heart issues and taking all these factors into account, a crushing sentence was not appropriate.

That was certainly an understatement, as Graham was only sentenced to a maximum of 18 years imprisonment with a non-parole period of 13 years. As he had already served over a year in pre-trial detention, this meant, if he behaved himself, he could be a free man by 2012. It would take nearly two decades

509 Justice Teague AO was a judge of the Supreme Court from October 1987 to February 2008. He was then appointed as head of the Bushfires Royal Commission into the February 2009 disasters that killed 179 people and destroyed thousands of homes and livestock.

510 *R v Graham* [2001] VSC 201-para 4.

though, for the actions of Colin Earl Graham to once again rear their ugly head.

Cold case detectives had not given up hope of finding the culprit responsible for the 1986 murder of Ina-Doris Warrick. While they clearly still had the Box Hill anaesthetist and, of course, Graham as suspects, what was interesting was the murder bore striking similarities to that of Hilary Stevens. In 2017, with Graham now a free man since 2012, a public appeal was made for any information that could assist in leading to the identity of the murderer. This appeal was complimented by a television episode titled, "Million Dollar Case", which promoted the reward on offer. The program also revealed that Graham had been imprisoned for the murder of Stevens, which prompted three people to contact police.

A former security guard, who had worked with Graham at a night club, stated that in 1999, he had told him about a nurse he was seeing who 'literally died in his arms.' Graham elaborated further, talking about 'all the blood' and, after a night out, how something happened back at her house. This would also be corroborated by two other witnesses, with one saying Graham told him he 'done a murder' and the other stating he said it was all over a 'denial of sex'.

This was enough for police to charge Graham with the murder of Warrick and he was remanded in custody in early 2018. In a remarkable turnaround, after being committed for trial in August 2019, Graham was released on bail in December 2020. Supreme Court Justice Elizabeth Hollingworth determined the Crown case against the accused was somewhat weak. Furthermore, Judge Hollingworth was perplexed at why the Box Hill anaesthetist had been discounted as a suspect by police. On that basis, Graham's time in custody was indeed onerous, releasing him on strict bail conditions which included that he reside with his parents.

The initial jury trial, concerning the charge of murdering Ina-Doris Warwick in which Graham entered a plea of not guilty, was discharged in March 2022. This was after the jury were unable to reach a verdict, following two days of deliberation. Graham was presented before a jury again in September 2022, with the Crown largely relying on the testimony of witnesses of the murder confessions made by the accused. In addition, they submitted that Graham was the last person to see her alive but conceded the knife found in his possession in 2018, was not the one that was used to stab Ina to death.

Defence counsel for Graham told the jury there was reasonable doubt of the accused being responsible and it was possible that her other lover, the anaesthetist, could not be ruled out. Counsel called out the alibi given by this person, noting there was evidence he had left his wife some nights, while she was asleep, to pay a visit to Warrick. He was also called to give evidence and explain why he did not tell anyone about finding her dead.

As to the so-called confessions made by Graham, apart from there being no evidence of motive, it was submitted the three witnesses only came forward hoping to collect the million-dollar reward. The jury were also told it was, in fact, the accused who contacted police when he found out Warrick had died, being upfront about taking her out for dinner earlier that evening.

It is important to note that under the rules of evidence, jurors cannot be told about the prior history of Graham and certainly not of his conviction for the murder of Stevens.[511] In

511 See *Evidence Act 2008*(Vic) –section 91- Exclusion of evidence of judgments and convictions.

addition, the comments of Justice Teague were also withheld, in which he referred to Graham as a brazen liar. Jurors were also not informed of the previous jury's inability to reach a verdict in the earlier same case trial. After hearing evidence from a total of 19 witnesses, the jury retired to consider its verdict. After less than a day of deliberations, they returned to the courtroom.

> His Honour: Jury foreperson, has the jury reached a verdict?
> Foreperson: We have your Honour; we find the defendant not guilty.
> His Honour: Thank you. Mr Graham, you may leave the dock.

Given he was found not guilty, it's probably best I make no further comment. However, I will leave the final word to a grieving Warrick family member, who told waiting media on leaving court, following the not guilty verdict:

'God will deal with him.'

50
NO BODY, NO PAROLE

In Australia's early days, the lucky country down under has not been so lucky for some people, due to the harshest and most debilitating punishments imposed. As you have read, not only were convicts hanged but others suffered the same fate well into the 20th century. Solitary confinement also used to be the order of the day for some, even with chains and iron masks. Fortunately, we no longer see floggings in our jails but to some that is a point of contention.

Arguably, today's sentencing laws, on the one hand, are legislated to be seen to be effective in that, 'You do the crime you do the time.' However, the sentence imposed must also be seen as humane, giving the offender the possibility of parole at some point. Even for murder, unless determined that the scale of the crime means life without any possibility of release, a life sentence for murder can also see a non-parole period fixed by the sentencing judge. In that respect, a minimum term would be handed down with, for example, 25-30 years to be served before being eligible for parole.

What does raise its ugly head though, is the refusal of a person convicted of murder to reveal the location of their deceased victim. This situation prolongs the emotional anguish experienced by the victims' families, who are left unable to achieve closure and lay their loved ones to rest in this endless journey. They remain uncertain about what occurred and continue to encounter frequent reminders of their loss, which makes moving forward difficult.

On that basis, why should any convicted murderer be released without revealing the location of the victim's remains? If such an offender was paroled back into the community, all that does is create further heartache for the grieving families and untold indignation, knowing the killer has no remorse whatsoever.

South Australia, Victoria, Western Australia, the Northern Territory and Queensland have all enacted the "no body, no parole" legislation.[512] In New South Wales, such laws came into effect in October 2022, largely in response to the case of Christopher Michael Dawson. He was convicted and sentenced in December 2022 for the murder of his wife

---

512 South Australian legislation is outlined in the *Correctional Services Act 1982*(SA) as amended in 2016. No Body, No Parole laws in Victoria were also introduced in late 2016 as per section 74AABA of the *Corrections Act 1986*(Vic) includes the same provision for those convicted of killing a police officer. Also in 2016 was Western Australia under section 66B of the *Sentence Administration Act 2003*(WA), with the Northern Territory courtesy of the *Parole Act 1971*(NT)-section 4B. Such legislation was introduced in Queensland in August 2017 as per the *Corrective Services (No Body, No Parole) Amendment Act 2017*(Qld)).

Lynette, who disappeared on or about 8 January 1982, never to be seen again.

It was alleged that Dawson, while working as a schoolteacher, began an extra-marital affair with one of his school students. This, understandably, caused friction between him and Lynette and, after marriage counselling, she suddenly disappeared, leaving behind their two young daughters. Dawson did not report her missing until six weeks later and that was only at the insistence of Lynette's mother.

The Director of Public Prosecutions did not pursue anyone, despite two coronial inquests in 2001 and 2003, determining that a person known to Lynette, most likely killed her. It was not until 2018 following a "Teacher's Pet Podcast",[513] that the Unsolved Homicide Unit arrested and charged Dawson. He still maintained his innocence, despite overwhelming circumstantial evidence, and was sentenced to a term of 24 years imprisonment, with a non-parole period of 18 years. This effectively meant his earliest release date would be around August 2042.[514]

The issue he faces though is not disclosing the location of her remains, which has now become a decisive factor, rather than just a consideration for the Adult Parole Board. Dawson appealed his conviction to the Court of Criminal Appeal, which was dismissed by all three judges.[515] In a last ditch bid to

513 This Australian Crime Podcast hosted by journalist Hedley Thomas in the following two years had almost 30 million downloads and achieved the number one slot, not only in Australia, but a number of overseas countries.

514 *R v Dawson* [2022] NSWSC 1632. Also see R v Dawson [2022] NSWSC 1131 for the facts set out by Justice Harrison in a judge alone trial for determining a guilty verdict beyond reasonable doubt.

515 *Dawson v R* [2024] NSWCCA 98.

gain a new trial, Dawson, now aged 77, lodged an application for special leave, which currently sits with the High Court of Australia.

Convicted rapist, Robert Adams, must have thought he got away with cold blooded murder, after it took almost 34 years to see him finally convicted. Adams was known to have a strong tendency to assault and even strangle women, when they rejected his sexual advances. In 1976, Adams pleaded guilty to the offence of rape for which he was sentenced to a term of imprisonment. This rape involved a brutal assault on a young woman, which would later lead a sentencing judge to comment that it bore striking similarities to his murder victims.

After casually meeting 33-year-old Sydney nurse, Mary Wallace, at a bar in Crows Nest, Sydney, Adams offered to drive her home in the early hours of Saturday, 24 September 1983. The were both intoxicated, with Mary barely able to stand, but Adams said he was a police officer and would look after her. Given his occupation, which was in fact a lie, Mary's friends had no issue with this "kind gentleman" looking after their friend. They waved them both goodbye, watching the vehicle driven away by Adams towards the suburb of Willoughby. They had no doubt that Mary was in good hands and Adams would safely see her home. Unfortunately, that was the last they ever saw of her.

When reported missing three days later, one of Mary's friends made a statement to police, which included an identikit picture of the man they thought would take care of her. This drawing bore a striking resemblance to Adams after police received further information that he was indeed the male last seen with Mary. On Thursday, 29 September 1983, he was taken into custody. He agreed he was with Mary and because he was very drunk, he had pulled over just around the corner from the Crows Nest bar. He fell asleep, after they had been "fooling around" and on waking up, Mary was nowhere to be seen.

Police accepted his explanation to a degree and released him without any charge, other than for possessing cannabis. They did, however, thoroughly search Adams' vehicle, which included vacuuming some hairs found inside the car's boot. The following day, they conducted a further examination of Mary's flat, taking fingerprints from what was now considered to be a potential crime scene, together with hair samples from a hairbrush belonging to her. Although Adams was considered a very strong person of interest, they were unable to locate Mary, or any evidence that, in fact, she may have been murdered.

In October 2002, with still no sign of what happened to Mary, NSW Police re-activated investigations into her disappearance. This included extracting and perusing, not only the witness statements but ensuring all the exhibits were still held securely and available for further examination. In addition, Adams was placed under covert surveillance but, again, there was nothing to incriminate him in anyway.

In 2010, further searches, including an excavation of Lane Cove National Park, together with inquiries of any use of her credit cards again found nothing. Also, to no avail, police even carried out a process of looking at the unidentified bodies database, of bodies previously found in NSW since Mary's disappearance, just in case one was, in fact, her.

The investigation by this stage was with the Unsolved Homicide Team and at a December 2010 coronial inquest, several witnesses gave evidence incriminating Adams, as they did later at his criminal trial. However, it was not until late

2013 that DNA testing compared the hairs found in the boot of Adams vehicle with those said to be from Mary's hairbrush.

The overall view of an expert hair analyst with the Australian Federal Police in Canberra was that the hairs vacuumed from the boot, were identical to the hairs taken from the hairbrush. To make sure the hairs were indeed from Mary, a swab was also taken from her sister, which revealed a slightly different mtDNA profile[516] but still a match with only a miniscule variation between the two siblings.

On the morning of 20 December 2013, after being taken into custody, Adams was charged with one count of murder. He told police during the record of interview about the stress and anguish he had suffered over many years, as a result of having this matter hanging over his head. Adams also said he had no doubt he would be acquitted. The problem he faced though was, when asked to explain the matching hair samples with one set found in his car boot, he had no answer.

Following a four week judge-alone trial in the Supreme Court of NSW, Adams was found guilty by Justice Button on 4 November 2016 of the murder of Mary Wallace.[517] On 3 March 2017, he appeared for sentencing and on the evidence presented at his trial, His Honour again emphasised that Adams strangled his victim in an effort to force her to have sex with him. After hearing testimony from three previous victims of Adams, the judge said:

---

516 Genetic material found in human cells is from two locations. Nuclear DNA from the cell's nucleus is most common. Mitochondrial DNA (mt) is similar to bacterial DNA and is passed down exclusively from the birth mother.

517 *R v Adams (No 6)* [2016] NSWSC 1565- judgment-verdict of guilty of murder.

> *...I consider that, if the deceased had readily consented to sexual contact with the offender, he would not have applied force to her person. Having said that, there is no doubt that, as at the date of the offence, the offender possessed a long-standing tendency to strangle young women if they rejected his sexual advances. The fatal act was a contingency that the offender believed was available to him.*[518]

Justice Button also stated Adams stored the deceased's body in the boot of his vehicle and, in the ensuing days, did his best to remove any trace of her from his vehicle, before disposing of the body. As to whether a life sentence should be imposed without the possibility of parole, His Honour stated:

> *...the offence cannot be assessed as other than extremely grave. Having said that, it did not feature an intention to kill. Nor did the offender commit a multiple murder; nor was this a murder committed by a person who had murdered before. Nor was it a cold-blooded contract killing; nor a murder that featured some exceptionally heinous act of cruelty, torture or mutilation...*[519]

I'm sure Mary's family would agree that nothing less than a life sentence without parole was more than appropriate. Nonetheless, Justice Button sentenced Adams to a head term of imprisonment of 20 years, with a non-parole period of 15 years. This meant the earliest possible release date for Adams would be 10 June 2030 at the age of 79. However, he has a slight problem. Unless he reveals the location of the remains

518 *R v Adams (No 7)* [2017] NSWSC 179- para 11.

519 Ibid- para 53.

of Mary, he won't be released until 2036, thanks to "no body, no parole".

Another convicted murderer, who will remain in jail with no chance of parole until she reveals the location of her victim, is Keli Lane. In late 2010, she was convicted of the 1996 murder of her newborn daughter, Tegan, together with three counts of making a false declaration. The prosecution argued that her motive was related to concerns that raising a young child could affect her ability to represent Australia in water polo at the 2000 Olympics. Lane was sentenced to a non-parole period of 13 years and five months, meaning it expired in May 2024.[520]

After serving her minimum term of imprisonment, Lane subsequently applied for release which was denied on the grounds that she had not cooperated with police to reveal the location of the deceased baby. Unless Lane is successful in any High Court appeal, she will remain incarcerated as sentenced for her full maximum prison term, meaning she will not be released until December 2028, at the age of 53. Lane continues to maintain though that she gave Tegan to her biological father soon after giving birth.

Daniel Cherry is also set to serve his full term of imprisonment, after his appeal to the High Court of Australia, against Queensland's "no body, no parole" legislation, was unsuccessful. On 8 November 2002, Cherry was found guilty and convicted by a jury of having murdered his wife Annette Cherry on 16 June 1997 in the suburb of Springsure. He was also found guilty of having murdered his stepdaughter, Kira Guise, on or about 23 July 1999.

Regarding the murder of his wife, the Crown case at trial

520 *R v Keli Lane* [2011] NSWSC 289. Also see appeal against conviction which was denied. *Lane v R* [2013] NSWCCA 317.

alleged he enlisted his other stepdaughter, 18-year-old Debbie Guise, to kill her mother. Cherry supplied her with a .45 calibre colt pistol, together with the ammunition and even showed her how to fire the weapon. Debbie was in a sexual relationship with Cherry, which Annette found out about during an argument a week before she was murdered. She immediately separated from him and was able to obtain interim custody orders of their two young sons. Cherry then made it well known if he did not get custody of them, he would kill Annette.

Cherry didn't muck around and procured Debbie to carry out the murder. After shooting her mother dead at her grandmother's house, she took herself and the pistol to the local police station and confessed. In August 1998, after two Supreme Court trials, Debbie was convicted of her mother's manslaughter. This was on the basis the jury accepted that she lacked the necessary intent to kill, saying the pistol had been given to her by a person with the name of "Macca". Debbie was jailed for a maximum of six years and, no doubt, Cherry surmised he had gotten away with being implicated in the murder of his wife.

With Debbie now behind bars, he began a full-time sexual relationship with his other stepdaughter, 17-year-old Kira. That didn't turn out the way he was hoping and, after she tried to end it, in July 1999 he also killed her. Another reason for her murder was Cherry believed she might not only reveal he had sex with her before she turned 16 but also that Kira knew about his role in her mother's murder. What better way to solve both problems but eliminate Kira, hoping her family and friends would think she had disappeared to start a new life elsewhere. Sadly, Kira was never seen again.

In late September 2000, police made numerous visits to

speak with Debbie in prison about her missing sister, Kira. After then incriminating Cherry in the murder of her mother, Debbie was released into police custody in May 2001 and then, at their instigation, contacted him. At this point, Cherry may have thought she wanted to resume a sexual relationship with him. After further informing police of her concerns regarding his possible involvement in her sister's disappearance, Debbie met Cherry at a local motel. However, he was unaware that the entire situation was actually part of a carefully orchestrated police operation, being recorded by undercover homicide investigators.

What it showed was Debbie trying to extract a confession from Cherry, first in respect of the murder of her mother:

> Debbie: But Rodney, I wouldn't have done it unless you hadn't made me…
> Cherry: Well, you can blame me for making you, Deb. I didn't make you.
> Debbie: But you told me to.
> Cherry: Okay, if you're gunna blame me, I'll go and leave you here.
> Debbie: But why did you give it to me (the pistol)? Why did you say go do it…?
> Cherry: I don't know the answer. This woman took everything and destroyed me. I'm completely destroyed… there would be 50 blokes she's been screwing in the last fucking 12 months of our life…don't squeal and ruin your life…the most important thing you've got to remember, mate, is stick to your story you told in the courtroom because you never know when you'll tell it to the wrong person, ever. Now Kira knows the fucking truth…

The conversation now turned to Kira, with Debbie asking Cherry why Kira knew the truth:

> Cherry: …because she worked it out a long time before.
> Debbie: How, did you tell her?
> Cherry: The only thing she doesn't know for sure is the gun, right, the rest she knows.

On telling Cherry she hadn't heard from Kira, even when she turned 21, Cherry stated they didn't know she was dead, followed by:

> Debbie: Have you heard from her?
> Cherry: No mate, I haven't heard jackshit from her, mate. I'm worried that she's in trouble or she's got herself bloody hurt or some fucking thing.

At this point in the conversation, after Cherry denied he ever had a sexual relationship with Kira, he showed Debbie a ring he was wearing. He offered it to her, saying Kira gave it to him on the promise he would always wear it. The only problem was, which would later come out in his trial, although the ring belonged to Kira, it was so highly valued by her that she would have never given it to Cherry.

The undercover surveillance video then showed Cherry moving towards Debbie, first sitting on the bed, then placing his hand on her head. That was enough for armed police who stormed through the motel door and took him into custody. On 20 May 2001, with Cherry flatly professing his innocence, he was charged with both murders and placed in custody on remand.

The evidence at his trial was overwhelming with the

Crown presenting a strong case in both murders. This was supported by, not only inconsistencies in the statements made by Cherry but testimony from Debbie, further evidenced by the videotaped motel conversation. The Crown also took testimony from a prisoner, who just happened to be on remand at the same time as Cherry. His evidence was also supported by handwritten notes he took of conversations he had with Cherry, including a discussion that police might fabricate evidence against him.

In that respect, he wrote down that Cherry said words to the effect:

> *...he didn't need police to fabricate the evidence, he knows where she is and she is and how she died... no one's going to find out...couldn't keep her mouth shut, just like her mother...*

This was followed by further notes of their conversation, after an agitated Cherry had read a newspaper article about the missing Kira, when he said:

> *...they've got no body, I've made sure of that... I've hidden the body...DNA is the only thing that is going to link me to Kira's death...*

The jury had no hesitation in finding Cherry guilty beyond reasonable doubt for both murders. On 2 December 2002, he was sentenced to two life terms of imprisonment, with a mandatory non-parole period of 20 years. In September 2004, his appeal for a new trial was dismissed, with the three Court of Appeal justices concurring there was no miscarriage of justice.[521]

521 *R v Cherry* [2004] QCA 328.

Cherry continued to maintain his innocence and, at his parole hearing in July 2022, he labelled his conviction nothing but a "kangaroo court".[522] His bid for parole was refused as were his further attempts in 2023. The problem he had was the parole board had no power or authority to consider his application as he was a no body, no parole prisoner. Cherry, of course, maintained Kira was still alive, supposedly, according to him, being seen in the town of Yeppoon in Central Queensland.

In a further bizarre twist, Cherry even claimed he had received a letter from Kira saying she was alive and well. The only problem there was her family and friends, for whatever reason, had not heard from her. Once again, the parole board would tell Cherry that as he had not cooperated with authorities to identify the location of her body, they could not and would not parole him.[523]

In perhaps an ominous sign for other convicted no body, no parole prisoners, Cherry took up the challenge all the way to the High Court of Australia. However, in April 2025, the High Court found in favour of the no body, no parole legislation. In that regard, the court said the legislation's inherent purpose was to encourage a prisoner to cooperate in locating a victim's

---

522 This term has been in play since the 19th Century meaning such a court is allegedly a sham and doesn't follow due process in order to ensure a fair trial, bouncing all over the place like a kangaroo.

523 Section 175L of the *Corrective Services Act 2006*(Qld) allows the Queensland Parole Board to make a 'no cooperation declaration' about a 'no body- no parole prisoner' in the event the board is not satisfied the prisoner has given satisfactory cooperation regarding the location of the victim's body or remains.

body or remains which, in turn, served the public interest and provided comfort to families.[524]

This means Cherry will see out the rest of his days in prison, unless he can provide fresh and compelling evidence that he was wrongly convicted.[525] The other solution is for him to cooperate with police and disclose where the remains of Kira are. I doubt very much that will happen, though. He could always petition the Governor of Queensland for a pardon but I also don't like his chances in that respect.

There is a contrary argument against no body, no parole laws, noting Australia is not on its own in enacting such legislation.[526] Proponents argue not all the remains of a missing person can be located, thanks to, not only animal activity but a declining environmental landscape. They also say such laws do more harm than good and denying parole is more of a punishment.

In some instances, it is suggested even when a convicted person is remorseful, the passage of time hinders them in remembering where the body might be located. By refusing parole, it can also have a negative impact on the convicted prisoner, where their period of incarceration should be focused on their rehabilitation. On release under stringent parole conditions, they can then comfortably reintegrate back into society.

---

524 *Cherry v Queensland* [2025] HCA 14

525 *The Criminal Code and Other Legislation (Double Jeopardy Exception and Subsequent Appeals) Amendment Act 2024*(Qld) enables an appeal in respect of a wrongful conviction.

526 The United Kingdom enacted in November 2020 the *Prisoners (Disclosure of Information About Victims) Act* 2020. The United States saw its first enactment of such legislation in Utah in 2021.

There is also an argument for individuals who have allegedly been wrongfully convicted and remain in prison without any knowledge of the victim's whereabouts, as they were not responsible for the crime. Arguments also revolve around other alternate solutions to give closure to families and loved ones of murder victims, whose remains have never been found. Victim support services are available to provide grief counselling and there is also a suggestion that perhaps police resources could be better allocated, especially in respect of search techniques and forensic analysis.

I'm not sure the family and friends of missing victims would totally agree with these contrasting views, as they live their loss on a daily basis. I will, however, let you be the judge and jury in that respect.

51
THE PORT ARTHUR MASSACRE

I have left this confronting chapter to last, not that it deserves any special recognition, other than in memory of the victims and their loved ones. Sadly, the horrific event which took place over two chilling and fateful days in April 1996 at Port Arthur is etched in our history. Like many other countries, Australia has seen its fair share of mass murders[527] but nothing like what would be inflicted by Martin John Bryant.

527 For example, the bodies in the barrels also known as the Snowtown murders saw 12 people in South Australia murdered between August 1992 and May 1999. The remains of eight of the victims were located in barrels filled with acid in a disused bank vault, with the other four found in separate locations. John Justin Bunting was the ringleader and together with Robert Wagner both were convicted and sentenced to life imprisonment without parole, with their two accomplices being imprisoned with lengthy non-parole periods.

The town of Port Arthur is located approximately 97 kilometres southeast of Hobart, Tasmania, which was originally known as Van Diemen's Land, with its name accorded around 1830 to Lieutenant Governor George Arthur. Apart from its early recognition for producing sawn off timber logs, it was also recognised for holding the worst type of recalcitrant offenders in its convict prison. From around 1877 and even to this day, it is also recognised as a popular tourist attraction. Unfortunately, on 28 April 1996 this historic site saw the massacre of 35 innocent people, many of whom were tourists.

Born on 7 May 1967, Bryant spent much of his childhood in the nearby beach town of Carnarvon Bay. He was known to be disruptive at school, even being suspended after torturing animals. Bryant used to tease his fellow students and by 1983, was on a disability pension due to mental issues. By 1987, he had become close friends with a rich, middle-aged eccentric woman and was residing with her. They then moved into a farm near the small township of Copping.

After she was killed in a car accident from a head-on collision when driving on the wrong side of the road, there was some suggestion that Bryant, who was a passenger in the vehicle, may have been responsible. He had a tendency of grabbing her steering wheel for no apparent reason and this was not the first time she had been involved in a car accident, with Bryant always being the passenger. After Bryant recovered from his serious injuries and being cleared by police of any wrongdoing, he was now quite wealthy, as he was the sole beneficiary of her estate.

Now with a reputation of being quite eccentric, wearing electric-blue suits with flared trousers, Bryant seemed to be living the high life and by 1995, he had travelled overseas on numerous occasions. At this stage, he was also a heavy drinker but he would later say he was very lonely, reportedly telling his next-door neighbour that he would, 'do something to make people remember him.'

Bryant certainly did that on the morning of Sunday, 28 April 1996, when he shot dead the owners of a bed and breakfast guest house known as "Seascape". Apparently, he blamed them for the depression and later suicide of his father who had been unsuccessful in bidding against them for the purchase of the guest house.

Bryant was armed with three high-powered weapons, including an Armalite-15 rifle fitted with a 30-shot magazine. They were concealed in his sports bag which also contained a hunting knife, two sets of handcuffs and a rope. In addition, he was carrying containers of petrol, a cigarette lighter and fire starters. Bryant was not a smoker, so he obviously had other plans besides death and mayhem, including causing damage to property. After killing the guest house owners, he arrived at the Port Arthur historic site at around 1pm and entered the Broad Arrow Café. It was a busy time for the business, with about 60 customers either seated or waiting outside for their takeaway meal order.

After consuming lunch and talking at random with many unsuspecting tourists, Bryant then removed the semi-automatic rifle from his carrying bag and opened fire, shooting the weapon from his hip. It would only take 15 seconds to discharge 17 rounds, which resulted in the deaths of 12 patrons and the wounding of 10 others. He then casually walked from the café to the adjacent gift shop before opening fire, this time shooting dead another eight victims. In the space of one and half minutes, Bryant had fired a total of 29 rounds and killing

20 people and wounding many others, who were lucky to escape the mayhem alive.

After changing magazines and reloading, he continued firing the weapon as he moved out of the historic building into the nearby car park. On seeing a bus driver sitting behind the wheel, he nonchalantly walked up to him and shot him in the back, killing him instantly. He continued to discharge several rounds at many potential victims who were screaming and trying to get away from him. One was shot dead and another three suffered gunshot wounds.

Not content, Bryant swapped the Armalite rifle for a SLR military style semi-automatic .308FN, which he had left in the boot of his Volvo motor vehicle. He sprayed numerous rounds from the car park into the adjacent dam near the historic ruins, then back towards the café. Two more visitors were killed and another six wounded, with others extremely lucky to escape unscathed.

On entering his vehicle and driving 300 metres down the road towards the toll booth, he saw a mother walking with her two young daughters. He alighted from his vehicle, shot the mother and her younger child dead, then chased the other daughter before fatally wounding her with a single shot.[528] On

528 The Mikac family were simply enjoying the sunshine and having a picnic when their lives were cut short. The husband and father was playing golf at a nearby course when he heard shots ring out, not knowing at the time what was taking place. The Allanah and Madeline Foundation was subsequently set up in memory of his two cherished daughters as a national charity to help children subjected to extreme violence and trauma. It was officially launched by the then Australian Prime Minister John Howard in April 1997.

reaching the toll booth, he murdered the four occupants of a BMW waiting to leave the site.

Bryant was so callous that he even pulled two of the female passengers from the vehicle, before shooting them at close range. He then transferred all his belongings from his own car into the BMW, including the Armalite rifle, its ammunition and the petrol containers. A driver in another vehicle approaching the toll booth saw what was happening and quickly reversed away. Luckily, he was fortunate enough to escape, despite shots fired in his direction.

Bryant observed two people in a white Toyota Corolla parked at a service station adjacent the toll booth. He drove the BMW near the front of the Corolla blocking their escape. Under gun point, he forced the male into the boot of the stolen BMW and after firing three fatal shots into the female passenger, he drove to the Seascape guest house.

After being removed from the car boot, the hostage was placed in handcuffs by Bryant who then set the BMW alight before entering the guest house. On learning of the massacre, a massive police and emergency services operation was put in place, with the guest house being surrounded by heavily armed police.[529]

Initially, they tried to negotiate with Bryant, thinking the owners of Seascape and his hostage were still alive. Indeed, during lengthy telephone conversations with Bryant, who was calling himself Jamie, he gave them the impression the

529 Police established a forward command post at the Tasmanian Devil Park at Taranna and members from both the Tasmania and Victoria Special Operations Group would be deployed, along with a Police Hostage Negotiation Team to numerous suitable observation points surrounding the Seascape Guest House.

hostages had not been harmed, even saying he had cooked them something to eat and had made them cups of tea. However, it wasn't long before police found out the three were already dead.

During the night, Bryant discharged his weapons on numerous occasions trying to keep police at bay before making a final desperate attempt to escape. At approximately 7.45am on Monday, 29 April 1996, after 18 long hours, the mayhem was finally about to end. Smoke was first seen coming from an upper storey window of the Seascape guest house, followed by extensive flames which ultimately destroyed the building.

After more gunfire, Bryant was observed wearing dark clothing but then appeared naked when dropping to the ground on his knees. Police wasted no time capturing Bryant who, by then, was suffering burns to his back and buttocks. He was taken to the Royal Hobart Hospital under heavy guard and treated for his burn injuries.

Detectives from the eastern police district CIB initially interviewed Bryant the following day when he was in hospital. On being questioned if he was the person responsible for the Port Arthur massacre, he stated he didn't know anything as he was surfing a long way from the historic site. After declining to participate in a video recorded interview, Bryant was formally charged with one initial count of murder of the woman he shot dead in the Toyota Corolla motor vehicle, with many more charges to follow.

On 4 July 1996, detectives formally interviewed Bryant when he was on remand at Risdon Prison. The interview was electronically recorded and was conducted in the absence of Bryant's lawyer. He agreed his client could be interviewed without his presence and, after being formally cautioned, a number of matters were put to Bryant. He initially agreed he owned the Armalite rifle and then made certain admissions to the kidnapping by placing the male in the boot of his vehicle. Bryant also agreed he had proceeded to Seascape and set it on fire.

The following extract of an edited selected questions and answers interview of his admissions, were subsequently played to the court[530] prior to sentencing:

> Q. Look Martin, you've obviously got a…a, an interest in firearms as well?
> A. Well, I have had an interest in firearms.
> Q. How many guns do you own?
> A. I own umm, a shotgun and a semi-automatic and another semi-automatic. Three altogether.
> Q. Where'd you get those guns?
> A. Oh, umm. I can't really say, I haven't got my lawyer here, so…
> Q. Well we have spoken to your lawyer and he knows that we're talking to you.
> A. He knows, he knows.
> Q. And aah, has no problem with that so, aah.
> A. Yeah, I got umm, one ooh, off a gun dealer and I also got two of 'em umm, got two off…. (inaudible).

After taking Bryant through further protracted questions and answers about the guns and his movements on the fateful day, the detectives turned to the kidnapping and subsequent

530 *The Queen v Martin Bryant*-In the Criminal Sittings of the Supreme Court held at Number 7 Court, Salamanca Place, Hobart, before His Honour the Chief Justice on Tuesday, the 19th Day of November 1996- Transcript of Proceedings.

events at Seascape. On admitting he held up a car that he liked, Bryant said:

> A…held up the person in the car and kidnapped him.
> Q. Kidnapped him?
> A. Mmm.
> Q. When you say held up.
> A.… No, I didn't really, didn't know whether I'd let you know you're not gunna let anyone else know. Yeah, no, I stopped the car, I was in the Volvo, I stopped the car on the corner, there was a nice-looking BMW and I asked them to get out of the car but the…
> Q. How many people were in it?
> A. There was a child in there, in the back and a lady and a man. The man, I got him out the car, I had my gun with me and I said I want to take your car, so I took his car. I got, then his wife or girlfriend got into the Volvo with the child and I left, I drove off.
> Q. So you drove away in the BMW?
> A. Yes.
> Q. With another male person?
> A. Yeah, he was in the boot, I put him in the boot of the car.

Bryant was then asked what he remembered when he drove into the Seascape Guest House:

> A. I remember skidding on some grass and I had a heap of petrol, had some petrol with me, I put some petrol in the BMW.
> Q. And what happened then?

A. Well, what happened then, I knocked on the door… but there was no answer. And what happened is I remember the explosion…I don't know whether I put the car on, lit the car up or not.
Q. Sorry?
A. I don't know whether I lit the car up or not but there was an explosion.
Q. Where was the man that was…?
A. He must've been trapped in the boot, the hostage.
After clarifying where Bryant had purchased the petrol, investigators continued with their questioning about Seascape.
Q.… You've got out of the BMW?
A. Mmmm
Q. Tipped petrol, where did you tip the petrol?
A. I don't recall because it was a vast explosion…
Q. Did you actually knock on the door at Seascape?
A. Mmm, few times, went around the back, knocked on the door, no answer.
Q. Do you remember talking to anyone that morning, the same morning at Seascape?
A. No.
Q. Did you go inside at Seascape?
A. No. You can ask me questions. It'd be interesting if I could hear some of yours…if you've got other things that you could tell me on your report…What have you got on your report? Is there other things that you've reckon I've done down there?
Q. Yes there are.
A. What like?
Q. Well, you see...

A. Tell me.
Q. If you could tell us.
A. No, I don't.

Unsatisfied with Bryant's version of what had transpired, police kept at him regarding the Seascape inferno:

Q. Back at, back to Seascape. What happened when no one answered the door?
A. I went around to the back.
Q. You went around to the back? And what did you do there?
A. No answer the door there either.
Q. No.
A. So next thing is, I must've played around with petrol.
Q. What do you mean you must've played around with petrol?
A. Set fire to the, to the car.
Q. Can you remember doing that? You say you must.
A. No I can't. Vaguely remember a flash and I must've been in the car when it went up 'cos I got burnt so.
Q. And you said to us earlier that you think the hostage at that stage must've been in the car, that's, is that correct or?
A. In the boot.
Q. Must've still been in the boot?
A. Yes.
Q. So you know Seascape's burnt down?
A. Yeah. Been informed.
Q. Who told you that?
A. A doctor and security guards.

Q. What else have they told you?
A. They said that people had been burnt inside there. Mmm. So, I don't know how many people were burnt inside the Seascape Guest House.

While he effectively admitted setting the fire at Seascape, Bryant's version of the theft of the BMW motor vehicle and the kidnapping victim was certainly at odds with what police knew had transpired. In addition, his response and demeanour certainly demonstrated a complete lack of remorse, notably demonstrated by fielding questions put to him by police. As to the deaths of the guest house owners, Bryant also tried to suggest he was not involved, but again police knew he was lying.

Regarding the guest house husband and wife and the kidnap victim, all three bodies were burnt beyond recognition. It would take dental records and a DNA analysis to confirm their identities. A subsequent postmortem revealed these badly burnt bodies had also suffered gunshot wounds. Following an examination of their trachea, toxicology results showed they had both died from gunshot wounds before the fire had started.

The BMW kidnap victim's body was also located in the remnants of the building. His hands were tied behind his back by two sets of handcuffs. He'd been shot twice and, as there was no evidence of smoke inhalation, his death also occurred before the guest house burnt down.

Regarding the events at the Port Arthur historical site, Bryant took it one step further again, with a complete denial throughout the interview. The following is another selected edit of the interview with Bryant and police:

Q. Martin, do you remember the 28th of April, Sunday the 28th of April this year?
A. Aah, no I don't. Was that the day I suppose everyone's talking about. Ohh, about the drama of me being in Royal Hobart Hospital, I think.
Q.… lots of people are saying they saw you in the Broad Arrow Café on Sunday, 28th of April.
A. Mm, that's untrue.
Q. And why do you say that, Martin?
A. Because I didn't, I drove straight past.
Q. Martin, I believe you went to the Broad Arrow Café at Port Arthur on Sunday the 28th.
A. That's nonsense…I didn't go to Port Arthur.
Q. See you, you've been pretty good with your memory really and a lot of things that we've been talking about, some things you're not recollecting, but you've very, very definite now that weren't at Port Arthur on that day.
A. Probably, because I've got a reasonably good memory.
Q. What would you say if I said that someone's identified you having a meal at the Broad Arrow Café?
A. Having a meal? I had a toasted sandwich at Nubeena and that was it.
Q. Martin, quite frankly, I find it very hard to believe what you're telling me.
A. Well, it's your word, I mean how come you don't believe me?
Q. …we've been speaking to a lot of people…who have identified a person answering your description at Port Arthur, at the Broad Arrow Café…at the toll booth and also at the service station where that Toyota Corolla was…bearing in mind your car, registered to you…was

also there at the toll booth and you're telling us that you weren't anywhere near it.
A. That's right, I drove straight past, so.
Q. ...how do you expect us to believe what you're telling us. Doesn't add up, does it? Doesn't make any sense.
A. It's silly, I mean, I wouldn't drive into Port Arthur on that day, so. I drove straight past Port Arthur that day.

Detectives then told Bryant exactly what he did on that fateful day, shooting dead 20 people in the café and injuring many more. It was suggested further that he killed more people in the car park, including the two children and their mother who were heading towards the toll booth. Bryant maintained that he was not responsible for killing a total of 35 people and injuring many others:

Q. ...a lot of people have identified a person with your description driving your car killing those 35 people.
A. ...All I know is other people have said to me, asked a couple of times whether I was at Port Arthur and I've said no because I wasn't there at Port Arthur that day.

In continuing to put forward a fanciful story that police had the wrong man, the other problem Bryant faced was two of his weapons were identified as being used in the mass shooting. When given that information, he made a comment which understandably infuriated detectives:

Q. ... with all the people that were shot, were either shot with those two weapons closest to us over there, your weapons.

A. Yeah…No, not the one with scope, I don't know that, never seen that, never seen that one before. Mmm, I'm not signing anything…not I until me lawyer sees me. I'm sure you'll find the person who caused all this. Me.
Q. I don't find that a very funny statement at all Martin, to be quite honest.
A. You should've put that on recording.
Q. Ohh, it's still recording at this present stage. So that is on the recording… like I said before…we are looking at the person responsible.
A. I must need a lawyer then…

Having been charged with the murder of no less than 35 people, the attempted murder of another 20 and a number of other charges,[531] Bryant engaged the services of high profile barrister, John Avery.[532] After numerous discussions long into the night between the lawyer and his client, who was still protesting his innocence, Bryant finally decided to plead guilty as charged.

Avery was credited with this change of plea, which was believed to be brought about by Bryant encouraged to draw pictures of what had taken place. No doubt though, Avery would have convinced the still unremorseful Bryant that the

531 Bryant was facing all up a total of 72 charges which included counts of aggravated assault, inflict grievous bodily harm and unlawfully setting fire to property.

532 Avery would also suffer a fall from grace after he was jailed in 2008 for fraudulent misappropriation and stealing of client funds. Part of a plea submission when being sentenced to four years and six months, was that representing Bryant had a significant impact on his life. Avery was released from prison in September 2012.

clear weight of evidence against him would result in a guilty verdict in any event.

On 22 November 1996, Bryant appeared before Supreme Court Chief Justice William Cox for sentencing. It was of no surprise that at the forefront of this case was Bryant's mental condition, which could point to an underlying factor of why he carried out such horrendous acts. Not for one moment did the court form the view that Bryant was not fit to stand trial[533] but they accepted his level of culpability was reduced due to an intellectual impairment. Psychiatric evidence tendered to His Honour determined that Bryant was of limited intellectual ability but was able to function reasonably well in the community, albeit somewhat of a social misfit.

In sentencing Bryant on each of the 35 counts of murder for the term of his natural life with no eligibility for parole, Chief Justice Cox said:

> *The prisoner has shown no remorse for his actions. Though he ultimately pleaded guilty, it has clearly been done in recognition of the undoubted strength of the evidence against him and amounts to little more than a case of bowing to the inevitable... Having regard to the nature and extent of his conduct, I cannot regard it as anything other than falling within the worst category of cases...I have no reason to hope and every reason to fear that he will remain indefinitely as disturbed and*

533 The law recognises that a person, by reason of a mental disease who is unable to understand the gravity of the offending, should not be held criminally responsible and therefore detention in a mental health facility is more appropriate. A diagnosis such as schizophrenia, psychosis or bipolar disorder is typical of such a condition.

insensitive as he was when planning and executing the crimes of which he now stands convicted...[534]

Apart from Bryant being jailed for life, the only other consolation, as a consequence of the Port Arthur tragedy, was the proposed radical overhaul of Australia's gun laws, thanks to then Prime Minister John Howard. The significant changes sought to create uniform gun laws and a database registry for all states and territories, courtesy of a National Firearms Agreement.

Its formidable provisions included a ban on automatic and semi-automatic weapons, strict storage requirements, together with mandatory licensing with a thorough background check of the applicant. In addition, two federally-funded buyback schemes, including large scale voluntary weapon surrender, saw over 650,000 firearms handed over, vastly reducing the number of guns in circulation throughout Australia. Unfortunately, the planned national registry was never signed off by all states and territories until 2023. This was largely as a result of the December 2022 shooting of three people, including two police officers in Wieambilla, Queensland.

In any event, the National Firearms Registry will not be fully operational until 2028. In the meantime, the lack of a uniform database keeping track of such weapons goes on unabated. According to The Australia Institute, in early 2025 they estimated there were four million guns in the hands of Australian civilians. Given there is no registry though, such figure could be indeed higher. We can only hope and pray that

---

534 *R v Martin Bryant*, Cox CJ 22 November 1996- Comments on passing sentence.

there will be no more mass shootings like we witnessed at Port Arthur.

For the time being, though, I rest my case Your Honour. Until we meet again in 'Another Question of Murder Down Under', it's time to put the pen down, say goodnight and turn out the light.

ACKNOWLEDGEMENTS

I must admit after retiring as a lawyer with several university degree notches on my belt, not to mention former miscreant clients who I kept out of prison, I thought becoming an author would be a breeze. After I finished my first manuscript, I had no doubt I would be picked up by at least one, if not more than one, Australian publisher. That certainly never happened and despite sending what I thought were 'brilliant further manuscripts', either you wouldn't get a response or at best, 'Thanks, but no thanks and good luck'. Unless you are a Colleen McCullough or a Tim Winton, publishers don't want to know you. On the other hand, unless you are a well-known recently retired AFL footballer, off you go to the world of self-publishing.

Not for one moment am I complaining but now, after completing my fourth book, and I hope you enjoyed it, the merry-go-round continues. As a self-published author, you look forward to receiving royalties from the well-known companies who, thankfully, advertise your book on their web site and on receipt of an order, print and post it. When the first royalty payment arrived, I was over the moon, but alas, it wouldn't even buy a cup of coffee. Such payments still arrive on a monthly basis and, as they slowly increase so I can buy a coffee, perhaps self-publishing does have its advantages but only time will tell.

Now that I have that off my chest, I must acknowledge the support I receive, not only from my family, but friends and acquaintances who purchase my books with no questions asked. Of course, they may well not read each book and again I say that with tongue in cheek, but your support is greatly appreciated.

Local bookstores such as Farrell's in Mornington, Petersen's in Hastings, Rosebud Book Barn and Antipodes in Sorrento, have been amazing in supporting, not only me but all other budding authors from our sunny seaside peninsula. A big thank you to them and also to Peter Marshall OAM, the Mornington and the Mount Martha Newsagencies and also Stories By The Sea Bookshop in Mt Eliza.

In reaching the "pinnacle" as a self-published author, the journey has not been an easy road and if it wasn't for Alana Lambert of Coven Press, I would still be going around in circles. Journalist, Samantha Elley is always a pleasure to deal with and, as usual in editing my books, she always finds a few embarrassing errors. Thank you so much to these two kind ladies and also to graphic designer, Melinda Childs of Studio Orchard, who is brilliant in designing the front and back covers. The finished product is then progressed by Revolution Print in Ballarat, Victoria and they also deserve a pat on the back.

My research can be attributed in part to Andrew Rule, Anthony Dowsley and Patrick Dowling of the Herald Sun and also John 'Sly of the Underworld' Silvester. I am the first to acknowledge they do pen interesting articles on crooks who have passed us by. My access to decisions of our courts and tribunals is thanks to AustLII, set up in 1995 as a joint program by the University of Technology and the University of New South Wales law schools. If you need to peruse the facts leading to the sentencing of those convicted of crimes, then this site is a must.

Finally, the love and support of my very patient wife, Michelle and our two sons continue unabated, particularly when I get frustrated as a "wanna-be author". Michelle spends countless hours well into the night perusing at times, my hapless writing and then attending to numerous rewrites of each paragraph. Without doubt, I love her to the moon and back.

November 2025

ROGUES GALLERY

Amos Atkinson	120	Gregory Brazel	120, 343
Sammy Hutchinson	120	Frankie Waghorn	120
Craig Minogue	121	Dieter Pfennig	128
John J. Powers	136	Frank Abbott	146
John D. Bowie	148	Billy McCulkin	162
John Stuart	163	James Finch	163
Garry R. Dubois	164	Vincent O'Dempsey	165
Warren McDonald	166	Raymond Edmunds	171
Bandali Debs	186	Frederick Boyle	203
Stephen J. Bradley	209	Christopher Lowery	213
Charles Ian King	213	Martha Needle	217
Lorraine Whyte	218	Alexander Lee	218
Darren Chalmers	231	Leonard J Warwick	239
Michael Guider	252	Robert Lowe	264, 310
Gregory K. Davies	265	David J. Birnie	274
Catherine M. Birnie	274	Peter J. Maloney	281
William P. Mitchell	281, 368	Frank Vitkovic	292
John Robert Glover	298	Peter Reid	312
Andrew P. Garforth	315	John R. Travers	322
Michael Murdoch	322	Michael Murphy	322
Gary Murphy	322	Les Murphy	322
Ivan 'The Rat' Milat	324	John W. Lindrea	338
Christopher Binse	343	Matthew Johnson	343
Carl Williams	343	Paul Haigh	358
Peter Dupas	358	Malcolm G. Baker	359
Malcolm Hungerford	364	William P. Mitchell	368
Peter Maloney	373	Paul Charles Denyer	378
Ashley Coulston	388	John P. Lascano	391
Martin Bryant	391, 548	Mark Lewis	400

Lindsey Rose	402	Ronald Waters	402
Simon Rochford	432	Phuong Canh Ngo	435
Mark Smith	445	Matthew De Gruchy	459
Mark Mala Valera	464, 483	Craig A. Merritt	469
Mark England	473	Karl M Hague	474
Keith A Schreber	484	Belinda van Krevel	487
Brendan Fernando	501	Vester Fernando	501
Robert C. Parsons	512	Matthew J. Harris	518
Colin Earl Graham	525	Chris M. Dawson	534
Robert Adams	536	Keli Lane	540
Daniel Cherry	540	Debbie Guise	541
John J. Bunting	548	Robert Wagner	548

POLICE TASK FORCES/OPERATIONS

LIST OF CASES

R v Ryan and Walker [1966] VR 553, Winneke, CJ, Hudson and McInerney, JJ, 8 June 1966.-Appeal dismissed	70
Ryan v The Queen [1966] HCA, 14 October 1966-Appeal dismissed	70
Ronald Joseph Ryan v A.G. for Victoria & O'Brien and I Grindlay, [1966] VicSC, Justice Menhennitt, 23 December 1966-Appeal dismissed	71
DPP v Walker [2016] VCC 160-Conviction and sentence	72
Regina v Keith Ryrie [1966] Unreported, VicSC 160,5 December 1966-Appeal dismissed	73
Priest v Deputy State Coroner & Anor [2010] VSC 449-Application in the interests of justice	93
Linda Jane Stilwell, Finding into Death With Inquest-Coroners Court Reference 2005/1489	93
The Queen v Barrie Robert Quinn [1975] Unreported, Vic Court of Criminal Appeal, 3 April 1975- Appeal dismissed	108
R v Haigh [1993] Unreported, Supreme Court of Victoria, Judge Coldrey, 26 May 1993, transcript sentencing remarks, page 173.	110
R v Haigh [2009] VSC 185-para 202- Application refused	112
Haigh v The Queen Unreported-Court of Appeal, Buchanan and Nettle JJA and Kyrou AJA, 19 April 2011-Appeal granted	112
R v Haigh [2012] VSC 617-Application refused	112
R v Bazley, James Frederick [1986] Unreported VicSC, 133, Judge Gray, 16 April 1986-Conviction and sentence	116
The Queen v Barrie Robert Quinn [1975] Unreported, VCCA, 3 April 1975	118
In the Matter of an Application for Bail by Alexander Tsakmakis, Unreported VicSC–Justice Kaye, 19 September 1978	118
The Queen v Alexander Tsakmakis, [1979] Unreported, VCCA, 24 October 1979- Appeal dismissed	119

LIST OF LEGISLATION

Criminal Procedure Act 1986	18, 248
Mental Health and Cognitive Impairment Forensic Provisions Act 2020	305
Sentencing Act 1989	318

Northern Territory

Criminal Code Act 1983	17, 413
Parole Act 1971	534

Queensland

Corrective Services Act 2006	545
Corrective Services (No Body, No Parole) Amendment Act 2017	169, 534
Crime and Corruption Act 2001	164
Criminal Code Act 1899	17, 166, 192, 195
Criminal Code (Double Jeopardy) Amendment Act 2007	199
Criminal Code and Other Legislation (Double Jeopardy Exception and Subsequent Appeals) Amendment Act 2024	199, 546
Police Powers and Responsibilities Act 2000	164

South Australia

Correctional Services Act 1982	534
Criminal Law Consolidation Act 1935	17, 130, 415
Criminal Law Consolidation (Double Jeopardy) Amendment Act 2008	199

Tasmania

Criminal Code Act 1924	17

Victoria

Western Australia

International

REFERENCES

PROLOGUE

- *Murder at Launceston,* Colonial Times and Tasmanian Advertiser, 6 January 1826
- *The Convict Lynch,* Sydney Herald, 2 May 1842
- *Registers of Coroners' Inquests and Magisterial Inquiries,* State Records of NSW 1842
- *Another Dead Body Found,* Sydney Morning Herald, 12 November 1892
- *The Mysterious Discoveries,* Sydney Morning Herald, 12 November 1892
- *Colonial History: Bushranging in Tasmania,* The Australasian, 29 November 1893
- *The Story of the Australian Bushrangers,* George E Boxall, Swan Sonnenschein & Co, 1899
- *Colonial History: Bushranging,* Sydney Sportsman, 18 June 1902
- *The Murder Trial,* The West Australian 15 September 1909
- *Family of Seven Perishes in Mysterious Village Fire - Gun Found By Side of Dead Man,* The Register News – Pictorial Adelaide SA, 27 Feb 1929
- *Father's Crime. Family Tragedy, Murder and Suicide. Hobart.* The Brisbane Courier 20 Mar 1929
- *The Hat Pin Murderers,* Truth Newspaper, 29 March 1953
- *They hanged a woman-killer of 3 in Perth,* The Daily Telegraph, 22 November 1953
- *Insanity and Injustice,* John P Bourke & David S Sonenberg, Jacaranda, 1969
- *Legal Executions in Western Australia*, Brian Purdue, Foundation Press 1993

- *Australia's Serial Killers,* Paul B. Kidd, Amazon 2000
- *A journey through hell's gates,* The Age, 29 October 2002
- *Family Homicide in Australia*, J Mouzos & Catherine Rushforth, Australian Institute of Criminology, 15 June 2003
- *Motives for Homicide*, Australian Institute of Criminology, 8 November 2005
- *Twelve Crimes That Shocked the Nation*, Alan J Whiticker, January 2005
- *A Compulsion to Kill: The Surprising Story of Australia's First Serial Killers*, Robert Cox, Glass House Books, 2014
- *The Abolition of Defensive Homicide; A Step Towards Populist Punitivism at the Expense of Mentally Impaired Offenders*, Madeline Ulbrick et al, 2016
- *Intimate Family Violence and the Abolition of Defensive Homicide*, Alexander Ross Davis, Insight-Thomson Reuters, 11 February 2018
- *Understanding What Drives Serial Killers,* Scott A Bonn Ph.D. 15 September 2019
- *The Legal Definition of Murder and the Different Degrees of Murder Charges*, Galbally Parker, 24 April 2023
- *The Black Hand Mafia*, Stories from the Archives, Queensland State Archives, 4 July 2023
- *Criminal Offence of Murder Across Australia*, Jarryd Bartle, 23 December 2023
- *Two of Queensland's most brutal unsolved murders may have been committed by the same killer,* Cira Jones, ABC News, 25 January 2025
- *Exhibition focuses on domestic violence murder that divided colonial Perth*, Emma Wynne, ABC Radio Perth, 7 May 2025
- *We interviewed 205 Australians convicted of murder and manslaughter. Alcohol's role was alarming*, Li Eriksson et al, The Conversation, 10 July 2025
- *Town Serially Unlucky*, Mark Butler, Herald Sun, 1 August 2025

CHAPTER 1: THE GUN ALLEY POSTHUMOUS PARDON

- *Colin Campbell Ross,* John Lack & Kevin Morgan, Australian Dictionary of Biography, Australian National University, 2005
- *Wrong Man Hanged,* Steve Waldon, The Age 9 July 2005
- *Gun Alley murder: posthumous pardon*, Hansard Parliament of Victoria, 2008
- *Ross cleared of murder nearly 90 years ago,* John Silvester, The Age, 27 May 2008
- *Man hanged for murder 86 years ago pardoned,* The Associated Press, 28 May 2008
- *Gun Alley: Murder, Lies and Failure of Justice*, Kevin Morgan, Hardie Grant Books(Australia), 2012
- *Murder by Numbers-Fascinating Figures Behind the World's Worst Crimes*, James Moore, History Press, 2018

CHAPTER 2: THE 'UNWITTEN LAW' ACQUITTAL

- *Audrey Jacob in Custody,* Mirror Perth WA, 5 September 1925
- *Audrey Jacob committed,* trove nla gov.au 1925
- *Audrey Jacob Reappears,* Truth Sydney NSW, 24 January 1926
- *A Great Perth Lawyer's Greatest Case,* Mirror Perth WA, 27 September 1952
- *Constructing gender in the press: The case of Audrey Jacob,* Caroline Ingram, School of Humanities, The University of Western Australia, 2019
- *How an 'unwritten Law', media spin and legal cunning saw Audrey Jacob get away with murder,* Emma Wynne, ABC Radio Perth, 2 August 2020
- *Audrey Jacob's 100yo 'murder' on the dance floor brought back to life*, Emma Wynne, ABC Radio Perth, 31 August 2025

CHAPTER 3: PYJAMA GIRL MYSTERY

- *New facts on pyjama girl: secret police file,* The Daily Telegraph, 19 January 1941

- *The Pyjama Girl Case,* Hugh Geddes, Sun Books Pty Ltd, 1978
- *Linda Agostini, (1905-1934),* Bruce Pennay, Australian Dictionary of Biography. Vol 13, National Centre of Biography, Australian National University, 1993
- *Antonio Agostini, (1903-1969),* Bruce Pennay, Australian Dictionary of Biography. Vol 13, National Centre of Biography, Australian National University, 1993
- *The Pyjama Girl Mystery*, Richard Evans, Scribe Publications Pty Ltd, 2004
- *The Pyjama Girl murder,* The Daily Telegraph, 5 November 2015
- *The Pyjama Girl was on public display on in Sydney for almost a decade. Her murder remains a mystery*, Helen Vnuk, Mamamia, 19 September 2020

CHAPTER 4: AUNT THALLY-THE COMFORT TOXIC TEA KILLER

- *Why Thallium May Be Banned,* The Sunday Herald, 28 June 1953
- *Caroline Grills, (1888-1960),* Stephen Garton, Australian Dictionary of Biography. Vol 14, National Centre of Biography, Australian National University, 1996
- *Murder, tried and true*, Sydney Morning Herald, 11 February 2003
- *Cinema Serial Killers,* Paul B Kidd, Five Mile Press, 2012
- *The Sydney aunty who poisoned her family,* Gillian Taylor, that's life Magazine, 31 August 2018

CHAPTER 5: LAST MURDERER TO BE FLOGGED

- *Constable's condition very low,* The Argus Melbourne, 1 February 1952
- *Police Draw Dragnet Tighter Round Killer of Constable,* The Argus Melbourne, 2 February 1952
- *Belief killer was migrant*, The Argus Melbourne, 4 February 1952

- *Tributes Paid to Police Constable*, The Age Melbourne, 5 February 1952
- *Shooting of Constable - Arrest Today likely*, The Argus Melbourne, 6 February 1952
- *Howell Murder Charge Laid*, The Argus Melbourne, 13 February 1952
- *O'Meally committed in police murder*, News, Adelaide SA, 13 March 1952
- *O'Meally guilty of Murder*, The Advertiser Adelaide SA, 24 May 1952
- *O'Meally sentenced to death*, The Argus Melbourne, 24 May 1952
- *O'Meally Loses Appeal*, Examiner Launceston, Tasmania, 23 July 1952
- *O'Meally To Make High Court Appeal*, The West Australian, 5 August 1952
- *Appeal by O'Meally to Full Court*, The Canberra Times, 12 August 1952
- *Queen's Medal For Constable Howell*, The Age Melbourne, 11 September 1952
- *O'Meally's Appeal*, The Herald Melbourne, 6 October 1952
- *O'Meally Refused Leave To Appeal*, Morning Bulletin, Rockhampton Qld, 7 October 1952
- *O'Meally will spend the rest of his life in Pentridge*, The Argus Melbourne, 28 January 1953
- *Two Criminals to Be Whipped*, The Advertiser, Adelaide, 1 November 1957
- *Lonely Lifer sees the Light of Day*, Geoff Walsh, The Age, 5 July 1979
- *The Man They Couldn't Break*, Alan Sharpe, Kingsclear Books, 1997
- *Pentridge: Behind The Bluestone Walls*, Richard Willis et al, Echo Publishing, Sydney, 2015

- *From the Archives 1957: Dramatic car chase after Pentridge Prison Escape*, The Age, 28 March 2019

CHAPTER 6: LAST ONE TO BE HANGED

- *Ryan, Walker committed for trial,* The Canberra Times, 5 February 1966
- *Ryan and Walker lose appeals over shot warder,* The Age, 9 June 1966
- *Murder appeal fails,* The Canberra Times, 6 December 1966
- *Ryrie goaled for 50 years,* The Canberra Times, 30 May 1967
- *End of appeals from the High Court to the Privy Council,* Parliamentary Education Office, 8 July 1975
- *Ryan Juror- 'We didn't want rope'*, The Sun, 14 August 1984
- *The Walker Interview*, The Truth, 25 January 1985
- *No 3 Capital Punishment,* Ivan Potas and John Walker, Australian Institute of Criminology, February 1987
- *Ronald Jopseh Ryan (1925-1967),* Mike Richards, Australian Dictionary of Biography. Vol 16, National Centre of Biography, Australian National University, 2002
- *The Hanged Man-The Life and Death of Ronald Ryan,* Mike Richards, Scribe Publications, Melbourne, 2002
- *Death penalty dead and buried,* The Sydney Morning Herald, 11 March 2010
- *Barry Dickins remembers last man hanged in Ryan at La Mama,* John Bailey, The Sydney Morning Herald, 23 November 2015
- *Notorious criminal Peter Walker is back in jail,* Olivia Lambert, news.com.au, 22 February 2016
- *Unseen footage of Ronald Ryan, Australia's last man hanged, reveals divided opinions on capital punishment*, Kelsie lorio, ABC News, 5 January 2020
- *1967: Ronald Ryan becomes the last person to be executed in Australia,* National Museum Australia, 18 September 2024

• *Eric Edgar Cooke terrorised the city of Perth for years before he was caught and executed*, Nine News, 26 October 2025

CHAPTER 7: THE GHASTLY MUTILATOR

• *Police Get Description of Mutilation Killer*, Canberra Times, 16 April 1962

• *Coroner Finds Body in Shop Was Hacketts*, Canberra Times, 18 July 1963

• *Compulsion To Kill 'Alleged at Inquest'*, Canberra Times, 5 December 1963

• *The Knick-Knack Man; Inside the Mind of Australia's Most Deranged Serial Killer*, Paul B. Kidd, Harper Collins Australia, 2002

• *The Mutilator serial killer who first struck in Brisbane*, Courier Mail, 13 May 2015

• *Murder spree ended when Mutilator 'rose from the dead'*, Daily Telegraph, 13 May 2015

• *William 'The Mutilator' MacDonald, NSW 's oldest prisoner, dead at 90*, The Sydney Morning Herald, 13 May 2015

• *The Mutilator dead at 90: William MacDonald who cut off victim's genitalia, was NSW's longest-serving prisoner*, Mark Morri, The Daily Telegraph, 13 May 2015

• *William, MacDonald 'The Mutilator', Sydney's Most Disturbed Serial Killer*, Eliot Lindsay, Murders Most Foul, 17 August 2022

CHAPTER 8: WAS HE AUSTRALIA'S MOST EVIL?

• *Man charged with picnic murders*, The Canberra Times, 29 May 1965

• *Killer of three will not hang*, The Sydney Morning Herald, 2 February 1966

• *Girl, 5, raped, murdered*, The Canberra Times, 18 April 1966

• *Second murder charge laid*, The Canberra Times, 22 April 1966

• *Accused denies any link with child murder,* The Canberra Times, 12 October 1966

• *Inquest on Adelaide Oval girls,* The Age, 10 July 1979

• *One man, so many faces of evil,* John Silvester, The Age, 22 April 2007

• *Court upholds child killer Percy's right to silence,* Sarah Farnsworth, ABC News, 7 October 2010

• *DNA clue could solve 47-year-old Wanda Beach murders,* Mark Morri, The Daily Telegraph, 24 February 2012

• *Derek Percy's mother Elaine admits she 'got rid of things' as cops investigated child serial killings,* Elissa Hunt, Herald Sun, 24 July 2013

• *A man called Percy, beast without mercy,* John Silvester, The Sydney Morning Herald, 27 July 2013

• *Child killer stays silent on death bed,* Rachel Olding, The Sydney Morning Herald, 24 July 2013

• *Linda Stilwell inquest: Notorious child killer Derek Percy caused 7yo's death, coroner finds,* ABC News, 30 October 2014

• *Child killer Derek Percy was linked to deaths of nine children,* ABC News, 30 October 2014

• *Derek Percy believed to be Australia's worst child serial killer*, NZ Herald, 1 April 2017

• *Innocence lost to little Allen's murder in Curtin,* Nichole Overall, Canberra City News, 23 September 2021

• *Derek Percy was one of Australia's longest serving prisoners. He's been called 'the most evil offender in our history',* Tiasha Debray, Mamamia, 12 February 2023

• *The Beaumont children's disappearance almost 60 years ago 'fundamentally changed society',* Daniel Keane, ABCNews, 18 February 2025

• *Last hope for Australia's longest cold case,* Holly Truelove, NewsWire, 22 February 2025

• *Claims of new evidence as final dig for bodies of Beaumont children begins*, Josh Hohne, Nine News, 22 February 2025

• *'We can't move on': Search renewed for Adelaide girls who vanished 50 years ago*, Zara Zadro, Nine News, 23 March 2025

CHAPTER 9: TWO MODEL PRISONERS

• *Father charged after 10 killed,* The Age, 7 September 1971

• *10 SHOT DEAD Husband is charged with wife's murder*, The Canberra Times, 7 September 1971

• *Death sentence for wife killer,* The Canberra Times, 24 November 1971

• *Man remanded on murder counts,* The Canberra Times, 28 November 1978

• *Mystery of the Homestead Murders,* David Knox, Crime Investigation Australia, 13 November 2009

• *Anniversary Of The Homestead Murders in Jerilderie,* Australia, Capt. McNeely, 22 September 2017

• *The secret life of Australia's on one of Australia's worst mass murderers. Killer who slaughtered TEN of his own family was released from prison and remarried under a secret identity*, Charlie Moore, Daily Mail Australia, 27 May 2018

• *The Margaret River shooting shows that we must stay vigilant about gun access,* Denise Cullen, The Guardian, 15 May 2018

• *Mass murderer who killed his seven biological kids remembered as a 'gentleman' by adopted children,* Express Digest, 2 June 2018

• *'To know the full story is horrendous': Stepchildren of mass murderer who slaughtered his wife and seven kids before raising a secret family reveal how they learned their 'loving dad' was one of Australia's worst serial killers*, Brooke Rolfe, Daily Mail Australia, 3 June 2018

• *Mummy's Turning Black: Murder at Summerfield Station,* Season 4, Ep.161. Bloody Murder-A True Crime Podcast, 6 July 2020

- *Clifford Bartholomew murdered his wife and 7 children. Then he had a second family*, Gemma Bath, Mamamia, 1 February 2025

CHAPTER 10: SERIAL KILLER PAUL STEVEN HAIGH

- *Two men jailed for life for murders,* The Canberra Times, 11 November 1980
- *Cruel killer wants hope,* Herald Sun, 26 January 2008
- *Brutal killer to appeal life term, James Campbell,* Sunday Herald Sun, 10 April 2011
- *Victoria's worst serial killer 'no longer a monster'* Nine News, 3 December 2012
- *Vic Serial Killer was 'victim of illness,* Belinda Merhab, The Sydney Morning Herald, 6 December 2012
- *Serial killer Paul Steven Haigh responsible for worst combination of murders, Supreme Court hears,* Paul Anderson, Herald Sun, 5 December 2012
- *Serial killer's parole bid refused,* Andrea Petrie, The Age, 13 December 2012
- *Inside the mind of our worst mass killer,* Herald Sun, 13 August 2015
- *Paul Steven Haigh, Australia's Serial Killer's Reign of Terror,* TrueCrimeArchives, 3 May 2025

CHAPTER 11: THE BBQ KING

- *Nine charges include two of murder,* The Canberra Times, 27 March 1974
- *In a gang started by Chopper's Christmas sausages,* Andrew Rule, The Sydney Morning Herald, 21 April 2010
- *Revenge served cold for 'BBQ King',* Herald Sun, 14 May 2012
- *Greek-Australian Killer Suspected in TV Chef's Murder in the '80's,* Areti Kotseli, Greek Reporter, 26 May 2012
- Serail Killer Alex *Tsakmakis suspected of cold case Manchester Unity triple execution murder,* Keith Moor, Herald Sun, 24 March 2013

- *Prison gangs flex their muscle inside and outside jail,* John Silvester, The Age, 28 April 2017
- *James 'Machine Gun' Bazley dies with his lips sealed over Donald Mackay murder,* Paige Cockburn, ABC News, 2 November 2018
- *'A very loyal, staunch friend': Crime Boss Mick Gatto pays tribute to feared assassin James 'Iceman' Bazley after the hitman dies aged 92,* Brooke Rolfe, Daily Mail Australia, 7 November 2018
- *The most Infamous Jail Killings in Victoria,* Lantern Ghost Tours, 24 May 2022
- *Alexander 'The Barbecue King' Tsakmakis,* Find A Grave, Memorial ID 142843372
- *Barry Robert Quinn,* Find A Grave, Memorial ID 140678018

CHAPTER 12: COLD CASES- PART ONE

- *Paedophile killer's house searched in link to teen's 29-year murder mystery,* Doug Robertson, The Advertiser, 2 July 2012
- *Queensland's cold case: Looking back at some of the state's most baffling cases,* Kym Agius and Elaine Ford, ABC News, 10 August 2014
- *Dieter Pfennig found guilty of 1983 murder of South Australian schoolgirl Louise Bell,* Nine News, 11 November 2016
- *Louise Bell trial: Dieter Pfennig sentenced to 35 years prison for the 1983 murder of Adelaide schoolgirl,* Claire Campbell, ABC News, 6 December 2016
- *'Real-life Wolf Creek': Man arrested over 1978 triple murders in Mt Isa,* Tim Arvier, Nine News, 12 April 2019
- *Investigative Genetic Genealogy: How does it Work?* Marc McDermott, Genealogy Explained, 8 July 2020
- *NT Police, AFP release facial reconstruction of 'The Woman in Yellow' whose remains were found in Darwin in 1987,* Sarah Spina-Matthews, 31 July 2023
- *The murder of Betty Shanks has haunted Brisbane for decades. After 72

years, it still remains unsolved, Ciara Jones, ABC News, 19 September 2024

- *Vanished in Coober Pedy: The unsolved disappearance of Karen Williams,* True Crime Avenue, 19 February 2025
- *Police name Kerryn Tate murder suspect as Terence John Fisher after cold case DNA breakthrough*, Garrett Mundy & Blake Kagi, ABC News, 13 March 2025
- *Kerryn Tate–1979 cold case breakthrough,* Government of Western Australia, 13 March 2025
- *Lisa Mott cold case investigation leads police back to panel van found in Collie bush,* Lily Krtistano, ABC News, 25 March 2025
- *Pre-inquest hearing begins for cold case murders of trio shot dead in Mount Isa bushland,* Talissa Signato, ABC News, 19 June 2025
- *Police's new weapon to crack open cold cases*, Cydonee Mardon, News.com.au 24 June 2025
- *Queensland police offer $500k reward for information about 1987 murder of Bundaberg taxi driver Bryan Hodgkinson*, Julius Dennis, ABC News, 2 July 2025
- *A young woman was murdered in Central Queensland 58 years ago. Her suspected killer never faced justice*, Ciara Jones, ABC News, 12 August 2025
- *Decades-old outback triple murder mystery brought back in the spotlight,* Robyn Wuth, Nine News, 7 October 2025
- *Police receive new information about one on WA's oldest cold cases,* Emily Bennett, Nine News, 29 October 2025
- *Investigative Genetic Genealogy,* Crime Stoppers Western Australia, 2025

CHAPTER 13: COLD CASES–PART TWO

- *'Hitman's planned victim felt marked for death',* John Silvester, The Age, 27 July 2004

- *'A mother, her daughter and a murder case that got away from all,* The Age, 18 June 2010
- *Digging up past to reveal scale of gay-hate deaths,* Paul Sheehan, The Sydney Morning Herald, 7 March 2013
- *Another twist in the Julie Garciacelay cold case, 40 years after she disappeared,* Nino Bucci, The Age, 7 January 2015
- *Dead end in brother's execution-style hits,* Herald Sun, 31 August 2017
- *Killers behind four execution-style Melbourne murders,* The Age, 31 August 2017
- *'It was murder': 1975 missing librarian case revolves around boxer, violent criminal and crime reporter,* Tammy Mills, The Age, 11 April 2018
- *Son says father could be mother-daughter Tapp killer,* Sky News Australia, 18 August 2018
- *Witness in William Tyrell inquest acquitted of murdering schoolgirl,* Sally *Rawsthorne, The Sydney Morning Herald, 11 March 2020*
- *'Victoria Police launch cold case hub with Jane Thurgood-Dove's murder unsolved',* News. com.au, 23 May 2021
- *Nancy Grunwaldt's sister, Frauke, tells of the pain of losing her older sister who disappeared from Tasmania's east coast almost 30 years ago,* Will Murray, ABC News, 1 August 2021
- *William Tyrell investigation reveals person of interest Frank Abbott has no alibi on day of disappearance,* Alex Chapman, 7News, 27 September 2021
- *Twins, 69, face sexual abuse charges,* Australian Senior News, 25 November 2021
- *Disgraceful' forensic failures exposed as Special Commission investigates deaths of three gay men in Sydney,* Hugo Timms, NCA NewsWire, 28 June 2023
- *'Fruitful' discussions in Avoca speak hope for justice for Terry Floyd,*

still missing after 48 years, Emma D'Ágostino, ABC News, 1 August 2023

- *Victoria Cafasso 1995 beach murder still unsolved as Tasmania Police conduct new searches, release image of car,* Meg Whitfield ABC News, 11 August 2023
- *No justice for Margert Tapp and little daughter,* Andrew Rule, Herald Sun, 17 August 2024
- *Newcastle graffiti marks Gordana Kotevski's abduction in 1994 as investigation continues*, Giselle Wakatama, ABC News, 24 November 2023
- *Renewed hope to solve 1975 Julie Garciacelay cold case following Easey Street breakthroughs,* Steve Vivian, ABC News, 18 October 2024
- *Hundreds of murder cases to be re-examined by special task force*, Amber Schultz, The Sydney Morning Herald, 12 December 2024
- *Police review hundreds of cold cases after hate crime inquiry,* Jordan Hirst, Q News, 15 December 2024
- *Victoria Police offer of $1 million reward for help in solving John Furlan cold case murder,* Cassie Zervos, 7 News, 2 March 2025
- *Victoria Police offer of $1 million reward in bid to solve 1998 carbombing murder,* ABC News, 3 March 2025
- *Police renew push to solve cold case disappearance of Jessica Small,* Claire Simmonds, ABC News, 7 May 2025
- *The man known only by a number: Police hope image will crack 30-year cold case,* Cassandra Morgan, The Age, 13 May 2025
- *William Tyrell 'person of interest' Frank Abbott has previously been acquitted of murder in disturbing 1968 case*, Dan Box and Nina Young, News com.au, 20 May 2025
- *Charges laid in shock 30-year-old case,* Duncan Evans, NewsWire 29 May 2025
- *Potentially significant breakthrough nearly 30 years after teenage girl disappeared*, Nine News, 30 May 2025

• *After half a century, nurse's startling new evidence- I Saw Missing Boy Talking To 'Shady Character',* John Kalia, Herald Sun, 9 June 2025

• *Police submit new evidence to coroner in Terry Floyd missing person cold case,* Sarah Lawrence, ABC News, 19 June 2025

• *'All I want is my daughter found': mum's Fresh Pain Over Cold Case Murder of Young Woman,* Tara Cosieto, Nine News, 2 July 2025

• *Cardiff mural keeps missing teenager Gordana Kotevski's story in the public eye,* Bridget Murphy and Ben Clifford, ABC News, 18 July 2025

• *Tasmania Police offers $1 million reward to crack Victoria Cafasso cold case murder,* Madeline Rojahn, ABC News, 10 October 2025

CHAPTER 14: JUSTICE FOR MY MUM

• *Roxlyn Bowie disappearance now subject of inquest,* Daily Liberal, 16 September 2014

• *Husband has history of violence: inquest,* Daily Liberal 17 September 2014

• *Roxlyn Bowie met with foul play: coroner,* Daily Liberal 19 September 2014

• *Roxlyn Bowie tip-off leads NSW investigators to comb Walgett dam,* Jamie McKinnell and Jean Kennedy, ABC News, 27 November 2018

• *Police launch forensic search and excavation over disappearance of Roxlyn Bowie,* Jenny Noyes & Rachel Clun, The Sydney Morning Herald, 27 November 2018

• *Forensic excavation at Walgett home-concludes Strike Force Maluka,* Mirage News, 22 March 2019

• *Cold case breakthrough: Husband of missing woman arrested almost 40 years later,* Rebecca Pocklington, ABC News, 5 October 2019

• *John Bowie charged with murder of wife Roxlyn Bowie, which happened 37 years ago,* ABC News, 5 October 2019

• *Justice Dina Yehia becomes first Greek Egyptian sworn into NSW Supreme Court,* The Greek Herald, 6 July 2022

- *Court hears murderer was an adulterer and violent' but not a killer*, Lucy Thackray and Olivia Ralph, ABC News, 28 September 2022
- *Alleged wife murderer was seen burning bra and pantyhose, court told*, Sarah Mc Phee, The Sydney Morning Herald, 5 October 2022
- *John Bowie found guilty in NSW Supreme Court of murdering wife, Roxlyn, 40 years ago*, Lucy Thackray, , ABC News, 31 October 2022
- *John Bowie sentenced to 24 years' jail for the murder of wife Roxlyn 40 years after she disappeared*, Olivia Ralph and Jamie McKinnell, ABC News, 17 March 2023

CHAPTER 15: MCCULKIN FAMILY MURDERS

- *McCulkin cold case: 40-year mystery leads to murder charges*, Kim Stephens, Brisbane Times, 19 October 2014
- *Shocking alleged confession to sickening cold-case killings of Brisbane mother and girls*, Michelle Rattray, Yahoo News, 25 November 2015
- *The McCulkin family murders: How police cracked the case four decades later*, Nine News, 28 May 2017
- *'Cold-blooded killer'* Vincent O'Dempsey and *Garry Dubois handed life sentences over McCulkin murders*, Nine News, 1 June 2017
- *McCulkin murders: Cold blooded killers* Vincent O'Dempsey, *Garry Dubois sentenced to life in jail*, Andrew Kos and Candice Prosser, ABC News, 1 June 2017
- *Convicted McCulkin killer Garry Dubois found dead in prison*, Paula Doneman, ABC News, 7 July 2021

CHAPTER 16: QUESTIONABLE LIFE AND TIMES OF 'MR STINKY

- *Murder-suspect picture issued*, The Canberra Times, 10 January 1980
- *Victim pleads with Mr Stinky: Admit Your Evil Deeds*, Geoff Wilkinson, Herald Sun, 27 July 1998
- *Still a mystery after 27 years*, The Age, 8 July 2003

- *Retired detectives back in the hunt,* John Silvester, The Age, 21 November 2005
- *Beaumaris girl's abductor still at large*, Bayside Leader, 4 June 2012
- *Mr Stinky still a suspect, 35 years later, in murder of Elaine Jones at Murray River camping spot,* Nino Bucci, The Age, 18 January 2015
- *Serial rapist and killer 'Mr Stinky' emerges as prime suspect in the vicious slashing murder of a mother on holiday 35 years ago, which left her two young girls as orphans,* Candace Sutton, Daily Mail Australia,19 January 2015
- *Police offer $6 million reward to catch Tynong North serial killer,* Loretta Florence, ABC News, 21 October 2017
- *Cold case detectives launch a fresh hunt for serial killer,* John Silvester, The Age, 21 October 2017
- *Detectives need new clues into decades old 'baffling' murder mystery,* Nine News, 21 October 2017
- *Person of intertest in six Frankston murders tells A Current Affair he's innocent,* Elizabeth Muling, Nine News, 8 March 2018
- *'Double murderer 'Mr Stinky' to plead guilty to historical rape charges,* ABC News, 3 May 2019
- *Jailed-for-life murderer and serail rapist Raymond 'Mr Stinky' Edmunds awaits further sentences*, Sarah Mc Phee, The Courier Mail, 21 September 2019
- *Prime suspect in 40-year Melbourne murder mystery dies*, John Silvester and Ashliegh McMillan, The Age, 30 August 2020
- *Unsolved murders a 40-year mystery,* Jake Pike, Bayside News, 19 April 2021
- *Killer's Acts Left An Awful Stench,* Andrew Rule, Sunday Herald Sun, 6 April 2025

CHAPTER 17: A QUESTION OF DOUBLE JEOPARDY

- *Hulls offers to examine double jeopardy,* The Age, 20 March 2004

• *NSW seeks to scrap double jeopardy principle*, Conor Duffy, The World Today, 7 September 2006

• *WA the next state to axe double jeopardy,* The Sydney Morning Herald, 8 September 2011

• *Victorian double jeopardy reform begins*, Melissa Iaria, The Age, 8 November 2011

• *Why Australia 'watered down' it's double jeopardy laws,* Elizabeth Byrne. ABC News, 7 May 2016

• *Bowraville murders: Man charged for second time over deaths of Aboriginal children,* ABC News, 9 February 2017

• *Double jeopardy: What is it? And why is it so import with the Bowraville murders,* Jessica Kidd, ABC News, 9 February 2017

• *Explaining double jeopardy,* Alison and Jillian Barrett, The Sydney Morning Herald, 10 August 2018

• *No retrial for the man acquitted over Bowraville murders,* Megan Palin, News.com.au 13 September 2018

• *The compelling case of the Bowraville murders and its implications for criminal law,* Craig Longman, Legal Services Journal, 1 May 2019

• *No retrial for man cleared of Qld murder,* Nine News, 3 December 2019

• *Investigating The Bowraville Murders: One of Australia's Worst Unsolved Serial Murder Cases,* Ally Pascoe, MarieClaire Australia, 4 November 2021

• *Police launch fresh search in cold case murder of Colleen Walker-Craig,* Claire Simmonds, ABC News, 24 October 2025

CHAPTER 18: REMAINS LEFT IN A DRUM

• *Man found guilty over body-in-drum case,* ABC News, 9 February 2008

• *Wife-in-drum killer faces life, Stephen Cauchi,* The Age, 10 February 2008

- *Sister of murdered wife welcomes guilty verdict on Cardiff man,* WalesOnline, 11 February 2008
- *Wife-in-barrel killer's plea,* The Age, 1 March 2008
- *21 years 'jail for 'body in barrel' murder,* ABC News, 18 March 2008
- *Killer who hid wife in drum loses appeal,* Melissa Iaria, The Sydney Morning Herald, 11 December 2009
- *Body in barrel kept in Fred Boyle's yard for 23 years,* Herald Sun, 6 October 2016
- *Boyle's body found in green metal barrel a decade ago,* Olivia Lambert, News. com.au, 31 October 2016

CHAPTER 19: I KILLED A GIRL LAST NIGHT

- *Revealed: Thrill killer Ian King's secret past,* Shannon Deery, Sunday Herald Sun 30 October 2014
- *Guilty verdict in 1983 murder,* SBS News, 9 October 2015
- *Guilty: Dog groomer: Stephen James Bradley murdered Michelle Buckingham in 1983,* Tammy Mills, The Age, 9 October 2015
- *Steven Bradley jailed for murdering teenager Michelle Buckingham in Shepparton in 1983*, ABC News, 22 December 2015
- *Jail for 'nightmare'1983 murder,* Megan Neil News.com.au, 22 December 2015
- *Cold case killer Stephen Bradley appeal sentence for Michelle Buckingham murder,* Jane Lee, The Age, 3 March 2017
- *Someone knows: How detectives and a change of conscience can crack a cold case*, John Silvester, The Age, 9 September 2022
- *A Crime So Revolting It Defiled Us All,* Andrew Rule, Sunday Herald Sun, 30 March 2025

CHAPTER 20: POISON MY LOVE

- *Execution of Martha Needle,* Burrows News, 26 October 1894
- *18 years jail for arsenic lunches,* Wayne Howell, Herald Sun, 4 May 2002

- *Lorraine Alice Whyte,* Offenders Exposed, 4 May 2002
- *The Arsenic Century: How Victorian Britain was Poisoned at Home, Work and Play,* James C. Whorton, Oxford University Press, 2010
- *Black Widows: Six Notorious felled killers who tuned on their loved ones,* Herald Sun, 25 November 2014
- *The Deadly truth: how scientists can end a murder's mystery*, John Silvester, The Age, 24 November 2018
- *Lorraine Moss held a heinous secret about the fate of her husband for 15 years but finally her unforgivable crime was uncovered,* Narelle Fraser Interviews, 1 August 2021
- *The black widow of Bendigo,* Life and Crimes with Andrew Rule, 18 February 2022
- *Murder, kidnapping, mysteries: the crimes that shocked Bendigo*, Lucy Williams, Bendigo Advertiser, 9 December 2023
- *Evil Deeds or Self-Defence? Sad tales of Woman Who Killed,* Andrew Rule, 13 July 2024

CHAPTER 21: TWO KIND DEFENCELESS AND INNOCENT WOMAN

- *Darren Chalmers sentenced to life in prison with 20 year minimum over Dianne Barrett murder, Joanna Menagh,* ABC News, 28 January 2021
- *WA man faces Victorian court over 1992 cold case death of Annette Steward,* Emily Woods, Nine News, 20 March 2023
- *Man admits to being a double killer with attacks decades apart,* Erin Pearson, The Age, 6 September 2023
- *Double killer Darren John Chalmers begs court to never be released as the chilling details of young mum found naked and strangled to death insider her home are told for the first time*, Liam Beatty, Daily Mail, 29 November 2023
- *Double killer Darren Chalmers urges judge to lock him up and throw away the key,* Erin Pearson, The Age, 29 November 2023

- *Killer handed second life sentence for murder of Geelong woman back in 1992,* Karen Sweeney, Nine News, 18 December 2023
- *Self-proclaimed monster Darren Chalmers who murdered two young women jailed for 'ultimate act of evil',* Erin Pearson, The Age, 18 December 2023

CHAPTER 22: THE FAMILY COURT BOMBER

- *Courts Church bomb linked to court blasts,* The Canberra Times, 9 April 1986
- *Man linked to bombed judges,* The Sydney Morning Herald, 12 February 1987
- *Investigation exposes the dad accused of an unsolved crime spree that killed four people,* Ross Coulthart, Daily Telegraph, 7 July 2013
- *Road to revenge,* The Sydney Morning Herald, 30 August 2014
- *Man charged over Sydney family law court bombings in 1980,* ABC News, 29 July *2015*
- *Ex-wife tells of alleged violent incident that sparked deadly bombings, shootings,* Angus Thompson, The Sydney Morning Herald, 19 July 2018
- *The accused is indigent alleged Family Court bomber broke, judge says,* Angus Thompson, The Sydney Morning Herald, 28 February 2019
- *Accused Family Court bomber claims his lawyer 'bullied him',* Angus Thompson, The Sydney Morning Herald, 18 June 2019
- *Leonard Warwick Family Court bomber found guilty of murdering three people in 1980's,* Jamie McKinnell, ABC News, 23 July 2020
- *A 40-year 'Ill-kept secret' exposed after justice served to the family court bomber Leonard Warwick,* Jamie McKinnell, ABC News, 24 July 2020
- *Sydney Family Court bombing cases,* The Senior, 3 September 2020
- *Family Court bomber destined to die in jail for 'calculated, violent murders',* ABC News, 3 September 2020
- *How police stumbled upon 'vital' evidence used to convict Family*

Court bomber Leonard John Warwick, Jamie Mc Kinnell, ABC News, 6 September 2023

- *Family Court bomber Leonard Warwick dies in jail aged 78,* Nine News, 14 February 2025
- *We won't give up fight for Rachelle*, Patrick Carlyon & Ashlea Hansen, Herald Sun, 22 March 2025

CHAPTER 23: ONE EVIL PREDATOR

- *Samantha Knight stalked before disappearing,* Philip Cornford, The Sydney Morning Herald, 11 April 2002
- *The deadly silence that doomed Samantha,* The Sydney Morning Herald, 8 June 2002
- *Killer's silence leaves chilling doubts,* Philip Cornford, The Sydney Morning Herald, 29 August 2002
- *Gone forever: Sam's grave yields only more mystery*, Philip Cornford, The Sydney Morning Herald, 12 July 2003
- *Forever Nine: The untold story of Bondi's Missing Schoolgirl, Samantha Knight,* Denise Hofman, Five Mile Press, 2013
- *Sex predator who killed Samantha Knight denied parole,* Tim Barass, Sun-Herald Sydney, 18 May 2014
- *Michael Guider, killer of Bondi schoolgirl Samantha Knight 'should never be released', News.com.au, 12 April 2017*
- *Samantha Knight's mother calls for killer and paedophile Michael Guider to remain in jail,* Nick Sas et al, ABC News, 25 May 2019
- *Serial paedophile Michael Guider who killed 9yo Samantha Knight dead in custody,* News.com.au, 7 September 2024

CHAPTER 24: ONLY A MATTER OF TIME

- *Body of girl, 6, found in gutter,* The Canberra Times, 8 November 1984
- *Murdered girl might have been drugged, coroner finds,* Rosemary Mullaly, The Age, 23 January 1986

- *Prisoner suspected in ex-wife's murder,* The Age, 11 February 2004
- *Hitman's planned victim felt marked for death,* John Silvester, The Age, 27 July 2004
- *Murder riddle lingers,* Andrew Rule, The Sydney Morning Hearld, 16 January 2010
- *Cold case files: Victoria Police secretly starts fresh investigation into 63 unsolved murders,* Keith Moor, Herald Sun, 7 December 2014
- *Gregory Keith Davies charged with murder, rape of Preston girl in 1984,* ABC News, 9 June 2016
- *Murder accused arrested at Melbourne retirement village,* Villages Info Centre, 24 June 2016
- *Kylie Maybury's killer trapped by a mix of new-age science, old fashioned policing,* John Silvester, The Age, 29 May 2017
- *'He hurt me really badly': Lucy was 14 when Kylie Maybury's killer turned on her,* Nino Bucci, The Age, 30 May 2017
- *Kylie's Killer Attacked 14 years Earlier,* Nino Bucci, The Age, 31 May 2017
- *Kylie's Murdered Molested Others, Relative Says,* Keith Moor, Herald Sun, 1 June 2017
- *Child rapist and killer has boiling water poured on groin in jail,* Nine News, 6 September 2017
- *Kylie Maybury's killer Gregory Keith Davies 'a marked man' as family describes decades of anguish,* Emma Younger, ABC News, 27 November 2017
- *Gregory Davies sentenced to life for rape, murder of 6yo Kylie Maybury in 1984,* Emma Younger, ABC News, 21 December 2017
- *Victoria Police launch cold case hub with Jane Thurgood-Dove's murder unsolved,* Evin Priest, News.com.au, 23 May 2021

CHAPTER 25: THE NOT SO LOVABLE BIRNIES

- *Couple charged,* Cyril Ayris, The West Australian, 12 November 1986

- *David and Caterine Birnie, The Visual Encyclopedia of Serial Killers*, Nigel Blundell and Susan Blackhall, eds, London, England PRC Ltd
- *Serail killer found hanged in cell,* The Sydney Morning Herald, 7 October 2005
- *Birnie prepared suicide, inquiry told,* Nicolas Perpitch, The Sydney Morning Herald, 18 December 2007
- *Killer Catherine Birnie given no hope of parole*, Nick Taylor, PerthNow, 14 March 2009
- *Evil serial killer David Birnie was 'a softie inside'-ex-prison guard*, Trevor Paddenburg, PerthNow, 13 November 2010
- *Serial killer Birnie to remain in WA jail,* Rebecca Le May, News.com.au, 29 March 2013
- *Perth serial killer Catherine Birnie deserves no mercy, Liam Bartlett,* PerthNow, 22 November 2015
- *I am a victim of my mother's crimes, says Catherine Birnie' son,* Tim Clarke, The West Australian, 22 April 2016
- *Are you going to rape or kill me?,* Debbie Schipp, news.com.au, 5 February 2017
- *How I escaped the house of horrors: Hostage of Australia's most evil killers tells how she fled*, Natasha Christian, Yahoo News, 8 February 2017
- *Stitch her up: Police thought Birnie escape victim was faking it,* Heather McNeil WA Today, 9 February 2017
- *Murder uncovered reveals more possible victims of David and Katherine Birnie,* Marika Dobbin-Thomas, The Sydney Morning Herald, 9 February 2017
- *Serial killer Catherine Birnie's parole 'no hope' Attorney-General John Quigley,* Kate Campell, PerthNow, 4 June 2017
- *The Moorhouse Murders: The chilling Serial Killer Couple Who May Have Inspired 'Hounds of Love,* Orrin Grey, The LineUp, 18 June 2018
- *WA attorney-general John Quigley, delays mass murderers parole eligibility,* Emily JB Smith, ABC News, 2 November 2024

CHAPTER 26: THE HODDLE STREET MASSACRE

- *Cain defends gun laws,* The Sydney Morning Herald, 11 August 1987
- *Mass killer Knight loses legal fight,* The Age, 8 October 2003
- *Even Julian Knight is entitled to basic human rights*, The Age, 25 November 2003
- *Hoddle Street killer banned from court,* The Age, 19 October 2004
- *Angry victims reject Knight's apology,* The Sydney Morning Herald, 27 June 2007
- *Hoddle Street killer won't be forgotten,* Jane Cowan, ABC News, 9 August 2007
- *Hoddle St judge firm on Knight,* Norrie Ross, Herald Sun, 9 August 2007
- *Law to stop criminals contacting victims,* The Age, 22 August 2007
- *Julian Knight's evil bid,* Liam Houlihan, Herald Sun, 14 June 2009
- *Insight editor Keith Moor, reconstructs the terrible events of the Hoddle Street massacre*, Keith Moor, The Australian, 17 February 2014
- *Confrontation with a killer*, Tess Lawrence, The Age, 16 September 2014
- *Ambush Now!: Inside Hoddle St killer's chilling handwritten murder manifesto*, Sunday Night, Yahoo News, 13 August 2017
- *Hoddle St killer Julian Knight loses final bid for freedom, will rot in jail,* Shae Mc Donald and Kaitlyn Offer, News.com.au, 17 August 2017
- *Melbourne's Hoddle Street massacre 35 years on*, Melissa Meehan, The Canberra Times, 9 August 2022
- *Hoddle Street massacre gunman seeks veterans' help,* Herald Sun, 1 May 2023
- *Hoddle Street mass killer Julian Knight moved to 'campus-style' prison with lower security,* April Glover, Nine News, 8 October 2025

CHAPTER 27: THE QUEEN STREET MASSACRE

- *Nine die in city rampage,* Innes Willox, The Age, 9 December 1987

- *Tem minutes of terror,* The Age, 9 December 1987
- *Merciless massacre carried out by a pleasant, well-liked man,* The Canberra Times, 10 December 1987
- *Killer leaves trail of carnage,* The Age, 10 December 1987
- *'Dial O', gasped dying man,* The Age, 10 December 1987
- *No drugs, alcohol in killer's body inquest told,* Peter Gregory, The Age, 16 September 1988
- *Prime target tells of Queen Street rampage,* Peter Gregory, The Age, 16 September 1988
- *Police action at Queen Street orderly: counsel,* The Age, 5 October 1988
- *Melbourne remembers Queen Street massacre,* The Age, 7 December 2007
- *30 years on from the Queen Street Massacre,* Damien Murphy, The Age, 7 December 2017
- *Pain remains 30 years after Vic massacre,* Nine News, 8 December 2017

CHAPTER 28: NO MORE GRANNIES

- *Police bungling allowed granny killer to strike one last time,* Ben Hills, The Sydney Morning Herald,30 November 1991
- *The Story of John Glover,* The Sydney Morning Herald, 9 August 1992
- *Suicide watch on 'sick' granny killer, Alex Mitchell, The* Sydney Morning Herald, 8 May 2005
- *Suburban serial killer,* Lindsay Simpson & Sandra Harvey, The Sydney Morning Herald, 9 September 2005
- *Granny killer takes evil secrets to his grave,* The Sydney Morning Herald, 10 September 2005
- *John Wayne Glover's despicable urge to fondle elderly women led to at least six vicious murders*, Paul Anderson, Herald Sun, 8 September 2015

• *John Wayne Glover aka 'The Granny Killer' stalked Sydney streets and killed at least six woman*, Andrew Koubaridis, News.com.au, 10 October 2015

• *From the Archives: The family man police say killed six elderly women, Jacquelyn Hole*, The Sydney Morning Herald, 28 March 2019

• *The Granny Killer: In 1989, Dorothy invited a kind stranger in for tea. He'd already killed two women*, Belinda Jepsen, Mamamia, 5 February 2021

CHAPTER 29: A CHURCH ELDER

• *Confidentiality & Disclosure of crime-related information*, Marilyn Mc Mahon, In-Psych, The Bulletin of the Australian Psychological Society Ltd, 1998

• *Freed killer 'under surveillance for life,* ABC News, 12 August 2004

• Evil killer *Robert Arthur Selby Lowe running jail sex ring,* Wayne Flower, Herald Sun, 6 December 2010

• *Mr Cruel Suspected of at Least a Dozen Attacks on Children,* Keith Moor, Herald Sun, 11 April 2012

• *The daily grind of a rotting soul,* John Silvester, The Age, 8 March 2014

• *Child killer Robert Arthur Selby Lowe pleads innocence from behind bars,* Jackie Quist, Seven News, 6 August 2014

• *Sheree Beasley's mother disgusted by killer's claim of innocence,* Brendan Roberts, Yahoo News, 7 August 2014

• *Sheree Beasley murder: Why paedophile Robert Arthur Selby Lowe and 'Mr Cruel' changed suburban life,* Paul Anderson, Herald Sun, 21 June 2015

• *Mornington Peninsula unites to remember Rosebud murder victim Sheree Beasly on anniversary of her death,* Herald Sun, Leader Community Newspapers, 24 June 2015

• *Change for Sheree-Call for Tougher Laws on Sexual Abuse,* Eddie Morton, Mornington Peninsula Leader, 30 June 2015

• *Evil paedophile who kidnapped, abused and murdered a six-year-old girl Sheree Beasley dies in prison*, Samuel Squire, Daily Mail Australia, 9 November 2021

• *Abducted in Broad Daylight: Sheree Beasley*, Emily G. Thompson, True Crime, 27 January 2023

CHAPTER 30: LIFE MEANS LIFE

• *Anita may have died in two minutes, Court told*, Richard Macey, The Sydney Morning Herald, 25 June 1986

• *Mrs Cobby 'Beaten Systematically'* The Canberra Times, 27 March 1987

• *Town shocked at schoolgirl's disappearance,* The Canberra Times, 21 August 1992

• *Angry crowd waits as man faces charge of killing Bargo girl,* The Canberra Times, 22 August 1992

• *Ebony's killer to spend rest of his life in jail,* The Canberra Times, 10 July 1993

• *Ebony's killer attacked by prisoners a second time,* The Canberra Times, 16 October 1993

• *Little Girls Lost: The Stories of Four of Australia's Most Horrific Child Murders and Their Families Fight for Justice*, Helen Reade, Five Mile Press, 2003

• *NSW sentencing laws to be simplified,* Anna Patty, The Sydney Morning Herald, *13 September 2013*

• *A life sentence for victims of crime,* William Verity, Illawarra Mercury, 17 April 2014

• *Mother recounts Ebony Simpson tragedy in new crime series*, William Verity, Illawarra Mercury, 17 April 2014

• *Ebony Simpson's abduction and murder by Andrew Peter Garforth placed in 'worst category' by judge,* The Daily Telegraph, 14 July 2015

• *Ebony Simpson's murder remembered 25 years on*, Ashleigh Tullis, The Sydney Morning Herald, 17 August 2017

• *How Are Prison Inmates Classified?* Ugar Nedim, Sydney Criminal Lawyers, 9 May 2020

• *The Monster in Bargo: The Tragic Case of Ebony Simpson*, Emily G. Thompson, True Crime, 10 January 2025

CHAPTER 31: IVAN 'THE RAT' MILAT

• *Suspect charged in seven murders,* Peter James Spielman, The Dispatch, 31 May 1994

• *Coroner blasts 'extraordinary' inquiries into missing women,* Ellen Connolly, The Sydney Morning Herald, 4 July 2002

• *I am what l am, My Live and Curious Times,* John Marsden, Penguin, 2004

• *Sins of the Brother: The Definitive Story of Ivan Milat and the Backpacker Murders*, Mark Wittaker & Les Kennedy, PanMacmillan, 2007

• *The nine bodies round in Belango forest,* the Australian, 22 November 2010

• *Does crime run in the Milat family tree*, Les Kennedy, The Sydney Morning Herald, 28 November 2010

• *Did Australia's backpacker killer have an accomplice?* Roger Maynard, The Independent, 30 January 2011

• *On the trail of a…serial killer,* Clive Small, The Sydney Morning Herald, 19 April 2014

• *Twenty-Five years ago the first victims of Backpacker killer Ivan Milat were found in Belango Forest*, Troy Lennon, The Daily Telegraph, 19 September 2017

• *Timeline of Ivan Milat's crimes and trial, Nine News,* 27 October 2019

• *The 'backpacker killer' and unanswered questions,* Gary Nunn, BBC News, 27 October 2019

• *Uncovered: The woman thought to be Ivan Milat's first victim as family says 'she has not been respected,* Ollie Buckley, Seven News, 18 March 2021

- *Fifty years on, family of strangled Canberra woman are no nearer to answers*, Raffaelli Ciccareli, Nine news, 12 May 2021
- *Teens Toni and Kay disappeared in 1979. Ivan Milat was working nearby at the time,* Nicole Morris, Mamamia, 29 July 2023
- *'Worst serial killer in nation's history' could be to blame for dozens of missing or murdered women, MP says*, April Glover, Nine News, 24 October 2024
- *Jeremy Buckingham calls for parliamentary inquiry into serial killer Ivan Milat,* Duncan Evans, NewsWire, 18 August 2025
- *NSW Premier Chris Minns says he won't 'rule out' parliamentary inquiry into Ivan Milat,* Nathan Schmidt, NewsWire, 20 August 2025
- *Police files link Milat to 58 cold cases over decades*, Samantha Locke, The Canberra Times, 22 August 2025
- *NSW inquiry into unsolved murders, missing persons will divert police resources, Homicide Squad chief says,* Mark Tobin, ABC News, 27 October 2025

CHAPTER 32: THE GATE CRASHER

- *Meet the man who murdered Carl Williams,* Steve Butcher, the Age, 30 September 2011
- *John Lindrea is a violent man who is on the run from police,* Olivia Lambert, News.com.au,30 March 2016
- *Double murderer with a history of 'extreme violence' is caught by police at a house after cutting off his ankle bracelet and going on the run for six weeks,* Daniel Peters, Daily Mail Australia, 10 May 2016
- *Chris Binse has taken one step to reform,* John Silvester, The Age 2 February 2018
- *Man jailed over Westmeadows pub robbery and siege in Melbourne's north,* Danny Tran, ABC News, 4 October 2021

- *Double murderer John Lindrea jailed for hold up at Melbourne Pub,* Adam Cooper, The Age, 4 October 2021
- *Infamous murderer behind terrifying armed hold up at tavern in Melbourne's north west,* Serena Seyfort, Nine News, 4 October 2021

CHAPTER 33: 'CAPTAIN BATHTUB'

- *Evil unmasked, Les Kennedy,* The Sydney Morning Herald, 27 November 2000
- *Murderer hoards violent TV images,* The Age, 7 February 2005
- *Balaclava Killer case reopened,* Greg Stolz, Courier Mail, 7 April 2008
- *Murder in Suburbia: Disturbing stories from Australia's dark heart,* Emily Webb, The Five Mile Press, 2014
- *Killers Bandali Debs and Ashely Mervyn Coulston linked to unsolved murders,* Mark Morri & Mark Butler, News,com.au, 10 March 2015
- *New DNA evidence suggest Ashley Coulston could be behind Balaclava murders,* News Corp Australia, 17 September 2018
- *'The worst criminal offences in Victorian history': the shocking murders of Ashley Coulston,* Yahoo News, 17 September 2018
- *Born bad: The 21 unexplained years when abductor and triple killer Ashley Coulston disappeared,* Sarah McPhee, News.com.au, 8 September 2019
- *Anne and Kerryn were interviewing for a new flatmate. They opened the door to their killer,* Nama Winston, Mamamia, 22 September 2019
- *What happened in missing years of a monster?,* Andrew Rule, Herald Sun, 31 July 2021
- *Captain Bathtub: Ashley Coulston's Burwood Triple Murders & Trans-Tasman Escape,* True Crime Archives, 16 April 2025

CHAPTER 34: ANOTHER WORST OF THE WORST

- *Shot Rampage Kills 6 In Australia,* San Jose Mercury News, 28 October 1992
- *Case Study: Malcolm Baker,* Justice Action, 5 September 2012

- *Get here now, all hell has broken loose,* Nicole Hogan, News.com.au, 25 October 2017
- *The toll of murder: How a mother whose daughters were killed turned to drugs and the streets,* Megan Palin, News.com.au, 4 November 2017
- *Justice Action calling for improved prisoner rights,* Eden Gillepsie, news.com.au, 28 November 2017
- *Malcolm George Baker: Mass murderer who killed his ex and six others in NSW Central Coast massacre dies behind bars,* Makayla Muscat, Dail Mail Australia, 23 June 2024

CHAPTER 35: THE TOMAHAWK CREEP

- *Throw Away the Prison Keys,* Nicole Cox, The Sunday Times, 18 May 2007
- *Keep the monster in prison says sister of murder victim Karen MacKenzie,* Yasmine Phillips, The Sunday Times, 2 February 2013
- *Greenough massacre still haunts WA police,* WA Today, 6 June 2013
- *Axe murderer William Patrick Mitchell 'wiped out a quarter of my family tree,* Andrew Koubaridis, News.com.au, 21 February 2016
- *Greenough killer's parole bid denied,* William Mitchell, News.com.au, 1 October 2017
- *Mitchell case prompts WA to introduce laws stripping 'worst killers' of parole rights,* Sebastian Neuweiler, ABC News, 9 December 2017
- *WA longest terms and the man who came close,* Nine News, 19 July 2019
- *The Greenough Family Massacre, Emily G Thompson*, True Crime, 17 August 2021
- *WA attorney-general John Quigley delays mass murderers' parole eligibility,* Emily Smith, ABCNews, 2 November 2024

CHAPTER 36: FRANKSTON SERIAL MURDERER

- *For the living, the pain of death goes on,* Alan Attwood, The Age,15 December 1993

- *Portrait of a Serial Killer,* Ian Munro, The Age, 28 August 1994
- *The Frankston Murders: The True Story of Serial Killer Paul Denyer,* Vikki Petraitis, Nivar Press, 1995
- *Why triple-killer Paul Denyer must never be released,* The Age, 14 January 2004
- *Stop pandering to 'sicko', says Doyle,* The Age, 28 June 2004
- *Serial killer's family shocked by letter,* The Age, 30 September 2004
- *The Job: Fighting Crime from the Frontline,* Charlie Bezzina, Slattery Media Group, 1 October 2011
- *Serial killer Paul Denyer quizzed on four jail rapes in just six weeks,* The Daily Telegraph, 25 July 2012
- *Paul Denyer letters,* Herald Sun, 29 October 2017
- *The Investigator who put the Gladiator behind bars,* John Silvester, The Age, 31 July 2021
- *Less than an hour after taking a life, Paul Denyer sat down to dinner at his girlfriend's house,* Belinda Jepson, Mamamia, 7 August 2021
- *Family of murdered schoolgirl warn Frankston serial killer will kill again if released,* Adelaide Lang, News.com.au, 27 October 2022
- *Frankston serial killer Paul Denyer denied parole three decades after murders,* ABC News, 10 May 2023

CHAPTER 37: A GUN FANATIC

- *Murder on the City's Streets,* Dandenong Star Journal, 21 August 1993
- *O'Reilly's in Thornbury robbery earlier today,* Enough Gun, By Wombat, 12 February 2018
- *The Investigator who put the Gladiator behind bars,* John Silvester, The Age, 31 July 2021

CHAPTER 38: VALENTINE'S DAY MURDERS

- *Lindsey Robert Rose arriving at NSW Supreme Court in handcuffs where he pleaded guilty to five murder charges,* Newspix News Ltd, 18 June 1998

• *Woman shot dead 'because she was there'*, The Sydney Morning Herald, 19 June 1998

• *Fed: First six inmates of the new Goulburn high risk jail,* AAP, 1 June 2001

• *Radical Muslims pay jail inmates,* Kate Sikora, The Daily Telegraph, 23 April 2007

• *Supermax crims 'letters of woe',* Neil Mercer, The Daily Telegraph, 7 October 2007

• *Election 2016: Senate hopeful Ron Waters seeks to make amends for link to Valentine's Day murders,* Candice Prosser, ABC News, 29 June 2016

• *Atoning for his sins: My father the multiple murderer,* Australian Story, ABC, 30 October 2017

• *Massage parlour where a serial killer shot dead a woman before slaughtering his girlfriend on Valentine's Day sells for $1.8 million,* Bryant Hevesi, Daily Mail Australia, 18 August 2018

• *Forensic Investigators: Lindsay Robert Rose,* Australian Crime, True Crime 9 June 2019

CHAPTER 39: A QUESTION OF INNOCENCE–PART ONE

• *The case against David Harold Eastman,* The Canberra Times, 4 November 1995

• *David Eastman appeal upheld,* The Sydney Morning Herald, 28 May 2003

• *Everlasting nightmare,* The Sydney Morning Herald, 13 September 2008

• *Not over: Chamberlain seeks justice from hearts of stone,* Lindsay Murdoch, The Sydney Morning Herald, 10 November 2010

• *New inquest must declare innocence,* Andrew Rule, Herald Sun, 20 December 2011

- *Dingo caused baby Azaria Chamberlain's death- coroner,* BBC News Asia, 11 June 2012
- *Terry O'Donnell is still on the Colin Winchester murder case*, Richard Guilliatt, The Australian, 25 February 2013
- *The devil in the detail, Christine Jackman,* The Canberra Times, 19 February 2014
- Eastman inquiry recommends *David Eastman's conviction be quashed, finds miscarriage of justice,* ABC News, 30 May 2014
- *How a strange, cruel life led to jail for David Eastman,* Keith Moor, Herald Sun, 31 May 2014
- *David Eastman freed from jail, conviction quashed for murder of AFP assistant commissioner Colin Winchester,* ABC News, 22 August 2014
- *Henry Keogh released on bail after 20 years in jail on Anna-Jane Cheney murder conviction,* Candice Marcus, ABC News, 21 December 2014
- *Murder charge against Henry Keogh accused of drowning fiancée in bath, dropped by SA DPP,* ABC News, 12 November 2015
- *The Eastman case: Implications for an Australian Criminal Case Review Commission*, David Hamer, Flinders Law Journal, 2015
- *Compo bid in SA bathtub murder conviction,* Nine News, 16 April 2017
- *Henry Keogh to get $2.5 million settlement for overturned murder conviction,* Isabel Dayman & Eugene Boisvert, ABC News, 1 July 2018
- *David Eastman found not guilty of murdering senior AFP officer nearly three decades ago,* Elizabeth Bryne, ABC News, 22 November 2018
- *David Eastman awarded more than $7 million for wrongful murder conviction, almost 20 years in jail,* Elizabeth Byrne, ABC News, 14 October 2019
- *Henry Keogh: Wrongful conviction, fight for Justice, and the Anna-Jane Cheney Case*, True Crime Archives, 21 April 2025

CHAPTER 40: A QUESTION OF INNOCENCE–PART TWO

- *Officers in Mallard case stood down, ABC News, 7 October 2008*
- *Murderer no more: Andrew Mallard and the Epic Fight that Proved his Innocence,* Colleen Egan, Allen & Unwin, June 2010
- *Labor MP John Quigley fined over Mallard case, ABC News, 2 November 2011*
- *Killer takes murder mystery to his grave,* West Yorkshire News, 11 July 2013
- *Simon Rochford's missing murder weapon discovery has 'stench of cover up': WA Opposition,* David Weber, ABC News, 12 September 2015
- *What was Andrew Mallard accused of doing and how did he prove his innocence?* ABC News, 20 April 2019
- *Family devastated by Andrew Mallard's death in LA in hit-and-run-crash,* The West Australian, 20 April 2019
- *The Wronged Man: Andrew Mallard,* Australian Story, ABC, 10 May 2019

CHAPTER 41: POLITICAL RIVALRY

- *Councillor looks to integration,* Bernard Lagan, The Sydney Morning Herald, 9 October 1987
- *The Newman Murder,* Four Corners, ABC, 19 September 1994
- *Ngo found guilty of Newman assassination,* Nick Grimm, Lateline, ABC, 29 June 2001
- *Report to the Chief Justice of NSW of the Inquiry into the Conviction of Phuong Canh Ngo for the Murder of John Newman,* David Patten: Judicial Officer, 14 April 2009
- *Ngo did mastermind MP's murder: inquiry,* Geesche Jacobsen, The Sydney Morning Herald, 17 April 2009
- *Political murder: Phuong Ngo to stay in jail,* Nonee Walsh and Antonette Collins, ABC News, 17 April 2009
- *On Deadly Ground: The Assassination of John Newman MP,* Tim Priest, New Holland Publishers, 2010

- *Murderer of NSW MP refused life sentence appeal,* Nine News, 12 December 2014
- *Almost 30 years on, the man convicted of killing politician John Newman deserves to be pardoned. Here is why*, Mac Halliday, Michael West Media,1 July 2023
- *Why Phuong Ngo Should Get Out Of Prison*, Carlotta McIntosh, Megaphone Oz, 5 September 2024

CHAPTER 42: IT WAS NO ACCIDENT

- *How could a father do this,* Herald Sun, 27 November 2017
- *Man who killed son and burnt wife sentenced for 26 years*, Stuart Walsh, AAP News, 12 June 2000

CHAPTER 43: ONE DISTURBED MIND

- *Before the High Court: The Case of the Improbable Murderer: De Gruchy v R,* Jeremy Gans, Informit, 1 March 2002
- *Murderers charged over NSW prison attack,* The Sydney Morning Herald, 18 March 2009
- *Matthew De Gruchy assaulted rapist brothers: police*, Angela Thompson, Illawarra Mercury, 5 November 2012
- *Notorious teen killer sends family chilling note ahead of parole hearing,* Yahoo News Australia, 20 April 2017
- *Matthew De Gruchy, who bludgeoned to death three family members, to have parole hearing,* Andrew Koubaridis, News.com.au, 21 April 2017
- Triple murderer *Matthew De Gruchy working at NSW abattoir,* Angela Thompson, The Sydney Morning Herald, 22 April 2017
- *Triple killer denied parole: 'Matthew is the stuff nightmares are made of',* Andrew Koubaridis, News.com.au, 26 May 2017
- *Matthew De Gruchy, who killed his family as a teenager, set to be released from jail,* Caitlin Duggan & Kelly Fuller, ABC News, 26 July 2019

- *Aussie 'sociopath', Mathew De B Gruchy, who wrote horror 'to-do list' to be released from jail,* Stephanie Bedo, News.com.au, 26 July 2019
- *Triple murderer Matthew De Gruchy walks free after two decades behind bars,* Cydonee Marden, The Sydney Morning Herald, 15 August 2019
- *Triple killer released from Sydney prison,* Nine News, 15 August 2019

CHAPTER 44: A BRUTAL ACT

- DPP v England [1998]-Unreported VSC, Justice Coldrey, 23 October 1998-Conviction and sentence
- DPP v England [1999] VSCA 95-Appeal upheld

CHAPTER 45: LIKE BROTHER LIKE SISTER

- *Terse words form judge dismissing lifer's appeal,* Sarah Crichton, The Sydney Morning Herald, 13 April 2002
- *Woman admits to inciting lover to kill father,* The Sydney Morning Herald, 10 February 2003
- *I hated my father, I wanted him dead,* The Sydney Morning Herald, 11 February 2003
- *Death-plot daughter puts on show for Parole Board,* Stephen Gibbs, The Sydney Morning Herald, 30 June 2006
- *Belinda Van Krevel set for freedom,* AAP, 19 May 2007
- *Death surrounds her,* Greg Bearup, The Sydney Morning Herald,31 May 2007
- *Wollongong's past may be too sordid for underbelly,* Jodie Minus, Illawarra Mercury, 6 June 2009
- *Femme fatale locked up again,* Alicia Wood, The Sydney Morning Herald, 29 August 2010
- *Belinda Van Krevel charged with boyfriend's stabbing,* Megan Levy, The Sydney Morning Herald, 5 July 2013
- *Death surrounds her,* Greg Bearup, The Sydney Morning Herald, 16 September 2014

- *She was named 'Australia's most evil woman'. But where is Belinda Van Krevel now?* Zara Mc Donald, True Crime, 3 March 2018
- *Frank Arkell: How a vicious murder unmasked a city's darkest secrets,* Nick McLaren, 26 June 2018
- *Belinda van Evil: Australia's scariest woman*, Charis Chang, News.com.au, 18 September 2018
- *Belinda Van Krevel, sister of Mark Valera, jailed for stabbing second partner,* Tim Fernandez, ABC News, 21 February 2024

CHAPTER 46: THE BROTHERLY FERNANDO COUSINS

- *How two cousins with a brotherly bond abduced a nurse, 21, from a country hospital before raping and almost beheading her in a crime of 'unbelievable savagery' that stunned a nation and stoked racial tensions,* Stephen Gibbs, Daily Mail Australia, 30 April 2020
- *Notorious Australian prisoner who killed his cousin after they were both jailed for raping and murdering a nurse gets 17 years on top of j his life sentence for another vicious jail stabbing caught on film,* Stephen Gibbs, Daily Mail Australia, 21 November 2021
- *Prison officer Lisa Brown recalls the day nurse-killer Vester Fernando tried to stab death a fellow inmate,* Stephen Gibbs, Daily Mail Australia,27 January 2024

CHAPTER 47: ONE OPEN AND SHUT CASE

- *Judge defends security*, Fergus Shiel, The Age, 12 December 1997
- *Private men, public anger: The men's rights movement in Australia,* Sarah Maddison, 1999
- *Shattered lives,* The Sydney Morning Herald, 17 September 2003
- *It's a Man's World: Claims of Provocation and Automatism in 'Intimate Homicides',* Bernadette Mc Sherry, Melbourne University Law Review 28: 2005

CHAPTER 48: THE WAGGA WAGGA STRANGLER

- *Strangler jailed,* The Daily Advertiser, 8 April 2000
- *Killer, Matthew James Harris,* profile on Killer Cloud, 8 February 2019
- *Matthew James Harris,* Woman's Day, 19 December 2022

CHAPTER 49: THE TWO CASES OF COLIN EARL GRAHAM

- *Homicide detectives urge callers to ring back after cold-case confession,* Tom Cowie, The Age, 6 April 2017
- *Married Melbourne man accused of stabbing lover 30 years ago fronts court,* Nine News, 29 July 2019
- *Man allegedly confessed to lover murder,* Nine News, 30 July 2019
- *Bail for accused killer as judge labels prosecution case 'weak',* Adam Cooper, The Age, 8 December 2020
- *Major development in nurse's cold case murder trial,* Caroline Schelle and Erin Lyons, The Australian, 11 March 2022
- *Cold case acquittal: Jury unaware accused murderer stabbed another woman to death,* Erin Pearson, The Age, 16 September 2022
- *Two murders, one accused, two verdicts: the case of Colin Earl Graham,* Erin Pearson, and Marta Pascual Juanola, The Age, 16 October 2022

CHAPTER 50: NO BODY NO PAROLE

- *Lies don't mean you're guilty, judge says in case of Keli Lane, accused of killing her baby,* Natsha Robinson, The Australian, 12 August 2010
- *Keli Lane scream's and collapses as jury find her guilty of murdering baby Tegan,* Kim Arlington, The Sydney Morning Herald, 13 December 2010
- *Absence of facts hindered police investigation into Tegan Lane's disappearance,* Michael Duffy, The National Times, 14 Dember 2010
- Keli Lane sentenced to 18 years for murder of Tegan, The Sydney Morning Herald, 15 April 2011

• *Lane dumped baby in bushland: Taxi driver,* Stephanie Gardiner, The Sydney Morning Herald, 18 April 2011

• *Keli Lane loses bid to fight baby murder conviction,* ABC News, 15 August 2014

• *Nurse's killer convicted after 33 years,* SBS News, 4 November 2016

• *The moment double murderer is caught in elaborate sting,* Laura Hedges, Daily Mail, 16 October 2018

• *Helen's Law receives Royal Assent,* Ministry of Justice, UK, 4 November 2020

• *How does Queensland's No Body No Parole Law Work?* Hannay Lawyers, 19 February 2021

• *Kangaroo trial: Convicted double murderer's court spray at parole hearing,* Blake Antrobus, NCA NewsWire,22 July 2022

• *'No body, no parole laws',* Lenny Roth, NSW Parliamentary Research Service, October 2022

• *Murderer Rodney Cherry's parole bid fails after refusal to help police find victims' body,* Katrina Beavan, ABC News, 19 July 2023

• *A case against 'no body, no parole laws' being adopted in Tasmania,* Isobel Bird, The Examiner, 6 October 2023

• *Reforms for double jeopardy and subsequent appeals,* The Queensland Cabinet and Ministerial Directory, 6 March 2024

• *Former Sydney teacher Chris Dawson loses appeal over conviction for murdering his wife Lynette Sims,* Jamie Mc Kinnell, ABC News, 13 June 2024

• *Wife killer's huge court move revealed,* Steve Zemek, News Wire, 15 February 2025

CHAPTER 51: THE PORT ARTHUR MASSACRE

• *Convicted murderer attacked in jail with cleaning fluid,* ABC News, 5 July 2003

• *Snowtown killers likely to die in jail,* Tony Hull, ABC News, 8 September 2003

- *Shedding light on Port Arthur killer,* The Age, 29 March 2006
- *Struggling with its massacre in silence,* The Sydney Morning Herald, 7 February 2007
- *Court told lawyer affected by Bryant case,* ABC News, 9 September 2008
- *Bryant's lawyer jailed over thefts,* Andrew Darby and Hobart, The Sydney Morning Herald, 19 September 2008
- *A dangerous mind: What turned Martin Bryant into a mass murderer,* Robert Wainwright & Paola Toataro, The Sydney Morning Herald, 27 April 2009
- *Bryant's mother defends her son,* The Sydney Morning Herald, 27 February 2011
- *Snowtown: Living with a death penalty,* The Age, 7 May 2011
- *Disgraced lawyer out of jail,* ABC News, 28 September 2012
- *Gun control, Change is possible-and fast,* Philip Alpers, CNN, 11 June 2014
- *The man behind the Port Arthur Massacre,* SBS, 27 April 2017
- *Rare prison photograph of a 'dim, fat, angry' Martin Bryant,* Candace Sutton, News.com.au, 15 March 2021
- *Walter shares how his girl's legacy is now helping other kids,* Emma Lovett, Woman's Day, 9 October 2024

PRINCIPAL REFERENCE WEBSITES

- www.abc.net.au
- www.afsa.gov.au
- www.asic.gov.au
- www.ato.gov.au
- www.austlii.edu.au
- www.childrenscourt.vic.gov.au
- www.countycourt.vic.gov.au
- www.fitzroy-legal.org.au
- www.legalaid.vic.gov.au
- www.magistratescourt.vic.gov.au
- www.supremecourt.vic.gov.au
- www.vcat.gov.au
- www.vocat.vic.gov.au
- www.1800respect.org.au
- www.wikipedia.org
- www.trove.nla.gov.au

ABOUT THE AUTHOR

Colin served in Vietnam as a National conscript during 1968-69. On his discharge from the Army, he resumed working for the Victoria Police Department as an unsworn member. In 1974, Colin was appointed Head of School Security for the Victorian Education Department in the prevention and detection of school crime.

He then entered the legal profession, being admitted to practice in 1996 as a Barrister and Solicitor mainly practicing in the areas of crime, family violence and industrial relations. He retired in 2022 and lives on the Mornington Peninsula in Victoria with his wife, Michelle.

www.ingramcontent.com/pod-product-compliance
Lightning Source LLC
LaVergne TN
LVHW052207200926
848481LV00001B/52
* 9 7 8 1 7 6 3 8 6 9 1 4 1 *